# WORLD MILITARY AVIATION
## Aircraft, Airforces & Weaponry

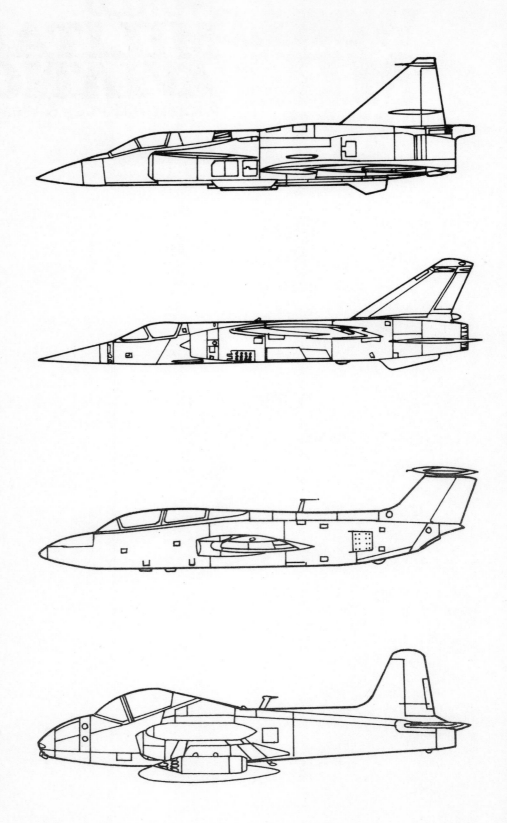

# WORLD MILITARY AVIATION

## Aircraft, Airforces & Weaponry

Edited by

**Nikolaus Krivinyi**

in collaboration with
Franz Kosar and Johann Kroupa
Illustrated by Franz Gruber
Translated by Elke C Weal

Arms and Armour Press, London

Published in 1973 by
Arms and Armour Press
Lionel Leventhal Limited
2-6 Hampstead High Street
London NW3 IPR

© J. F. Lehmanns Verlag, Munchen,
   1972
Revisions and corrections
   © J. F. Lehmanns Verlag,
   Munchen, 1973
English language edition © Lionel
   Leventhal Limited, 1973

Updated and revised from
*Taschenbuch Der Luftflotten.*

SBN 85368 279 8

Printed in Great Britain by
Lowe & Brydone (Printers) Ltd., Thetford, Norfolk

# Contents

# Introduction

The world balance of power fluxes and changes, and so does the role of aircraft in modern warfare. There is a tendency among the N.A.T.O. countries to decrease the size of their present technical and strategic superiority over the countries of the Eastern Blocs because of the very high costs involved. Time will tell whether this trusting act at a time of *détente* is realistic.

While the major powers talk of reducing their Air Force sizes, the Latin-American, the Middle Eastern and African countries are at present involved in their own individual arms races. Latin America is currently replacing equipment, much of it of World War II vintage, with the most up-to-date the world can offer. The volatile situation in the Middle East necessitates the purchase of sophisticated equipment by the countries involved—who in some cases are finding that without massive foreign aid and foreign pilots the aircraft cannot be kept in the air. The African states, as they become more mature, appear to feel that their weaponry must also be equal to the sophisticated nations, and with the increasing uneasiness of that continent they may well find themselves having to employ their new purchases. However it seems doubtful whether some of these countries have the skill to even maintain their aircraft on the ground and will not be able to actually use their costly equipment without support from the West or Soviet Bloc. The expenditure of large sums on equipment which cannot be used is, alas, nothing new when national pride is at stake.

The balance of power between the Soviet Union and China is hardly likely to alter in the coming years. China is only very slowly establishing herself in the field of technical development—particularly in terms of high-quality equipment. It is interesting that those Soviet prototypes which were unveiled at the 1967 Domodedowo Air Show have not as yet appeared in the operational units of the Soviet airforce. As it seems unlikely that these types will be on the production line in the near future,

they were not included in this volume, which is complete in its coverage of aeroplanes and helicopters operational at the present time.

Some years ago it was put forward that by the 1970s wars would be only fought with rockets alone. But this is demonstrably not so. Aircraft of all types still continue to play a major part in warfare, as shown by the conflicts in Vietnam and the Middle East, where without the air superiority maintained by the U.S.A. and Israel there may have been completely different military conclusions.

Meanwhile the sophistication (and cost) of modern war is ever increasing. Today considerable importance is attached to precise air reconnaissance and Electronic-Counter-Measures in all modern operations. New weapons, such as guided missiles and 'smart bombs', can be employed effectively against large scale guerilla operations and in standard conventional wars such as the Indo-Pakistan wars of 1965 and 1971; but become next to useless against small raids and sabotage groups, which to some extent seems to be the pattern of conflict for the mid-1970s (such as Northern Ireland, Mozambique, etc.).

At present V.T.O.L. projects, even though expensive, are under strong consideration by the major powers, with both the U.S.A. and Great Britain employing the Harrier strike fighter. In the near future the U.S.S.R. could well have in service a similar aircraft on its new aircraft carriers, and Great Britain will be using a version of the Harrier on its proposed Through Deck Cruisers.

The swing-wing developments (F-111, Mirage G and MiG-23) are again expensive and up to now have not proved entirely successful, as illustrated by the unsatisfactory performance of the F-111 in Vietnam. It seems, however, as though the swing-wing plane will yet again have a new lease of life as with Great Britain, West Germany and Italy continue development of the M.R.C.A.

# Airforces

## ABU DHABI

**Air force** (Abu Dhabian Air force)
men 800
squadrons 4
operational aircraft 31 and
helicopters 8
**Organisation**
1 strike fighter squadron with Mirage 5
1 strike fighter squadron with Hunter FGA.76 and
  FR.76A
1 transport squadron with DHC-4 and BN-2
1 helicopter squadron with Alouette III and S.A.330
**Major bases**
Abu Dhabi, Sharjah
**Military training aid from**
Great Britain
**Equipment**
Fighters and strike fighters
12 Dassault Mirage 5
9 Hawker Hunter FGA.76
1 Hawker Hunter T.76A
Reconnaissance aircraft
1 Hawker Hunter FR.76A
Transports
4 DeHavilland Canada DHC-4
4 Britten-Norman BN-2
Helicopters
5 Aérospatiale Alouette III
3 Aérospatiale S.A.330
**Army**
6,000 men
**Navy**
200 men

## AFGHANISTAN

**Air force**
men 5,000
squadrons 11
operational aircraft 146 and
helicopters 24
**Organisation**
2 fighter squadrons with MiG-21
1 fighter squadron with MiG-19
3 strike fighter squadrons with MiG-17
1 strike fighter squadron with Su-7
1 bomber squadron with Il-28
2 transport squadrons with Il-14
1 helicopter squadron with Mi-4
– trainer squadrons with Yak-11 and Yak-18
fighter and strike fighter squadrons each with 12-15
  aircraft
**Major bases**
Herat, Jalalabad, Kandahar, Mazar-i-Sharif, Pagram,
  Sherpur, Shindand
**Military training aid from**
Soviet Union
**Foreign Air Forces in Afghanistan**
Soviet Union
**Equipment**
Fighters and strike fighters
45 Mikoyan MiG-17
12 Mikoyan MiG-19
30 Mikoyan MiG-21
12 Sukhoi Su-7
Bombers
10 Ilyushin Il-28
Transports
10 Antonov An-2
25 Ilyushin Il-14
2 Ilyushin Il-18

Helicopters
6 Mil Mi-1
18 Mil Mi-4
Trainers
approx 45 aircraft, inc Yakovlev Yak-11 and Yak-18,
  Mikoyan MiG-15UTI
**Programme**
Replacement of further Mikoyan MiG-17 by Mikoyan
  MiG-21 and Sukhoi Su-7 strike fighters
**Army**
80,000 men
**Army Aviation**
The Air Force is a component part of the Army

## ALBANIA

**Air force**
men 4,000
squadrons 8
operational aircraft 65 and
helicopters 10
**Organisation**
1 fighter squadron with F-8 (MiG-21)
1 fighter squadron with F-6 (MiG-19)
2 strike fighter squadrons with F-4 (MiG-17)
2 strike fighter squadrons with MiG-15
1 transport squadron with An-2 and Il-14
1 helicopter squadron with Mi-1 and Mi-4
Fighter and strike fighter squadrons each with 10-12
  aircraft
**Major bases**
Berat/Kucove, Durazzo/Shiyak, Tirana, Valona
**Military training aid from**
China
**Equipment**
Fighters and strike fighters
20 Mikoyan MiG-15
15 Shenyang F-4 (MiG-17)
10 Shenyang F-6 (MiG-19)
10 Shenyang F-8 (MiG-21)
Transports
3 Antonov An-2
3 Ilyushin Il-14
Helicopters
2 Mil Mi-1
8 Mil Mi-4
Trainers
Yakovlev Yak-11 and Yak-18; Mikoyan MiG-15UTI
**Programme**
Replacement of Mikoyan MiG-15 and MiG-17 strike
  fighters by 25-30 Shenyang F-8 (MiG-21)
**Army**
35,000 men
**Navy**
3,000 men

## ALGERIA

**Air force**
men 4,000
squadrons 16
operational aircraft 130 and
helicopters 50
**Organisation**
3 fighter squadrons with MiG-21F
3 strike fighter squadrons with MiG-17
2 strike fighter squadrons with MiG-15
2 bomber squadrons with Il-28
1 transport squadron with An-12 and Il-18
3 helicopter squadrons with Mi-4
2 helicopter squadrons with S.A. 330
fighter, strike fighter and bomber squadrons each with

10–12 aircraft
**Major bases**
Algiers, Biskra, Boufarak, Dar-el-Beider, Maison Blanche, Marine, Mers-el-Kebir, Oran, Oukar, Paul-Cazelles, Sidi-bel-Abbès
**Military training from**
Egypt (UAR), France, Soviet Union
**Equipment**
Fighters and strike fighters
20 Mikoyan MiG–15
40 Mikoyan MiG–17
36 Mikoyan MiG–21F and MiG–21UTI
Bombers
20 Ilyushin Il–28
Transports
8 Antonov An–12
3 Ilyushin Il–18
Helicopters
20 Aérospatiale S.A.330
30 Mil Mi–4
Trainers
55–60 aircraft, inc Yakovlev Yak–11, Yakovlev Yak–18, Mikoyan MiG–15UTI, 26 Potez-Air Fouga C.M. 170
2 Army
53,000 men
3 Navy
3,200 men

# ARGENTINE

**Air force** (Fuerza Aérea Argentina)
men 21,000
squadrons 11
operational aircraft 170 and
helicopters 26
**Organisation**
1 strike fighter squadron with Mirage IIIEA
1 strike fighter squadron with F–86F
1 strike fighter squadron with A–4P
1 strike fighter squadron with A–4F
1 bomber squadron with Canberra B.62
1 transport squadron with F.27
1 transport squadron with C–130E and DC–6
1 transport squadron with C–47
1 transport squadron with DHC–6
1 helicopter squadron with OH–6A
1 helicopter squadron with UH–1H
– trainer squadrons with T–28A
– trainer squadrons with T–34B
– trainer squadrons with M.S. 760
**Major bases**
Chamical, Comodoro Rivadavia, El Palomar, El Plumerillo, Mar del Plata, Mendoza, Moron, Paranã, Reconquista, Rio Gallegos, Santa Fé, Tandil, Villa Reynolds
**Military training aid from**
United States (?)
**Equipment**
Fighters and strike fighters
10 Dassault Mirage IIIEA
2 Dassault Mirage IIIDA
25 McDonnell Douglas A–4P
16 McDonnell Douglas A–4F
20 North American F–86F
Bombers
9 English Electric Canberra B.62
2 English Electric Canberra T.64
Transports
6 Beechcraft C–45
4 Canadair CC–106
20 DeHavilland Dove
5 DeHavilland Canada DHC–6
10 Douglas C–47
3 Douglas DC–6
20 FMA I.A. 50
11 Fokker-VFW F.27
1 Fokker-VFW F.28
1 Hawker Siddeley H.S.748

5 Lockheed C–130E
Liaison and reconnaissance aircraft
approx 35 aircraft, inc Beechcraft Bonanza, 30 (?) Cessna 182, 1 Cessna 320, and 3 (?) De Havilland Canada DHC–2
Helicopters
3 Bell 47G
1 Bell 47J
8 Bell UH–1H
12 Hughes OH–6A
2 Hughes 500M
Trainers
25 Beechcraft T–34B
35 FMA I.A. 35
12 Morane-Saulnier M.S. 760
24 North American T–28A
**Programme**
3 further Lockheed C–130 transports and 6 Aérospatiale S.A. 315B helicopters on order, purchase of 80 further Dassault Mirage III strike fighters and production of 80 FMA I.A. 58 Pucará ground-attack aircraft planned. 50 FMA I.A. 58 are reportedly already on order.
**Army**
85,000 men
**Army Aviation** (Comando de Aviación Ejército)
– men
– squadrons
50 operational aircraft and 12 helicopters
**Organisation**
—
**Equipment**
Helicopters
6 Bell UH–1H
6 Fairchild-Hiller FH–1100
Liaison and AOP aircraft
2 Cessna 310
13 Cessna U–17A
4 Piper Apache
7 Piper L–21A
Transports
approx 25 aircraft, inc 14 (?) Aero Turbo Commander
3 Beechcraft C–45
3 DeHavilland Canada DHC–6
**Programme**
Aquisition of additional helicopters and phasing out of all fixed-wing aircraft with the exception of 3 DeHavilland Canada DHC–6 transports.
**Navy**
34,000 men
1 aircraft carrier
**Naval Aviation** (Comando de Aviación Naval)
3,000 men
8 squadrons
80 operational aircraft and
26 helicopters
**Organisation**
1 strike fighter squadron with A–4Q
1 ground-attack squadron with MB.326K
1 ground-attack squadron with T–28D
1 maritime reconnaissance and ASW squadron with SP–2H
1 maritime reconnaissance and ASW squadron with S–2A
1 transport squadron with C–47 and C–54
1 helicopter squadron with S–61D–4
1 helicopter squadron with Bell 47 and Alouette III
**Major Bases**
Commandante Espora, Ezeiza, Puerto Belgrano, Punta de Indio, Trelew, Ushuaia
**Equipment**
Fighters and strike fighters
16 McDonnell Douglas A–4Q
Ground-attack aircraft
12 Aermacchi MB.326K
20 North American T–28D Fennec
Maritime reconnaissance and ASW aircraft
3 Grumman HU–16B
6 Grumman S–2A

4 Lockheed SP–2H
Transports
approx 20 (?) aircraft, inc Beechcraft C–45
1 DeHavilland Canada DHC–6
8 (?) Douglas C–47
2 Douglas C–54D
1 FMA I.A.50
2 Hawker Siddeley H.S.125/400
Liaison and AOP aircraft
2 DeHavilland Canada DHC–2
3 Fairchild-Hiller (Pilatus) PC–6A
Helicopters
4 Aérospatiale Alouette III
6 Bell 47D
6 Bell 47G and J
6 Hughes 500M
4 Sikorsky S–61D–4
Trainers
approx 20 aircraft, inc Beechcraft T–11
2 (?) Grumman TF–9J
12 (?) North American T–6G
some North American T–28A
**Programme**
2 Westland Lynx HAS.2 helicopters on order
**Coast guard** (Prefectura Nacional Maritima)
8,000 men
Transports
5 Short Skyvan 3M
Helicopters
1 Bell 47G
2 Bell 47J
6 Hughes 500M
**Aircraft factories**
FMA (Fábrica Militar de Aviones), known as DINFIA
    in period 1957–1968

## AUSTRALIA

**Air force** (Royal Australian Air Force)
men 22,500
squadrons 15
operational aircraft 211 and
helicopters 61
**Organisation**
2 strike fighter squadrons with Mirage IIIOA
2 strike fighter squadrons with Mirage IIIOF
2 strike fighter squadrons with F–111C
1 maritime reconnaissance and ASW squadron with P–3B
1 maritime reconnaissance and ASW squadron with
    SP–2H
2 transport squadrons with DHC–4
1 transport squadron with C–130A
1 transport squadron with C–130E
1 transport squadron with BAC 1–11, Falcon, H.S.748 and
    C–47
1 helicopter squadron with UH–1B and UH–1D
1 helicopter squadron with UH–1H
– trainer squadrons with CA–25 and Vampire T.35
– trainer squadrons with MB.326H
**Major bases**
Amberley, Brisbane, Edinburgh, Darwin, East Sale,
    Fairbarn, Learmonth (?), Pearce, Richmond, Townsville,
    Williamtown
**Equipment**
Fighters and strike fighters
40 Dassault (Commonwealth CA–29) Mirage IIIOF
45 Dassault Mirage IIIOA
15 Dassault Mirage IIID
24 General Dynamics F–111C
Maritime reconnaissance and ASW aircraft
10 Lockheed SP–2H
10 Lockheed P–3B
Transports
2 BAC 1–11
3 Dassault Falcon 20
3 DeHavilland Canada DHC–3
22 DeHavilland Canada DHC–4
10 Douglas C–47

2 Hawker Siddeley H.S.748C.2
12 Lockheed C–130A
12 Lockheed C–130E
Helicopters
18 Bell UH–1B
2 Bell UH–1D
29 Bell UH–1H
12 Boeing Vertol CH–47C
Trainers
75 Aermacchi MB.326H
30 Commonwealth CA–25 Winjeel
30 DeHavilland Vampire T.35
8 Hawker Siddeley H.S.748T.2
**Programme**
Replacement of Lockheed SP–2H reconnaissance aircraft
    by 10 (8 ?) Lockheed P–3C or Hawker Siddeley Nimrod
    MR.1, of Lockheed C–130A transports by 12 Lockheed
    C–130E, of Commonwealth CA–25 trainers by 37 AESL
    Airtrainer CT.4.   12 further Bell UH–1H helicopters on
    order.
**Army**
31,000 men
**Army Aviation** (Australian Army Aviation Corps)
– men
3 squadrons
28 operation aircraft and
105 helicopters
**Organisation**
3 (?) helicopter squadrons with OH–58B and Bell 47G
**Equipment**
Helicopters
30 Bell 47G–3
75 (55 ?) Bell OH–58B
Liaison and reconnaissance aircraft
16 Cessna 180
12 Pilatus PC–6A
**Programme**
Replacement of Bell 47G helicopters by Bell OH–58B.
    11 GAF Nomad transports on order, delivery from
    1973/74
**Navy**
17,000 men
1 aircraft carrier
**Naval Aviation** (Royal Australian Navy, Fleet Air Arm)
1,500 men
4 squadrons
26 operational aircraft and
26 helicopters
**Organisation**
1 strike fighter squadron with A–4G
1 maritime reconnaissance and ASW squadron with S–2E
1 helicopter squadron with UH–1D and UH–1B
1 helicopter squadron with Wessex Mk. 31
1 trainer squadron with MB.326H
**Equipment**
Fighters and strike fighters
8 McDonnell Douglas A–4G
2 McDonnell Douglas TA–4G
Maritime reconnaissance and ASW aircraft
14 Grumman S–2E
Transports
2 Hawker Siddeley H.S.748
Helicopters
1 Bell UH–1B
4 Bell UH–1D
1 Westland Scout
20 Westland Wessex Mk. 31B
Trainers
approx 25 aircraft, inc 10 Aermacchi MB.326H,
    DeHavilland Sea Venom FAW.53, DeHavilland
    Vampire T.34
**Programme**
Phasing out of DeHavilland Sea Venom FAW.53 and
    Vampire T.34 trainers.  Replacement of Westland
    Wessex helicopters by 10 Westland Sea King Mk.50
    from 1974.  Procurement of further 15 Westland Sea
    King planned

**Aircraft factories**
CA (Commonwealth Aircraft Corporation)
GAF (Government Aircraft Factories)

# AUSTRIA

**Air force** (Österreichische Luftstreitkräfte)
men 3,500
squadrons 6
operational aircraft 2 and
helicopters 58
**Organisation**
1 transport squadron with Skyvan 3M and DHC–2
1 helicopter squadron with AB.206A
2 helicopter squadrons with AB.204B
1 helicopter squadron with Alouette II
1 helicopter squadron with Alouette III
3 trainer squadrons with Saab 105 OE
1 trainer squadron with Saab 91D
1 trainer squadron with C.M.170
The Saab 105 OE trainer squadrons are also to be used
in the ground-attack role
**Major bases**
Graz-Thalerhof, Langenlebarn, Linz-Hörsching, Zeltweg
**Military training aids from**
Sweden
**Equipment**
Transports
2 Short Skyvan 3M
Liaison and AOP aircraft
18 Cessna O–1A and E
2 DeHavilland Canada DHC–2
Helicopters
10 Aérospatiale Alouette II
12 Aérospatiale Alouette III
22 Agusta-Bell AB.204B
12 Agusta-Bell AB.206A
2 Sikorsky S–65 OE
Trainers
16 Saab 91D
38 Saab 105 OE
**Programme**
Formation of one fighter squadron with Northrop F–5E?
Phasing out of Cessna O–1 and DeHavilland Canada
DHC–2 liaison and AOP aircraft and of Aérospatiale
Alouette II helicopters. Purchase of new helicopters
(8 Aérospatiale Alouette III, 6 Agusta-Bell AB.206A, 1
Sikorsky S–650E?) and an additional Short Skyvan 3M
transport?
**Army**
36,000 men

# BAHREIN

**Armed Forces**
Police force only with 2 Westland Scout helicopters.

# BANGLA DESH

**Air force**
– men
– squadrons
– operational aircraft and
4 helicopters
**Organisation**
—
**Bases**
Chittagong, Comilla, Tezgaon (Dacca), Jessore
**Military training aid from**
India, Soviet Union
**Equipment**
Transport
1 DeHavilland Canada DHC–4
Liaison and AOP aircraft
Some aircraft, type unknown
Helicopters
3 Aérospatiale Alouette III
2 Westland Wessex H.U. Mk. 5
**Programme**
Formation of one strike fighter squadron (with 10
8 Mikoyan MiG–21F and 2 MiG–21UTI)

**Army**
– men
**Navy**
– men

# BELGIUM

**Air force** (Force Aérienne Belge/Belgische Luchtmacht)
men 20,000
squadrons 11
operation aircraft 215 and
helicopters 8
**Organisation**
2 fighter squadrons with F–104G
2 strike fighter squadrons with F–104G
3 strike fighter squadrons with Mirage 5–BA
1 reconnaissance squadron with Mirage 5–BR
1 transport squadron with C–130H
1 transport squadron with C–47 and DC–6
1 helicopter squadron with S–58C and H–34A
– trainer squadrons with SF.260MB
– trainer squadrons with C.M.170
1 trainer squadron with T–33A
fighter, strike-fighter and reconnaissance squadrons each
with 18 aircraft
**Major bases**
Beauvechain, Bierset, Florennes, Kleine, Brogel, Melsbroek
**Equipment**
Fighters and strike fighters
62 Dassault Mirage 5–BA
16 Dassault Mirage 5–BD
70 Lockheed F–104G
9 Lockheed TF–104G
Reconnaissance aircraft
26 Dassault Mirage 5–BR
Transport
1 Dassault Falcon 20
5 Douglas C–47
4 Douglas DC–6
some Fairchild C–119G
some (9?) Hunting Pembroke
12 Lockheed C–130H
Helicopters
4 Sikorsky H–34A
4 Sikorsky S–58C
Trainers
12 Lockheed T–33A
35 Potez-Air Fouga C.M.170
35 SIAI-Marchetti SF.260MB
**Programme**
Phasing out of Faircrild C–119C transports.
2 Dassault Falcon 20 crew trainers on order.
Purchase of 12 light transports (IAI–201 Arava or Short
Skyvan 3M) under consideration. Seeking replacements
for Potez-Air Fouga C.M.170 trainer (Dassault-Dornier
Alpha Jet or Saab 105G?), and for Lockheed F–104G
strike fighter (Dassault Mirage F1, Northrop P.530
Cobra or Saab 37?). Licence-production of 33 Saab
105 trainers by SABCA under consideration. Replacement of Sikorsky H–34A and S–58C helicopters by 6
Westland Sea King?
**Army**
66,000 men
**Army aviation** (Aviation Légère de la Force Térrestre)
– men
4 squadrons
5 (?) operational aircraft and
80 helicopters
**Organisation**
4 helicopter squadrons with Alouette II
**Equipment**
Helicopters
80 Aérospatiale Alouette II
Liaison and AOP aircraft
some Dornier Do–27D
**Navy**
4,200 men
**Naval Aviation**
5 helicopters

10

3 Aérospatiale Alouette III and
2 Sikorsky S–58C
**Aircraft factories**
SABCA Fairey, (Société Anonyme Belge de Constructions
   Aéronautiques Fairey)

## BOLIVIA

**Air force** (Fuerza Aérea Boliviana)
men 1,800
squadrons 5
operational aircraft 35 and
helicopters 15
**Organisation**
1 ground-attack squadron with F–51D
1 ground-attack squadron with T–28A
2 transport squadrons with C–47 and Convair 440
1 liaison squadron with Cessna 185
1 helicopter squadron with Hughes 500M
– trainer squadrons with T–6G
**Bases**
Charana, Colcapima, El Tejar, El Trompillo, La Florida,
   La Paz, Puerto Suarez, Santa Cruz
**Military training aid from**
United States
**Equipment**
Ground-attack aircraft
10 North American (Cavalier) F–51D
Transport
some Beechcraft C–45
6 Convair 440
12 Douglas C–47
1 Douglas C–54
Liaison and AOP aircraft
6 Cessna 172
7 Cessna 185
Helicopters
3 Hiller OH–23D
12 Hughes 500M
Trainers
13 Lockheed T–33A–N
13 North American T–6G
4 (10?) North American T–28A
**Programme**
Aquisition of modern strike fighters
18 Embraer EMB–326–GB (Aermacchi MB.326GB)
   trainers on order
**Army**
20,000 men

## BRAZIL

**Air force** (Fôrça Aérea Brasileira)
men 30,000
squadrons 17
operational aircraft 190
helicopters 41
**Organisation**
1 strike fighter squadron with Mirage IIIEBR
1 strike fighter squadron with A–4F
3 ground-attack squadrons with MB.326GB and T–33
1 bomber squadron with B–26K
1 maritime reconnaissance squadron with HU–16A
1 maritime reconnaissance and ASW squadron with P–2E
1 maritime reconnaissance and ASW squadron with S–2A
   and CS2F–1
1 transport squadron with C–130E
2 transport squadrons with DHC–5
2 transport squadrons with C–47, C–54 and DC–6B
1 transport squadron with C–119G
1 transport squadron with BAC 1–11, H.S.125, H.S.748
   and Viscount
3 liaison squadrons with C–42/L–42 and O–1E
1 helicopter squadron with UH–1D and Bell 206A
– trainer squadrons with T–23
– trainer squadrons with T–37C
**Major Bases**
Anapolis, Balterra, Belem, Cachijo, Combica, Fortaleaza,
   Galeat, Guarantiqueta, Jacreacanga, Natal, Porto Alegre,
Recife, Rio de Janeiro, Salvador, Santa Cruz, Santarem,
   Sao Paulo
**Military training aid from**
United States
**Equipment**
Fighters and strike fighters
12 Dassault Mirage IIIEBR
4 Dassault Mirage IIIDBR
15 McDonnell Douglas A–4F
Bombers
15 Douglas (On Mark) B–26K
Maritime reconnaissance and ASW aircraft
8 Convair PBY–5A
12 Grumman HU–16A
10 Grumman S–2A and CS2F–1
8 Lockheed P–2E
Transports
2 BAC 1–11
some Beechcraft C–45
24 DeHavilland Canada DHC–5
30 Douglas C–47
5 Douglas C–54
4 Douglas DC–6B
12 Fairchild C–119G
10 Hawker Siddeley H.S.125
6 Hawker Siddeley H.S.748
10 Lockheed C–130E
2 Vickers Viscount
Liaison and AOP aircraft
approx 60 aircraft, inc Cessna O–1E, 40 Neiva C–42 and
   L–42, 5 Pilatus PC–6
Helicopters
10 Bell 47G
5 Bell 48J
7 Bell 206A
6 Bell UH–1D
8 Bell UH–1H
5 Bell SH–1D
Trainers
approx 300 aircraft, inc 70 Aerotec T–23, 40 Cessna
   T–37C, 30 Embraer-Aermacchi MB.326GB, 60 Fokker
   S.11 and S.12, 15 Lockheed T–33, 50 North American
   T–6G, 18 North American T–28C, Pilatus P–3, 7 Potez-
   Air Fouga C.M.170–2
**Programme**
Further 30 Dassault Mirage IIIEBR strike fighters
   reportedly already on order. Formation of 4 strike
   fighter squadrons with 48 Northrop F–5E. Replacement
   of Lockheed P–2E maritime reconnaissance and ASW
   aircraft by 8 Breguet Br.1150 or Lockheed P–3C from
   1973/74. 80 Embraer Bandeirante transports on order.
   Foreign-built trainers to be replaced by Brazilian-built
   machines from 1972/73: 112 Embraer-Aermacchi
   MB.326GB (TF.26 Xavante) and 150 Neiva T–25
   trainers delivered or on order. The MB.326GB is to
   replace the Lockheed T–33A in the ground-attack
   squadrons.
**Army**
120,000 men
**Navy**
44,350 men
1 aircraft carrier
**Naval Aviation** (Fôrca Aéronatale)
– men
3 squadrons
36 helicopters
**Organisation**
1 ASW squadron with SH–3D and SH–34G
1 helicopter squadron with Whirlwind 3
1 helicopter squadron with FH–1100
**Equipment**
Helicopters
6 Fairchild-Hiller FH–1100
9 Hughes 269
4 Sikorsky SH–3D
5 Sikorsky SH–34J
3 Westland Wasp AS.1

7 Westland Whirlwind 3
The shipboard ASW squadron with S-2A and CS2F-1 is
 subordinated to the Air Force.
**Programme**
30 Aérospatiale S.A.341 helicopters on order, delivery
 from 1974.
**Aircraft factories**
Aerotec, Embraer (Emprêsa Brasileira de Aéronautica
 SA), Neiva

## BRUNEI

**Air force**
Part of the Army
**Army**
– men
Army Aviation (Askar Melaya Diraja Brunei)
– men
2 squadrons
1 operational aircraft and
8 helicopters
**Organisation**
1 helicopter squadron with Bell 205A and Bell 212
1 helicopter squadron with Bell 206A
**Equipment**
Helicopters
2 Bell 205A
4 Bell 206A
2 Bell 212
Transport
1 Hawker Siddeley H.S.748

## BULGARIA

**Air force**
men 22,000
squadrons 18
operational aircraft 165 and
helicopters 40
**Organisation**
3 fighter squadrons with MiG-21
3 fighter squadrons with MiG-19
4 strike fighter squadrons with MiG-17
2 reconnaissance squadrons with MiG-17 and Il-28
2 transport squadrons with Il-14, Il-12 and Li-2
1 transport squadron with An-2
3 helicopter squadrons with Mi-4
– trainer squadrons with Yak-11 and Yak-18
– trainer squadrons with L-29 and MiG-15UTI
Fighter, strike fighter and reconnaissance squadrons each
 with 10–12 aircraft
**Major bases**
Balchik, Burgas, Ignatiev, Karlovo, Plovdiv, Sofia,
 Tolbuchin, Yambol
**Military training aid from**
Soviet Union
**Equipment**
Fighters and strike fighters
40–45 Mikoyan MiG-17
30 Mikoyan MiG-19
40 Mikoyan MiG-21 and MiG-21UTI
Bombers
8–10 Ilyushin Il-28
Reconnaissance aircraft
15–20 Mikoyan MiG-17
Transports
8 Antonov An-2
6 Ilyushin Il-12
10 Ilyushin Il-14
4 Ilyushin Il-18
1–2 Li-2 (Soviet copy of Douglas C-47)
Liaison and AOP aircraft
some L-60 and PZL-104
Helicopters
10 Mil Mi-1
30 Mil Mi-4
Trainers
approx 100 aircraft, inc Aero L-29, Yakovlev Yak-11 and
 Yak-18, Mikoyan MiG-15UTI

**Programme**
Re-equipment of further Mikoyan MiG-17 strike fighter
 squadrons with Mikoyan MiG-21, replacement of Mil
 Mi-4 helicopters by Mil Mi-8
**Army**
117,000 men
**Navy**
9,000 men
**Naval Aviation**
6 Mil Mi-4 and Mi-1 helicopters

## BURMA

**Air force** (Union of Burma Air Force)
men 6,500
squadrons 6
operational aircraft 28 and
helicopters 38
**Organisation**
1 strike fighter squadron with F-86F
1 transport squadron with DHC-3
1 transport squadron with C-47
1 liaison squadron with U-17A
1 helicopter squadron with Alouette III
1 helicopter squadron with HH-43B
1 helicopter squadron with Bell 47G
– trainer squadrons with DHC-1 and Provost T.53
1 trainer squadron with T-33 and Vampire T.55
**Major bases**
Hmawbi, Kengtung, Mandalay, Meiktila, Mingaladon
 (Rangoon), Myitkyina
**Military training aid from**
United States
**Equipment**
Fighters and strike fighters
12 North American F-86F
Transports
4 Beechcraft C-45
6 DeHavilland Canada DHC-3
6 Douglas C-47
Liaison and AOP aircraft
10 Cessna U-17A
Helicopters
13 Aérospatiale Alouette III
9 Kaman HH-43B
13 Kawasaki-Bell 47G
3 Kawasaki-Vertol KV-107
Trainers
10 DeHavilland Canada DHC-1
3 DeHavilland Vampire T.55
30 Hunting Provost T.53
10 Lockheed T-33
**Army**
130,000 men
**Navy**
7,000 men

## CAMBODIA

**Air force** (Aviation Nationale Khmer)
men 2,500
squadrons 4
operational aircraft 60(?) and
helicopters 20
**Organisation**
1 ground-attack squadron with A-1
1 night ground-support squadron with AC-47
1 transport squadron with C-47
1 liaison squadron with 0-1
1 helicopter squadron with UH-1D
1 trainer squadron with T-37B
1 trainer squadron with T-6G
**Bases**
Battambang, Pochentong (Pnom Penh), Seam Reap
**Military training aid from**
United States, Vietnam (South)
**Equipment**
Ground-attack aircraft
18(?) Douglas A-1

12

some North American T–28D
Night ground support aircraft
6 Douglas AC–47
14 Helio AU–24A
Transports
2 Antonov An–2
some(?) Dassault M.D.315
12 Douglas C–47
1 Douglas C–54
1 Ilyushin Il–14
Liaison and AOP aircraft
10 Cessna 0–1
2 DeHavilland Canada DHC–2
Helicopters
2 Aérospatiale Alouette II
18 Bell UH–1D
Trainers
6 Cessna T–37B and T–37C
6(?) North American T–6G
2(?) Potez–Air Fouga C.M.170
**Programme**
Formation of new ground-attack squadrons (with Cessna
    A–37?) and helicopter squadrons with Bell UH–1
**Army**
175,000 men
**Navy**
1,600 men

## CAMEROON

**Air force**
men 3,000
squadrons —
operational aircraft 3 and
helicopter 1
**Organisation**
—
**Base**
Bangui
**Military aid from**
France
**Equipment**
Transports
1 Douglas C–47
2 DeHavilland Canada DHC–4
Liaison and AOP aircraft
2 Max Holste M.H.1521M
Helicopter
1 Aérospatiale Alouette II
**Army**
3,000 men
**Navy**
200 men

## CANADA

**Air force**
men 34,000
squadrons 14
operational aircraft 338 and
helicopters 6
**Organisation**
3 fighter squadrons with F–101B
2 strike fighter squadrons with CF–104
2 strike fighter squadrons with CF–5A
1 ECM squadron with CF–100
1 reconnaissance squadron with CF–104
2 transport squadrons with C–130E
1 transport squadron with Falcon 20
1 transport squadron with DHC–6
1 transport squadron with Boeing 707–320C
1 trainer squadron with CF–104D
1 trainer squadron with TF–101B and T–33A–N
1 trainer squadron with T–33A–N
– trainer squadrons with Musketeer and DHC–1
– trainer squadrons with CL–41
fighter, strike fighter and reconnaissance squadrons each
    with 16–18 aircraft

**Major bases**
Bagotville, Calgary, Chatham, Cold Lake, Comox,
    Edmonton, Gagetown, Halifax, Montreal, Moose Jaw,
    Namao, North Bay, Ottawa, Petawawa, Rivers, St.
    Hubert, Toronto, Trenton, Uplands, Valcartier,
    Winnipeg
**Equipment**
Fighters and strike fighters
14 Canadair CF–100
65 Canadair CF–104 (F–104G)
25 Canadair CF–104D (TF–104G)
71 Canadair CF–5A (Northrop F–5A)
44 Canadair CF–5B (Northrop F–5B)
60 McDonnell F–101B
6 McDonnell TF–101B
Some CF–104 and 74 CF–5 have been mothballed
Transports
5 Boeing 707–320C
7 Dassault Falcon 20
8 DeHavilland Canada DHC–6
17 Douglas C–47
23 Lockheed C–130E
Helicopters
6 Boeing Vertol CH–113
Trainers
25 Beechcraft Musketeer Sport
170 Canadair CL–41A
150(?) Canadair T–33A–N
9 Convair CC–109
40 DeHavilland Canada DHC–1
**Programme**
Purchase of further 1–2 Boeing 707–320C transports and
    tankers planned. Douglas C–47 transports and
    DeHavilland Canada DHC–1 trainers to be phased out.
**Army**
34,000 men
**Army Aviation**
— men
— squadrons
85 operational aircraft and
140 helicopters
**Organisation**
4 helicopter squadrons with CUH–1N (UH–1N) and
    COH–58A (OH–58A)
1 helicopter squadron with CH–113A
– liaison and AOP squadrons with O–1A and O–1E
1 transport squadron with DHC–5
6 transport squadrons with DHC–3
**Equipment**
Helicopters
74 Bell COH–58A (OH–58A)
10 Bell CUH–1H (UH–1H)
50 Bell CUH–1N (UH–1N)
some Boeing Vertol CH–113
Liaison and AOP aircraft
24 Cessna O–1A and O–1E
4 Cessna L–19L
some Cessna 172
Transports
38 DeHavilland Canada DHC–3
15 DeHavilland Canada DHC–5
**Programme**
Phasing out of Cessna L–19L and Cessna 172 liaison
    aircraft
**Navy**
14,000 men
**Naval aviation**
— men
6 squadrons
52 operational aircraft and
38 helicopters
**Organisation**
4 maritime reconnaissance and ASW squadrons with
    CL–28
1 maritime reconnaissance and ASW squadron with
    CS2F–2 (S–2A)
1 ASW squadron with CHSS–2 (SH–3A)

1 trainer squadron with CL–28
**Equipment**
Maritime reconnaissance and ASW aircraft
30 Canadair CL–28
6 DeHavilland Canada–Grumman CS2F–2 (S–2A)
9 Grumman CSR–110 (HU–16B)
Helicopters
38 Sikorsky CHSS–2 (SH–3A)
**Programme**
Replacement of Canadair CL–28 maritime reconnaissance
    and ASW aircraft from 1975 (by 30 Lockheed P–3?)
**Aircraft factories**
Canadair, DeHavilland and Canada (DHC)

## CENTRAL AFRICAN REPUBLIC

**Air force** (Force Aérienne Centrafricaine)
men 100
squadrons —
operational aircraft 2 and
helicopters 1
**Organisation**
—
**Base**
Bangui
**Military training aid from**
France
**Equipment**
Transports
1 Dassault Falcon 20
1 Douglas C–47
Liaison and AOP aircraft
8 Aermacchi AL.60C5
3 Max Holste M.H.1521M
Helicopters
1 Aérospatiale Alouette II
**Army**
700 men

## CEYLON (SRI LANKA)

**Air force** (Sri Lanka Air Force)
men 1,600
squadrons 4
operational aircraft 17
helicopters 16
**Organisation**
1 strike fighter squadron with MiG–17
1 transport squadron with Dove and Heron
1 helicopter squadron with Bell 47G
1 helicopter squadron with Bell 206A
1 trainer squadron with DHC–1
1 trainer squadron with Provost T.51
**Bases**
Banderanaike (Ratmalana–Colombo), China Bay,
    Katunayake
**Military training aid from**
Great Britain, Soviet Union
**Equipment**
Fighters and strike fighters
5 Mikoyan MiG–17
Transports
5 DeHavilland Dove
4 DeHavilland Heron
3 Scottish Aviation Twin Pioneer CC.2
Liaison and AOP aircraft
10 Cessna, type unknown
Helicopters
6 Bell 47G
10 Bell 206A
Trainers
9 DeHavilland Canada DHC–1
8 Hunting Provost T.51
1 Mikoyan MiG–15UTI
The Mikoyan MiG–17 strike fighters are not in service
    owing to lack of pilots
**Army**
5,000 men
**Navy**
2,000 men

## CHAD

**Air force** (Escadrille Tchadienne)
men 400
squadrons 3
operational aircraft 16 and
helicopters 15
**Organisation**
1 ground attack squadron with A–1D
1 transport squadron with N.2501
1 helicopter squadron with H–34
**Base**
Fort Lamy
**Military training aid from**
France
**Equipment**
Ground-attack aircraft
5 Douglas A–1D
Transports
1 Douglas C–47
10 Nord N.2501
Liaison and AOP aircraft
3 Max Holste M.H.1521M
Helicopters
approx 15 machines inc 1 Aérospatiale Alouette II,
    Aérospatiale Alouette III, Sikorsky H–34
**Army**
2,500 men

## CHILE

**Air force** (Fuerza Aérea de Chile)
men 8,000
squadrons 11
operational aircraft 120 and
helicopters 27
**Organisation**
2 strike fighter squadrons with Hunter FGA.71 and FR.10
1 bomber squadron with B–26
1 maritime reconnaissance squadron with HU–16B
2 transport squadrons with C–47
1 transport squadron with Beechcraft 99A
1 transport squadron with DHC–3
1 transport squadron with DHC–6
1 liaison squadron with Cessna 180
1 liaison squadron with DHC–2
1 helicopter squadron with UH–12E
1 helicopter squadron with UH–19
– trainer squadrons with T–6G and T–34
– trainer squadrons with T–33A, T–37B, T–37C and
    Vampire T.55
**Major bases**
Bahia, Catalina, Balmaceda, Chamiza, Cerro Moreno, El
    Bosque, Iquique, Los Cerillos, Los Condores, Maquehue,
    Punta Arenas, Puerto Montt, Quintero
**Equipment**
Fighters and strike fighters
18 Hawker Hunter FGA.71
3 Hawker Hunter T.72
Bombers
12 Douglas B–26
Reconnaissance aircraft
4 Hawker Hunter FR.10
Maritime reconnaissance and ASW aircraft
14 Grumman HU–16B
Transports
some Beechcraft C–45
9 Beechcraft 99A
12 DeHavilland Canada DHC–3
7 DeHavilland Canada DHC–6
25 Douglas C–47
3 Douglas DC–6B
1 Hawker Siddeley H.S.748
3 Lockheed C–130E
Liaison and AOP aircraft
5 Beechcraft Twin Bonanza
10 Cessna 180
4 Cessna 0–1
20 DeHavilland Canada DHC–2

Helicopters
10 Bell 47D, G and J
2 Bell UH–1D
10 Hiller UH–12E
5(?) Sikorsky S–55T
Trainers
45(?) Beechcraft T–34
10 Cessna T–37B and T–37C
6 DeHavilland Sea Vampire T.22
5 DeHavilland Vampire T.55
8 Lockheed T–33A
20 North American T–6G
**Programme**
Replacement of Hawker Hunter FGA.71 strike fighters by
18 Northrop F–5A and 3 Northrop F–5B(?). Purchase
of 20 McDonnell Douglas A–4 strike fighters?
**Army**
38,000 men
**Army aviation**
– men
1 liaison and AOP squadron with 8 aircraft (type
unknown)
**Navy**
15,000 men
**Naval aviation** (Aviation Naval)
– men
– squadrons
– operational aircraft and
6 helicopters
**Organisation**
—
**Equipment**
Helicopters
2 Bell 47G
4 Bell 206A
Transports
some Beechcraft C–45
Trainers
some Beechcraft T–34

## CHINA

**Air force** (Chung–Kuo Zhen Min Tsie–Fang Tsun Pu–tai):
men 180,000
squadrons approx 220 (250?)
operational aircraft 2,900–3,000 and
helicopters —
**Organisation**
150 strike fighter squadrons with F–4 (MiG–17), F–6
(MiG–19) and F–8 (MiG–21)
36–40(?) strike fighter squadrons with F–2 (MiG–15)
20(?) bomber squadrons with Il–28 and Tu–16
– maritime reconnaissance and ASW squadrons with Be–6
– transport squadrons with An–2 and Fongshu 2
– transport squadrons with Il–14 and Il–18
– helicopter squadrons with Mi–1 and Mi–4
– trainer squadrons with Yak–11 and Yak–18
– trainer squadrons with MiG–15UTI
**Major bases**
Canton, Changsha, Chengchow, Chienchiao, Futshau,
Hsincheng, Hungchiao, Kunming, Kwangchan, Lhasa,
Liencheng, Luchiao, Nanhai, Nanking, Peking, Pingtau,
Shenyang, Sian, Tenghai, Tsaochiao, Wuhan
**Equipment**
Fighters and strike fighters
100 Shenyang F–2 (MiG–15)
1,500 Shenyang F–4 (MiG–17)
800 Shenyang F–6 (MiG–19)
100(?) Shenyang F–8 (MiG–21)
200(?) Shenyang F–9
Bombers
150 Ilyushin Il–28
some Tu–4
100 Tupolev Tu–16
Reconnaissance aircraft
—
Maritime reconnaissance and ASW aircraft
Beriev Be–6
Transports

approx 400 aircraft, inc Antonov An–2, Fongshu 2,
Ilyushin Il–14, Ilyushin Il–18, Li–2 (C–47 copy)
Liaison and AOP aircraft
—
Helicopters
approx 300 machines, inc Mil Mi–1, Mil Mi–4
Trainers
Yakovlev Yak–11
Yakovlev Yak–18
300 Mikoyan MiG–15UTI
**Programme**
Purchase of 20 Hawker Siddeley Harrier strike fighters?
**Army**
2,500,000 men
**Navy**
160,000 men
**Naval aviation**
16,000 men
– squadrons
380 operational aircraft and
100 helicopters
**Organisation**
– strike fighter squadrons with F–2 (MiG–15) and
F–4 (MiG–17)
– bomber squadrons with Il–28
**Equipment**
Fighters and strike fighters
100 Shenyang F–2 (MiG–15)
200 Shenyang F–4 (MiG–17)
Bombers
80 Ilyushin Il–28
Helicopters
approx 100 machines
Trainers
approx 150 aircraft
**Aircraft factories**
Fongshu, Shenyang

## CHINA (TAIWAN)

**Air force** (Chung–Kuo Kung Chuan)
men 80,000
squadrons 16
operational aircraft 355 and
helicopters 16
**Organisation**
2 fighter squadrons with F–104G
1 fighter squadrons with F–104A
3 strike fighter squadrons with F–5A
1 strike fighter squadrons with F–86F
3 strike fighter squadrons with F–100D
1 reconnaissance squadron with RF–104G and RF–101C
1 maritime reconnaissance and ASW squadron with
HU–16B and PBY–5A
2 transport squadrons with C–47
2 transport squadrons with C–119G
1 transport squadron with C–46
1 helicopter squadron with Hughes 500M
1 helicopter squadron with UH–19
– trainer squadrons with T–6G and T–28A
– trainer squadrons with T–33A
Fighter and strike fighter squadrons each with 18–25
aircraft
**Major bases**
Chiai, Hsinchu, Kung K'uang, Ping tung, T'ai–chung,
T'ai–nan, Taipei, Tao–yuan
**Military training aid from**
United States
**Foreign Air Forces in China (Taiwan)**
5 American squadrons:
2 strike fighter squadrons with F–4
3 transport squadrons with C–130
**Equipment**
Fighters and strike fighters
18 Lockheed F–104A
45 Lockheed F–104G and TF–104G
20 North American F–86F
75 North American F–100D and F–100F

70 Northrop F–5A and F–5B
Reconnaissance aircraft
8 Lockheed RF–104G
some Martin RB–57
4 McDonnell RF–101C
Maritime reconnaissance and ASW aircraft
some Convair PBY–5A and Grumman HU–16B
Transports
1 Boeing 720B
20 Curtiss-Wright C–46
40 Douglas C–47
1–2 Douglas DC–6
35 Fairchild C–119G
Helicopters
3 Bell 47G
6 Hughes 500M
7 Sikorsky UH–19
Trainers
approx 70 aircraft, inc 40 Pazmany/CAF PL–1B,
    Lockheed T–33A, North American T–28A
45 Northrop F–5 strike fighters reportedly lent to
    Vietnam (South) in November 1972
**Programme**
Replacement of North American F–86F strike fighters by
    Northrop F–5E. 21 Bell UH–1H helicopters on order
**Army**
390,000 men
**Army aviation**
50 Bell UH–1H helicopters
2 Kawasaki KH–4 helicopters
10 Pazmany/CAF PL–1B trainers
**Navy**
35,000 men
**Naval Aviation**
1 maritime reconnaissance and ASW squadron with 9
    Grumman S–2A
**Marines**
35,000 men
**Aircraft factories**
AIDC/CAF (Aero-Industry Development Center, Chinese
    Air Force)

## COLOMBIA

**Air force** (Fuerza Aérea Colombiana)
men 6,000
squadrons 9
operational aircraft 65 and
helicopters 50
**Organisation**
1 strike fighter squadron with Mirage 5–COA
1 strike fighter squadron with F–86F and CL–13B
1 bomber squadron with B–26B and C
1 maritime reconnaissance squadron with PBY–5A
1 transport squadron with C–47
1 transport squadron with C–54 and C–130E
1 liaison squadron with DHC–2
1 liaison squadron with PC–6 and PC–6A
1 helicopter squadron with OH–6A
1 helicopter squadron with HH–43B
1 helicopter squadron with UH–1B
– trainer squadrons with T–6G, T–34A and T–41D
1 trainer squadron with T–37C
**Major bases**
Baranquilla, Bogotá, Cali, Melgar, Palanquero
**Military training aid from**
United States
**Equipment**
Fighters and strike fighters
4 Canadair CL–13B Sabre Mk.6
14 Dassault Mirage 5–COA
2 Dassault Mirage 5–COD
6 North American F–86F
Bombers
6 Douglas B–26B and C
Reconnaissance aircraft
2 Dassault Mirage 5–COR
Maritime reconnaissance aircraft

8 Convair PBY–5A
Transports
1 Aero Commander 560A
3 Beechcraft C–45H
4 DeHavilland Canada DHC–3
6 Douglas C–47
3 Douglas C–54
1 Fokker F.28
4 Hawker Siddeley H.S.748
2 Lockheed C–130E
Liaison and AOP aircraft
10 DeHavilland Canada DHC–2
6 Pilatus PC–6 and PC–6A
Helicopters
6 Bell 47D
8 Bell 47G
2 Bell 47J
1 Bell 212
6 Bell UH–1B
4 Hiller OH–23G
12 Hughes OH–6A
6 Hughes TH–55A
6 Kaman HH–43B
Trainers
30 Beechcraft T–34A
10 Cessna T–37C
30 Cessna T–41D
4 Lockheed T–33A
20 North American T–6G
**Army**
50,000 men
**Navy**
7,200 men

## CONGO (BRAZZAVILLE)

**Air force**
men 200
squadrons —
operational aircraft 9 and
helicopter 1
**Organisation**
—
**Base**
Brazzaville
**Military training aid from**
France, Soviet Union
**Equipment**
Transport
3(?) Antonov An–24
1 Douglas C–47
5(?) Ilyushin Il–14
Liaison and AOP aircraft
3 Max Holste M.H.1521M
Helicopter
1 Aérospatiale Alouette II
**Army**
1,400 men
**Navy**
200 men

## CONGO (KINSHASA)

**Air force** (Force Aérienne Zaïroise)
men 850
squadron 6
operational aircraft 29 and
helicopters 40
**Organisation**
1 ground-attack squadron with MB.326GB
1 transport squadron with C–47
1 transport squadron with C–54 and C–130H
1 helicopter squadron with Alouette III
2 helicopter squadrons with S.A.330
1 trainer squadron with T–28D
2 trainer squadrons with SF.260MC and T–6G
**Major bases**
Kamina, Kinshasa, Kinsangani, Kolwezi
**Military training aid from**

Italy
**Equipment**
Ground-attack aircraft
15 Aermacchi MB.326GB
Transports
9 Douglas C–47
2(4?) Douglas C–54
1 Douglas DC–6
2 Lockheed C–130H
Liaison and AOP aircraft
2 Auster AOP
2 Dornier Do–27
Helicopters
8 Aérospatiale Alouette III
30 Aérospatiale S.A.330
some Bell 47G
Trainers
8 North American T–6G
5 North American T–28D
some Piaggio P.148 and Potez-Air Fouga C.M.170
12 SIAI–Marchetti SF.260MC
**Programme**
Further 12 SIAI–Marchetti SF.260MC trainers on order.
Phasing out of North American T–6G trainers. Purchase
of 15 Dassault Mirage III strike fighters under consideration. Procurement of further Lockheed C–130H
planned.
**Army**
49,000 men
**Navy**
200 men

## COSTA RICA

**Air Force**
Component part of army
**Army**
1,200 men
**Army aviation**
some Cessna U–17A liaison aircraft

## CUBA

**Air force** (Fuerza Aérea Revolucionaria)
men 12,000
squadrons 19
operational aircraft 210 and
helicopters 30
**Organisation**
6 fighter squadrons with MiG–21
2(?) fighter squadrons with MiG–19
5 strike fighter squadrons with MiG–17
1 strike fighter squadron with MiG–15
2 transport squadrons with Il–14
1 transport squadron with An–24
2 helicopter squadrons with Mi–4
fighter and strike fighter squadron each with 10–12
aircraft
**Major bases**
Camaguey, Havanna, San Antonio, Santa Clara
**Military training aid from**
Soviet Union
**Equipment**
Fighters and strike fighters
12 Mikoyan MiG–15
60 Mikoyan MiG–17
20(?) Mikoyan MiG–19
80 Mikoyan MiG–21 and MiG–21UTI
Transports
approx 45 aircraft, inc Antonov AN–2, Antonov An–24
and Ilyushin Il–14
Helicopters
6(?) Mil Mi–1 and 24 Mil Mi–4
Trainers
approx 100 aircraft, inc Mikoyan MiG–15UTI and
Zlin 226
**Army**
90,000 men
**Navy**

6,000 men

## CYPRUS

**Air force** (Cyprus National Guard, Air Wing)
men —
squadrons —
helicopters 2
**Organisation**
—

**Bases**
Akrotiri, Dhekelia
**Military training aid from**
Great Britain, Greece, Turkey
**Foreign Air Forces in Cyprus**
5 British squadrons:
1 fighter squadron with Lightning F.6
2 bomber squadrons with Vulcan B.2
1 transport squadron with C–130K
1 helicopter squadron with Whirlwind HAR.10 and
Wessex HC.2
In addition 2 further squadrons with detachments
sometimes based on Malta
1 reconnaissance squadron with Canberra PR.9
1 maritime reconnaissance and ASW squadron with
Nimrod MR.1
**Equipment**
Helicopters
1 Agusta-Bell AB.47J
1 Fairchild–Hiller FH–1100
**Army**
15,000 men
**Navy**
– men

## CZECHOSLOVAKIA

**Air force** (Ceskoslovenské Letectvo)
40,000 men
– squadrons
500 operational aircraft and
90 helicopters
**Organisation**
12 fighter squadrons with MiG–21
6 fighter squadrons with MiG–19
18 strike fighter squadrons with Su–7 and MiG–17
3 bomber squadrons with Il–28
– transport squadrons with An–2
– transport squadrons with Il–14
– transport squadrons with An–24
– helicopter squadrons with Mi–4
– helicopter squadrons with Mi–8
– trainer squadrons with L–29
– trainer squadrons with Zlin 226 and Zlin 326
Fighter, strike fighter and bomber squadrons each with
10–12 aircraft
**Major bases**
Barca, Bechyne, Brünn (Brno), Cakovice, Cáslav, Ceské,
Budejovice (Bohemian=Budweis), Chocen, Dobrany,
Eger (Cheb), Ivanka/Slovakia, Kbley near Prague,
Klecany, Kunovice, Letnany, Lucenec/Slovakia, Milovice,
Mimon, Mosnov, Muchovo, Otrokovice, Pardubitz
(Pardubice), Prerau, Piestany/Slovakia, Pilsen (Plzen),
Poprad/Slovakia, Preschau, Pressburg (Bratislava),
Ruzyne near Prague, Saaz (Zatec), Sliac, Spisska–Nova
Ves
**Military training aid from**
Soviet Union
**Foreign Air Forces in Czechoslovakia**
approx 400 Soviet fighters, strike fighters and
reconnaissance aircraft
**Equipment**
Fighters and strike fighters
30 Mikoyan MiG–17
75 Mikoyan MiG–19
150 Mikoyan MiG–21 and MiG–21UTI
160 Sukhoi Su–7 and Su–7UTI
Bombers
30 Ilyushin Il–28 and Il–28UTI

Transports
approx 50 aircraft, inc Antonov An–2, Antonov An–24,
 Ilyushin Il–14, Ilyushin Il–18, Lisunov Li–2
Liaison and AOP aircraft
L–60, LET L–200 Morava
Helicopters
approx 90 machines, inc Mil Mi–1 Mil Mi–4 Mil Mi–8
Trainers
approx 300(?) aircraft, inc 150 Aero L–29, Mikoyan
 MiG–15UTI, Yakovlev Yak–18(?), Zlin 226, Zlin 326
**Programme**
Replacement of Mikoyan MiG–17 strike fighters by
 Sukhoi Su–7 and, from 1975, replacement of Aero
 L–29 trainers by 100 Aero L–39
**Army**
145,000 men
**Aircraft factories**
Aero, Avia, Letov, Zlin

## DAHOMEY

**Air force** (Force Aérienne du Dahomey)
men 150
squadrons —
operational aircraft 2 and
helicopter 1
**Organisation**
—
**Base**
Porto Novo
**Military training aid from**
France
**Equipment**
Transports
1 Aero Commander 500B
1 Douglas C–47
Liaison and AOP aircraft
2 Max Holste M.H.1521M
Helicopter
1 Aérospatiale Alouette II
**Army**
2,000 men
**Navy**
100 men

## DENMARK

**Air force** (Kongelige Danske Flyvevåben)
men 9,600
squadrons 8
operational aircraft 131 and
helicopters 8
**Organisation**
2 fighter squadrons with F–104G
2 strike fighter squadrons with F–100D
1 strike fighter squadron with Saab 35XD
1 reconnaissance squadron with Saab 35XD
1 transport squadron with C–47 and C–54
1 helicopter squadron with S–61A
1 trainer squadron with DHC–1
1 trainer squadron with T–33A
fighter squadron and strike fighter squadrons each with
 20 aircraft, reconnaissance squadron with 16 aircraft
**Major bases**
Aalborg, Karup, Kastrup, Odense, Skrydstrup, Tirstrip,
 Vaerløse, Vandel
**Military training aid from**
United States
**Equipment**
Fighters and strike fighters
15 Canadair CF–104 (F–104G)
7 Canadair CF–104D (TF–104G)
18 Lockheed F–104G
4 Lockheed TF–104G
25 North American F–100D
6 (12?) North American F–100F
40 Saab 35XD
6 Saab 35XT
Transports

6 Douglas C–47
3 Douglas C–54
Helicopters
8 Sikorsky S–61A
Trainers
25 DeHavilland Canada DHC–1
25 Lockheed T–33A
**Programme**
Reduction of personnel strength to 6,970 men and the
 number of fighters and strike fighters from 112 to 72.
 Replacement of Douglas C–47 and C–54 transports by
 3 Lockheed C–130H and of DeHavilland Canada
 DHC–1 trainers (by Saab MFI 17?). Disbandment of
 both trainer squadrons
**Army**
27,000 men
**Army Aviation** (Haerens Flyvetjeneste)
1 squadron with 12 Hughes 500M helicopters and
2 Piper L–18C liaison aircraft
**Programme**
3 Hughes 500M helicopters on order(?). Formation of a
 helicopter squadron with 8 further helicopters
**Navy**
6,500 men
**Naval Aviation** (Sovaernets Flyvevaesen)
8 Aérospatiale Alouette III helicopters

## DOMINICAN REPUBLIC

**Air force** (Aviasión Militar Dominicana)
men 3,000
squadrons 5
operational aircraft 44 and
 helicopters 11
**Organisation**
1 strike fighter squadron with Vampire Mk.1 and Mk.50
1 ground-attack squadron with F–51D
1 bomber squadron with B–26
1 transport squadron with C–46 and C–47
1 helicopter squadron with OH–6A
– trainer squadrons with T–69
**Bases**
Azua, Barahona, La Romana, La Vega, Monte Cristi,
 Puerta Plata, Saibo, San Isidor, Santiago, Santo
 Domingo
**Military training aid from**
United States
**Equipment**
Fighters and strike fighters
15 DeHavilland Vampire Mk.1 and Mk.50
Ground-attack aircraft
15 North American F–51D
Bombers
3 Douglas B–26
Maritime reconnaissance and ASW aircraft
2 Convair PBY–5A
Transports
5 Curtiss C–46
5 Douglas C–47
Liaison and AOP aircraft
3 DeHavilland Canada DHC–2
Helicopters
2 Aérospatiale Alouette II
1 Aérospatiale Alouette III
6 Hughes OH–6A
2 Sikorsky UH–19
Trainers
approx 25 aircraft, inc Beechcraft T–11 and
North American T–6G
**Army**
12,000 men
**Army Aviation**
3 Cessna 170 liaison aircraft
**Navy**
3,800 men

## ECUADOR

**Air force** (Fuerza Aérea Ecuatoriana)
men 3,500

squadrons 4
operational aircraft 45 and
helicopters 4
**Organisation**
1 strike fighter squadron with F–80C
1 bomber squadron with Canberra B.6
1 reconnaissance squadron with Meteor FR.9
1 transport squadron with C–47
– trainer squadrons with T–6G, T–28A and T–41A
– trainer squadrons with T–33
**Bases**
Latacunga, Loja, Manta, Quito, Riobamba, Salinas
**Military training aid from**
United States
**Equipment**
Fighters and strike fighters
10 Lockheed F–80C
Bombers
5 English Electric Canberra B.6
Reconnaissance aircraft
8 Gloster Meteor FR.9
Maritime reconnaissance and ASF aircraft
2 Convair PBY–5A
Transports
6 Beechcraft C–45
8 Douglas C–47
2 Douglas DC–6B
3 Hawker Siddeley H.S.748
1 Short Skyvan 3M
Liaison and AOP aircraft
2 Cessna 180
2 Fairchild-Hiller Porter
Helicopters
3 Bell 47G
1 Fairchild-Hiller FH–1100
Trainers
approx 25 aircraft inc 12 Cessna T–41A, North American
 T–6G and T–28A, Lockheed T–33A
**Programme**
Replacement of Lockheed F–80C strike fighters and
 Gloster Meteor FR.9 reconnaissance aircraft (by 12
 SEPECAT Jaguar strike fighters?). Formation of one
 ground-attack squadron with 8 BAC–167 Strikemaster
 Mk.89 ground-attack aircraft. 6 Aérospatiale Alouette
 III helicopters on order.
**Army**
12,800 men
**Navy**
3,700 men
**Naval aviation** (Aviacion Naval Ecuatorianas)
1 Cessna 177 liaison aircraft

## EGYPT (UAR)

**Air force** (Al Quwwat Aljawwiya Ilmisriya)
men 25,000
squadrons 41
operational aircraft 515 and
helicopters 140
**Organisation**
10 fighter squadrons with MiG–21
2 fighter squadrons with MiG–19
8 strike fighter squadrons with Su–7
12 strike fighter squadrons with MiG–17
1 bomber squadron with Il–28
1 bomber and reconnaissance squadron with Tu–16
4 transport squadrons with Il–14
2 transport squadrons with An–12
– helicopter squadrons with Mi–4
– helicopter squadrons with Mi–6
– helicopter squadrons with Mi–8
– trainer squadrons with Yak–11, Yak–18 and Zlin 226
– trainer squadrons with L–29 and MiG–15UTI
**Major bases**
Alexandria, Almaza, Assuan, Beni Sueif, Bilbeis, Cairo-
 West, El Mansura, El Minya, Heliopolis, Heluan,
 Hurghada, Inchas, Luxor, Ras Banas
**Military training aid from**

Soviet Union
**Foreign Air Forces in Egypt**
12–15 Soviet fighter squadrons with approx 150 Mikoyan
 MiG–21MF, Sukhoi Su–11 and some Mikoyan MiG–25
**Equipment**
Fighters and strike fighters
150 (?) Mikoyan MiG–17
20 (?) Mikoyan MiG–19
130 Mikoyan MiG–21
20 (?) Mikoyan MiG–21UTI
100 Sukhoi Su–7
Bombers
10 Ilyushin Il–28
18 (25?) Tupolev Tu–16
Transports
20 Antonov An–12
some (5?) Antonov An–26
40 Ilyushin Il–14
Helicopters
some Mil Mi–1
40 Mil Mi–4
20 Mil Mi–6
80 Mil Mi–8
Trainers
approx 150 aircraft, inc Aero L–29, Hispano HA–200,
 Mikoyan MiG–15UTI, Yakovlev Yak–11, Yakovlev
 Yak–18, Zlin 226
**Programme**
Replacement of Mikoyan MiG–19 fighters by Mikoyan
 MiG–21 (or Mikoyan MiG–25) and replacement of
 Mikoyan MiG–17 strike fighters by Sukhoi Su–7
**Army**
275,000 men
**Navy**
14,000 men
**Missile troops**
4,000 men
**Aircraft factories**
Heluan Aircraft Factory

## EL SALVADOR

**Air force** (Fuerza Aérea Salvadoreña)
men 1,000
squadrons 3
operational aircraft 15 and
helicopters 1
**Organisation**
1 ground-attack squadron with F–51D
1 ground-attack squadron wih F4U–5
1 transport squadron with C–47
– trainer squadrons with T–6G and T–34
**Base**
Ilopango
**Military training aid from**
United States
**Equipment**
Ground-attack aircraft
10 (?) North American (Cavalier) F–51D
4 Vought F4U–5
Transports
4 Douglas C–47
1 Douglas DC–4
Helicopter
1 Fairchild-Hiller FH–1100
Trainers
approx 20 aircraft, inc Beechcraft T–11, Beechcraft T–34
 and 10 North American T–6G
**Army**
4,500 men
**Navy**
130 men

## ETHIOPIA

**Air force**
men 2,200
squadrons 8
operational aircraft 57 and

helicopters 12
**Organisation**
1 fighter squadron with F–5A
1 fighter squadron with F–86F
1 ground-attack squadron with T–28D
1 bomber squadron with Canberra B.52
1 transport squadron with C–47 and C–54
1 transport squadron with C–119K
1 helicopter squadron with Alouette III
1 helicopter squadron with AB.204B
1 trainer squadron with Saab 91B and C
1 trainer squadron with T–28A
1 trainer squadron with T–33
**Major bases**
Asmar, Bishiftu, Debre Zeit, Harar, Jijiga
**Military training aid from**
United States
**Equipment**
Fighters and strike fighters
11 North American F–86F
10 Northrop F–5A
Ground-attack aircraft
13 North American T–28D
Bombers
4 English Electric Canberra B.52
Transports
4 Douglas C–47
2 Douglas C–54
2 Fairchild C–119G
10 (?) Fairchild C–119K
2 DeHavilland Dove
1 Ilyushin Il–14
Helicopters
5 Aérospatiale Alouette III
5 Agusta Bell AB.204B
2 Mil Mi–8
Trainers
11 Lockheed T–33
15 North American T–28A
20 Saab 91B and C
**Army**
39,000 men
**Army aviation**
1 helicopter squadron with UH–1H
helicopters
6 Bell UH–1H
**Navy**
1,400 men

# FINLAND

**Air Force** (Suomen Ilmavoimat)
men 3,000
squadrons 5
operational aircraft 63 and
helicopters 13
**Organisation**
3 strike fighter squadrons with MiG–21F
1 ground-attack squadron with C.M.170
1 transport squadron with C–47 and DHC–2
1 trainer squadron with Saab 91D
– trainer squadrons with C.M.170
strike fighter squadrons each with 12 aircraft
**Major bases**
Kuopio, Luonetjärvi, Pori, Rovaniemi, Utti
**Military training aid from**
Soviet Union
**Equipment**
Fighters and strike fighters
35 Mikoyan MiG–21F
4 Mikoyan MiG–21UTI
Ground-attack aircraft
12 armed Potez–Air Fouga C.M.170
Bombers
2 Ilyushin Il–28
Transports
8 Douglas C–47
2 Hunting Pembroke C.53

Liaison and AOP aircraft
some DeHavilland Canada DHC–2
Helicopters
1 Aérospatiale Alouette II
4 Agusta–Bell AB.204B
1 Agusta–Bell AB.206A
3 Mil Mi–4
2 Mil Mi–8
Trainers
4 Mikoyan MiG–15UTI
55 Potez-Air Fouga C.M.170
28 Saab 91D
**Programme**
12 Saab 35XS Draken strike fighters on order. 6 older Saab 35Bs strike fighters on loan from Swedish Air Force from 1972/73 until delivery of Saab 35XS. Replacement of Douglas C–47 transports, Mi–4 helicopters as well as Mikoyan MiG–15UTI and Saab 91D trainers.
**Army**
31,400 men
**Navy**
2,000 men

# FRANCE

**Air force** (Armée de l'Air)
101,000 men
51 squadrons
645 operational aircraft
70 helicopters
**Organisation**
3 fighter squadrons with Mirage IIIC
2 fighter squadrons with Vautour IIN
2 fighter squadrons with Super Mystère B2
6 strike fighter squadrons with Mirage IIIE
2 strike fighter squadrons with Mirage 5–F
1 strike fighter squadron with Mirage IIIB
2 strike fighter squadrons with F–100D
2 strike fighter squadrons with Mystère IVA
9 bomber squadrons with Mirage IVA
3 reconnaissance squadrons with Mirage IIIR and IIIRD
1 ECM squadron with N.2501
3 transport squadrons with C.160F
4 transport squadrons with N.2501
1 transport squadron with DC–6 and DC–8
3 tanker squadrons with KC–135F
2 transport squadrons with C–47, DC–6 and N.262
1 transport squadron with N.262
4 helicopter squadrons with H–34 and Alouette II
– trainer squadrons with C.M.170 and T–33A
– trainer squadrons with M.S.760
fighter and strike fighter squadrons each with 12–16, and reconnaissance squadrons each with 18 aircraft
**Major Bases**
Aix-en-Provence, Avord, Bordeaux, Bretigny, Cambrai, Chartres, Cognac, Creil, Dijon, Etampes, Istres, Le Bourget, Limoges, Metz, Mont-de-Marsan, Nancy-Ochey, Nîmes, Orange, Orléans-Bricy, Pau, Reims, St. Dizier, Strasbourg, Toul-Rosières, Toulouse, Tours, Villacoublay
**Equipment**
Fighters and strike fighters
40 Dassault Mirage IIIC
120 Dassault Mirage IIIE
25 (?) Dassault Mirage IIIB
50 Mirage 5–F
30 Dassault Mystère IVA
25 Dassault Super Mystère B2
30 North American F–100D and F–100F
25 Sud-Aviation S.O.4050 Vautour IIN
Bombers
45 Dassault Mirage IVA
Reconnaissance and ECM aircraft
60 Dassault Mirage IIIR and IIIRD
1 Douglas DC–8
8 Nord N.2501
Transports

6 Aérospatiale N.262A
18 Aérospatiale N.262C
1 Aérospatiale S.E.210 Caravelle III
11 Boeing KC–135F
10 (?) Dassault M.D.315
6 Douglas DC–6
3 Douglas DC–8
80 Nord N.2501
50 Transall C.160F
Liaison and AOP aircraft
approx 80 (100?) aircraft, inc
10 Cessna 310
12 Cessna 411
Max Holste M.H.1521M
Helicopters
52 Aérospatiale Alouette II
13 Aérospatiale Alouette III
1 Aérospatiale S.A.321
4 Bell 47G
Trainers
approx 800 (?) aircraft, inc 1 Dassault Falcon 20, Lockheed T–33A, some Morane-Saulnier M.S.733, Morane-
Saulnier M.S.760, Potez-Air Fouga C.M.170 and C.M.
170–2

**Programme**
Replacement of Sud Aviation S.O.4050 Vautour IIN
fighters by Dassault Mirage F1 (85 aircraft on order),
replacement of Dassault Mystère IVA and North American F–100 strike fighters by SEPECAT Jaguar (50
strike fighters and 40 strike trainers). Further 20
Dassault Mirage IIIRD reconnaissance aircraft, 9
Aérospatiale S.A.330 helicopters and 2 Dassault Falcon
10 transports also on order. Deliveries of aircraft to
commence from 1972/73. The Jaguar order has reportedly been increased to 200 aircraft

**Army**
327,000 men
**Army aviation** (Aviation Légère de l'Armée de Terre–
ALAT)
4,500 (?) men
– squadrons
150 operational aircraft and
490 helicopters
**Organisation**
20 (?) helicopter squadrons with Alouette II
5 (?) helicopter squadrons with Alouette III
7 (?) helicopter squadrons with S.A.330
– (?) helicopter squadrons with CH–34A
helicopter squadrons each with 10 machines
**Equipment**
Helicopters
229 Aérospatiale Alouette II
84 Aérospatiale Alouette III
130 Aérospatiale S.A.330
8 Bell 47G
40 Sikorsky CH–34A
Liaison and AOP aircraft
approx 150 aircraft, inc Cessna 0–1, Max Holste M.H.
1521M, Nord 3400, Piper L–18
Trainers
Nord 3200
**Programme**
Acquisition of 166 Aérospatiale S.A.341 helicopters to
replace older types from 1972–1977
**Navy**
68,000 men
2 aircraft carriers
1 helicopter carrier
1 helicopter cruiser
**Naval aviation** (Aéronautique Navale—L'Aéronavale)
12,000 men
17 squadrons
230 operational aircraft and
82 helicopters
**Organisation**
2 fighter squadrons with F–8E(FN)
3 strike fighter squadrons with Etendard IV–M

1 reconnaissance squadron with Etendard IV–P
4 maritime reconnaissance and ASW squadrons with
Br.1150
2 maritime reconnaissance and ASW squadrons with
Br.1050
1 maritime reconnaissance and ASW squadron with P–2H
1 helicopter squadron with S.A.321
2 helicopter squadrons with Alouette II and III
1 helicopter squadron with SH–34J
– trainer squadrons with M.S.733 and M.S.760
**Bases**
Landivisiau, Lann–Bihoue, Lanveoc–Poulmic, Lorient,
Nîmes-Garons, St. Mandrier, St. Raphaël
**Equipment**
Fighters and strike fighters
50 Dassault Etendard IV–M
32 Vought F–8E (FN)
Reconnaissance aircraft
15 Dassault Etendard IV–P
Maritime reconnaissance and ASW aircraft
60 (?) Breguet Br.1050
38 Breguet Br.1150
15 Lockheed P–2H
Transports
21 Aérospatiale N.262A
Liaison aircraft
10 Piper PA–31 Navajo
Helicopters
22 Aérospatiale Alouette II
22 Aérospatiale Alouette III
22 Aérospatiale S.A.321
16 Sikorsky SH–34J
Trainers
some Morane-Saulnier M.S.733,
Morane-Saulnier M.S.760, Potez-Air Fouga C.M.175
**Programme**
Replacement of Dassault Etendard IV strike fighters and
reconnaissance aircraft by Dassault Super Etendard
strike fighters? 80 Aérospatiale Westland W.G. 13 heli-
copters on order, delivery from 1972/73.
**Aircraft factories**
Aérospatiale (Société Nationale Industrielle Aérospatiale
— S.N.I.A.S., formed in 1970 by the merger of Sud-
Aviation and Nord-Aviation. Sud-Aviation had taken
over Morane-Saulnier in 1966 and Potez in 1967).
Breguet (combined with Dassault since 1971). Dassault/
Breguet (Avions Marcel Dassault/Breguet Aviation).
Max Holste. Nord-Aviation, see Aérospatiale. Potez-
Air Fouga, see Aérospatiale. Sud-Aviation, see Aéro-
spatiale.

## GABON

**Air force** (Force Aérienne Gabonnaise)
men 100(?)
squadrons –
operational aircraft 8 and
helicopters 4
**Organisation**
—
**Base**
Libreville
**Military training aid from**
France
**Equipment**
Transports
3 Aérospatiale N.262
1 Dassault Falcon 20
1 Douglas C–47
1 Douglas DC–6B
2 NAMC YS–11A (?)
Liaison and OAP aircraft
2 Cessna 337
2 Max Holste M.H.1521M
Helicopters
3 Aérospatiale Alouette III
1 Aérospatiale S.A.330
**Army**

600 men
**Navy**
100 men

# GERMANY (EAST)

**Air force**
31,000 men
24 squadrons
305 operational aircraft and
30 helicopters
**Organisation**
11 fighter squadrons with MiG–21 and MiG–19
7 strike fighter squadrons with Su–7
1 bomber squadron with Il–28
1 transport squadron with Il–14
2 transport squadrons with An–2 and An–14
2 helicopter squadrons with Mi–4 and Mi–8
– trainer squadrons with Yak–11, Yak–18 and Zlin 226
– trainer squadrons with L–29 and MiG–15UTI
fighter, strike fighter and bomber squadrons each with
   10–12 aircraft
**Major Bases**
a) **East German:** Buatzen, Bergen, Brandenburg-Briest,
   Cottbus, Dessau, Drewitz, Jänschwalde-Ost, Jocksdorf,
   Kamenz, Marxwalde (earlier Neuhardenberg), Neu-
   brandenburg, Peenemünde, Prenzlau, Preschen, Rothen-
   burg, Strausberg-Eggersdorf
b) **Soviet:** Altenburg, Alt-Lermewitz, Brusin, Finow,
   Fürstenwalde, Gross-Dölln, Grossenhain, Jüterbog,
   Köthen, Merseburg, Neuruppin, Oranienburg, Parchim,
   Puettnitz, Rechlin-Lärz, Stendal, Spremberg, Welzow,
   Werneuchen, Wittenberge, Wittstock, Wünsdorf-Zossen
   (?), Zerbst
**Military training aid from**
Soviet Union
**Foreign Air Forces in East Germany**
Approx 800 (920?) Soviet operational aircraft (680 fighters
   strike fighters, reconnaissance aircraft and light bombers
   plus 120 transports) and 120 Soviet helicopters
**Equipment**
Fighters and strike fighters
approx 150 Mikoyan MiG–21 and Mikoyan MiG–19
20 Mikoyan MiG–21UTI
approx 80 Sukhoi Su-7
10 Sukhoi Su–7UTI
**Bombers**
12 Ilyushin Il 28
Transports
approx 35 (30?) aircraft, inc
20 Antonov AN–2 and Antonov An–14
10 Ilyushin Il–14M
1–2 Ilyushin Il–18
some Li–2 (copy of C–47 [Dakota])
1–2 Tupolev Tu–124
Liaison and AOP aircraft
some Yakovlev Yak–12, L–60 and PZL–104
Helicopters
approx 30 aircraft, inc Mil Mi–1, Mi–4 and Mi–8
Trainers
approx 100 (120?) aircraft, inc Aero L–29, Mikoyan
   MiG–15UTI, Yakovlev Yak–11, Yakovlev Yak–18,
   Zlin 226
**Programme**
Replacement of older trainers by 100 Aero L–39 from
   1975
**Army**
95,000 men
**Navy**
17,000 men
**Naval aviation**
1 helicopter squadron with Mi–4 helicopters
8 (10?) Mil Mi–4

# GERMANY (WEST)

**Air force** (Deutsche Luftwaffe)
men 104,000
squadrons 37

operational aircraft 1,240 and
helicopters 184
**Organisation**
4 fighter squadrons with F–104G
11 strike fighter squadrons with F–104G
10 strike fighter squadrons with G.91R.3
4 reconnaissance squadrons with RF–4E
6 transport squadrons with C.160D
2 helicopter squadrons with UH–1D
1 trainer squadron with T–37B and T–38A
fighter squadrons each with 15 aircraft, strike fighter
   squadrons (F–104G) each with 15–18, strike fighter
   squadrons (G.91) each with 21
**Bases**
a) **German:** Ahlhorn, Bremgarten, Büchel, Celle,
   Fürstenfeldbruck, Hohn, Husum, Jever, Lager Lech-
   feld, Landsberg, Leck, Leipheim, Manching/Ingolstadt,
   Memmingen, Neubiberg, Neuburg/Donau, Nörvenich,
   Oldenburg, Pierdsfeld, Rheine–Hopsten, Sobernheim,
   Wittmundhaven
b) **American:** Bitburg, Hahn, Ramstein, Rhein-Main
   (Frankfurt), Spangdahlem, Zweibrücken
c) **British:** Brüggen, Gütersloh, Lahrbruch, Wildenrath
d) **Canadian:** Baden-Söllingen, Lahr
**Military training aid from**
United States
**Foreign Air Forces in Germany**
a)   12 American squadrons:
8 strike fighter squadrons with F–4C, F–4D and F–4E
2 reconnaissance squadrons with RF–4C
1 special-duties squadron with EC–135, C–130A and B
1 transport squadron with C–130E
1 AOP squadron with 0–2A
b)   11 British squadrons:
2 fighter squadrons with Lightning F.2A
4 strike fighter squadrons with F–4M
3 strike fighter squadrons with Harrier GR.1 and GR.1A
2 bomber squadrons with Buccaneer S.2B
1 transport and liaison squadron with Pembroke C.1,
   Devon C.2 and Basset CC.1
1 helicopter squadron with Wessex HC.2
c)   4 Canadian squadrons:
2 strike fighter squadrons with CF–104
1 reconnaissance squadron with CF–104
1 helicopter squadron with COH–58A (OH–58A)
**Equipment**
Fighters and strike fighters
300 Fiat G.91R.3
39 Fiat G.91T.3
480 Lockheed F–104G
118 Lockheed TF–104G
Reconnaissance and ECM aircraft
2 MBB–HFB 320
88 McDonnell Douglas RF–4E
18 North American Rockwell OV–10C (also as target-
   tugs)
Transports
4 Boeing 707–320C
3 Boeing 737–100
101 Dornier Do–28D
some Douglas C–47
2 Douglas DC–6B
3 Lockheed JetStar
8 MBB–HFB 320
82 (90?) Transall C.160D
Liaison and AOP aircraft
some Dornier Do–27
some Piper L–18C
Helicopters
30 Aérospatiale Alouette II
24 Bell 47G–2
130 Bell UH–1D
Trainers
47 Cessna T–37B
some Lockheed T–33A
45 Northrop T–38A
some Piaggio P.149D and Potez–Air Fouga C.M.170

**Programme**
175 McDonnell Douglas F–4F strike fighters on order
(delivery from 1973/74) 4 MBB–HFB 320 ECM aircraft
on order (delivery 1975) plus 5 Boeing 737–100 transports to replace Convair 440/640
**Army**
327,000 men
**Army Aviation** (Heeresflieger)
9,000 men
28 squadrons
6 operational aircraft and
540 helicopters
**Organisation**
15 helicopter squadrons with Alouette II
7 helicopter squadrons with UH–1D
6 helicopter squadrons with CH–53DG
**Equipment**
Helicopters
256 Aérospatiale Alouette II
204 Bell UH–1D
16 Sikorsky CH–34A
64 Sikorsky CH–53DG
Liaison and AOP aircraft
6 Dornier Do–27
**Programme**
Sikorsky CH–34A helicopters are gradually being withdrawn from service. 46 further Sikorsky CH–53DG
helicopters on order, delivery from 1973/1974
**Navy**
36,000 men
**Naval aviation** (Marineflieger)
6,000 men
7 squadrons
150 operational aircraft and
30 helicopters
**Organisation**
3 strike fighter squadrons with F–104G
1 reconnaissance squadron with F–104G
2 maritime reconnaissance and ASW squadrons with
Br.1150
1 helicopter squadron with SeaKing Mk.41
Strike fighter and reconnaissance squadrons each with
18 aircraft, maritime reconnaissance and ASW
squadrons each with 6
**Bases**
Eggebek, Jagel, Kiel-Holtenau, Nordholz
**Equipment**
Fighters and strike fighters
100 Lockheed F–104G
10 Lockheed TF–104G
Maritime reconnaissance and ASW aircraft
20 Breguet Br.1150
Transports
20 Dornier Do–28D
Helicopters
some Sikorsky SH–34G
22 Westland Sea King Mk.41
**Programme**
Replacement of Lockheed F–104G strike fighters (by
McDonnell Douglas F–4 strike fighters and recon-
naissance aircraft ?) planned
**Aircraft Factories**
Dornier, MBB (Messerschmitt–Bolkow–Blohm),
VFW (Vereinigte Flugtechnische Werke)–Fokker

# GHANA

**Air force**
men 1,100
squadrons 5
operational aircraft 33 and
helicopters 10
**Organisation**
1 ground-attack squadron with MB.326F
1 transport squadron with BN–2A
1 transport squadron with DHC–3
1 transport squadron with DHC–4 and Heron
1 liaison squadron with DHC–2

1 helicopter squadron with Wessex Mk.53 and
Whirlwind 3
1 trainer squadron with Bulldog and HT–2
**Bases**
Accra, Kumasi, Tamale, Takoradi
**Military training aid from**
Great Britain
**Equipment**
Ground-attack aircraft
6 Aermacchi MB.326F
Transports
8 Britten–Norman BN–2A
3 DeHavilland Heron
7 DeHavilland Canada DHC–3
8 DeHavilland Canada DHC–4
1 Hawker Siddeley H.S.125
Liaison and AOP aircraft
1 Cessna 337
11 DeHavilland Canada DHC–2
Helicopters
2 Bell 212
3 Hughes 269
2 Westland Wessex Mk.53
3 Westland Whirlwind Srs.3
Trainers
some DeHavilland Canada DHC–1
4 HAL HT–2
6 Scottish Aviation Bulldog
**Programme**
Further 9 Aermacchi M.B.326 ground-attack aircraft on
order
**Army**
16,500 men
**Navy**
1,000 men

# GREAT BRITAIN

**Air Force** (Royal Air Force, RAF)
109,800 men
79 squadrons
900 operational aircraft and
150(?) helicopters
**Organisation**
5 fighter squadrons with Lightning F.6
4 fighter squadrons with Lightning F.3
2 fighter squadrons with Lightning F.2A
1 fighter squadron with F–4K
8 strike fighter squadrons with F–4M
5 strike fighter squadrons with Harrier GR.1 and GR.3
2 strike fighter squadrons with Hunter FGA.9
1 strike fighter squadron with Hunter F.6 and T.7
4 bomber squadrons with Buccaneer S.2B and S.2A
7 bomber squadrons with Vulcan B.2
1 reconnaissance squadron with Victor B.(SR)2
1 reconnaissance squadron with Canberra PR.9
2 ECM squadrons with Canberra B.15, B.16 and E.15
1 ECM squadron with Canberra B.6 and Nimrod R.1
5 maritime reconnaissance and ASW squadrons with
Nimrod MR.1
1 maritime reconnaissance and ASW squadron with
Shackleton AEW.2
3 tanker squadrons with Victor K.1A and K.2
6 transport squadrons with C–130K
2 transport squadrons with Britannia C.1 and C.2
1 transport squadron with Andover C.1
1 transport squadron with Belfast C.1
1 transport squadron with VC10
1 transport squadron with Comet C.4
5 transport squadrons with Devon C.2, Pembroke C.1,
H.S.125, Basset CC.1 and Whirlwind HAR.10
3 helicopter squadrons with Whirlwind HAR.10
2 helicoper squadrons with S.A.330
4 helicopter squadrons with Wessex HC.2
17 trainer squadrons, variously equipped with DHC–1,
Jet Provost T.3, T.4 and T.5, and Gnat T.1
fighter, strike fighter, bomber and reconnaissance
squadrons each with 8–12 aircraft, maritime recon-

naissance squadrons each with 6–8 aircraft

**Major Bases**

a) **British:** Abingdon, Ballykelly, Bawtry, Benson, Binbrook, Brampton, Brawdy, Brize Norton, Chivenor, Church Fenton, Coltishall, Coningsby, Cottesmore, Finningley, Honington, High Wycombe, Kinloss, Leuchars, Linton-on-Ouse, Lossiemouth, Lyneham, Marham, Northolt, Oakington, Odiham, Scampton, Stanmore, St. Mawgan, Thorney Island, Topcliffe, Upavon, Waddington, Wattisham, West Raynham, Wittering, Wyton, Yeovilton

b) **American:** Alconbury, Bentwaters, Lakenheath, Mildenhall, Upper Heyford, Wethersfield, Woodbridge

**Foreign Air Forces in Great Britain**

17 American squadrons

6 strike fighter squadrons with F–4C, F–4D and F–4E

3 strike fighter squadrons with F–111E

3 reconnaissance squadrons with RF–4C

1 electronic reconnaissance squadron with RC–135C, D and U

1 special-duties squadron with EC–135H and J

1 transport squadron with C–130E

1 tanker squadron with KC–135A

1 air-rescue squadron with HH–53C, HC–130T and N

**Equipment**

Fighters and strike fighters

30 BAC Lightning F.2A

67 BAC Lightning F.3 and F.6

20 BAC Lightning T.4 and T.5

30 Hawker Hunter F.6, T.7 and T.7A

20 Hawker Hunter FGA.9 and FR.10

65 Hawker Siddeley Harrier GR.1 and GR.3

13 Hawker Siddeley Harrier T.2

30 McDonnell Douglas F–4K

110 McDonnell Douglas F–4M

Bombers

40(?) English Electric Canberra B.2, B.6, B.15 and B.16

35 Hawker Siddeley Buccaneer S.2A

45 Hawker Siddeley Buccaneer S.2B

50 Hawker Siddeley Vulcan B.2

Reconnaissance and ECM aircraft

8 Handley Page Victor B.(SR)2

3 Hawker Siddeley Nimrod R.1

20(?) English Electric Canberra PR.7, PR.9 and E.15

Maritime reconnaissance and ASW aircraft

12 Avro Shackleton AEW.2

30(?) Avro Shackleton MR.2 and MR.3

46 Hawker Siddeley Nimrod MR.1

Transports

14 BAC VC10

20 Bristol Britannia C.1 and C.2

5 DeHavilland Comet C.4

some DeHavilland Devon C.2

some DeHavilland Dove

20 Handley Page Victor K.1A

16 Handley Page Victor K.2

30 Hawker Siddeley Andover C.1 and CC.2

4 Hawker Siddeley H.S.125 CC.1

2 Hawker Siddeley H.S.125–600

25 Hunting Pembroke C.1

63 Lockheed C–130K

10(?) Scottish Aviation Twin Pioneer CC.2

10 Short Belfast C.1

Liaison and AOP aircraft

20 Beagle Basset CC.1

some Scottish Aviation Pioneer CC.1

Helicopters

approx 140(?) aircraft, inc

40 Aérospatiale S.A.330

12 Westland Sioux HT.2

60 Westland Wessex HC.2 and HCC.4

– Westland Whirlwind HAR.10

Trainers

approx 450(?) aircraft, inc BAC Jet Provost T.3 and T.4, 100 BAC Jet Provost T.5, DeHavilland Vampire T.11, DeHavilland Canada DHC–1, English Electric Canberra T.4, T.11, T.17, T.19, T.22 and TT.18, Handley Page Hastings T.5, 35 Hawker Siddeley Argosy, Hawker

Siddeley Dominie T.1, Hawker Siddeley Gnat T.1, Vickers Varsity T.1

**Programme**

165 SEPECAT Jaguar GR.1 strike fighters and 35 Jaguar T.2 strike trainers, 15 Hawker Siddeley Harrier GR.3 strike fighters, 9 Aérospatiale S.A.341D helicopters, 25 Westland WG.13 helicopters, 132 Scottish Aviation Bulldog T.1 trainers and 26 Scottish Aviation Jetstream trainers on order. Acquisition of 175 Hawker Siddeley H.S.1182 strike trainers from 1976 planned.

**Army**

180,500 men

**Army aviation** (Army Air Corps)

– men

18 squadrons

42 operational aircraft and

305 helicopters

**Organisation**

– helicopter squadrons with Sioux AH.1

– helicopter squadrons with Scout AH.1

– liaison and AOP squadrons with DHC–2 and Scout AH.1

– liaison and AOP squadrons with DHC–2

squadrons each with 12–18 aircraft

**Equipment**

Helicopters

12 Aérospatiale Alouette II

120 Westland Scout AH.1

175 Westland Sioux AH.1

Liaison and AOP aircraft

2 Auster AOP.9

40(24?) DeHavilland Canada DHC–2

Trainers

20 DeHavilland Canada DHC–1

**Programme**

150 Westland WG.13 Lynx helicopters to replace Westland Scout AH.1 by 1975, plus 30 Aérospatiale S.A.341B helicopters on order. Orders for approx a further 250 S.A.314B expected to follow

**Navy**

82,000 men

1 aircraft carrier

2 helicopter carriers

**Naval aviation** (Fleet Air Arm, FAA)

– men

13 squadrons

85 operational aircraft and

240 helicopters

**Organisation**

1 fighter squadron with F–4K

1 strike fighter squadron with Buccaneer S.2C and S.2D

1 maritime reconnaissance and ASW squadron with Gannet AEW.3

1 transport squadron with Heron, Sea Devon C.20 and Wessex HU.5

3 helicopter squadrons with Wessex HU.5

5 helicopter squadrons with Sea King HAS.1

1 helicopter squadron with Wasp HAS.1

2 trainer squadrons with Hunter T.8, GA.11 and Sea Vixen FAW.2

1 trainer squadron with Sea Prince T.1

5 helicopter training squadrons with Wessex HAS.1, HAS.3 and HU.5, Sea King HAS.1, Wasp HAS.1, Whirlwind HAS.7 and Hiller HT.2

Fighter and strike fighter squadrons each with 12 aircraft

**Bases**

Culdrose, Lee-on-Solent, Portland, Prestwick, Yeovilton

**Equipment**

Fighters and strike fighters

15 Hawker Siddeley Buccaneer S.2C and S.2D

20(?) Hawker Siddeley Sea Vixen FAW.2

12 McDonnell Douglas F–4K

Maritime reconnaissance and ASW aircraft

15 Fairy Gannet AEW.3

Transports

4 DeHavilland Heron

10 DeHavilland Sea Devon C.20

2 Hawker Siddeley H.S.125 CC.1

some Hunting Sea Prince C.1 and C.2

Liaison aircraft
some Fairey Gannet COD.4
Helicopters
12 Hiller HT.2
5 Westland Scout AH.1
53 Westland Sea King HAS.1
20 Westland Sioux AH.1
25(?) Westland Wasp HAS.1
100(?) Westland Wessex HAS.1, HAS.3 and HU.5
25(?) Westland Whirlwind HAS.7 and HAR.9
Trainers
approx 40 (60?) aircraft, inc 9 DeHavilland Canada
    DHC-1, some English Electric Canberra T.4, T.22 and
    TT.18, – Hawker Hunter T.8 and GA.11, 8 Hunting
    Sea Prince T.1
**Programme**
100 Westland WG.13 and 21 Aérospatiale S.A.341
    helicopters on order
**Aircraft Factories**
BAC (British Aircraft Corporation), Fairey (Britten–
    Norman), Hawker Siddeley, Scottish Aviation, Short,
    Westland

## GREECE

**Air force** (Elliniki Aeroporia)
men 23,000
squadron 16
operational aircraft 280 and
helicopters 27
**Organisation**
1 fighter squadron with F-102A
2 strike fighter squadrons with F-104G
3 strike fighter squadrons with F-84F
4 strike fighter squadrons with F-5A
1 reconnaissance squadron with RF-5A
1 maritime reconnaissance and ASW squadron with
    HU-16B
2 transport squadrons with N.2501D
1 helicopter squadron with Bell 47G
1 helicopter squadron with AB.205 and UH-19D
1 trainer squadron with T-37B
1 trainer squadron with T-33A-N
fighter, strike fighter and reconnaissance squadrons each
    with 16-18 aircraft
**Major bases**
Achialos (Volos), Araxos, Eleusis, Larissa, Nea Ankhialos,
    Peloponnessus, Sedes, Suda (Crete), Tanagra, Tatoi,
    Thiva
**Military training aid from**
United States
**Foreign Air Forces in Greece**
1 American ASW squadron with P-3 on Crete and
    sometimes 1 American strike fighter squadron with F-4
**Equipment**
Fighters and strike fighters
20 Convair F-102A
5 Convair TF-102A
31 Lockheed F-104G
18(?) Lockheed TF-104G
60 Northrop F-5A
20 Northrop F-5B
54 Republic F-84F
Reconnaissance aircraft
18 Northrop RF-5A
Maritime reconnaissance and ASW aircraft
14 (8?) Grumman HU-16B
Transports
some Douglas C-47
1 Grumman Gulfstream 1
40 Nord N.2501D
Helicopters
6 Agusta–Bell AB.205
1 Agusta–Bell AB.206A
10 Bell 47G
10 Sikorsky UH-19D
Trainers
approx 60 aircraft, inc Canadair (Lockheed) T-33A-N,

Cessna T-37B, Cessna T-41A and 21 Cessna T-41D
**Programme**
Replacement of Republic F-84F strike fighters by 36
    McDonnell Douglas F-4E and further Northrop F-5.
    Purchase of 49 Dassault Mirage 5 strike fighters(?)
**Army**
118,000 men
**Army aviation** (Aeroporia Stratou)
approx 20 aircraft, inc Cessna U-17A, Aero (North
    American Rockwell) Commander 680 FL and Piper
    L-21 liaison aircraft and Bell 47G helicopters
**Navy**
18,000 men

## GUATEMALA

**Air force** (Fuerza Aérea de Guatemala)
men 1,000
squadrons 4
operational aircraft 23 and
helicopters 10
**Organisation**
1 ground-attack squadron with A-37B
1 ground-attack squadron with F-51D
1 transport squadron with C-47
1 helicopter squadron with UH-1D
– trainer squadrons with T-6G and T-33A
**Bases**
La Aurora (Guatemala City), Puerto Barrios, Puerto San
    Jose
**Military training aid from**
United States
**Equipment**
Ground-attack aircraft
8 Cessna A-37B
8 North American (Cavalier) F-51D
Transports
6 Douglas C-47
1 Douglas C-54
Helicopters
6 Bell UH-1D
1 Hiller OH-23G
3 Sikorsky H-19
Trainers
approx 15 aircraft, inc North American T-6G and
    Lockheed T-33A
**Army**
7,800 men
**Navy**
200 men

## GUINEA

**Air force** (Force Aérienne de Guinée)
men 500
squadrons 1
operational aircraft 12 and
helicopter 1
**Organisation**
1 strike fighter squadron with MiG-17
**Base**
Conakry
**Military training aid from**
Soviet Union
**Equipment**
Fighters and strike fighters
5 Mikoyan MiG-17
Transports
1-2 Antonov An-14
4 Ilyushin Il-14
2 Ilyushin Il-18
Helicopters
1 Bell 47G
Trainers
some Aero L-29 and Yakovlev Yak-18
**Army**
5,000 men
**Navy**
150 men

## GUYANA

**Army**
2,000 men
**Army aviation**
2 Britten-Norman BN-2 transports
2 Helio H-295 Super Courier liaison aircraft

## HAITI

**Air force** (Corps d'Aviation d'Haiti)
men 250
squadrons 2
operational aircraft 9
**Organisation**
1 ground-attack squadron with F-51D
1 transport squadron with C-45 and C-47
**Base**
Bowen Field (Port-au-Prince)
**Equipment**
Ground-attack aircraft
4 North American F-51D
Transports
2 Beechcraft C-45
Trainers
2 North American T-6G
2 North American T-28A
**Army**
5,000 men
**Navy**
250 men

## HONDURAS

**Air force** (Fuerza Aérea Hondurena)

men 1,200
squadrons 4
operational aircraft 20 and
helicopters 2
**Organisation**
1 ground-attack squadron with F4U
1 ground-attack squadron with F-51D
1 bomber squadron with B-26C
1 transport squadron with C-47
– trainer squadrons with T-6G and T-33A
**Bases**
San Pedro Sula, Tegucigalpa
**Military training aid from**
United States
**Equipment**
Ground-attack aircraft
Total of 12 aircraft, inc 6 Vought F4U-4, F4U-5 and
    F4U-5N plus 5 North American F-51D
Bombers
some Douglas B-26C(?)
Transports
4 Douglas C-47
1 Douglas C-54
Liaison and AOP aircraft
some Cessna 180 and Cessna 185
Helicopters
2 Sikorsky H-19
Trainers
approx 15 aircraft, inc some Beechcraft T-11, 3 Lockheed
    T-33A, some North American T-6G
**Army**
3,500 men
**Navy**
40 men

## HUNGARY

**Air force** (Magyar Légierö)
12,500 men
17 squadrons
165 operational aircraft and
25 helicopters
**Organisation**
3 fighter squadrons with MiG-21
3 fighter squadrons with MiG-19

5 strike fighter squadrons with Su-7 and MiG-17
1 reconnaissance squadron with MiG-17
1 transport squadron with An-2
1 transport squadron with Il-14 and Li-2
1 helicopter squadron with Mi-8
2 helicopter squadrons with Mi-4 and Mi-1
– trainer squadrons with Yak-11 and Yak-18
– trainer squadrons with L-29 and MiG-15UTI
fighter, strike fighter and reconnaissance squadrons each
    with 10–12 aircraft
**Major bases**
a) **Hungarian:** Budapest, Debrecen, Estergom, Kaposvàr,
    Kiskunfélegyháza, Miskolc, Nyiregyháza, Pécs, Szeged,
    Szolnok
b) **Soviet:** Dombovàr, Györ (Raab), Papa, Székesfehérvàr
    (Stuhlweissenburg), Szombathely (Steinamanger), Tököl
**Military training aid from**
Soviet Union
**Foreign Air Forces in Hungary**
approx 250 (200?) Soviet fighters, strike fighters and
    reconnaissance aircraft
**Equipment**
Fighters and strike fighters
some Mikoyan MiG-17
30 Mikoyan MiG-19
40 Mikoyan MiG-21 and MiG-21UTI
55 Sukhoi Su-7 and Su-7UTI
Bombers
some Ilyushin Il-28
reconnaissance aircraft
10 Mikoyan MiG-17
Transports
10 Antonov An-2
10 Ilyushin Il-14
6 (copy of C-47 [Dakota]) Li-2
Helicopters
approx 25 machines, inc Mil Mi-1, 6 Mil Mi-4, Mil
    Mi-8, WSK SM-2
Trainers
approx 95 (80?) aircraft, inc Aero L-29, Mikoyan MiG-
    15UTI, Yakovlev Yak-11, Yakovlev Yak-18
**Programme**
Replacement of Mikoyan MiG-17 strike fighters by
    Sukhoi Su-7 plus acquisition of transports to replace
    Antonov An-2 and Ilyushin Il-14
**Army**
90,000 men
**Navy**
500 men

## ICELAND

No national armed forces
**Coast guard** (Lanhelgisgaezlan)
1 Fokker VFW F.27 transport
3 helicopters: 2 Bell 47J, 1 Sikorsky S-62C
**Foreign Air Forces in Iceland**
1 American fighter squadron with
F-4 based at Keflavik

## INDIA

**Air Force** (Bharatiya Vayu Sena)
92,000 men
58 squadrons
911 operational aircraft and
205 helicopters
**Organisation**
8 fighter squadrons with Gnat
8 fighter squadrons with MiG-21
6 strike fighter squadrons with Hunter F.56
6 strike fighter squadrons with Su-7
2 strike fighter squadrons with HF-24
2 strike fighter squadrons with Mystère IVA
4 bomber squadrons with Canberra B.(I)58 and B.66
1 reconnaissance squadron with Canberra PR.57
1 maritime reconnaissance and ASW squadron with
L.1049G
2 transport squadrons with An-12

2 transport squadrons with C–47
3 transport squadrons with C–119G
1 transport squadron with DHC–3
1 transport squadron with DHC–4
1 transport squadron with H.S.748
1 transport squadron with Il–14
1 transport squadron with Tu–124 and H.S.748
4 liaison squadrons with HAOP–27
4 helicopter squadrons with Alouette III
4 helicopter squadrons with Mi–4
7 (?) trainer squadrons with T–6G and Vampire T.55
1 strike fighter trainer squadron with Hunter T.66
– trainer squadrons with HJT–2
– trainer squadrons with DHC–1 and HT–2
fighter and strike fighter squadrons each with 12–18
  aircraft
**Major bases**
Adilabad, Agartala, Agra, Ahmedabad, Akola, Alir,
Allahabad, Ambala, Amritsar, Arkonam, Asansol,
Aurangabad, Bangalore, Baroda, Barrackpore, Belgaum,
Benares, Bhawi, Bhopal, Bhubaneshwar, Bhuj, Bidar,
Bikaner, Bilaspur, Calcutta, Chakalia, Cochin, Dum
Dum, Ferozepore, Gaya, Gorakpur, Gurgaon, Gwalior,
Hyderabad, Iharsuguda, Imphal, Jaipur, Jammu,
Jamnagar, Jodhpur, Jubbulpore, Kalaikunda, Kanpur,
Kolar, Kumbhirgram, Lalitpur, Lucknow, Madras,
Madura, Manipur Road, Mohanbari, Nagpur, Palam,
Pali, Poona, Raichur, Raipur, Rajah Mundry, Rampur-
hat, Ranchi, Saharanpur, Santa Cruz, Satna, Srinagar,
Tamaram, Tanjore, Tezpur, Tiruchirappalli, Trivandrum
Utterlai, Vijayawada, Visakhapatnam, Warangal
**Military training aid from**
Soviet Union
**Equipment**
Fighter and strike fighters
25 Dassault Mystère IVA
45 HAL HF–24
180 Hawker Hunter F.56 and T.66
160 Hawker Siddeley Gnat
200 Mikoyan MiG–21 and MiG–21UTI
75 Sukhoi Su–7 and Su–7UTI
Bombers
60 English Electric Canberra B.(I)58
8 English Electric Canberra B.66
11 English Electric Canberra T.4
2 English Electric Canberra T.67
Reconnaissance Aircraft
10 English Electric Canberra PR.57
Maritime reconnaissance and ASW aircraft
8 Lockheed L.1049G Super Constellation
Transports
34 Antonov An–12
25 DeHavilland Canada DHC–3
15 DeHavilland Canada DHC–4
55 Douglas C–47
60 Fairchild C–119G
25 Hawker Siddeley H.S. 748
20 Ilyushin Il–14
3 Tupolev Tu–124
Helicopters
90 Aérospatiale Alouette III
20 Aérospatiale S.A.315B
10 Bell 47G
80 Mil Mi–4
some Mil Mi–8
1 Sikorsky S–62A
Trainers
**approx** 300 aircraft, inc DeHavilland Vampire T.55,
  DeHavilland Canada DHC–1, 60 HAL HJT–16, HAL
  HT–2, North American T–6G
**Programme**
Expansion to 45 fighter and strike fighter squadrons
  intended. Formation of 15 fighter squadrons with
  Mikoyan MiG–21 plus planned replacement of Dassault
  Mystère IVA strike fighters by Mikoyan MiG–21
  fighters and strike fighters. Replacement of Douglas
  C–47, Fairchild C–119G and Ilyushin Il–14 transports

(by Hawker Siddeley H.S. 748?)
**Army**
860,000 men
**Army aviation**
– men
– squadrons
70 operational aircraft and
35 helicopters
**Organisation**
—
**Equipment**
Helicopters
15 Aérospatiale Alouette III
20 Mil Mi–8
Liaison and AOP aircraft
20 Auster AOP.9
50 HAL HAOP–27
**Navy**
40,000 men
1 aircraft carrier
**Naval aviation**
– men
5 squadrons
32 operational aircraft
30 helicopters
**Organisation**
1 strike fighter squadron with Sea Hawk FGA.6, Mk.100
  and Mk.101
1 ASW squadron with Br.1050
2 helicopter squadrons with Alouette III
1 helicopter squadron with Sea King Mk.42
1 trainer squadron with HJT–16
1 trainer squadron with Hughes 300 and Alouette III
**Equipment**
Fighters and strike fighters
20 Armstrong Whitworth Sea Hawk FGA.6, Mk.100
  and Mk.101
Maritime reconnaissance and ASW aircraft
11 Breguet Br.1050
Transports
1 DeHavilland Devon
Helicopters
2 Aérospatiale Alouette II
18 Aérospatiale Alouette III
4 (6?) Hughes 300
6 Westland Sea King Mk.42
Trainers
some DeHavilland Vampire T.55
7 HAL HJT–16
15 HAL HT–2
**Programme**
Replacement of Armstrong Whitworth Sea Hawk strike
  fighters. Formation of 2–3 new ASW squadrons by
  1973/74; further Westland Sea King Mk.42 helicopters
  on order
**Aircraft factories**
HAL (Hindustan Aeronautics Ltd.)

## INDONESIA

**Air force** (Angkatan Udara Republik Indonesia)
35,000 men
13 squadrons
145 operational aircraft and
27 helicopters
**Organisation**
1 fighter squadron with MiG–21
1 strike fighter squadron with CA–27
1 strike fighter squadron with MiG–17 and MiG–19
1 ground-attack squadron with F–51D
2 bomber squadrons with Tu–16
1 bomber squadron with Il–28
1 bomber squadron with B–26B and B–25J
1 transport squadron with C–130B and An–12
1 transport squadron with Il–14 and C–47
3 helicopter squadrons with Mi–4 and Mi–6
6 trainer squadrons with T–6G, L–29 and MiG–15UTI
Of the fighter, strike fighter, ground-attack and bomber

squadrons only the ground-attack squadron with F–51D and 1 bomber squadron with B–26B and B–25J are operational. All others are grounded due to lack of spares.

**Bases**
Amboina, Balikpapan, Denpasar, Djkarta, Husein (Bandung), Lombok, Medan, Palembang, Semerang

**Military training aid from**
Australia

**Equipment**
Fighters and strike fighters
16 Commonwealth CA–27 Sabre Mk.32 (F–86F)
15 Mikoyan MiG–17
some Mikoyan MiG–19
15 Mikoyan MiG–21
Ground-attack aircraft
10 North American F–51D
Bombers
4 Douglas B–26B
10 Ilyushin Il–28
5 North American B–25J
22 Tupolev Tu–16
Transports
6 Antonov An–12
7 DeHavilland Canada DHC–3
6 Douglas C–47
10 Ilyushin Il–14
8 Lockheed C–130B
2 Lockheed JetStar
some Scottish Aviation Twin Pioneer CC.1 and CC.2
3 Short Skyan 3M
Liaison and AOP aircraft
5 Cessna 401A
2 Cessna 402A
5 Cessna T207 Turbo–Skywagon
56(?) PZL–104 Wilga
Helicopters
4 Aérospatiale Alouette III
2 Bell 204B
16 Mil Mi–4
6 Mil Mi–6
1 Sikorsky S–61A
Trainers
approx 60(?) aircraft, inc Aero L–29, AESL Airtourer T.6, 20 Mikoyan MiG–15UTI, North American T–6G, Yakovlev Yak–11(?)

**Programme**
Replacement of those Mikoyan MiG–17 and Mikoyan MiG–19 fighters and strike fighters still on hand by a further 12 Commonwealth CA–27 Sabre Mk.32 strike fighters (donated by Australia)

**Army**
140,000 men
**Army aviation** (Angkatan Daraf Republik Indonesia)
some Aérospatiale Alouette III helicopters(?)

**Navy**
30,000 men
**Naval aviation** (Angkatan Laut Republik Indonesia)
– men
2 squadrons
30 operational aircraft and
15 helicopters
**Organisation**
1 strike fighter squadron with MiG–19 and MiG–21
1 maritime reconnaissance and ASW squadron with HU–16D and PBY–5A
**Equipment**
Fighters and strike fighters
approx 20 Mikoyan MiG–19 and Mikoyan MiG–21
Maritime reconnaissance and ASW aircraft
some Convair PBY–5A
5 Grumman HU–16D
Transports
some Douglas C–47(?)
Helicopters
3 Aérospatiale Alouette II
3 Aérospatiale Alouette III

4 Bell 47G
**Programme**
Replacement of Convair PBY–5A maritime reconnaissance aircraft by 4 GAF Nomad 22 1973/74
**Aircraft factories**
Lipnur (Lembaga Industri Penerbangan Nurtanio)

# IRAN

**Air force** (Nirou Havai Shahanshahiyé Irân)
35,000 men
15 squadrons
245 operational aircraft and
37 helicopters
**Organisation**
2 fighter squadrons with F–4D
1 fighter squadron with F–86F and Sabre Mk.6
6 strike fighter squadrons with F–5A
1 reconnaissance squadron with RF–5A
1 transport squadron with C–47
1 transport squadron with C–130B
1 transport squadron with C–130E
1 liaison squadron with O–2A
1 helicopter squadron with AB.206A
1 helicopter squadron with S.A.321
– trainer squadrons with T–6G
– trainer squadrons with T–33A
fighter, strike fighter and reconnaissance squadrons each with 16–20 aircraft
**Major Bases**
Abu Musa, Ahwaz, Banda Abbas, Bushehr, Chah Bahar, Doshan-Tappeh, Galeh-Marghi, Ishafan, Kish, Mashhad, Mehrabad, Schiras, Täbris
**Military training aid from**
United States, Italy
**Equipment**
Fighters and strike fighters
32 McDonnell Douglas F–4D
20 North American F–86F and Canadair Sabre Mk.6
100 Northrop F–5A
20 Northrop F–5B
Reconnaissance aircraft
9(?) Lockheed RT–33A
4 McDonnell Douglas RF–4E
12 Northrop RF–5A
Transports
8 Beechcraft C–45
6 Boeing 707–320C
5 Douglas C–47
3 North American Rockwell TurboCommander 681B
8 Lockheed C–130B
14 Lockheed C–130E
Liaison and AOP aircraft
12 Cessna O–2A
5 DeHavilland Canada DHC–2
Helicopters
16 Aérospatiale S.A.321
2 Agusta (Meridionali)–Boeing Vertol CH–47C
10 Agusta–Bell AB.206A
5 Agusta–Bell AB.212
4 Kaman HH–43B
Trainers
30 Beechcraft Bonanza F32C
Lockheed T–33
North American T–6G
Approx 30 Northrop F–5 strike fighters reportedly lent to Vietnam (South) in November 1972
**Programme**
32 McDonnell Douglas F–4E, 141 Northrop F–5E strike fighters and 16 Northrop F–5B strike trainers on order, plus 10 Fokker–VFW F.27M and 4(10?) Fokker–VFW F.27 Mk.600 transports to replace Douglas C–47, and 30 Lockheed C–130H transports. Approx 70 further McDonnell Douglas F–4 strike fighters to be acquired by 1975. In addition 202 Bell AH–1J attack helicopters and 287 Bell 214A (similar to UH–1H) helicopters on order; delivery from 1974–1978
**Army**

175,000 men
**Army aviation** (Gordan Havanirouz)
– men
– squadrons
55 operational aircraft and
92 helicopters
**Organisation**
– helicopter squadrons with AB.205
– helicopter squadrons with AB.206A
1 helicopter squadron with CH–47C
1 helicopter squadron with HH–43B
– liaison and AOP squadrons with Cessna 185
**Equipment**
Helicopters
47 Agusta–Bell AB.205
23 Agusta–Bell AB.206A
8 Kaman HH–43B
14 (20?) Agusta (Meridionali)–Boeing Vertol CH–47C
Liaison and AOP aircraft
45 Cessna 185
6 Cessna 310
some Piper L–18
**Navy**
13,000 men
**Naval aviation**
– men
1 squadron
31 helicopters
**Organisation**
1 ASW squadron with SH–3D
**Equipment**
Helicopters
4 Agusta–Bell AB.205
11 Agusta–Bell AB.206A
6 Agusta–Bell AB.212
10 Agusta–Sikorsky SH–3D
**Programme**
4 (6?) Lockheed P–3F maritime reconnaissance and ASW aircraft on order, delivery from 1974. Formation of a transport squadron with 8 aircraft?

## IRAQ

**Air force**
9,800 men
19 squadrons
225 operational aircraft and
45 helicopters
**Organisation**
4 fighter squadrons with MiG–21
1 fighter squadron with MiG–17
3 strike fighter squadrons with Su–7
2 strike fighter squadrons with Hunter F.6 and FGA.59
1 ground-attack squadron with Jet Provost T.52
1 bomber squadron with Tu–16
1 transport squadron with An–2
1 transport squadron with An–12
1 transport squadron with An–26
1 helicopter squadron with Wessex Mk.52
2 helicopter squadrons with Mi–4
1 helicopter squadron with Mi–8
– trainer squadrons with DHC–1 and Provost
**Major bases**
Basra, Habbaniya, Kirkuk, Mossul, Raschid, Shaiba
**Military training aid from**
Soviet Union
**Equipment**
Fighters and strike fighters
30 Hawker Hunter F.6, FGA.59 and T.69
15 Mikoyan MiG–17
60 Mikoyan MiG–21
50 Sukhoi Su–7
Ground attack aircraft
16 BAC Jet Provost T.52
Bombers
some Ilyushin Il–28
8 Tupolev Tu–16
Transports

12 Antonov An–2
6 Antonov An–12
10 Antonov An–26
2 DeHavilland Heron
some (14?) Ilyushin Il–14
2 Tupolev Tu–124
Helicopters
4 Mil Mi–1
20 Mil Mi–4
12 Mil Mi–8
9 Westland Wessex Mk.52
Trainers
approx 50 aircraft, inc Aero L–29, DeHavilland Canada DHC–1, Hunting Provost T.53, Mikoyan MiG–15UTI and Yakovlev Yak–18
**Programme**
Purchase of 54(?) Dassault Mirage 5 strike fighters planned, 3 Britten-Norman BN–2A transports on order
**Army**
85,000 men
**Navy**
2,000 men

## IRELAND (EIRE)

**Air force** (Irish Army Air Corps)
men 550
squadron 1
operational aircraft 2 and
helicopters 5
**Organisation**
1 Liaison and AOP squadron with FR172H
**Bases**
Baldonnel, Gormanston
**Equipment**
Liaison and AOP aircraft
8 Reims–Cessna FR 172H
Transports
2 DeHavilland Dove
Helicopters
5 Aérospatiale Alouette III
Trainers
approx 15 aircraft, inc 6 DeHavilland Canada DHC–1 and 6 Hunting Provost T.51 and T.53
**Programme**
1 Aérospatiale Alouette III helicopter on order
**Army**
11,700 men
**Navy**
500 men

## ISRAEL

**Air force** (Heil Avir le Israel)
10,000 men (20,000 after mobilisation)
23 squadrons
400 operational aircraft and
50 helicopters
**Organisation**
3 fighter squadrons with Mirage IIICJ
3 (4?) strike fighter squadrons with F–4E and RF–4E
2 strike fighter squadrons with A–4E
4 strike fighter squadrons with A–4H
1 strike fighter squadron with Mystère IVA
1 strike fighter squadron with Super Mystère B2
1 bomber squadron with Vautour IIA
2 transport squadrons with N.2501
1 transport squadron with C–47
1 transport squadron with KC–97G and Stratocruiser
2 helicopter squadrons with Bell 205
1 helicopter squadron with HH–53C
1 helicopter squadron with S.A.321K
– trainer squadrons with C.M.170
**Bases**
Bir Gifgafa, Bir Thamada, Ekron, El Arish, Gebel Libni, Haifa, Hatzerim, Jerusalem, Lod, Ramat David, Tel Aviv
**Military training aid from**
United States (?)

## Equipment
**Fighters and strike fighters**
50 Dassault Mirage IIICJ
3 Dassault Mirage IIIBJ
20 Dassault Mystère IVA
9 Dassault Super Mystère B2
43 McDonnell Douglas A–4E
90 McDonnell Douglas A–4H
10 McDonnell Douglas TA–4H
115 (?) McDonnell Douglas F–4E
**Bombers**
10 Sud-Aviation S.O.4050 Vautour IIA and Vautour IIN
**Reconnaissance aircraft**
6 (?) McDonnell Douglas RF–4E
**Transports**
3 Boeing KC–97G
6 Boeing Stratocruiser
10 Douglas C–47
2 Lockheed C–130E
20 Nord N.2501
**Liaison and AOP aircraft**
approx 30 aircraft, inc Cessna U206C Turbo-Skywagon,
    Dornier Do–27, Piper L–18C
**Helicopters**
5 Aérospatiale Alouette II
9 (12?) Aérospatiale S.A.321K
25 Bell 205
10 Sikorsky HH–53C
**Trainers**
approx 100 aircraft, inc Fokker S.11 (?), 65 Potez-Air
    Fouga C.M.170
**Programme**
Phasing out of Dassault Mystère IVA and Super Mystère
    B2 strike fighters. Acquisition of further modern
    American strike fighters, 50 (?) McDonnell Douglas
    A–4N and 42 McDonnell Douglas F–4, as well as new
    STOL transports. Introduction of 24 new Israeli-built
    fighters, IAI Barak?
**Army**
61,500 men (275,000 after mobilisation)
**Navy**
4,500 men (8,000 after mobilisation)
**Aircraft factories**
IAI (Israel Aircraft Industries)

## ITALY

**Air force** (Aeronautica Militare Italiana)
73,000 men
23 squadrons
565 operational aircraft and
163 helicopters
**Organisation**
7 fighter squadrons with F–104S
4 strike fighter squadrons with F–104G
4 strike fighter squadrons with G.91R.1
4 strike fighter squadrons with G.91Y
1 transport squadron with C–130H
2 transport squadrons with C–119G and C–119J
1 transport squadron with C–47, Convair 440 and DC–6
– helicopter squadrons with AB.47G and AB.47J
– helicopter squadrons with AB.204B
– trainer squadrons with P.148 and S.11
– trainer squadrons with MB.326 and MB.326G
fighter, strike fighter and reconnaissance squadrons each
    with 15–18 aircraft
**Major bases**
Aviano, Brindisi, Cameri, Gervia, Ciampino, Decimom-
    annu (Sardinia), Ghedi, Gioia del Colle, Grazzanise,
    Grosseto, Istrana/Treviso, Piacenza, Pisa, Rimini,
    Sigonella (Sicily), Treviso, Villafranca
**Foreign Air Forces in Italy**
2 American squadrons: 1 American strike fighter squadron
    with F–4 and 1 maritime reconnaissance and ASW
    squadron with P–3 (on Sicily)
**Equipment**
**Fighters and strike fighters**
72 Fiat G.91R.1

50 Fiat G.91T.1
75 Fiat G.91Y
95 Lockheed F–104G
18 Lockheed TF–104G
160 Lockheed F–104S
**Transports**
some Beechcraft C–45(?), Convair 440,
Douglas C–47 and Douglas DC–6
25 Fairchild C–119G and J
14 Lockheed C–130H
45 Piaggio P.166M
**Liaison and AOP aircraft**
24 SIAI–Marchetti S.208M
**Helicopters**
90 Agusta–Bell AB.47G and J
60 (40?) Agusta–Bell AB.204B
3 Agusta–Bell AB.205
2 Agusta–Bell AB.206A
8 Agusta (Meridionali)–Boeing Vertol CH–47C
**Trainers**
approx 250 aircraft, inc 90 Aermacchi MB.326,
90 Aermacchi MB.326G, some Fokker S.11,
50 (?) Piaggio P.148
**Programme**
Further 40 Lockheed F–104S fighters ordered in 1972.
    Phasing out of Fairchild C–119 transports, to be re-
    placed by 44 Fiat G.222, delivery from 1974
**Army**
295,000 men
**Army aviation** (Aviazione Leggera dell Esercito)
– men
– squadrons
150 operational aircraft and
300 helicopters
**Organisation**
– helicopter squadrons with AB.47G and AB.47J
– helicopter squadrons with AB.204B
– helicopter squadrons with AB.205
– helicopter squadrons with AB.206A
– helicopter squadrons with CH–47C
– liaison and AOP squadrons with O–1E
– liaison and AOP squadrons with L–18C
– liaison and AOP squadrons with L–21B
**Equipment**
125 Agusta–Bell AB.47G and J
50 Agusta–Bell AB.204B
30 Agusta–Bell AB.205
70 Agusta–Bell AB.206A
26 Agusta (Meridionali)–Boeing Vertol CH–47C
**Liaison and AOP aircraft**
approx 150 aircraft, inc 100 Cessna O–1E plus Piper
    L–18C and Piper L–21B
**Programme**
Replacement of American-built liaison aircraft by Italian
    designs (20 Aerfer Aermacchi AM.3C and 100 SIAI–
    Marchetti SM.1019)
**Navy**
45,000 men
1 helicopter cruiser
**Naval aviation** (Aviazione per la Marina)
– men
9 squadrons
40 operational aircraft and
76 helicopters
**Major bases**
Catania, Naples, Trapani
**Organisation**
3 maritime reconnaissance and ASW squadrons with
    Br.1150 and S–2F
1 maritime reconnaissance squadron with HU–16A
2 ASW squadrons with SH–3D
2 ASW squadrons with AB.204B and AB.212ASW
1 helicopter squadron with AB.47J and AB.204B
**Equipment**
**Maritime reconnaissance and ASW aircraft**
18 Breguet Br.1150
15 Grumman S–2F

some Grumman HU–16A
Helicopters
2 Agusta A.106
10 Agusta-Bell AB.47G and J
28 Agusta–Bell AB.204B
12 Agusta–Bell AB.212ASW
24 Agusta–Sikorsky SH–3D
**Programme**
Phasing out of Grumman S–2F maritime reconnaissance
and ASW aircraft. 20 Agusta-Sikorsky HH–3F helicopters on order, delivery from 1974/75 (?)
**Aircraft factories**
Aerfer-Industrie Aerospaziali Meridionali, Aermacchi
(Aeronautica Macchi), Agusta (Construzioni Aero-
nautiche Giovanni Agusta), Fiat, Piaggio, SIAI–
Marchetti

## IVORY COAST

**Air force** (Force Aérienne de la Côte d'Ivoire)
men 300
squadrons –
operational aircraft 6 and
helicopters 6
**Organisation**
—
**Base**
Port Bouet (Abidjan)
**Military training aid from**
France
**Equipment**
Transports
1 Aero Commander 500
1 Dassault Falcon 20
2 Douglas C–47
2 Fokker F.27
Liaison and AOP aircraft
2 Cessna 337
4 Max Holste M.H.1521M
Helicopters
2 Aérospatiale Alouette II
3 Aérospatiale Alouette III
1 Aérospatiale S.A.330
Trainers
2 Cessna 150 (?)
**Programme**
Formation of strike fighter squadrons
**Army**
4,000 men
**Navy**
200 men

## JAMAICA

**Air force** (Jamaica Defence Force Air Wing)
men 250
squadrons –
operational aircraft 1 and
helicopters 3
**Organisation**
—
**Base**
Up Park Camp (Kingston)
**Military training aid from**
Great Britain
**Equipment**
Transport
1 DeHavilland Canada DHC–6
Liaison and AOP aircraft
1 (2?) Cessna 185
Helicopters
2 Bell 47G
1 Bell 206A
**Army**
1,000 men
**Navy**
50 men

## JAPAN

**Air force** (Koku Jietai)
41,700 men
21 squadrons
465 operational aircraft and
22 helicopters
**Organisation**
1 fighter squadron with F–4EJ
6 fighter squadrons with F–104J
8 strike fighter squadrons with F–86F
1 reconnaissance squadron with RF–4EJ
2 transport squadrons with C–46D
1 transport squadron with YS–11
1 helicopter squadron with KV–107
1 helicopter squadron with S–62A
10(?) trainer squadrons with either T–34 or T–1 and
T–33A
fighter and strike fighter squadrons each with 18–25
aircraft
**Bases**
Chitose, Hachinoe, Hayakuri, Iruma, Iwakumi, Kadena
(Okinawa), Kasuga, Komaki, Komatsu, Matsushima,
Misawa, Naha (Okinawa), Nyutbaru, Tachikawa,
Tsuiki, Yokota
**Military training aid from**
United States
**Foreign Air Forces in Japan**
a) 8 American squadrons in Japan: 6 strike fighter
squadrons with F–4C and D, 1 reconnaissance squadron
with RF–4C, 1 ECM squadron with EB–57E and RC–
130B
b) 6 American squadrons on Okinawa: 3 strike fighter
squadrons with A–7D and 3 transport squadrons with
C–130
**Equipment**
Fighters and strike fighters
160 Lockheed F–104J
12 Lockheed F–104DJ
15 McDonnell Douglas F–4EJ
200 North American F–86F
Reconnaissance aircraft
14 McDonnell Douglas RF–4EJ
some North American RF–86F
Transports
30 Curtiss-Wright C–46D
16 Mitsubishi MU–2E
13 NAMC YS–11
2 Kawasaki C–1
Liaison aircraft
5 Beechcraft Queen Air
Helicopters
14 Kawasaki-Vertol KV–107
8 Mitsubishi-Sikorsky S–62A
Trainers
approx 350 aircraft, inc 100 Fuji-Beechcraft T–34,
40 Fuji T–1, 170 (?) Lockheed T–33A
**Programme**
Replacement of Lockheed F–104J fighters by 128 Mc-
Donnell Douglas F–4EJ from 1973/74. Acquisition of
following aircraft planned from 1972–1976:
46 McDonnell Douglas F–4EJ fighters, 68 Mitsubishi
F–1 strike fighters and 59 Mitsubishi T–2 strike
trainers; 25 Kawasaki C–1 transports to replace the
obsolete Curtiss C–46; 12 additional Mitsubishi MU–2;
60 new trainers (Fuji FA–200 or Fuji KM–2?) to
replace Fuji-Beechcraft T–34; further 12 Kawasaki-
Vertol KV–107 helicopters
**Army**
180,000 men
**Army aviation**
– men
– squadrons
120 (?) operational aircraft and
218 helicopters
**Organisation**
– helicopter squadrons with Bell 47 and OH–6J
– helicopter squadrons with UH–1B

– helicopter squadrons with KV–107
**Equipment**
Helicopters
70 Fuji-Bell UH–1B
60 Kawasaki-Bell 47G
39 Kawasaki-Hughes OH–6J
7 Kawasaki-Hughes TH–55J
42 Kawasaki-Vertol KV–107
Liaison and AOP aircraft
– Cessna O–1
– Piper L–21
Transports
10 Mitsubishi MU–2C
**Programme**
Acquisition of 190 helicopters (55 Fuji-Bell UH–1H, 79 Kawasaki-Hughes OH–6J, 20 Kawasaki-Vertol KV–107, 36 Kawasaki-Hughes TH–55J) and 5 Mitsubishi MU–2 transports planned from 1972–1976
**Navy**
39,000 men
**Naval aviation**
– men
12 squadrons
130 operational aircraft and
76 helicopters
**Organisation**
4 maritime reconnaissance and ASW squadrons with P–2J and P–2H
3 maritime reconnaissance and ASW squadrons with S–2F
1 maritime reconnaissance and ASW squadron with PS–1
3 ASW squadrons with SH–3A
1 ASW squadron with SH–34J
**Bases**
Hachinoe, Komatsijima, Kanoya, Ohminato, Shimofusa, Tateyama, Tokushima
**Equipment**
Maritime reconnaissance and ASW aircraft
5 Grumman HU–16
50 Grumman S–2F
60 Kawasaki-Lockheed P–2H and Kawasaki P–2J
9 Shin Meiwa PS–1
Transports
6 NAMC YS–11
Liaison and AOP aircraft
30 Beechcraft 65 Queen Air
Helicopters
some Bell 47G
6 Kawasaki-Vertol KV–107
2 Mitsubishi-Sikorsky S–61A
8 Mitsubishi-Sikorsky S–62A
43 Mitsubishi-Sikorsky SH–3A
some Mitsubishi-Sikorsky SH–34J
Trainers
5 Fuji-Beechcraft T–34
27 Fuji KM–2
**Programme**
Acquisition of 46 maritime reconnaissance and ASW aircraft (43 Kawasaki P–2J, 3 Shin Meiwa SS–2), 48 helicopters (5 Kawasaki-Hughes OH–6J, 5 Kawasaki-Vertol KV–107, 4 Mitsubishi-Sikorsky S–61A, 34 Mitsubishi-Sikorsky SH–3A), 9 liaison aircraft (Fuji KM–2?), and 3 trainers (Beechcraft King Air C.90) planned from 1972–1976. Purchase of 15 Grumman E–2C early warning and maritime patrol aircraft under consideration
**Aircraft factories**
Fuji (Fuji Heavy Industries Ltd), Kawasaki (Kawasaki Aircraft Co Ltd), Mitsubishi (Mitsubishi Heavy Industries Ltd), NAMC (Nihon Aeroplane Manufacturing Co), Shin Meiwa

## JORDAN

**Air force** (Al Quwwat Aljawwiya Almalakiya Alurduniya)
men 4,000
squadrons 5
operational aircraft 39 and
helicopters 7

**Organisation**
2 fighter squadrons with F–104A
1 strike fighter squadron with Hunter FGA.9 and FGA.73
1 transport squadron with C–47
1 helicopter squadron with Alouette III
**Major bases**
Amman, Aqaba, Mafrak
**Equipment**
Fighters and strike fighters
9 Hawker Hunter FGA.9
4 Hawker Hunter FGA.73
2 Hawker Hunter T.66B
15 Lockheed F–104A
2 Lockheed F–104B
Transports
1 Dassault Falcon 20
2 DeHavilland Dove
4 Douglas C–47
Helicopters
7 Aérospatiale Alouette III
Trainers
approx 10 aircraft, inc DeHavilland Vampire T.11 and 4 (5?) DeHavilland Canada
**Programme**
Introduction of further 16 Lockheed F–104A fighters. Replacement of Hawker Hunter FGA.9 and FGA.73 strike fighters by 24 Northrop F–5E strike fighters and 6 Northrop F–5B strike trainers. Acquisition of some Northrop T–38 (?) trainers
**Army**
58,000 men
**Navy**
250 men

## KENYA

**Air force**
men 620
squadrons 2
operational aircraft 13 and
helicopters 2
**Organisation**
1 ground-attack squadron with BAC 167
1 transport squadron with DHC–4
1 liaison squadron with DHC–2
1 trainer squadron with DHC–1 and Bulldog
**Bases**
Eastleigh (Nairobi), Mombasa, Nanyuki
**Military training aid from**
Great Britain
**Equipment**
Ground-attack aircraft
6 BAC 167 Strikemaster Mk.87
Transports
1 Aero Commander 680F
6 DeHavilland Canada DHC–4
Liaison and AOP aircraft
7 DeHavilland Canada DHC–2
Helicopters
2 Bell 47G
Trainers
5 DeHavilland Canada DHC–1
5 Scottish Aviation Bulldog
**Army**
6,300 men
**Navy**
250 men

## KOREA (NORTH)

**Air force**
30,000 men
27 squadrons
390 operational aircraft and
25 helicopters
**Organisation**
6 fighter squadrons with MiG–21
1 fighter squadron with MiG–19

6 strike fighter squadrons with MiG–17
3 strike fighter squadrons with MiG–15
3 strike fighter squadrons with Su–7
3 bomber squadrons with Il–28
2 transport squadrons with Il–12 and Il–14
1 transport squadron with Li–2
2 helicopter squadrons with Mi–4
– trainer squadrons with Yak–11 and Yak–18
– trainer squadrons with MiG–15UTI
fighter, strike fighter and bomber squadrons each with
    12–15 aircraft
**Major bases**
Pyöng-ni, Pyöngyang, Pyöngyang-East, Saamcham,
    Sinuiju, Sunan, Taechon, Uijû, Wonsan
**Military training aid from**
Soviet Union
**Equipment**
Fighters and strike fighters
30 Mikoyan MiG–15
100 Mikoyan MiG–17
15 Mikoyan MiG–19
90 Mikoyan MiG–21
some Mikoyan MiG–21UTI
30 Sukhoi Su–7 and Su–7UTI
Bombers
40 Ilyushin Il–28 and some Ilyushin Il–28UTI
Transports
approx 40 aircraft, inc Antonov An–2, Ilyushin Il–12,
    Ilyushin Il–14, (copy of C–47 [Dakota])
Liaison and AOP aircraft some PZL–104
Helicopters
some Mil Mi–1
20 Mil Mi–4
Trainers
approx 70 aircraft, inc Mikoyan MiG–15UTI plus
    Yakovlev Yak–11 and Yak–18
**Programme**
Replacement of Mikoyan MiG–15 and MiG–17 strike
    fighters by Sukhoi Su–7
**Army**
360,000 men
**Navy**
12,500 men

## KOREA (SOUTH)

**Air force** (Republic of Korea Air Force)
24,500 men
13 squadrons
230 operational aircraft and
15 helicopters
**Organisation**
1 fighter squadron with F–4D
1 fighter squadron with F–86D
3 strike fighter squadrons with F–5A
3 strike fighter squadrons with F–86F
1 reconnaissance squadron with RF–86F
2 transport squadrons with C–46, C–47 and C–54
– liaison squadrons with O–1
1 helicopter squadron with UH–1D
1 helicopter squadron with UH–19
– trainer squadrons with T–28
– trainer squadrons with T–33
fighter and strike fighter squadrons each with 18–25
    aircraft
Approx 45 Northrop F–5 strike fighters were reportedly
    lent to Vietnam (South) in 1972, in return the United
    States made available 18 McDonnell Douglas F–4C
    fighters
**Major bases**
Chinhae, Chongju, Chunchon, Hoengsong, Kananung,
    Kimpo, Kunsan, Osan, Pohang, Pusan, Pyong-taek,
    Saechon, Seoul, Suwon, Taegu
**Military training aid from**
United States
**Foreign Air Forces in Vietnam (South)**
4 American strike fighter squadrons with F–4
**Equipment**
Fighters and strike fighters

18 McDonnell Douglas F–4D
20 North American F–86D
75 North American F–86F
70 Northrop F–5A and some (10?) F–5B
Reconnaissance aircraft
10 North American RF–86F
Transports
approx 35 aircraft, inc Curtiss-Wright C–46, Douglas
    C–47, Douglas C–54 and some Aero Commander 500
Liaison and AOP aircraft
Cessna O–1 and 1–2 Beechcraft U–21A
Helicopters
2 Bell 212
5 Bell UH–1D
2 Kawasaki KH–4
6 Sikorsky UH–19
Trainers
approx 90 aircraft, inc Lockheed T–33A and North
    American T–28A
**Programme**
Acquisition of further McDonnell Douglas F–4 and
    Northrop F–5 strike fighters plus newer helicopters
**Army**
560,000 men
**Navy**
16,750 men
**Marines**
33,000 men

## KUWAIT

**Air force** (Kuwait Air Force)
men 800
squadrons 4
operational aircraft 37 and
helicopters 4
**Organisation**
1 fighter squadron with Lightning F.53
1 strike fighter squadron with Hunter FGA.57
1 ground-attack squadron with BAC 167
1 helicopter squadron with AB.205
1 trainer squadron with Jet Provost T.51
**Base**
Kuwait
**Military training aid from**
Great Britain
**Equipment**
Fighter and strike fighters
12 BAC Lightning F.53
2 BAC Lightning T.55
4 Hawker Hunter FGA.57
2 Hawker Hunter T.67
Ground-attack aircraft
12 BAC 167 Strikemaster Mk.83
Transports
2 DeHavilland Canada DHC–4
1 Hawker Siddeley Argosy
2 Lockheed L–100–20
Helicopters
4 Agusta-Bell AB.205
Trainers
4 BAC Jet Provost T.51
**Programme**
Purchase of 32 Vought F–8H and F–8K or 16 McDonnell
    Douglas F–4 strike fighters under consideration
**Army**
4,500 men
**Navy**
200 men

## LAOS

**Air force**
men 2,150
squadrons 5
operational aircraft 85 and
helicopters 35
**Organisation**
3 ground-attack squadrons with T–28D

1 night ground-support squadron with AC–47
1 transport squadron with C–47
– liaison squadrons with DHC–2 and U–17A
**Major bases**
Chieng Khouang, Savannakhet, Pakse, Vientiane
**Military training aid from**
United States
**Foreign Air Forces in Laos**
Two CIA–operated "Airlines", composition and strength
  unknown
"Air America" — for ground-support operations and
  training
"Continental Air Services" — for supply missions
**Equipment**
Ground-attack aircraft
60 North American T–28D
Night ground-support aircraft
8 (10?) Douglas AC–47
Transports
12 Douglas C–47
Liaison and AOP aircraft
some Cessna O–1
3 DeHavilland Canada DHC–2
10(?) Cessna U–17A
Helicopters
approx 35 aircraft, inc 2 Aérospatiale Alouette II,
4 Aérospatiale Alouette III (?),
some Bell UH–1D and
24 Sikorsky UH–34D
Trainers
approx 30 aircraft, inc 6 Cessna T–41B, 7 Cessna T–41D
  and 5 North American T–6G
**Army**
52,600 men
**Navy**
400 men

## LEBANON

**Air force** (Force Aérienne Libanaise)
men 1,000
squadrons 3
operational aircraft 20 and
helicopters 8
**Organisation**
1 fighter squadron with Mirage IIIEL
1 strike fighter squadron with Hunter F.6 and FGA.9
1 helicopter squadron with Alouette II and Alouette III
1 trainer squadron with DHC–1 and C.M.170–2
**Bases**
Beirut, Rayak, Tripoli
**Military training aid from**
France
**Equipment**
Fighters and strike fighters
6 Dassault Mirage IIIEL
2 Dassault Mirage IIIBL
4 Hawker Hunter F.6
4 Hawker Hunter FGA.9
2 Hawker Hunter T.69
Transports
1 DeHavilland Dove
Helicopters
3 Aérospatiale Alouette II
5 Aérospatiale Alouette III
Trainers
10 DeHavilland Canada DHC–1
4 Potez-Air Fouga C.M.170–2
**Army**
14,000 men
**Navy**
250 men

## LIBYA

**Air force** (Al Quwwat Aljawwiya Al Libiyya)
3,000 men
6 squadrons
36 (?) operational aircraft and

21 helicopters
**Organisation**
1 fighter squadron with Mirage 5
1 fighter squadron with F–5A
1 transport squadron with C–47
1 transport squadron with C–130E
1 helicopter squadron with Alouette III
1 helicopter squadron with S.A.321
**Bases**
Benina (Benghazi), El Adem, El Awai, Wheelus (Tripolis)
**Military training aid from**
Egypt
**Foreign Air Forces in Libya**
a number of Egyptian squadrons
**Equipment**
Fighters and strike fighters
– Dassault Mirage 5–D
10 Dassault Mirage 5–DD
– Dassault Mirage 5–DE
7 Northrop F–5A
2 Northrop F–5B
Reconnaissance aircraft
– Dassault Mirage 5–DR
Transports
1 Dassault Falcon 20
9 Douglas C–47
6 Lockheed C–130E
1 Lockheed JetStar
Helicopters
3 Aérospatiale Alouette II
10 Aérospatiale Alouette III
8 Aérospatiale S.A.321
Trainers
3 Lockheed T–33A
**Programme**
On order: 98 fighters and strike fighters (32 Dassault
  Mirage 5–DE, 58 Dassault Mirage 5–D, 8 Northrop
  F–5A) plus 10 Dassault Mirage 5–DR reconnaissance
  aircraft. Approx 80 Dassault Mirage 5 delivered by
  mid–1973; of which over 10 already lost in accidents.
  The majority of Mirage 5 are inoperative owing to lack
  of pilots and ground personnel.
**Army**
20,000 men
**Army aviation**
Liaison and AOP aircraft
2 Auster AOP.6 (?)
Helicopters
3 Agusta-Bell AB.47G
2 (5?) Agusta-Bell AB.206A
**Navy**
1,000 men

## MADAGASCAR (MALAGASY)

**Air force** (Armée de L'Air Malgache)
men 200
squadron 1
operational aircraft 5 and
helicopters 4
**Organisation**
1 transport squadron with C–47 and M.H.1521M
**Bases**
Diego-Suarez, Ivato (Tananarive)
**Military training aid from**
France
**Foreign Air Forces in Madagascar**
1 French squadron: 1 transport squadron with N.2501
**Equipment**
Transports
3 Douglas C–47
2 Dassault M.D.315
Liaison and AOP aircraft
2 Max Holste M.H.1521M
Helicopters
1 Aérospatiale Alouette II
2 Aérospatiale Alouette III
1 Bell 47G

**Army**
3,700 men
**Navy**
200 men

## MALAWI

**Air force**
men 100 (?)
squadron 1
operational aircraft 6
**Organisation**
1 transport squadron with C–47 and Pembroke
**Base**
Blantyre (?)
**Military training aid from**
Great Britain
**Equipment**
Transports
4 Douglas C–47
2 Hunting Pembroke
**Army**
1,200 men

## MALAYSIA

**Air force** (Tentera Udara Diraja Malaysia)
men 4,000
squadrons 9
operational aircraft 55 and
helicopters 40
**Organisation**
1 strike fighter squadron with CA–27
2 transport squadrons with DHC–4
1 transport squadron with Dove and Heron
1 transport squadron with Herald
2 helicopter squadrons with Alouette III
2 helicopter squadrons with S–61A–4
2 trainer squadrons with CL–41G
1 trainer squadron with Bulldog
**Bases**
Butterworth, Kuala Lumpur, Kuantan, Kuching, Labuan
**Military training aid from**
Australia, Great Britain
**Foreign Air Forces in Malaysia**
2 Australian strike fighter squadrons with Mirage IIIO
**Equipment**
Fighters and strike fighters
17 Commonwealth CA–27 Sabre Mk.32 (F–86F)
Transports
5 DeHavilland Dove
2 DeHavilland Heron
12 DeHavilland DHC–4
8 Handley Page Herald 401
2 Hawker Siddeley H.S.125
Liaison and AOP aircraft
6 Scottish Aviation Pioneer
Helicopters
24 Aérospatiale Alouette III
16 Sikorsky S–61A–4
Trainers
20 Canadair CL–41G
6 DeHavilland Canada DHC–1
12 Hunting Provost T.51
15 Scottish Aviation Bulldog
**Programme**
Formation of second strike fighter squadron with 16 Northrop F–5E, delivery 1973/74. Phasing out of DeHavilland Canada DHC–1 and Hunting Provost T.51 trainers
**Army**
43,000 men
**Navy**
3,000 men

## MALI

**Air force** (Force Aérienne du Mali)
men 200
squadrons –

operational aircraft 7 and
helicopters 2 (?)
**Organisation**
—
**Base**
Bamako
**Equipment**
Fighters and strike fighters
3 Mikoyan MiG–17
Transports
2 Antonov An–2 (?)
2 Douglas C–47
Liaison and AOP Aircraft
1 Max Holste M.H. 1521M
Helicopters
2 (?) Mil Mi–4
Trainers
1 Mikoyan MiG–15UTI
some Yakovlev Yak–12 and Yakovlev Yak–18 (?)
**Army**
3,500 men
**Navy**
40 men

## MALTA

**Air force**
men 250
squadrons –
helicopters 5
**Organisation**
—
**Bases**
Hal Far, Luqa, Takali
**Military training aid from**
Germany, Great Britain
**Foreign Air Forces on Malta**
2 British squadrons:
1 reconnaissance squadron with Canberra P.R.9
1 maritime reconnaissance and ASW squadron with Nimrod MR.1
**Equipment**
Helicopters
4 Bell 47G
1 Bell 206A
**Army**
1,250 men
**Navy**
500 men

## MAURITANIA

**Air force** (Force Aérienne de la Republique Islamique de la Mauritanie)
men 100
squadrons –
operational aircraft 1
**Organisation**
—
**Base**
Nouakchott
**Military training aid from**
France
**Equipment**
Transports
1 (3?) Douglas C–47
Liaison and AOP aircraft
1 Aermacchi AL.60
2 Max Holste M.H.1521M
**Army**
1,400 men

## MEXICO

**Air force** (Fuerza Aérea Mexicana)
men 6,000
squadrons 6
operational aircraft 43 and
helicopters 31

**Organisation**
1 strike fighter squadron with Vampire F.3
1 transport squadron with C–47
1 transport squadron with C–54
1 liaison squadron with LASA–60
1 liaison squadron with Musketeer Sport
1 helicopter squadron with Alouette III
1 helicopter squadron with Bell 47G
1 helicopter squadron with Bell 206A
3 trainer squadrons with T–6G
2 trainer squadrons with T–28A
1 trainer squadron with T–33A
1 trainer squadron with T–34A
**Bases**
Cozumel, El Cipres, Guadalajara, Ixtepec, Pie de la
    Cuesta, Puebla, Santa Lucia
**Military training aid from**
United States
**Equipment**
Fighters and strike fighters
12 DeHavilland Vampire F.3
3 DeHavilland Vampire T.11
Transports
5 Beechcraft C–45
3 Britten-Norman BN–2
6 Douglas C–47
5 Douglas C–54
2 Douglas C–118A
5 IAI–201 Arawa
1 Lockheed JetStar
1 Mitsubishi MU–2
Liaison and AOP aircraft
18 Lockheed-Azcarate LASA–60
Helicopters
6 Aérospatiale Alouette III
3 Aérospatiale S.A.330
14 Bell 47G
5 Bell 206A
2 Bell 212
1 Hiller OH–23G
Trainers
20 Beechcraft Musketeer Sport
15 Beechcraft T–11
10 Beechcraft T–34A
15 Lockheed T–33A
45 North American T–6G
30 North American T–28A
**Army**
54,000 men
**Navy**
13,200 men
**Naval aviation** (Armada de Mexico, Departemento de
    Aeronautica)
– men
– squadrons
5 operational aircraft and
9 helicopters
**Organisation**
—

**Base**
Balbuena
**Equipment**
Maritime reconnaissance aircraft
5 Convair PBY–5A
Helicopters
4 Aérospatiale Alouette II
1 Bell 47G
4 Bell 47J

## MONGOLIAN PEOPLE'S REPUBLIC

**Air force** (Part of the army)
men 1,000
squadron 1
operational aircraft 40 and
helicopters 10
**Organisation**
1 strike fighter squadron with MiG–15

**Major bases**
Sayn Shanda, Ulan Bator
**Military training aid from**
Soviet Union
**Foreign Air Forces in the Mongolian People's Republic**
Several Soviet fighter, strike fighter and reconnaissance
    squadrons
**Equipment**
Fighters and strike fighters
10 Mikoyan MiG–15
Transports
approx 30 aircraft, inc Antonov An–2, Antonov An–26,
    Ilyushin Il–12, Ilyushin Il–14, Tupolev Tu–104
Liaison and AOP aircraft
some PZL–104
Helicopters
approx 10 aircraft, inc Mil Mi–1 and Mil Mi–4
Trainers
approx 30 aircraft, inc Mikoyan MiG–15UTI, Yakovlev
    Yak–11 and Yakovlev Yak–18
**Army**
28,000 men

## MOROCCO

**Air force** (Al Quwwat Aljawwiya Almalakiya Marakishiya)
men 4,000
squadrons 3
operational aircraft 45 and
helicopters 32
**Organisation**
1 strike fighter squadron with F–5
1 transport squadron with C–119G and C–47
1 helicopter squadron with AB.205
1 trainer squadron with T–28D
1 trainer squadron with C.M.170
– trainer squadrons with T–6G
**Bases**
Kénitra, Marrakesh, Meknes, Nouasseur, Salé (Rabat)
**Military training aid from**
United States
**Equipment**
Fighters and strike fighters
12 Mikoyan MiG–17
10 Northrop F–5A
4 Northrop F–5B
Bombers
2 Ilyushin Il–28
Transports
some Douglas C–47
10 (6?) Fairchild C–119G
Liaison and AOP aircraft
2 Beechcraft Twin Bonanza
4 Max Holste M.H.1521M
Helicopters
4 Aérospatiale Alouette II
24 Agusta-Bell AB.205
4 Bell 47G
Trainers
2 Mikoyan MiG–15UTI
35 North American T–6G
25 North American T–28D
20 Potez-Air Fouga C.M.170
The Soviet aircraft (Il–28, MiG–15UTI, MiG–17) have
    been mothballed
**Army**
52,000 men
**Army aviation**
3 Aérospatiale Alouette III helicopters
**Navy**
1,500 men

## NEPAL

**Air force** (Part of the army)
men 500
squadrons –
operational aircraft 5 and
helicopters 1

**Organisation**
—
**Base**
Katmandu
**Military training aid from**
Great Britain, United States
**Equipment**
Transports
3 DeHavilland Canada DHC–3
2 Short Skyvan 3M
Helicopter
1 Aérospatiale Alouette III
**Army**
25,000 men

## NETHERLANDS

**Air force** (Koninklijke Nederlandse Luchtmacht)
men 21,500
squadrons 9
operational aircraft 215
**Organisation**
2 fighter squadrons with F–104G
2 strike fighter squadrons with F–104G
3 strike fighter squadrons with NF–5A
1 reconnaissance squadron with RF–104G
1 transport squadron with F.27M and F.27
1 strike fighter trainer squadron with NF–5B
fighter, strike fighter and reconnaissance squadrons each
    with 18 aircraft
**Major bases**
Eindhoven, Gilze Rijen, Leeuwarden, Soesterberg,
    Twente, Valkenburg, Volkel
**Military training aid from**
Canada
**Foreign Air Forces in the Netherlands**
1 American fighter squadron with F–4E
**Equipment**
Fighters and strike fighters
80 Lockheed F–104G
15 Lockheed TF–104G
70 Canadair (Northrop) NF–5A
30 Canadair (Northrop) NF–5B
Reconnaissance aircraft
18 Lockheed RF–104G
Transports
9 Fokker-VFW F.27M
3 Fokker-VFW F.27
Trainers
10 Fokker S.11
**Programme**
Seeking replacement for Lockheed F–104G strike fighters
    (Saab 37, Northrop P–530 Cobra or Dassault Mirage
    F1?)
**Army**
76,000 men
**Army aviation** (Groep Lichte Vliegtuigen)
– men
3 squadrons
15 (?) operational aircraft and
70 helicopters
**Organisation**
2 helicopter squadrons with Alouette III
1 helicopter squadron with Alouette III and DHC–2
**Equipment**
Helicopters
70 Aérospatiale Alouette III
Liaison and AOP aircraft
9 DeHavilland Canada DHC–2
some Piper L–21
**Navy**
20,000 men
**Naval aviation** (Marine Luchtvaartdienst)
2,000 men
4 squadrons
34 operational aircraft and
18 helicopters
**Organisation**

1 maritime reconnaissance and ASW squadron with
    S–2N
1 maritime reconnaissance and ASW squadron with
    SP–2H
1 maritime reconnaissance and ASW squadron with
    Br.1150
1 helicopter squadron with AB.204B
1 trainer squadron with Br.1150, S–2N and SP–2H
**Equipment**
Maritime reconnaissance and ASW aircraft
8 Breguet Br.1150
12 Grumman S–2N
13 Lockheed SP–2H
Helicopters
7 Agusta-Bell AB.204B
11 Westland Wasp
Trainers
5 Beechcraft TC–45
9 Fokker S.11
**Aircraft factories**
Fokker (N.V. Koninklijke Nederlandse Vliegtuigen-
    fabriek Fokker)—united with German VFW concern

## NEW ZEALAND

**Air force** (Royal New Zealand Air Force)
men 4,250
squadrons 7
operational aircraft 50 and
helicopters 24
**Organisation**
1 strike fighter squadron with A–4K
1 ground-attack squadron with BAC 167
1 maritime reconnaissance and ASW squadron with
    P–3B
1 transport squadron with C–130H
1 transport squadron with C–47
1 transport squadron with Bristol Freighter Mk.31M
1 transport squadron with Bristol Freighter Mk.31M
    and UH–1H
1 helicopter squadron with Bell 47G, UH–1D and
    UH–1H
– trainer squadrons with T–6G, Airtourer and Devon
    C.1
**Bases**
Hobsonville, Ohakea, Whenuapai, Wigram
**Equipment**
Fighters and strike fighters
10 McDonnell Douglas A–4K
4 McDonnell Douglas TA–4K
Ground-attack aircraft
10 BAC 167 Strikemaster Mk.88
Maritime reconnaissance and ASW aircraft
5 Lockheed P–3B
Transports
3 (9?) Bristol Freighter Mk.31M
6 (17?) DeHavilland Devon C.1
6 Douglas C–47
1 Fokker–VFW F.27
5 Lockheed C–130H
Helicopters
11 Bell 47G
5 Bell UH–1D
8 Bell UH–1H
Trainers
4 AESL Airtourer T.6
some DeHavilland Canada DHC–1
16 North American T–6G
**Programme**
Replacement of Bristol Freighter Mk.31M (by several
    DeHavilland Canada DHC–5?) and Douglas C–47
    transports
**Army**
5,500 men
**Navy**
2,900 men
**Naval aviation**
3 Westland Wasp helicopters

**Aircraft factories**
AESL (Aero Service Ltd)

## NICARAGUA

**Air force** (Fuerza Aérea, Guardia Nacional)
men 1,500
squadrons 3
operational aircraft 26 and
helicopters 5
**Organisation**
1 ground-attack squadron with F–51D
1 bomber squadron with B–26
1 transport squadron with C–45 and C–47
1 trainer squadron with T–28A
1 trainer squadron with T–33A
**Bases**
Managua, Puerto Cabezas
**Military training aid from**
United States
**Equipment**
Ground-attack aircraft
15 North American F–51D
Bombers
4 Douglas B–26
Transports
4 Beechcraft C–45
3 Douglas C–47
Liaison and AOP aircraft
10 Cessna 180
Helicopters
1 Hughes 269
4 Hughes 500M
Trainers
some Beechcraft T–11
6 Lockheed T–33A
4 North American T–6G
6 North American T–28A
**Army**
5,400 men
**Army aviation**
2 Cessna U–17A
**Navy**
200 men

## NIGER

**Air force** (Force Aérienne de Niger)
men 150
squadrons –
operational aircraft 6
**Organisation**
—
**Base**
Niamey
**Military training aid from**
France
**Equipment**
Transports
1 Aero Commander 500B
1 Douglas C–47
4 Nord N.2501
Liaison and AOP aircraft
2 Cessna 337
3 Max Holste M.H.1521M
**Army**
2,000 men

## NIGERIA

**Air force**
men 3,000
squadrons –
operational aircraft 30 and
helicopters 3
**Organisation**
—
**Bases**
Kano, Lagos
**Military training aid from**

Soviet Union
**Equipment**
Fighters and strike fighters
4 Mikoyan MiG–15
8 Mikoyan MiG–17
Bombers
3 Ilyushin Il–28
Transports
5 Dornier Do–28
3 Douglas C–47
6 Fokker–VFW F.27
Liaison and AOP aircraft
some Dornier Do–27
some Do–28
Helicopters
2 Westland Whirlwind 2
1 Westland Whirlwind 3
Trainers
8 Aero L–29
2 Mikoyan MiG–15UTI
10 Piaggio P.149D
**Programme**
20 Scottish Aviation Bulldog trainers on order, delivery
    1973/74
**Army**
75,000 men
**Navy**
2,000 men

## NORWAY

**Air force** (Kongelige Norske Flyvåpen)
men 9,400
squadrons 12
operational aircraft 145 and
helicopters 39
**Organisation**
2 fighter squadrons with F–104G
3 strike fighter squadrons with F–5A
1 reconnaissance squadron with RF–5A
1 maritime reconnaissance and ASW squadron with
    P–3B
1 transport squadron with C–130H
2 helicopter squadrons with AB.204B
1 helicopter squadron with AB.204B and DHC–6
1 trainer squadron with Saab 91B
1 trainer squadron with T–33A
fighter and strike fighter squadrons each with 16,
    reconnaissance squadrons each with 12 aircraft
**Major bases**
Banak, Bardufoss, Bodø, Gardermoen, Orlandet, Rygge,
    Sola
**Military training aid from**
United States
**Equipment**
Fighters and strike fighters
35 Lockheed F–104G
2 Lockheed TF–104G
54 Northrop F–5A
20 Northrop F–5B
Reconnaissance aircraft
14 Northrop RF–5A
Maritime reconnaissance and ASW aircraft
5 Lockheed P–3B
Transports
2 Dassault Falcon 20
3 DeHavilland Canada DHC–6
4 Douglas C–47
6 Lockheed C–130H
Liaison and AOP aircraft
approx 20 aircraft, inc Cessna O–1E and Piper L–18C
Helicopters
29 Agusta-Bell AB.204B
10 Westland Sea King Mk.43
Trainers
15 Lockheed T–33A
20 Saab 91B
**Army**

18,000 men
**Navy**
8,500 men

## OMAN

**Air force** (Sultan of Oman's Air Force)
men 500
squadrons 3
operational aircraft 45 and
helicopters 12
**Organisation**
1 strike fighter squadron with Hunter FGA.76
1 ground-attack squadron with BAC 167
1 transport squadron with Skyvan 3M and DHC-4
1 helicopter squadron with AB.205
**Bases**
Azaiba, Bait-al-Falaj (Muscat), Salalah
**Military training aid from**
Great Britain
**Equipment**
Fighters and strike fighters
12 Hawker Hunter FGA.76
Ground-attack aircraft
15 BAC 167 Strikemaster Mk.82
Transports
3 DeHavilland Canada DHC-4
10 Short Skyvan 3M
5 Vickers Viscount 800
Liaison and AOP aircraft
4 DeHavilland DHC-2
Helicopters
8 Agusta-Bell AB.205
4 Agusta-Bell AB.206A
**Army**
3,000 men
**Navy**
200 men

## PAKISTAN

**Air force**
men 17,000
squadrons 18
operational aircraft 258 and
helicopters 8
**Organisation**
4 fighter squadrons with F-6 (MiG-19)
1 fighter squadron with F-104A
1 strike fighter squadron with Mirage IIIEP and IIIRP
2 strike fighter squadrons with Mirage 5-PA
4 strike fighter squadrons with F-86F
2 bomber squadrons with B-57B
1 reconnaissance squadron with RT-33A and RB-57
1 transport squadron with C-47
1 transport squadron with C-130B
1 helicopter squadron with Alouette III
fighter and strike fighter squadrons each with 14–16
   aircraft
**Major bases**
Chaklala, Chitral, Drigh Road, Gilgit, Kohat, Korangi,
   Lahore, Malir, Masroor (Karachi), Mauripur,
   Miranshah, Peshawar, Risalpur, Samundri, Sargodha
**Military training aid from**
China, United States
**Equipment**
Fighters and strike fighters
17 Dassault Mirage IIIEP
3 Dassault Mirage IIIDP
28 Dassault Mirage 5-PA
2 Dassault Mirage 5-PD
4 Lockheed F-104A
2 Lockheed M-104B
55 North American F-86F and Canadair CL-13B
   Sabre 6
60 Shenyang F-6 (MiG-19)
Bombers
16 Martin B-57B
Reconnaissance aircraft

3 Dassault Mirage IIIRP
4 Lockheed RT-33A
2 Martin RB-57
Maritime reconnaissance and ASW aircraft
4 Grumman HU-16A
Transports
1 Aero Commander
1 Dassault Falcon 20
8 Douglas C-47
1 Fokker-VFW F.27
7 Lockheed C-130B
Liaison and AOP aircraft
1 Beechcraft Travel Air
1 Beechcraft Twin Bonanza
10 (12?) DeHavilland Canada DHC-2
Helicopters
4 Aérospatiale Alouette III
4 Kaman HH-43B
Trainers
approx 75 aircraft, inc 20 Cessna T-37B, Lockheed
   T-33A, 4 Mikoyan MiG-15UTI, North American
   T-6G
**Programme**
Formation of new strike fighter squadrons with 50–100
   Shenyang F-6 (MiG-19) or Shenyang F-8 (MiG-21)
   strike fighters (?). New American aid deliveries (?):
   Lockheed F-104 and Northrop F-5 (?) strike fighters,
   Martin B-57 bombers plus Grumman S-2 maritime
   reconnaissance and ASW aircraft (?)
**Army**
365,000 men
**Army aviation**
Helicopters
8 Aérospatiale Alouette III
15 Bell 47G
12 Mil Mi-8
Liaison and AOP aircraft
some Beechcraft Twin Bonanza, Cessna 172, Cessna
   Skymaster, 50 (?) Cessna O-1A and O-1E, some
   DeHavilland Canada DHC-2
**Navy**
10,000 men
**Naval aviation**
4 Aérospatiale Alouette III helicopters
**Programme**
3 Westland Sea King Mk.45 helicopters on order

## PANAMA

**Air force** (Fuerza Aérea Panamena)
men 60
squadrons –
operational aircraft 1 (?) and
helicopters 5
**Organisation**

—

**Bases**
Albrook, France Field, Tocumen (Panama City)
**Military training aid from**
United States
**Foreign Air Forces in Panama**
Some American trainer squadrons
**Equipment**
Transports
1 DeHavilland Canada DHC-6 (?)
Helicopters
2 Bell UH-1H
3 Fairchild-Hiller FH-1100
**Army**
4,700 men
**Navy**
30 men

## PARAGUAY

**Air force** (Fuerza Aérea del Paraguay)
men 800
squadron 1
operational aircraft 9 and

helicopters 7
**Organisation**
1 transport squadron with C–47 and C–54
**Base**
Campo Grande (Asunción)
**Military training aid from**
United States
**Equipment**
Transports
1 Convair 240
1 DeHavilland Canada DHC–3
1 DeHavilland Canada DHC–6
4 Douglas C–47
2 Douglas C–54
Liaison and AOP aircraft
4 Piper L–4
Helicopters
4 Bell 47G
3 Hiller OH–23G
Trainers
approx 15 aircraft, inc 1 Morane-Saulnier M.S.760 and
   10 North American T–6G
**Programme**
20 Aerotec T–23 trainers on order
**Army**
17,500 men
**Navy**
1,900 men

## PERU

**Air force** (Fuerza Aérea del Peru)
9,000 men
11 squadrons
125 operational aircraft and
43 helicopters
**Organisation**
1 strike fighter squadron with Mirage 5–P
1 strike fighter squadron with F–86F
1 strike fighter squadron with Hunter F.52
2 bomber squadrons with Canberra B.72 and B.(I)78
1 maritime reconnaissance and ASW squadron with
   HU–16B
1 transport squadron with C–130E
1 transport squadron with DHC–5
1 transport squadron with DHC–6
– liaison squadrons with Queen Air A80
1 liaison squadron with Cessna 185 and DHC–2
1 helicopter squadron with Alouette II and Alouette III
1 helicopter squadron with UH–1D
– trainer squadrons with T–33A
– trainer squadrons with T–37B
– trainer squadrons with T–41A
**Bases**
Ancon, Arequipa, Chiclayo, Cusco, Iquitos, Las Palmas,
   Lima, Pisco, Talava, Trujillo
**Equipment**
Fighters and strike fighters
12 Dassault Mirage 5–P
2 Dassault Mirage 5–DP
14 Hawker Hunter F.52
2 Hawker Hunter T.62
some Lockheed F–80C
10 North American F–86F
Bombers
20 English Electric Canberra B.72, B.(I)78 and T.74
Maritime reconnaissance and ASW aircraft
4 Grumman HU–16B and some Lockheed PV–2
Transports
16 DeHavilland Canada DHC–5
11 DeHavilland Canada DHC–6
3 Fokker-VFW F.28 Mk.1000
6 Lockheed C–130E plus some Curtiss-Wright C–46
   Douglas C–47 and Douglas C–54
Liaison and AOP aircraft
approx 30 aircraft, inc 18 Beechcraft Queen Air A80,
   some Cessna 185, 6 DeHavilland Canada DHC–2, 1
   Pilatus PC–6A

Helicopters
6 Aérospatiale Alouette II
10 Aérospatiale Alouette III
2 Bell 212
9 Bell UH–1D
13 Bell UH–1H
2 Hiller OH–23G
1 (?) Mil Mi–8
Trainers
6 Beechcraft T–34
25 Cessna T–37B
19 Cessna T–41A
8 (?) Lockheed T–33A
15 North American T–6G
**Programme**
Purchase of 25 FMA I.A.58 Pucará ground-attack aircraft under consideration. Phasing out of obsolete
   Curtiss-Wright C–46, Douglas C–47 and Douglas C–54
   transports. Acquisition of further helicopters
**Army**
35,500 men
**Army aviation**
8 Bell 47G helicopters
**Navy**
7,700 men
**Naval aviation** (Naval Aviacion Armada Peruana)
4 helicopters
2 Aérospatiale Alouette III
2 Bell 47G

## PHILIPPINES

**Air force** (Philippine Air Force)
men 9,000
squadrons 6
operational aircraft 91 and
helicopters 29
**Organisation**
1 fighter squadron with F–86D
2 strike fighter squadrons with F–86F
1 strike fighter squadron with F–5A
1 transport squadron with C–47
1 helicopter squadron with UH–19, H–34 and S–62A
2 trainer squadrons with T–34
**Bases**
Batangas, Cebu, Clark Field, Florida Blanca, Legaspi,
   Lipa, Manila, San Fernando, San Jose, Sibuyan,
   Tacloban, Zamboanga
**Military training aid from**
United States
**Foreign Air Forces in the Philippines**
6 American squadrons:
3 strike fighter squadrons with F–4
3 transport squadrons with C–130
**Equipment**
Fighters and strike fighters
15 North American F–86D
24 North American F–86F
20 Northrop F–5A
2 Northrop F–5B
Transports
1 Aero Commander 500
9 Douglas C–47
1 Fokker-VFW F.27
4 Lockheed L–100–20
4 NAMC YS–11
Helicopters
12 Bell UH–1D
8 Fairchild-Hiller FH–1100
2 Mitsubishi-Sikorsky S–62A
2 Sikorsky H–34
5 Sikorsky UH–19
Trainers
30 Fuji-Beechcraft T–34
3 Lockheed T–33A
8 North American T–28A
6 SIAI-Marchetti SF.260M
**Programme**

26 SIAI-Marchetti SF.260W ground-attack aircraft and
26 SIAI-Marchetti SF.260M trainers to be ordered ?
Introduction of new helicopters (Bell UH–1H ?)
**Army**
17,600 men
**Navy**
6,000 men

## POLAND

**Air force** (Polskie Lotnictwo Wojskowe)
55,000 men
66 squadrons
640 operational aircraft and
40 helicopters
**Organisation**
36 fighter squadrons with MiG–17, MiG–19 and MiG–21
12 strike fighter squadrons with MiG–17 and Su–7
4 bomber squadrons with Il–28
6 reconnaissance squadrons with MiG–17, MiG–21 and
Il–28
4 transport squadrons with An–2, An–12 and Il–14
4 helicopter squadrons with Mi–4 and Mi–8
– trainer squadrons with Yak–11 and Yak–18
– trainer squadrons with MiG–15UTI and TS–11
fighter, strike fighter and reconnaissance squadrons each
with 10–12 aircraft
**Major bases**
Allenstein (Olsztyn), Breslau, Bromberg ( Bydgoszcz),
Cracow, Danzig, Deblin, Elbing (Elblag), Graudenz
(Grudziadz), Hohensalza (Inowtoclaw), Hirschberg
(Jelenia Gora), Krosno, Kutno, Liegnitz, Lublin,
Mielce, Poznan, Radom, Rastenburg, Rzeszow,
Schrode (Sroda), Siedlce, Stettin, Stolp (Slupsk),
Swidnik, Thorn (Torun), Warsaw
**Military training aid from**
Soviet Union
**Foreign Air Forces in Poland**
approx 250 Soviet fighters, strike fighters and
reconnaissance aircraft
**Equipment**
Fighters and strike fighters
approx 220 Mikoyan MiG–17
over 250 (200?) Mikoyan MiG–19 and Mikoyan
MiG–21 plus Mikoyan MiG–21UTI
80 Sukhoi Su–7B
**Bombers**
45 Ilyushin Il–28
**Transports**
approx 45 aircraft, inc Antonov An–2, Antonov An–12,
Ilyushin Il–12, Ilyushin Il–14, Ilyushin Il–18, Li–2 (copy
of C–47 [Dakota])
Liaison and AOP aircraft
PZL–104
**Helicopters**
approx 40 machines, inc Mil Mi–1, Mil Mi–4, Mil Mi–8,
WSK SM–1, WSK SM–2
**Trainers**
approx 200 aircraft, inc Mikoyan MiG–15UTI, PZL
TS–11, Yakovlev Yak–11, Yakovlev Yak–18
**Army**
190,000 men
**Navy**
20,000 men
**Naval aviation** (Morskie Lotnictwo Wojskowe)
– men
4 squadrons
50 operational aircraft and
10 (?) helicopters
**Organisation**
3 strike fighter squadrons with MiG–17
1 bomber squadron with Il–28
**Equipment**
Fighters and strike fighters
40 Mikoyan MiG–17
Bombers
8–10 Ilyushin Il–28
Helicopters

some Mil Mi–2 and Mil Mi–4
Trainers
some Mikoyan MiG–15UTI and Yakovlev Yak–11
**Aircraft factories**
PZL (Polskie Zaklady Lotnicze), WSK (Wytwornia
Sprzetu Komunikacyjnego)

## PORTUGAL

**Air force** (Força Aérea Portuguesa)
21,000 men
10 squadrons
160 operational aircraft and
95 helicopters
**Organisation**
1 fighter squadron with F–86F
2 strike fighter squadrons with G.91R.4
1 strike fighter squadron with F–84G
1 bomber squadron with B–26
1 maritime reconnaissance and ASW squadron with P–2E
2 transport squadrons with N.2501
1 transport squadron with C–47
1 transport squadron with DC–6
– liaison squadrons with Do–27
– liaison squadrons with D5/160
– helicopter squadrons with Alouette III
3 trainer squadrons with T–6G
1 trainer squadron with T–33A
1 trainer squadron with T–37C
fighter and strike fighter squadrons each with 16–18
aircraft
The majority of the Portuguese squadrons are stationed
in the Portuguese overseas provinces of Angola,
Mozambique and Portuguese-Guinea. Only the F–86F
fighter squadron, the F–84G strike fighter squadron
and the P–2E maritime reconnaissance and ASW
squadron are based permanently in Portugal itself
**Major bases**
Alverca, Jacinto, Lisbon-Portela, Monte Real, Montijo,
Ita, Porto, Sintra, Tancos
**Foreign Air Forces in Portugal**
1 American rescue squadron with HC–130H in the
Azores and German trainer squadrons in Beja
**Equipment**
Fighters and strike fighters
35 Fiat G.91R.4
18 North American F–86F
18 Republic F–84G
Bombers
7 Douglas B–26
Maritime reconnaissance and ASW aircraft
10 Lockheed P–2E
Transports
15 Beechcraft C–45
2 Boeing 707–320C
16 Douglas C–47
3 (?) Douglas C–54
4 Douglas HC–54D
10 Douglas DC–6A and B
22 Nord N.2501
Liaison and AOP aircraft
11 Dornier Do–27
90 (?) OGMA-Auster D5/160
some Cessna L–21B
some Max Holste M.H.1521M
Helicopters
5 Aérospatiale Alouette II
approx 80 Aérospatiale Alouette III
11 Aérospatiale S.A.330
Trainers
25 Cessna T–37C
13 Lockheed T–33
35 North American T–6G
some DeHavilland Canada DHC–1
**Army**
179,000 men
**Navy**
18,000 men

**Aircraft factories**
OGMA (Oficinas Gerais de Material Aeronáutico)

## QATAR

**Air force** (Qatar Public Security Force Air Wing)
men 250 (?)
squadron 1
operational aircraft 6 and
helicopters 2
**Organisation**
1 strike fighter squadron with Hunter FGA.78
**Base**
Doha
**Military training aid from**
Great Britain
**Equipment**
Fighters and strike fighters
6 Hawker Hunter FGA.78
Helicopters
2 Westland Whirlwind 3
**Army**
1,600 (?) men

## RHODESIA

**Air force** (Rhodesian Air Force)
men 1,200
squadrons 5
operational aircraft 45 and
helicopters 8
**Organisation**
1 strike fighter squadron with Hunter FGA.57
1 strike fighter squadron with Vampire FB.9
1 bomber squadron with Canberra B.2
1 transport squadron with C–47 and DC–4
1 liaison squadron with AL.60
1 helicopter squadron with Alouette III
1 trainer squadron with Provost T.52
1 trainer squadron with Vampire T.55
**Bases**
New Sarum (Salisbury), Thornhill (Gwelo)
**Equipment**
Fighters and strike fighters
11 DeHavilland Vampire FB.9
12 Hawker Hunter FGA.57
2 Hawker Hunter T.52
Bombers
10 English Electric Canberra B.2
2 English Electric Canberra T.4
Transports
4 Douglas C–47
4 Douglas DC–4M
Liaison and AOP aircraft
4 (7?) Aermacchi AL.60
1 Beechcraft Baron
some Cessna 185
Helicopters
8 (12?) Aérospatiale Alouette III
Trainers
15 DeHavilland Vampire T.55
12 Hunting Provost T.52
**Army**
3,500 men

## RUANDA

**Air force**
men 150
squadrons –
operational aircraft 2 and
helicopters 2
**Organisation**
—

**Base**
Kigali
**Military training aid from**
Belgium
**Equipment**
Transports
2 Douglas C–47

Liaison and AOP aircraft
3 Aerfer-Aermacchi AM.3C
Helicopters
2 Aérospatiale Alouette III
**Programme**
Purchase of 3 Potez-Air Fouga C.M.170 trainers
**Army**
2,500 men

## RUMANIA

**Air force** (Fortele Aériene ale Republicii Socialiste
    România)
men 21,000
squadrons 18
operational aircraft 190 and
helicopters 30
**Organisation**
3 fighter squadrons with MiG–21F and PF
3 fighter squadrons with MiG–19
6 strike fighter squadrons with Su–7 and MiG–17F
1 bomber squadron with Il–28
2 transport squadrons with Il–12, Il–14 and Li–2
1 helicopter squadron with Mi–4
1 helicopter squadron with Mi–8
fighter, strike fighter and bomber squadrons each with
    10–12 aircraft, transport and helicopter squadrons
    each with 8–10 aircraft
**Major bases**
Arad, Bacau, Baneasa, Buzau, Calarasi, Constanza,
    Craiova, Galatz, Grosswardein (Oradea Mare), Jassy,
    Klausenburg (Cluj), Kronstadt (Brasov), Mamaia,
    Neppendorf (Turnisor), Otopeni, Popesti-Leordeni,
    Sathmar (Satu Mare), Tecuci, Temesvár (Timisoara),
    Zilistea
**Military training aid from**
Soviet Union
**Equipment**
Fighters and strike fighters
40 Mikoyan MiG–17F
40 Mikoyan MiG–19
40 Mikoyan MiG–21F and PF plus MiG–21UTI
30 Sukhoi Su–7 and Su–7UTI
Bombers
10 Ilyushin Il–28
Transports
10 Antonov An–2
some Ilyushin Il–12
6 Ilyushin Il–14
1 Ilyushin Il–18
10 Li–2 (C–47 [Dakota] copy)
In addition there are 55 aircraft of the national airline
    Tarom available for military employment. These in-
    clude 3 Antonov An–24, 6 BAC 111, 3 Boeing 707–
    302C (on order, delivery 1974), 18 Ilyushin Il–14, 11
    Ilyushin Il–18 and some Li–2 transports
Liaison and AOP aircraft
some LET L–200 Morava and some L–60
Helicopters
approx 30 machines, inc some Mil Mi–1, 10 Mil Mi–4,
    12 Mil Mi–8, some WSK SM–2
Trainers
approx 120 aircraft, inc Aero L–29, Mikoyan MiG–15UTI
    Yakovlev Yak–11, Yakovlev Yak–18
**Programme**
Re-equipment of further MiG–17 squadrons with MiG–
    21PF and MF fighters and Su–7 strike fighters. 50
    Aérospatiale Alouette III helicopters (Rumanian
    licence-built) on order, delivery from 1972/73
**Army**
165,000 men
**Navy**
9,000 men
**Naval aviation**
4 (?) Mil Mi–4 helicopters
**Aircraft factories**
IRMA (Intreprinderea de Reparat Material
    Aeronautic)

## SAUDI-ARABIA

**Air force** (Al Quwwat Aljawwiya Assu'udiya)
men 5,000
squadrons 9
operational aircraft 97 and
helicopters 43
**Organisation**
2 fighter squadrons with Lightning F.53
1 strike fighter squadron with F–86F
2 ground-attack squadrons with BAC 167
2 transport squadrons with C–130E
2 helicopter squadrons with AB.205 and AB.206A
1 trainer squadron with Cessna 172 and T–41A
1 trainer squadron with T–33A
**Bases**
Dhahran, Jedda, Khamis Mushayt, Riyadh, Tabuk,
   Taif
**Military training aid from**
Great Britain, United States
**Equipment**
Fighters and strike fighters
2 BAC Lightning F.52
32 BAC Lightning F.53
2 BAC Lightning T.54
6 BAC Lightning T.55
15 North American F–86F
Ground-attack aircraft
21 BAC 167 Strikemaster Mk.80
Transports
2 Douglas C–118
11 Lockheed C–130E
4 Lockheed KC–130H
2 Lockheed Jet Star
Liaison and AOP aircraft
1 Cessna 421
Helicopters
2 Aérospatiale Alouette III
25 Agusta-Bell AB.205
16 Agusta-Bell AB.206A
Trainers
approx 30 aircraft, inc Beechcraft T–34, 8 Cessna 172
   and T–41A, DeHavilland Canada DHC–1, 13 Lockheed
   T–33A, North American T–28A
A number of BAC Lightning strike fighters have been
   mothballed
**Programme**
30 Northrop F–5E strike fighters and 20 Northrop F–5B
   strike trainers on order to replace North American
   F–86F strike fighters and Lockheed T–33A trainers.
   Formation of a further ground-attack squadron with
   10 BAC 167
**Army**
35,000 men
**Navy**
1,000 men

## SENEGAL

**Air force** (Armée de l'Air du Sénégal)
men 200
squadrons —
operational aircraft 2 and
helicopters 2
**Organisation**
—
**Base**
Yoff (Dakar)
**Military training aid from**
France
**Foreign Air Forces in Senegal**
1 French transport squadron with 6 N.2501 transports
**Equipment**
Transports
2 Douglas C–47
Liaison and AOP aircraft
4 Max Holste M.H.1521M
Helicopters
1 Aérospatiale Alouette II

1 Agusta-Bell AB.47G
**Army**
5,500 men
**Navy**
200 men

## SINGAPORE

**Air force** (Singapore Air Defence Command)
men 1,500
squadrons 5
operational aircraft 45 and
helicopters 8
**Organisation**
2 strike fighter squadrons with Hunter FGA.74 and
   FR.74
1 ground-attack squadron with BAC 167
1 transport squadron with Skyvan 3M
1 liaison squadron with SF.260MS
1 helicopter squadron with Alouette III
**Bases**
Seletar, Tengah
**Military training aid from**
Australia, Great Britain
**Foreign Air Forces in Singapore**
4 British Nimrod MR.1 maritime reconnaissance aircraft
   plus a New Zealand transport squadron with Bristol
   freighter Mk.31M and 3 UH–1H and 1 British helicopter squadron with Wessex HC.2
**Equipment**
Fighters and strike fighters
20 Hawker Hunter FGA.74
2 Hawker Hunter T.75
Ground-attack aircraft
15 BAC 167 Strikemaster Mk.84
Reconnaissance aircraft
2 Hawker Hunter FR.74
Transports
6 Short Skyvan 3M
Liaison and AOP aircraft
8 Cessna 172K
Helicopters
8 Aérospatiale Alouette III
Trainers
6 AESL Airtourer T.6/24
16 SIAI-Marchetti SF.260MS
**Programme**
Formation of new strike fighter squadrons with
   McDonnell Douglas A–4B, 40 aircraft on order
**Army**
16,000 men
**Navy**
600 men

## SOMALI

**Air force** (Cuerpo Aeronautico del Somalia)
men 2,000
squadrons 2
operational aircraft 30
**Organisation**
1 strike fighter squadron with MiG–15 and MiG–17
1 transport squadron with An–2 and C–47
1 trainer squadron with Yak–11
**Bases**
Berbera, Mogadisho
**Military training aid from**
Soviet Union
**Equipment**
Fighters and strike fighters
12 Mikoyan MiG–15
6 Mikoyan MiG–17
Bombers
some Ilyushin Il–28(?)
Transports
3 Antonov An–2
2 Antonov An–24
1 Beechcraft C–45
2 Douglas C–47

Liaison aircraft
1 Helio Courier
Trainers
15 Yakovlev Yak–11 and Yakovlev Yak–18
2 Mikoyan MiG–15UTI
3 Piaggio P.148
**Army**
13,000 men
**Navy**
300 men

## SOUTH AFRICA

**Air force** (Suid-Afrikaanse Lugmag)
8,000 men
15 squadrons
162 operational aircraft and
90 helicopters
**Organisation**
1 fighter squadron with Mirage IIICZ
1 strike fighter squadron with Mirage IIIEZ
1 strike fighter squadron with Sabre Mk.6
1 bomber squadron with Canberra B.(I)12
1 bomber squadron with Buccaneer S.50
1 maritime reconnaissance and ASW squadron with
    Shackleton MR.3
1 maritime reconnaissance squadron with P.166S
1 transport squadron with C–47
1 transport squadron with C–47 and DC–4
1 transport squadron with C–47 and H.S.125
1 transport squadron with C.160Z and C–130B
2 liaison squadrons with AM.3C and Cessna 185
2 helicopter squadrons with Alouette III
1 helicopter squadron with S.A.321L
1 helicopter squadron with S.A.330
6 trainer squadrons with MB.326M and T–6G
**Major bases**
Bloemspruit, Dunnottar, Durban, Grand Central, Malan
    (Cape Town), Pietersberg, Port Elizabeth, Potchefs-
    troom, Waterkloof, Ysterplaat, Youngsfield, Zwartkop
**Equipment**
Fighters and strike fighters
18 Canadair CL–13B Sabre Mk.6
16 Dassault Mirage IIICZ
16 Dassault Mirage IIIEZ
3 Dassault Mirage IIIBZ
4 Dassault Mirage IIIDZ
20 DeHavilland Vampire FB.5 and FB.9
**Bombers**
6 English Electric Canberra B.(I)12
3 English Electric Canberra T.4
12 Hawker Siddeley Buccaneer S.50
Reconnaissance aircraft
4 Dassault Mirage IIIRZ
Maritime reconnaissance and ASW aircraft
7 Avro Shackleton MR.3
9 Piaggio P.166S
Transports
20 Douglas C–47
4 Douglas DC–4
4 Hawker Siddeley H.S.125
7 Lockheed C–130B
9 Transall C.160Z
1 Vickers Viscount
Liaison and AOP aircraft
40 Aerfer-Aermacchi AM.3C
some Cessna 185
Helicopters
5 Aérospatiale Alouette II
50 (70?) Aérospatiale Alouette III
15 Aérospatiale S.A.321L
20 Aérospatiale S.A.330
Trainers
200 Aermacchi MB.326M
20 DeHavilland Vampire T.11 and T.55
100 North American T–6G
some DeHavilland FB.5 and FB.9 strike fighters and
    North American T–6G trainers "mothballed" as

reserve equipment
**Programme**
Replacement of Canadair CL–13B Sabre Mk.6 strike
fighters by further 18 Dassault Mirage IIIEZ from
the end of 1973. Acquisition of further 9 Piaggio
P.166S maritime reconnaissance aircraft. Also seeking
replacement model for Avro Shackleton MR.3 maritime reconnaissance and ASW aircraft (15 Breguet
Br.1150 or Hawker Siddeley Nimrod MR.1?). Approx
50 further Aermacchi MB.326M trainers (or Aermacchi
MB.326K ground-attack aircraft) are on order and in
process of delivery. Licence-construction of French
Dassault Mirage IIIE and Mirage F1 strike fighters
planned. 18 Dassault Mirage F1 reportedly ordered in
1972; delivery from 1975(?)
**Army**
32,000 men
**Navy**
4,250 men
12 Westland Wasp helicopters
**Programme**
Further 8 Westland Wasp helicopters on order
**Aircraft factories**
Atlas (Atlas Aircraft Corporation of South Africa)

## SOUTH YEMEN

**Air force**
men 400
squadrons 3
operational aircraft 17 and
helicopters 6
**Organisation**
1 strike fighter squadron with MiG–17
1 transport squadron with C–47 and DHC–2
1 helicopter squadron with Sioux AH.1
1 trainer squadron with BAC 145 and BAC 167
**Base**
Aden
**Military training aid from**
Soviet Union
**Equipment**
Fighters and strike fighters
10 Mikoyan MiG–17
Ground-attack aircraft
4 BAC 167 Strikemaster Mk.81
Transports
3 Douglas C–47
Liaison and AOP aircraft
6 DeHavilland Canada DHC–2
Helicopters
6 Westland Sioux AH.1
Trainers
4 (8?) BAC 145 Jet Provost T.52
**Programme**
Replacement of Mikoyan MiG–17 strike fighters by
    Mikoyan MiG–21
**Army**
10,000 men
**Navy**
150 men

## SOVIET UNION

**Air Force** (Voenno-Vozdushnye Sily, VVS)
550,000 men
– squadrons
10,000 operational aircraft and
1,750 helicopters
**Organisation**
– fighter squadrons with MiG–17, MiG–19 and MiG–21
– fighter squadrons with Su–9, Su–11 and MiG–25
– fighter squadrons with Yak–25, Yak–28P and Tu–28
– strike fighter squadrons with MiG–17, MiG–19 and
    Su–7
– bomber squadrons with Il–28 and Yak–28
– bomber squadrons with Tu–20 and Mya–4
– bomber squadrons with Tu–16 and Tu–22
– reconnaissance squadrons with Il–28R and Yak–28

– reconnaissance squadrons with Tu-20
– transport squadrons with An-12
– transport squadrons with Il-18
– transport squadrons with An-2 and An-14
– transport squadrons with An-24 and An-26
– transport squadrons with Il-14 and Li-2
– liaison squadrons with Yak-12
– helicopter squadrons with Mi-1, Mi-3 and Mi-2
– helicopter squadrons with Mi-4 and Mi-8
– helicopter squadrons with Mi-6 and Mi-10
– trainer squadrons with Yak-11 and Yak-18
– trainer squadrons with L-29 and MiG-15UTI
fighter, strike fighter and reconnaissance squadrons each
   with 10–12, bomber squadrons each with 9 aircraft
**Bases**
approx 500 airfields, inc approx 300 in European
(Western) Russia and nearly 90 in northern latitudes.
**Equipment**
Fighters and strike fighters
approx 6,500 (6,000?) aircraft, inc Mikoyan MiG–17,
   Mikoyan MiG–19, Mikoyan MiG–21 and MiG–21UTI,
   Mikoyan MiG–25, Sukhoi Su–7 and Su–7UTI, Sukhoi
   Su–9 and Su–9UTI, Sukhoi Su–11, Tupolev Tu–28,
   Yakovlev Yak–25, Yakovlev Yak–28P
Bombers
approx 1,500 (1,800?) aircraft, inc Ilyushin Il–28 and
   Il–28U, 90 Myasischev Mya–4, 500 Tupolev Tu–16,
   100 Tupolev Tu–20, 200 Tupolev Tu–22 and Tu–22U
Reconnaissance aircraft
approx 300 (500?) aircraft, inc Ilyushin Il–28R, Tupolev
   Tu–20, Yakovlev Yak–28
Transports
approx 1,700 aircraft, inc Antonov An–2, An–8, 400
   Antonov An–12, An–14, 10 Antonov An–22, An–24,
   An–26, Ilyushin Il–14, 400 Ilyushin Il–18, Li–2 (copy of
   C–47). In addition there are approx 275 aircraft of the
   national airline Aeroflot available for military
   employment. These include Tupolev Tu–104, Tu–114,
   Tu–124 and Tu–134 transports
Liaison and AOP aircraft
approx 300(?) aircraft, inc Yakovlev Yak–12 and PZL–104
Helicopters
approx 1,750 machines, inc Mil Mi–1, Mi–2, Mi–3,
   Mi–4, Mi–6, Mi–8, Mi–10, Mi–12. Of these approx
   800 are subordinated to the Shock Armies
Trainers
approx 4,500 aircraft, inc Aero L–29, Mikoyan
   MiG–15UTI, Yakovlev Yak–11 and Yak–18
**Programme**
A whole series of new aircraft are under development,
inc Mikoyan fighters and strike fighters (Faithless,
Fearless, Flipper and Flogger), Tupolev bombers
(Backfire) Ilyushin transports (Il–76 Candid) and Mil
helicopters (Mi–12 Homer). The introduction of new
models with operational units is expected from the
mid-seventies.
**Army**
approx 800 of the 1,750 Air Force helicopters are
   available to the Shock Armies
**Navy**
475,000 men
2 helicopter carriers
**Naval Aviation** (Aiatsija–Voenno Morskovo Flota,
   AVMF)
7,500 men
– squadrons
·830 operational aircraft and
200 helicopters
**Organisation**
– bomber squadrons with Tu–16 and Tu–22
– bomber squadrons with Il–28T
– reconnaissance squadrons with TU–16 and Mya–4
– reconnaissance squadrons with Tu–20
– maritime reconnaissance and ASW squadrons with
   Be–6, Be–10 and Be–12
– maritime reconnaissance and ASW squadrons with
   Il–38

– helicopter squadrons with Ka–18, Ka–20 and Ka–25
– helicopter squadrons with Mi–4
**Equipment**
Bombers
40 Ilyushin Il–28T
200 Tupolev Tu–16
100 Tupolev Tu–22
Reconnaissance aircraft
20(?) Myasischev Mya–4
100 Tupolev Tu–16
50 Tupolev Tu–20
Maritime reconnaissance and ASW aircraft
50 Beriev Be–6
20(?) Beriev Be–10
75 Beriev Be–12
25 (140?) Ilyushin Il–38
Transports
approx 150 aircraft, inc Ilyushin Il–14, Ilyushin Il–18, Li–2
Helicopters
approx 200 machines, inc Kamov Ka–15, Kamov Ka–18,
   Kamov Ka–20, Kamov Ka–25, 100 Mil Mi–4
Trainers
approx 150 aircraft
**Programme**
Replacement of Tupolev Tu–16 bombers by Tupolev
   Tu–22 and of Beriev Be–6 and Be–10 maritime recon-
   naissance and ASW aircraft by Beriev Be–12
**Missile Troops**
200,000 men
**Aircraft factories**
Antonov (An), Beriev (Be), Ilyushin (Il), Kamov (Ka),
   Mikoyan-Gurevich (MiG), Mil (Mi), Myasischev
   (Mya), Sukhoi (Su), Tupolev (Tu), Yakovlev (Yak)

## SPAIN

**Air force** (Ejército del Aire Español)
33,500 men
18 squadrons
302 operational aircraft and
20 helicopters
**Organisation**
2 fighter squadrons with F–4C(S)
1 strike fighter squadron with F–86F
2 strike fighter squadrons with Mirage IIIEE
2 strike fighter squadrons with SF–5A
1 ground-attack squadron with HA–220
1 maritime reconnaissance and ASW squadron with
   HU–16B
1 transport squadron with DHC–4 and DHC–5
2 transport squadrons with C–47
1 transport squadron with C–54
i transport squadron with C.207
1 transport squadron with C–130E
2 helicopter squadrons with Bell 47
1 helicopter squadron with UH–19D and Whirlwind 1
1 strike fighter trainer squadron with SF–5B
12 trainer squadrons with I–115, T–34 and HA–100
3 trainer squadrons with HA–200
1 trainer squadron with T–6G
1 trainer squadron with T–33A
fighter and strike fighter squadrons each with 12–24
   aircraft
**Major bases**
Albacete, Badajos, Getafe, Madrid/Torrejón, Malaga,
   Matacan/Salamanca, Rota/Jerez, Sanjurio/Valenzuela,
   Sevilla/Morón, Valencia/Manises, Valladolid/Villan-
   ubla, Zaragoza
**Military training aid from**
United States
**Foreign Air Forces in Spain**
8 American squadrons:
3 strike fighter squadrons with F–4E
1 electronic reconnaissance squadron with EA–3B
1 electronic reconnaissance squadron with RC–135C,
   D and U
1 tanker squadron with KC–135A
1 transport squadron with C–130, VC–118B and C–1A

1 air-rescue squadron with HC–130H and CH–3E
**Equipment**
Fighters and strike fighters
24 Dassault Mirage IIIEE
6 Dassault Mirage IIIDE
34 CASA SF–5A (Northrop F–5A)
36 CASA SF–5B (Northrop F–5B)
36 McDonnell Douglas F–4C(S)
13 North American F–86F
Ground-attack aircraft
25 Hispano HA–220
Maritime reconnaissance and ASW aircraft
11 (7?) Grumman HU–16B
3 Lockheed P–3B
Transports
20 CASA C.207
4 Convair 440
3 Boeing KC–97L
12 DeHavilland Canada DHC–4
6 DeHavilland Canada DHC–5
50 Douglas C–47
10 Douglas C–54
6 Lockheed C–130E
2 Lockheed KC–130
Liaison and AOP aircraft
approx 60 aircraft, inc AISA I–11B, 7 Beechcraft Baron,
  Cessna O–1B, Dornier Do–27
Helicopters
20 Bell 47D and G
Trainers
approx 200 aircraft, inc AISA I–115, 25 Beechcraft T–34,
  Hispana HA–100, 55 Hispano HA–200, Lockheed
  T–33A, 25 North American T–6G
**Programme**
Acquisition of 15 Dassault Mirage F1 fighters. 40
  CASA C.212 Aviocar transports on order to replace
  Douglas C–47
**Army**
220,000 men
**Army aviation** (Aviación Ligera del Ejército de Tierra,
  ALET)
– men
4 squadrons
– operational aircraft and
50 helicopters
**Organisation**
2 helicopter squadrons with AB.47G and AB.206A
1 helicopter squadron with UH–1B
1 helicopter squadron with UH–1H
**Equipment**
Helicopters
6 Agusta-Bell AB.47G
12 Bell UH–1B
16 Bell UH–1H
16 Agusta-Bell AB.206A
Liaison and AOP aircraft
some Cessna O–1E and Dornier Do–27
**Programme**
22 helicopters (6 Boeing Vertol CH–47C, 16 Bell
  OH–58A) on order
**Navy**
47,500 men
1 helicopter carrier
**Naval aviation** (Arma Aérea de la Marina)
– men
5 squadrons
54(?) helicopters
**Organisation**
3 ASW squadrons with AB.204B, SH–3D and SH–19
2 helicopter squadrons with Bell 47 and Hughes
  500ASW
**Equipment**
Liaison aircraft
2 Piper PA–24 Comanche
2 Piper PA–30 Twin Comanche
**Helicopters**
4 Agusta-Bell AB.204B
4 Bell AH–1G

16 Bell 47G
5 Hughes 500ASW
10 Sikorsky SH–3D
5 Sikorsky SH–19
10(?) Sikorsky SH–34J
**Aircraft factories**
AISA (Aeronautica Industrial, S.A.), CASA (Construc-
  ciones Aeronauticas S.A.), Hispano (La Hispano-
  Aviación, S.A.)

## SRI LANKA—see Ceylon

## SUDAN
**Air force** (Silakh Al–Jawwiya As–Sudan)
men 1,500
squadrons 2
operational aircraft 41 and
helicopters 10
**Organisation**
1 strike fighter squadron with MiG–21
1 strike fighter squadron with F–4 (MiG–17)
1 liaison squadron with PC–6A
1 trainer squadron with BAC 145
**Bases**
Juba, Khartoum, Malakal, Port Sudan
**Military training aid from**
Soviet Union
**Equipment**
Fighters and strike fighters
16 Mikoyan MiG–21
8 Shenyang F–4 (MiG–17)
Transports
6 Antonov An–12
5 Antonov An–24
3(?) Fokker–VFW F.27M
3 Hunting Pembroke C.54
Liaison and AOP aircraft
12 Pilatus PC–6A
Helicopters
total of 10 Mil Mi–4 and Mil Mi–8
Trainers
3 BAC 145 Jet Provost T.51
4 BAC 145 Jet Provost T.52
5 BAC 145 Jet Provost T.55
3 Hunting Provost T.53
**Army**
35,000 men
**Navy**
600 men

## SWEDEN
**Air force** (Flygvåpnet)
men 16,000 (50,000 after mobilization)
squadrons 36
operational aircraft 550
helicopters 17
**Organisation**
13 fighter squadrons with Saab 35F
4 fighter squadrons with Saab 35D
2 fighter squadrons with Saab 35A and B
5 strike fighter squadrons with Saab 32A
3 strike fighter squadrons with Saab 37
3 reconnaissance squadrons with Saab 35E
2 reconnaissance squadrons with Saab 32C
1 transport squadron with C–47 and C–130E
1 helicopter squadron with BV–107
6 trainer squadrons with Saab 105
– trainer squadrons with Bulldog
fighter, strike fighter and reconnaissance squadrons each
  with 12–15 aircraft
**Major bases**
Angelholm, Barkarby, Kallinge, Kalmar, Karlsborg,
  Luleå, Malmslätt, Norrköping, Nyköping, Ostersund,
  Söderhamn, Såtenäs, Tullinge, Uppsala, Västerås
**Equipment**
Fighters and strike fighters
100 Saab 32A
approx 300 Saab 35A, B, D and F
Reconnaissance and ECM aircraft

2 Gates Learjet 24
30 Saab 32C
42 Saab 35E
Transports
2 Aérospatiale S.E.210 Caravelle
7 Douglas C–47
some Hunting Pembroke C.52
2 Lockheed C–130E
Helicopters
1 Aérospatiale Alouette II
6 Agusta-Bell AB.204B
10 Boeing Vertol BV–107
Trainers
80 Saab 91B and C
130 Saab 105A
20 Saab 105B
58 Scottish Aviation Bulldog
**Programme**
150 Saab 37 strike fighters and 25 Saab 37 strike trainers
  on order to replace Saab 32A strike fighters. Delivery
  started in mid–1972.
**Army**
47,000 men (600,000 after mobilization)
**Army aviation**
– men
– squadrons
37 operational aircraft and
32 helicopters
**Organisation**
– helicopter squadrons with AB.204B
– helicopter squadrons with AB.206A
– liaison and AOP squadrons with Bulldog
**Equipment**
Helicopters
12 Agusta-Bell AB.204B
20 Agusta-Bell AB.206A
Liaison and AOP aircraft
5 Dornier Do–27A–4
12 Piper L–21B
20 Scottish Aviation Bulldog
**Programme**
Piper L–21B liaison and AOP aircraft to be phased out
**Navy**
11,500 men (50,000 after mobilization)
**Naval aviation**
– men
2 squadrons
30 helicopters
**Organisation**
2 helicopter squadrons with Alouette II and Vertol 107
**Equipment**
Helicopters
10 Aérospatiale Alouette II
10 Agusta-Bell AB.206A
3 Boeing-Vertol BV–107
7 Kawasaki-Vertol KV–107
**Aircraft factories**
MFI (A.B. Malmö Flygindustri), Saab (Svenska
  Aeroplan A.B.)

## SWITZERLAND

**Air force** (Schweizerische Flugwaffe)
men 10,000 men (50,000 after mobilization)
squadrons 25
operational aircraft 290
helicopters 112
**Organisation**
2 fighter squadrons with Mirage IIIS
5 fighter squadrons with Hunter Mk.58
11 strike fighter squadrons with Venom FB.50
1 reconnaissance squadron with Mirage IIIRS
1 transport squadron with Ju–52/3m
4 helicopter squadrons with Alouette II, Alouette III,
  plus PC6 and PC–6A
1 helicopter squadron with AB.47G, Do–27H
– trainer squadrons with P–2 and P–3
– trainer squadrons with Vampire T.55
fighter, strike fighter and reconnaissance squadrons

each with 12–15 aircraft
**Major bases**
Alpnach, Buochs, Dübendorf, Emmen, Interlaken,
  Magadino, Meiringen, Payerne, Sion
**Equipment**
Fighters and strike fighters
2 Dassault Mirage IIIB
1 Dassault Mirage IIIC
36 Dassault Mirage IIIS
140 DeHavilland Venom FB.50
90 Hawker Hunter Mk.58
Reconnaissance aircraft
18 Dassault Mirage IIIRS
Transports
3 Junkers Ju–52/3m
Liaison and AOP aircraft
3 Beechcraft Twin Bonanza
6 Dornier Do–27H–2
12 Pilatus PC–6
15 Pilatus PC–6A–1 and H–2
Helicopters
29 Aérospatiale Alouette II
83 Aérospatiale Alouette III
Trainers
30 DeHavilland Vampire T.55
40 North American T–6G
26 Pilatus P–2
73 Pilatus P–3
**Programme**
60 Hawker Hunter Mk.58A strike fighters on order;
  delivery by 1973/1974. Seeking replacement for
  obsolete DeHavilland Venom FB.50 strike fighters.
  Acquisition of new helicopters (Aérospatiale S.A.330
  or Agusta-Bell AB.205 or Agusta-Bell AB.212)
**Army**
21,000 men (550,000 after mobilization)
**Aircraft factories**
Eidgenössisches Flugzeugwerk Emmen, FFA (Flug- und
  Fahrzeugwerke Altenrhein), Pilatus Flugzeugwerke

## SYRIA

**Air force** (Al Quwwat al–Jawwija al Arabia as–Suriya)
men 10,000
squadrons 16
operational aircraft 180(?) and
helicopters 34(?)
**Organisation**
6 fighter squadrons with MiG–21
4 strike fighter squadrons with MiG–17
2 strike fighter squadrons with Su–7
1 transport squadron with C–47
1 transport squadron with Il–14
1 helicopter squadron with Mi–4
1 helicopter squadron with Mi–8
– trainer squadrons with Yak–11 and Yak–18
– trainer squadrons with L–29
**Major bases**
Aleppo, Chliye, Damascus–Mezze, Dumeyr, El Rasafa,
  Hama, Palmyra, Sahl es Sahra
**Military training aid from**
Soviet Union
**Equipment**
Fighters and strike fighters
50 Mikoyan MiG–17
80 Mikoyan MiG–21
30 Sukhoi Su–7
Transports
6 Douglas C–47
8 Ilyushin Il–14
4(?) Ilyushin Il–18
3(?) Li–2 (C–47 copy)
Helicopters
4 Mil Mi–1
8 Mil Mi–4
22 Mil Mi–8
Trainers
approx 30 aircraft, inc Aero L–29, Yakovlev Yak–11
  and Yakovlev Yak–18

47

**Army**
100,000 men
**Navy**
1,750 men

## TANZANIA

**Air force** (Tanzanian People's Defence Force Air Wing)
men 500
squadrons 2
operational aircraft 18(?)
**Organisation**
1 strike fighter squadron with F–4 (MiG–17)
1 transport squadron with DHC–4
**Bases**
Arusha, Mbeya, Mikumi (Dar-es-Salaam), Tabora, Zanzibar
**Military training aid from**
China
**Equipment**
Fighters and strike fighters
6–8 Shenyang F–4 (MiG–17)
Transports
1 Antonov An–2
10 DeHavilland Canada DHC–4
Liaison and AOP aircraft
2 Cessna 310Q
3 DeHavilland Canada DHC–2
5 Piper PA–28–140 Cherokee
Trainers
7 Piaggio P.149D
**Programme**
Formation of second strike fighter squadron with 12 Shenyang F–6 (MiG–19). Some Soko G–2 trainers on order
**Army**
10,000 men
**Navy**
600 men

## THAILAND

**Air force**
25,000 men
14 squadrons
190 operational aircraft and
100 helicopters
**Organisation**
1 fighter squadron with F–86L
1 strike fighter squadron with F–86F
1 strike fighter squadron with F–5A
2 ground-attack squadrons with T–28D
2 ground-attack squadrons with OV–10C
1 night ground-support squadron with AC–47
1 transport squadron with C–47
1 transport squadron with C–123B
3 helicopter squadrons with UH–1H
1 helicopter squadron with CH–34C
1 trainer squadron with T–6G
1 trainer squadron with T–37B
**Major bases**
Bangkok, Don Muang, Kokekathion, Khorat, Nakhon Phanom, Nam Phong, Nongkai, Prachuab, Sattahip, Takhli, Ubon, Udon Thani, Utapao
**Military training aid from**
United States
**Foreign Air Forces in Thailand**
27 American squadrons:
12 strike fighter squadrons with approx 250 F–4 and F–111 strike fighters
6 bomber squadrons with over 80 B–52 bombers
1 night ground-support squadron with AC–130A
3 reconnaissance and ECM squadrons with EC–121 and EB–66
2 reconnaissance squadrons with RF–4C
1 tanker squadron with KC–135A
2 helicopter squadrons with HH–3
Part of the American squadrons are to be withdrawn in 1973/74
**Equipment**

Fighters and strike fighters
14 North American F–86F
20 North American F–86L
25 Northrop F–5A and F–5B
Ground-attack aircraft
40 North American T–28D
30 North American Rockwell OV–10C
Night ground-support aircraft
some Douglas AC–47
13 Fairchild Au–23A
Reconnaissance aircraft
2 Lockheed RT–33A
Transports
5 Beechcraft C–45
20 Douglas C–47
2 Douglas C–54
13 Fairchild C–123B
2 Hawker Siddeley H.S.748
Liaison and AOP aircraft
approx 20(?) aircraft, inc Cessna O–1 and Piper L–18C
Helicopters
50 Bell UH–1H
3 Kaman HH–43B
16 Kawasaki KH–4
4 Kawasaki-Vertol KV–107
20 Sikorsky CH–34C
some Sikorsky UH–19
Trainers
approx 50 aircraft, inc AESL Airtourer T.6, DeHavilland Canada DHC–1, 8 Cessna T–37B, 6 Lockheed T–33A, 20 North American T–6G
**Programme**
Replacement of North American F–86 fighters and strike fighters by Northrop F–5E. 36 trainers (24 AESL Air trainer CT.4, 12 SIAI–Marchetti SF.260MT) on order. Considering acquisition of further (43?) SIAI–Marchetti SF. 260MT to replace existing DeHavilland Canada DHC–1 and North American T–6G trainers
**Army and Border Guard**
130,000 men
– men
3 squadrons
18(?) operational aircraft and
44 helicopters
**Organisation**
1 helicopter squadron with UH–1B
1 helicopter squadron with UH–1D
1 helicopter squadron with FH–1100
**Equipment**
Helicopters
10 Bell UH–1B
11 Bell UH–1D
3 Bell 206A
13 Fairchild Hiller FH–1100
6 Hiller OH–23G
1 Mitsubishi-Sikorsky S–62A
Liaison and AOP aircraft
some Cessna O–1
Transports
3 DeHavilland Canada DHC–4
some Dornier Do–28D
3 short Skyvan 3M
**Programme**
5 Fairchild AU–23A night ground-support aircraft on order
**Navy**
21,500 men
**Naval aviation**
– men
1 squadron
10(?) operational aircraft
**Organisation**
1 maritime reconnaissance and ASW squadron with HU–16 and S–2F
**Equipment**
Maritime reconnaissance and ASW aircraft
some Grumman HU–16
6 Grumman S–2F

## TOGO

**Air force** (Force Aérienne Togolaise)
men 100
squadrons –
operational aircraft 1 and
helicopter 1
**Organisation**
—

**Base**
Lome
**Military training aid from**
France
**Equipment**
Transports
1 (2?) Douglas C–47
Liaison and AOP aircraft
2 Max Holste M.H.1521M
Helicopters
1 Aérospatiale Alouette II
**Army**
1,500 men
**Navy**
250 men

## TUNISIA

**Air force** (Armeé de l'Air Tunisienne)
men 1,000
squadrons 1
operational aircraft 15 and
helicopters 6
**Organisation**
1 strike fighter squadron with F–86F
1 trainer squadron with MB.326B
1 trainer squadron with Saab 91D
1 trainer squadron with T–6G
**Major bases**
Bizerta, El Aouina (Tunis), Monastir
**Military training aid from**
United States
**Equipment**
Fighters and strike fighters
12 North American F–86F
Transports
3 Dassault M.D.315
Helicopters
2 Aérospatiale Alouette II
4 Aérospatiale Alouette III
Trainers
8 Aermacchi MB.326B
12 North American T–6G
12 Saab 91D
**Army**
20,000 men
**Navy**
800 men

## TURKEY

**Air force** (Türk Hava Kuvvetleri)
43,000 men
21 squadrons
414 operational aircraft and
10 helicopters
**Organisation**
2 fighter squadrons with F–102A
4 fighter squadrons with F–5A
6 strike fighter squadrons with F–100D and F
1 strike fighter squadron with F–84F
2 strike fighter squadrons with F–104G
1 reconnaissance squadron with RF–5A
1 reconnaissance squadron with RF–84F
2 transport squadrons with C.160D and C–47
1 transport squadron with C–47, C–54D and Viscount
1 transport squadron with C–130E
– trainer squadrons with T–34 and T–6G
– trainer squadrons with T–37C and T–33A
fighter, strike fighter and reconnaissance squadrons each
   with 18–25 aircraft
**Major bases**

Adana, Balikesir, Bandirma, Cigli (Izmir), Diyarbakir,
   Esenboga, Eskisehir, Etimesgut, Incirlik, Izmir, Merzi-
   fon, Murted, Yesilkoy
**Military training aid from**
United States
**Foreign Air Forces in Turkey**
1 American strike fighter squadron with F–4
**Equipment**
Fighters and strike fighters
35 Convair F–102A
3 Convair TF–102A
33 Lockheed F–104G
4 Lockheed TF–104G
125 North American F–100D and F–100F
100 Northrop F–5A and F–5B
18 Republic F–84F
Reconnaissance aircraft
20 Northrop RF–5A
20 Republic RF–84F
Transports
6 Beechcraft C–45
6 (?) Dornier Do–28
10 Douglas C–47
3 Douglas C–54D
8 Lockheed C–130E
20 Transall C.160D
3 Vickers Viscount 794
Liaison and AOP aircraft
some Piper L–18C
Helicopters
approx 10 machines, inc Agusta-Bell AB.204B and
   Agusta-Bell AB.206A
Trainers
24 Beechcraft T–34
5 Beechcraft T–42A
23 Cessna T–37C
19 Cessna T–41D
30 Lockheed T–33A
40 North American T–6G
**Programme**
Replacement of existing Republic F–84F strike fighters,
   Republic RF–84F reconnaissance aircraft and North
   American F–100 strike fighters by McDonnell Douglas
   F–4 and Northrop F–5 strike fighters and reconnaissance
   aircraft. Initially 36 F–4E strike fighters and 42 (?)
   F–5E strike fighters to be delivered from 1973/74. 2
   Britten-Norman BN–2 transports for aerial photographic
   duties on order
**Army**
360,000 men
**Army aviation**
– men
– squadrons
30 operational aircraft and
65 helicopters
**Organisation**
– helicopter squadrons with AB.204B
– helicopter squadrons with AB.206A
– liaison and AOP squadrons with DHC–2
– liaison and AOP squadrons with Do–27
– liaison and AOP squadrons with U–17
**Equipment**
Helicopters
some Bell 47G(?)
20 (?) Agusta-Bell AB.204B
40 Agusta-Bell AB.206A
Liaison and AOP aircraft
approx 30 aircraft, inc Cessna U–17, DeHavilland Canada DHC–2, Dornier Do–27, 2 Dornier Do–28D, Piper
   L–18B and C
**Navy**
37,500 men
**Naval aviation**
– men
1 squadron
22 operational aircraft and
3 helicopters

**Organisation**
1 (2?) maritime reconnaissance and ASW squadrons with
S–2E and S–2D
**Equipment**
Maritime reconnaissance and ASW aircraft
8 Grumman S–2D
12 Grumman S–2E
2 Grumman TS–2A
Helicopters
3 Agusta-Bell AB.205

## UGANDA
**Air force**
men 600
squadrons 2
operational aircraft 13 and
helicopters 15
**Organisation**
1 strike fighter squadron with MiG–15 and MiG–17
1 transport squadron with C–47
1 trainer squadron with C.M.170
**Bases**
Arua, Entebbe, Gulu, Kampala, Nakasongola
**Military training aid from**
Czechoslovakia, Egypt, Libya, Soviet Union
**Equipment**
Fighters and strike fighters
5 Mikoyan MiG–17
Transports
1 DeHavilland Canada DHC–4
5 Douglas C–47
1 IAI Commodore Jet 1123
1 Nord N.2501(?)
Liaison and AOP aircraft
4 Cessna 180
1 Piper Aztec
5 Piper L–18
Helicopters
6 Agusta-Bell AB.205
4 Agusta-Bell AB.206A
2 Bell 205A
1 Bell 212
2 Westland Scout
Trainers
5 Aero L–29
2 Mikoyan MiG–15UTI
4 Piaggio P.149D
8 Potez-Air Fouga C.M.170
**Programme**
Formation of an additional strike fighter squadron with
8 aircraft, type unknown (donated by Libya)
**Army**
16,000 men

## UAR (United Arab Republic) — see Egypt

## UNITED STATES
**Air force** (United States Air Force, USAF)
660,000 men
over 225 squadrons
over 5,170 operational aircraft and
360 helicopters
**Organisation**
7 fighter squadrons with F–101, F–102 and F–106A
70 strike fighter squadrons with A–7, A–37, F–4 and
F–111
7 ground-attack and night ground-support squadrons
with A–1, AC–47, AC–119 and AC–130
26 bomber squadrons with B–52D, F, G, and H
4 bomber squadrons with FB–111A
1 reconnaissance squadron with U–2 and SR–71
13 reconnaissance squadrons with RF–4C
14 reconnaissance and ECM squadrons with EB–66,
EC–47, EC–121, O–2A, OV–10A and helicopters
13 transport squadrons with C–141A
4 transport squadrons with C–5A
3 transport squadrons with C–9A, VC–135 and
helicopters
17 transport squadrons with C–123K, C–130, C–118 and

C–7A
38 tanker squadrons with KC–135A
– helicopter squadrons with HH–3E, HH–53B and C
– helicopter squadrons with UH–1F, H and N
– helicopter squadrons with CH–3E
As part of America's foreign alliance commitments a
number of squadrons are permanently based overseas
Fighter, strike fighter and reconnaissance squadrons each
with 18–25, bomber squadrons each with 15, transport
squadrons each with 16, and tanker squadrons each
with 10 aircraft
**Major bases**
Altus AFB (= Air Force Base)/Okla., Andrew AFB/Md.,
Atlantic City/N.J., Baltimore/Md., Barksdale AFB/La.,
Beale AFB/Calif., Bergstrom AFB/Tex., Blytheville
AFB/Ark., Cannon AFB/N.M., Carswell AFB/Tex.,
Castle AFB/Calif., Davis-Monthan AFB/Ariz., Dyess
AFB/Tex., Eglin AFB/Fla., Eielson AFB/Alaska, Elling-
ton AFB/Tex., Elmendorf AFB/Alaska, Elssworth AFB/
S.D., England AFB/La., Fairchild AFB/Wash., George
AFB/Cal., Grand Forks AFB/N.D., Griffiss AFB/N.Y.,
Grissom AFB/Ind., Holloman AFB/N.M., Homestead
AFB/Fla., Hurtlburt Field/Fla., Kincheloe AFB/Mich.,
Langley AFB/Va., Little Rock AFB/Ark., Lockbourne
AFB/Ohio, Loring AFB/Maine, Luke AFB/Ariz., Mal-
strom AFB/Mont., March AFB/Calif., Mather AFB/
Calif., McConnell AFB/Kan., McDill AFB/Fla., Minot
AFB/N.D., Mountain Home AFB/Id., Myrtle Beach
AFB/S.C., Nellis AFB/Nev., Offutt AFB/Neb., Pease
AFB/N.H., Plattsburg AFB/N.Y., Pope AFB/N.C.,
Richards Gebaur AFB/Mo., Robins AFB/Ga., Sawyer
AFB/Mich., Sewart AFB/Tenn., Seymour Johnson AFB/
N.C., Shaw AFB/S.C., Travis AFB/Calif., Vandenberg
AFB/Calif., F. E. Warren AFB/Wyo., Whiteman AFB/
Mo., Wright-Patterson AFB/Ohio, Wurtsmith AFB/
Mich.
**Equipment**
Fighters and strike fighters
approx 2,500 aircraft, inc Convair F–102A and TF–102A,
Convair F–106A and F–106B; 300 General Dynamics
F–111A, D, E and F; 1,800 McDonnell Douglas F–4C,
D and E; 75 McDonnell Douglas F–101B and F;
Vought A–7D
Ground-attack and night ground-support aircraft
approx 170 aircraft, inc Cessna A–37A, Douglas A–1,
Douglas AC–47, Douglas B–26K (A–26A), Fairchild
AC–119G and K, Lockheed AC–130
Bombers
390 Boeing B–52D, F, G, and H, 65 General Dynamics
FB–111A
Reconnaissance and ECM aircraft
approx 700 aircraft, inc Boeing E–3A, Boeing RC–135,
Douglas EB–66, Douglas EC–47, Lockheed EC–121, 12
Lockheed SR–71, 30 (?) Lockheed U–2, Lockheed
WC–130E, Martin EB–57E, 20 Martin RB–57, 350 Mc-
Donnell Douglas RF–4C, North American Rockwell
OV–10A
Transports
approx 1,300 aircraft, inc Aero U–4B, 30 Boeing C–135B,
390 Boeing KC–135A, 5 Boeing VC–137, 100 DeHavil-
land Canada C–7A (DHC–4), Douglas C–47, Douglas
C–54, Douglas C–118, Fairchild C–119G and J, Fair-
child C–123K, 75 Lockheed C–5A, Lockheed C–121,
300 Lockheed C–130B, E and H, 11 (?) Lockheed C–
140A and VC–140, 260 Lockheed C–141A, 30 McDonnell Douglas C–9A
Liaison and AOP aircraft
approx 700 aircraft, inc Beechcraft U–8F, Cessna O–1,
Cessna O–2A and B, Cessna U–3A and B, Helio U–10A,
B and D
Helicopters
approx 360 machines, inc 100 Bell UH–1F, Bell UH–
1H, 75 Bell UH–1N, Bell OH–13, 50 Kaman HH–43B
and F, 80 Sikorsky CH–3E and CH–53C, 20 Sikorsky
HH–3E, 8 Sikorsky HH–53B, 30 Sikorsky HH–53C
Trainers
approx 2,400 aircraft, inc Beechcraft T–34, Beechcraft

T-42A, Cessna T-37, Cessna T-41, Convair T-29, Lockheed T-33, North American T-28, Northrop T-38A

In addition the American Air Force also holds over 2,700 "mothballed" aircraft in reverse, amongst them the following:

Fighters and strike fighters
Convair F-102A and TF-102A, General Dynamics F-111A, Lockheed F-104A, McDonnell F-101B and CF-101B, North American F-86, North American F-100C, Republic F-84F

Ground-attack and night ground-support aircraft
Douglas A-1E, Douglas B-26K (A-26A)

Bombers
Boeing B-52, Douglas B-66, General Dynamics FB-111A, Martin B-57

Reconnaissance and ECM aircraft
Lockheed EC-121, Republic RF-84F

Maritime reconnaissance and ASW aircraft
Grumman HU-16

Transports
Boeing C-97, Boeing KC-135A, Douglas C-47, Douglas C-54, Douglas C-124, Douglas C-133, Fairchild C-119, Fairchild C-123, Lockheed C-121

Liaison and AOP aircraft
Cessna O-1E, Cessna U-3, Helio U-10

Trainers
Lockheed T-33A

**Programme**
Re-equipment of further strike fighter and ground-attack squadrons with Vought A-7D (in all 645 aircraft delivered or on order). Introduction of the new McDonnell Douglas F-15 fighter (729 aircraft planned from 1973/74), the new Fairchild A-10A ground-attack aircraft (10 pre-production models on order, delivery from 1974, total 720 aircraft planned), and of the North American Rockwell B-1 bomber (252 aircraft planned from 1976/77). Replacement of older transports, helicopters and trainers by newer types

**Air National Guard, ANG**
87,000 men
85 squadrons
1,500 operational aircraft
**Organisation**
6 fighter squadrons with F-101B
9 fighter squadrons with F-102A
4 fighter squadrons with F-106A
1 fighter squadron with F-104A
19 strike fighter squadrons with F-100C and D
4 strike fighter squadrons with F-105B and D
1 strike fighter squadron with F-4C
3 ground-attack squadrons with A-37B
1 bomber squadron with B-57G
3 special-duties squadrons with C-119C and U-10D
3 reconnaissance squadrons with RF-101C
3 reconnaissance squadrons with RF-4C
1 ECM squadron with EC-121
5 transport squadrons with C-124C
11 transport squadrons with C-130A and B
1 transport squadron with C-121
1 transport squadron with C-123K
9 tanker squadrons with KC-97L
5 AOP squadrons with O-2
**Programme**
Re-equipment of Convair M-102A fighter squadrons with Convair F-106A

**Air Force Reserve**
47,000 men
30 squadrons
400 operational aircraft
**Organisation**
6 transport squadrons with C-124
18 transport squadrons with C-130
2 transport squadrons with C-119
1 transport squadron with C-123K
3 other special-duties squadrons

**Army**
804,000 men

**Army aviation** (United States Army Aviation)
– men
approx 200 squadrons
1,750 (?) operational aircraft and
9,750 (?) helicopters
**Organisation**
– reconnaissance squadrons with OV-1 and RU-21
– helicopter squadrons with AH-1G and AH-1Q
– helicopter squadrons with OH-6A, OH-58A and OH-23
– helicopter squadrons with UH-1, CH-34 and UH-19
– helicopter squadrons with CH-47 and CH-54A
– liaison and AOP squadrons with O-1, DHC-2 and U-7
– liaison and AOP squadrons with U-8 and U-21
– transport squadrons with DHC-3
– trainer squadrons with T-41B and T-42A
– trainer squadrons with TH-55A and TH-13S
**Equipment**
Reconnaissance and ECM aircraft
Beechcraft RU-21A, B, C, D, E and F, 320 Grumman OV-1A, B, C and D
Transports
some Aero U-9C and D plus Beechcraft C-45, 75 DeHavilland Canada DHC-3 (U-1A), 30 Douglas C-47
Liaison and AOP aircraft
approx 1,000 aircraft, inc Beechcraft U-21A and F, Beechcraft U-8D and F, Cessna O-1, DeHavilland Canada DHC-2 (U-6A), Piper U-7A and B
Helicopters
approx 9,750 machines, inc 600 Bell AH-1G and AH-1Q, 400 Bell CH-13G, H and S and TH-13S, 3,500 Bell UH-1B, C, D and H, 2,000 Bell OH-58A, 500 Boeing Vertol CH-47A, B and C, 250 Hiller OH-23F and G, 1,200 Hughes OH-6A, 600 Hughes TH-55A, 400 Sikorsky CH-34A and C, 50 Sikorsky CH-54A, 100 Sikorsky UH-19B, D and F
Trainers
50 Beechcraft T-42A. 200 Cessna T-41B
**Programme**
Replacement of older Bell OH-13 and TH-13, Hiller OH-23, Sikorsky CH-34 and Sikorsky UH-19 helicopters. Development of new attack helicopters

**Navy**
602,000 men
14 aircraft carriers
2 ASW carriers
7 helicopter carriers

**Naval aviation** (United States Naval Aviation)
– men
193 squadrons
3,890 (?) operational aircraft and
1,300 helicopters
**Organisation**
24 fighter squadrons with F-4
11 fighter squadrons with F-8
21 strike fighter squadrons with A-4
18 strike fighter squadrons with A-7
12 bomber squadrons with A-6
8 special-duties squadrons with A-4, F-8, S-2, C-54 and H-34
10 reconnaissance squadrons with RA-5C
1 reconnaissance squadron with RA-3B
1 reconnaissance squadron with RF-8G and F-8H
1 reconnaissance and ground-attack squadron with OV-10A
4 reconnaissance and ECM squadrons with RA-3B, EC-121M, WP-3A, EA-3B and EC-130Q
8 ECM squadrons with EA-6B, EKA-3B and KA-3B
13 maritime reconnaissance squadrons with E-2 and E-1B
24 maritime reconnaissance and ASW squadrons with P-3
14 maritime reconnaissance and ASW squadrons with S-2
8 transport squadrons with C-1A, C-2A, C-54, C-118, C-130, C-131 and VC-118
7 helicopter squadrons with UH-2, CH-46, UH-46 and SH-2
5 helicopter squadrons with SH-3

2 helicopter squadrons with RH–53D
1 helicopter squadron with UH–1
9 trainer squadrons with T–1A, T–2, T–28, T–34 and
  TC–45
11 trainer squadrons with TA–4J, TF–9J and TS–2A
1 trainer squadron with TH–1L and TH–57A
fighter and bomber squadrons each with 12 aircraft, strike
  fighter squadrons each with 14, reconnaissance
  squadrons each with 5–6, ECM squadrons each with
  10–15, maritime reconnaissance and ASW squadrons
  each with 9–10

**Major bases**
NAS Almeda/Cal. (NAS=Naval Air Station), NAS Bar-
bers Point/Hawaii, NAS Brunswick/Me., NAS Cecil
Field/Fla., NAS China Lake/Cal., NAS Corpus Christi/
Tex., NAS Jacksonville/Fla., NAS Key West/Fla., NAS
Lakehurst/N.J., NAS Lemoore/Cal., NAS Miramar/Cal.,
NAS Moffett Field/Cal., NAS Norfolk/Va., NAS North
Island/Cal., NAS Oceana/Va., NAS Patuxent River/Md.,
NAS Pensacola/Fla., NAS Point Mugu/Cal., NAS Whid-
bey Island/Cal.

**Equipment**
Fighters and strike fighters
approx 1,950 aircraft, inc 470 McDonnell Douglas A–4E,
  F, L, M and TA–4F and TA–4J, 650 McDonnell Doug-
  las F–4B, G, J and N, 520 Vought A–7A, B, C and E,
  300 Vought F–8H, J, K and L
Bombers
approx 520 aircraft, inc 190 (?) Douglas A–3B, EA–3B,
  KA–3B and EKA–3B, 250 (?) Grumman A–6A and
  A–6C, 36 Grumman A–6E, 20 Grumman EA–6B, 20
  Grumman KA–6D
Reconnaissance and ECM aircraft
approx 500 aircraft, inc Grumman E–1B, Grumman E–2B
  and C, Lockheed EP–3E and WP–3A, Lockheed
  EC–121K and M, Lockheed WC–121N, North American
  Rockwell OV–10A, North American Rockwell RA–5C,
  Vought RF–8G
Maritime reconnaissance and ASW aircraft
approx 620 (?) aircraft, inc Grumman HU–16, Grumman
  S–2E and G, 250 Lockheed P–3A, B and C
Transports
approx 300 (?) aircraft, inc Convair C–131, Douglas C–47
  and C–117, Douglas C–54, Douglas C–118 and VC–118,
  Grumman C–1A, Grumman C–2A, Lockheed C–130, 8
  McDonnell Douglas C–9B
Liaison aircraft
20 Piper U–11A
Helicopters
approx 1,300 machines, 45 Bell TH–1L, 40 Bell
  TH–57A, 27 Bell UH–1K, 8 Bell UH–1L, 40 Bell UH–
  1N, Boeing Vertol CH–46D, E and F plus UH–46D,
  20 Kaman UH–43C, 130 Kaman UH–2C, 70 Kaman
  HH–2C and D, 20 Kaman SH–2D, Sikorsky RH–53D,
  270 Sikorsky SH–3A, D, G and H, Sikorsky SH–34G
  and J
Trainers
approx 1,450 aircraft, inc Beechcraft T–34, Beechcraft
  TC–45, Convair T–29, Grumman TF–9J, Grumman
  TS–2A, North American Rockwell T–2B and C, North
  American Rockwell CT–39E, Lockheed T–33B
In addition United States Naval Aviation also holds over
1,500 "mothballed" aircraft in reserve, amongst them:
Fighters and strike fighters
Grumman TF–9, McDonnell Douglas A–4, Vought A–7A,
  Vought F–8
Ground-attack aircraft
Douglas A–1
Bombers
Douglas A–3
Reconnaissance aircraft
Grumman E–1, Lockheed EC–121 and WC–121,
  McDonnell Douglas RF–4B, North American Rockwell
  RA–5C, Vought RF–8
Maritime reconnaissance and ASW aircraft
Grumman HU–16, Grumman S–2, Lockheed P–2 and SP–2
Transports

Beechcraft C–45, Douglas C–47, Douglas C–54, Douglas
  C–117D, Grumman C–1A, Lockheed C–121
Helicopters
Sikorsky H–34
Trainers
Beechcraft T–34, Lockheed T–1A, Lockheed T–33B,
  North American Rockwell T–2

**Programme**
Replacement of McDonnell Douglas F–4B fighters by
  F–4J and the newly-developed Grumman F–14 (301
  aircraft planned, delivery from 1973/74), replacement
  of McDonnell Douglas A–4 strike fighters by Vought
  A–7, replacement of Grumman S–2 maritime reconnaissance and ASW aircraft by 191 Lockheed S–3A from
  1973/74, acquisition of over 100 ASW helicopters
  (LAMPS-programme) to operate from destroyers

**Naval Air Reserve, NAR**
– men
47 squadrons
475 operational aircraft and
75 helicopters
**Organisation**
4 fighter squadrons with F–8K
10 strike fighter squadrons with A–4C, A–4L and A–7A
2 reconnaissance squadrons with RF–8G
2 ECM squadrons with EKA–3B
4 maritime reconnaissance squadrons with E–1B
12 maritime reconnaissance and ASW squadrons with
  P–3A, SP–2E and SP–2H
6 maritime reconnaissance and ASW squadrons with S–2E
3 transport squadrons with C–118
4 helicopter squadrons with SH–3A
**Marine Corps**
196,000 men
**Marine Corps Aviation**
– men
58 squadrons
680 operational aircraft and
550 helicopters
**Organisation**
12 strike fighter squadrons with F–4B and F–4J
6 strike fighter squadrons with A–4E and A–4M
3 strike fighter squadrons with AV–8A
6 bomber squadrons with A–6A
3 reconnaissance squadrons with RF–4B and EA–6B
3 reconnaissance and ground-attack squadrons with
  OV–10A, UH–1E and AH–1J
3 transport squadrons with KC–130F
1 helicopter squadron with AH–1J
3 helicopter squadrons with UH–1E and AH–1J
12 helicopter squadrons with CH–46D and CH–46F
6 helicopter squadrons with CH–53A ad CH–53D
2 strike fighter trainer squadrons with F–4B and F–4J
3 strike fighter trainer squadrons with TA–4F and TA–4J
1 strike fighter trainer squadron with AV–8A
1 bomber trainer squadron with A–6A and TC–4C
1 helicopter trainer squadron with CH–46D and CH–53C
fighter squadrons each with 15 aircraft, strike fighter
  squadrons each with 20, bomber squadrons each with
  12, reconnaissance squadrons each with 18 (and 12 helicopters), transport squadrons each with 12 aircraft and
  helicopter squadrons each with 18–24 helicopters
**Equipment**
Fighters and strike fighters
100 Hawker Siddeley AV–8A (Harrier Mk.50),
8 Hawker Siddeley AV–8B (Harrier Mk.51),
150 McDonnell Douglas A–4E and A–4M,
40 (?) McDonnell Douglas TA–4F and TA–4J,
180 McDonnell Douglas F–4B and F–4J
Bombers
40 Grumman A–6A
Reconnaissance aircraft
20 Grumman EA–6A, 30 McDonnell Douglas RF–4B,
60 North American Rockwell OV–10A
Transports
some Douglas C–54, Douglas C–117, 40 Lockheed
  KC–130F, Grumman C–1A

Helicopters
45 Bell AH–1J, 100 Bell UH–1E and UH–1N
190 Boeing Vertol CH–46D and CH–46F
200 (?) Sikorsky CH–53A and CH–53D
some Sikorsky VH–3A, UH–34D and UH–34E
**Programme**
Replacement of older McDonnell Douglas A–4 strike
fighters. Replacement of McDonnell Douglas F–4B
strike fighters by 138 McDonnell Douglas F–4J. Replacement of Bell UH–1E helicopters by UH–1N (in
all 67 delivered or on order). 20 Bell AH–1J helicopters
on order, delivery 1974/75
**Marine Corps Aviation Reserve**
– men
34 squadrons
– operational aircraft and
– helicopters
**Organisation**
5 fighter squadrons with F–8
10 strike fighter squadrons with A–4
1 reconnaissance squadron with RF–8G
2 reconnaissance and ground-attack squadrons with
OV–10A
3 transport squadrons with C–119
1 helicopter squadron with AH–1G
12 helicopter squadrons with CH–46A and UH–34
**Coast Guard**
38,000 men
**Coast Guard Aviation**
– men
– squadrons
46(?) operational aircraft and
89 helicopters
**Organisation**

**Equipment**
Maritime reconnaissance aircraft
28 Grumman HU–16E
Transports
1 Grumman VC–4A, 1 Grumman VC–11A, 1 Lockheed
C–130E, 12 Lockheed HC–130B, 3 Lockheed HC–130H
Helicopters
40(?) Sikorsky HH–3F, 50(?) Sikorsky HH–52A
Sikorsky HH–52A
**Programme**
Further 18 Sikorsky HH–3F helicopters on order
**Aircraft factories**
Beechcraft, Bell, Boeing, Boeing Vertol, Cessna, Douglas
(now merged with McDonnell), Fairchild Hiller, Gen-
eral Dynamics (Convair), Grumman, Helio, Hiller,
Hughes, Kaman, Lockheed, McDonnell Douglas, North
American Rockwell, Northrop, Piper, Sikorsky, Vought
(earlier Ling Temco Vought, LTV)

## UPPER VOLTA
**Air force** (Force Aérienne de Haute-Volta)
men 50
squadrons –
operational aircraft 2
**Organisation**
—
**Base**
Quagadougou
**Military training aid from**
France
**Equipment**
Transports
1 Aero Commander 500B
1 (2?) Douglas C–47
Liaison and AOP aircraft
1 Cessna 337
2 Max Holste M.H.1521M
**Army**
1,750 men

## URUGUAY
**Air force** (Fuerza Aérea Uruguaya)
men 1,600

squadrons 3
operational aircraft 33 and
helicopters 2
**Organisation**
1 strike fighter squadron with F–80C
1 transport squadron with C–47
1 transport squadron with C–46 and F–27M
1 liaison squadron with U–17A
1 liaison squadron with OH–23F and L–21A
1 trainer squadron with T–6G and T–34
**Bases**
Carrasco, Laguna del Sauce, Melilla
**Equipment**
Fighters and strike fighters
6 Lockheed F–80C
Transports
3 Beechcraft C–45
2 Beechcraft Queen Air A–65
5 Curtiss-Wright C–46
13 Douglas C–47
2 Fairchild-Hiller FH–227B
2 Fokker-VFW F.27M
Liaison and AOP aircraft
2 Cessna 182D Skylane
8 Cessna U–17A
1 DeHavilland Canada DHC–2
2 Piper L–21A
Helicopters
2 Hiller OH–23F
Trainers
10 Beechcraft T–34
6 Lockheed T–33A
10 North American T–6G
**Army**
12,000 men
**Navy**
1,800 men
**Naval aviation** (Aviación Naval)
3 Grumman S–2A maritime reconnaissance and ASW
aircraft
2 Piper L–18 liaison aircraft
2 Bell 47G helicopters
3 Sikorsky SH–34J helicopters
1 Beechcraft T–34 trainer

## VENEZUELA
**Air force** (Fuerzas Aéreas Venezolanas)
men 9,000
squadrons 9
operational aircraft 140 and
helicopters 18
**Organisation**
2 fighter squadrons with F–86K
1 strike fighter squadron with F–86F
1 ground-attack squadron with OV–10E
2 bomber squadrons with Canberra B.82 and B.(I)88
1 transport squadron with C–130H, C–47 and C–54
1 transport squadron with C–123B
1 helicopter squadron with Alouette III
**Major bases**
La Carlota, Maiquetia, Maracaibo, Maracay, Maturin
**Military training aid from**
United States
**Equipment**
Fighters and strike fighters
some DeHavilland Vampire FB.5 and Venom FB.4
18 North American F–86F
38 North American F–86K
Ground-attack aircraft
16 North American Rockwell OV–10E
Bombers
6 English Electric B.82
8 English Electric Canberra B.(I)88
2 English Electric Canberra T.84
Reconnaissance aircraft
2 English Electric Canberra PR.83
Maritime reconnaissance and ASW aircraft
some Grumman HU–16A (?)

Transports
15 Douglas C–47
3 Douglas C–54
18 Fairchild C–123B
1 Hawker Siddeley H.S.748
4 Lockheed C–130H
Liaison and AOP aircraft
6 Beechcraft Queen Air B–80
2 Cessna 180
12 Cessna 182N
Helicopters
1 Aérospatiale Alouette II
5 Aérospatiale Alouette III
6 (?) Bell 47G
4 Bell UH–1D
2 Sikorsky UH–19
Trainers
approx 80 aircraft, inc 15 BAC Jet Provost T.52, Beech-craft T–11 (?), 30 Beechcraft T–34, 6 DeHavilland Vampire T–55, North American T–6G (?), 12 North American Rockwell T–2D
**Programme**
13 Dassault Mirage IIIEV strike fighters and 2 Dassault Mirage IIIDV strike trainers on order (delivery mid-1973). Also 18 Canadair CF–5A strike fighters and 2 CF–5D strike trainers on order
**Army**
20,000 men
**Army aviation**
20 helicopters
**Equipment**
15 Aérospatiale Alouette III
3 Bell 47G
2 Sikorsky UH–19
**Navy**
7,000 men
**Naval aviation**
3 Bell 47J (?) helicopters

## VIETNAM (NORTH)

**Air force**
men 10,000
squadrons 18
operational aircraft 180 and
helicopters 20
**Organisation**
3 fighter squadrons with MiG–21
2 fighter squadrons with F–6 (MiG–19)
5 strike fighter squadrons with MiG–17
1 strike fighter squadron with MiG–15
1 bomber squadron with Il–28
1 transport squadron with An–2
2 transport squadrons with Il–2, Il–4, Li–2
2 helicopter squadrons with Mi–4
1 helicopter squadron with Mi–6
– trainer squadrons with Yak–11
– trainer squadrons with MiG–15UTI
**Bases**
Bai Thuong, Dien Bien Phu, Dong Hoi, Gia Lam, Hoa Lac, Kep, Na San, Phuc Yen, Quang Lang, Vinh
**Military training aid from**
China, Soviet Union
**Equipment**
Fighters and strike fighters
10 (?) Mikoyan MiG–15
70 Mikoyan MiG–17
27 Shenyang F–8 (Mikoyan MiG–19)
40 Mikoyan MiG–21 and MiG–21UTI
Bombers
8 Ilyushin Il–28
Transports
8 Antonov An–2
3 Antonov An–24
6 Ilyushin Il–12
10 Ilyushin Il–14
3 Li–2 (copy of C–47)
Helicopters
some Mil Mi–1

12 Mil Mi–4
5 (6?) Mil Mi–6
Trainers
approx 40 aircraft, inc 10 (?) Mikoyan MiG–15UTI, Yakovlev Yak–11, Yakovlev Yak–18
**Army**
480,000 men
**Navy**
3,000 men

## VIETNAM (SOUTH)

**Air force**
men 50,000
squadrons 41
operational aircraft 630 and
helicopters 670
**Organisation**
1 strike fighter squadron with F–5A
7 ground-attack squadrons with A–37B
3 ground-attack squadrons with A–1
1 reconnaissance squadron with RF–5A and EC–47
1 night ground-support squadron with AC–47
2 night ground-support squadrons with AC–119G and K
2 transport squadrons with DHC–4
1 (?) transport squadron with C–47
1 transport squadron with C–119G
3 transport squadrons with C–123K
2 transport squadrons with C–130E
4 liaison squadrons with O–1
1 liaison squadron with U–17B
15 helicopter squadrons with UH–1B, D and H
2 (3?) helicopter squadrons with CH–47A and C
strike fighter and ground-attack squadrons each with 15–20 aircraft
**Major bases**
Bien Hoa, Binh Thuy, Cam Ranh Bay, Chulai, Dalat, Da Nang, Nha Trang, Phan Rang, Pleiku, Qui Nhon, Tanh Sonh Nhut (Saigon)
**Military training aid from**
United States
**Equipment**
Fighters and strike fighters
140 Northrop F–5A and B
Ground-attack aircraft
220 Cessna A–37A and B
65 Douglas A–1E, H and J
Night ground-support aircraft
20 Douglas AC–47
30 Fairchild AC–119G and K
Reconnaissance aircraft
some Douglas EC–47
some Northrop RF–5A
Transports
30 DeHavilland Canada DHC–4
20 (?) Douglas C–47
15 Fairchild C–119G
45 Fairchild C–123K
32 Lockheed C–130A
Liaison and AOP aircraft
60 Cessna O–1
20 Cessna U–17B
7 DeHavilland Canada DHC–2
Helicopters
620 (900?) Bell UH–1B, D and H
50 Boeing Vertol CH–47A and C
Trainers
some Cessna T–37B and 18 Cessna T–41
A number of the Northrop F–5A strike fighters and the Cessna A–37B ground-attack aircraft, the Lockheed C–130E transports as well as the Bell UH–1 and Boeing Vertol CH–47 helicopters are inoperative due to lack of pilots
**Programme**
Replacement of Douglas A–1 ground-attack aircraft by 72 Northrop F–5E strike fighters. 8 strike fighter squadrons with F–5 and 10 ground-attack squadrons with A–37 to be in service by 1974. Formation of further helicopter squadrons with UH–1 and CH–47. Formation

of one maritime reconnaissance squadron with 8 Fairchild C–119G from 1974

**Army**
410,000 men
**Navy**
31,000 men
**Marines**
15,000 men

## YEMEN

**Air force**
men 500 (?)
squadrons 2
operational aircraft 25 (?) and
helicopters 6–8 (?)
**Organisation**
1 strike fighter squadron with MiG–17
1 bomber squadron with Il–28
**Bases**
Hodeida, Sana, Taiz
**Military training aid from**
Egypt, Soviet Union
**Equipment**
Fighters and strike fighters
10–12 Mikoyan MiG–17
Bombers
6–8 Ilyushin Il–28
Transports
some Douglas C–47 and Ilyushin Il–14
Helicopters
some Mil Mi–1 and Mil Mi–4
Trainers
some Yakovlev Yak–11
**Army**
14,500 (?) men

## YUGOSLAVIA

**Air force** (Jugoslovensko Ratno Vazduhoplovstvo)
20,000 men
26 squadrons
320 operational aircraft and
57 helicopters
**Organisation**
6 fighter squadrons with MiG–21F and MiG–21PF
4 fighter squadrons with F–86D and F–86E(M)
4 strike fighter squadrons with F–84G
2 ground-attack squadrons with Jastreb
2 ground-attack squadrons with Kraguj
2 reconnaissance squadrons with RT–33A and RF–86F
1 transport squadron with C–47
1 transport squadron with Il–14
– liaison squadrons with UTVA–60 and UTVA–66
1 helicopter squadron with Alouette III
1 helicopter squadron with Whirlwind 2
1 helicopter squadron with Mi–4
1 helicopter squadron with Mi–8
– trainer squadrons with Aero 2 and Aero 3
– trainer squadrons with Galeb and T–33A
fighter, strike fighter, ground-attack and reconnaissance
  squadrons each with 12–15 aircraft
**Major bases**
Agram, Batajnica (Belgrade), Cattaro, Cerklje, Laibach,
  Mostar, Neusatz, Niksic, Nish, Pleso, Pola, Salusani,
  Sarajevo, Skoplje, Sombor, Titograd, Tuzla, Vrsac
  (Werschitz), Zemun
**Military training aid from**
Soviet Union (?)
**Equipment**
Fighters and strike fighters
80 Mikoyan MiG–21F and MiG–21PF
some Mikoyan MiG–21UTI
50 North American F–86D and F–86E(M)
60 Republic F–84G
Ground-attack aircraft
30 Soko J–1 Jastreb
30 Soko P–2 Kraguj
Reconnaissance aircraft

25–30 Lockheed RT–33A and North American RF–86F
Transports
1 Aérospatiale S.E.210 Caravelle
15 Douglas C–47
4 Douglas DC–6B
13 Ilyushin Il–14
1 Ilyushin Il–18
some Li–2(?)
3 Yakovlev Yak–40
Liaison and AOP aircraft
some Cijan Kurir, L–60
UTVA 60 and UTVA 66, Yakovlev Yak–12A
Helicopters
20 Aérospatiale Alouette III
15 Mil Mi–4
12 Mil Mi–8
10 Westland Whirlwind 2
Trainers
approx 200 aircraft, inc Aero 2, 60 (?) Aero 3,
50 Lockheed T–33A, 60 Soko G–2A Galeb and
some Type 214–D
**Programme**
Replacement of Republic F–84G strike fighters by Soko
  J–1 Jastreb ground-attack aircraft and modern strike
  fighters (Mikoyan MiG–21?) intended
**Army**
195,000 men
**Navy**
18,000 men
**Aircraft factories**
Soko (Preduzece Soko), UTVA (Fabrika Aviona UTVA)

## ZAÏRE — see Congo (Kinshasa)

## ZAMBIA

**Air force**
men 1,000
squadrons 4
operational aircraft 19 and
helicopters 6
**Organisation**
1 ground-attack squadron with MB.326GB
1 ground-attack squadron with Jastreb
1 transport squadron with DHC–4 and C–47
1 liaison squadron with DHC–2 and Pembroke C.1
1 helicopter squadron with AB.205
1 trainer squadron with SF.260MZ
1 trainer squadron with Bulldog
**Bases**
Balovale, Lusaka, Mbala (Abercorn), Mumbwa, Siluwe
**Military training aid from**
Italy
**Equipment**
Ground-attack aircraft
6 Aermacchi MB.326GB
4 Soko J–1 Jastreb
Transports
4 DeHavilland Canada DHC–4
2 Douglas C–47
1 Hawker Siddeley H.S.748
2 Hunting Pembroke C.1
Liaison and AOP aircraft
5 DeHavilland Canada DHC–2
Helicopters
5 Agusta-Bell AB.205
1 Agusta-Bell AB.212
Trainers
5 DeHavilland Canada DHC–1
8 Scottish Aviation Bulldog
8 SIAI-Marchetti SF.260MZ
2 Soko G–2A Galeb
**Programme**
Further 9 Aermacchi MB.326GB ground-attack aircraft
  on order
**Army**
5,000 men

# Aircraft

## FMA I.A. 35 'HUANQUERO'

**Type**
Navigation trainer
(Type IA)
**Weights**
empty 7,716 lb (3,500 kg)
normal 12,566 lb (5,700 kg)
**Performance**
maximum speed at 9,843 ft (3,000 m) 225 mph
  (362 km/hr)
maximum cruising speed at 9,843 ft (3,000 m) 217 mph
  (350 km/hr)
range 975 miles (1,570 km)
ferry range 1,317 miles (2,120 km)
initial rate of climb 19.7 fps (6.0 m/sec)
service ceiling 20,998 ft (6,400 m)
**Dimensions**
wing span 64 ft 3 in (19.60 m)
length overall 45 ft 10¼ in (13.98 m)
height overall 12 ft 1½ in (3.70 m)
wing area 452.1 sq ft (42.00 sq m)
**Power plant**
Two 620 hp I.A. 19 R El Indio piston engines
**Armament**
Type IB: Two 12.7 mm machine guns, max underwing
  weapon load 440 lb (200 kg) e.g. four 110 lb (50 kg)
  bombs or rockets
**Payload**
Type IA: 3 man crew, 4 trainees and 1 instructor
Type II: 3 man crew and 7 troops or freight
**Variants**
Type IB: Bombing/gunnery trainer with uprated (750 hp)
  engines
Type IV: Photo-reconnaissance aircraft
**First flights**
Prototype: 21 September 1953
1st production model: 27 March 1957
**Production**
31 built of all variants from 1956–1965
**In service**
Argentine

## FMA I.A. 50 'GUARANI II'

**Type**
Light transport
**Weights**
empty 8,650 lb (3,924 kg)
maximum 16,204 lb (7,350 kg)
**Performance**
maximum speed at sea level 310 mph (500 km/hr)
maximum cruising speed 305 mph (491 km/hr)
range w.m.p. 1,240 miles (1,995 km)
ferry range 1,600 miles (2,575 km)
initial rate of climb 43.9 fps (13.4 m/sec)
service ceiling 41,000 ft (12,500 m)
**Dimensions**
wing span 64 ft 1 in (19.53 m)
length overall 48 ft 9 in (14.86 m)
height overall 19 ft 0¾ in (5.81 m)
wing area 450 sq ft (41.81 sq m)
**Power plant**
Two 930 hp Turbomeca Bastan VI–A turboprops
**Payload**
2 man crew and 10–15 troops or max 3,300 lb (1,500 kg)
  freight
**First flights**
Prototype: 23 April 1963
**Production**
2 prototypes, 1 pre-production and 28 production models
  from 1966–1971
**In service**
Argentine

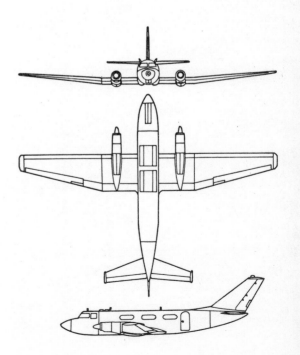

## FMA I.A. 58 'PUCARA'

**Type**
Two-seat light ground-attack aircraft
**Weights**
empty 7,826 lb (3,550 kg)
maximum 13,668 lb (6,200 kg)
**Performance**
maximum speed at 9,840 ft (3,000 m) 323 mph (520 km/hr)
maximum cruising speed at 9,840 ft (3,000 m) 299 mph (482 km/hr)
ferry range 1,890 miles (3,040 km)
initial rate of climb 59.1 fps (18.0 m/sec)
service ceiling 27,170 ft (8,280 m)
**Dimensions**
wing span 47 ft 6¾ in (14.50 m)
length overall 45 ft 7¼ in (13.90 m)
height overall 17 ft 2¼ in (5.24 m)
wing area 326.1 sq ft (30.30 sq m)
**Power plant**
Two 1,022 hp Turbomeca Astazou XVIG turboprops
**Armament**
Two 20 mm Hispano cannon and four 7.62 mm FN machine guns and max 2,200 lb (1,000 kg) weapon load on 3 hard points
**First flights**
Prototype: 20 August 1969
**Production**
2 prototypes, series production from 1973, over 80 delivered or on order to date
**In service**
Argentine

## GAF 'NOMAD' 22

**Type**
Light transport
**Weights**
empty 4,670 lb (2,118 kg)
maximum 8,000 lb (3,629 kg)
**Performance**
maximum speed at sea level 213 mph (341 km/hr)
maximum cruising speed 202 mph (325 km/hr)
range 1,060 miles (1,706 km)
initial rate of climb 25.0 fps (7.6 m/sec)
service ceiling 24,000 ft (7,315 m)
**Dimensions**
wing span 54 ft 0 in (16.46 m)
length overall 41 ft 2½ in (12.56 m)
height overall 17 ft 11¼ in (5.47 m)
wing area 320.0 sq ft (29.70 sq m)
**Power plant**
Two 416 hp Allison 250–B17 turboprops
**Armament**
Weapon load on 4 hard points, e.g., two-four weapon packs each containing one 7.62 mm Minigun with 1,500 rpg or four rocket launchers each containing seven 70 mm rockets or two rocket launchers each containing 70 mm rockets
**Payload**
2 man crew and 13 troops or max 3,200 lb (1,451 kg) freight
**Variants**
Nomad 24: Civil variant with lengthened fuselage
**First flights**
Prototype: 23 July 1971
**Production**
2 prototypes, series production from 1973, 20 delivered or on order to date
**In service**
Australia, Indonesia

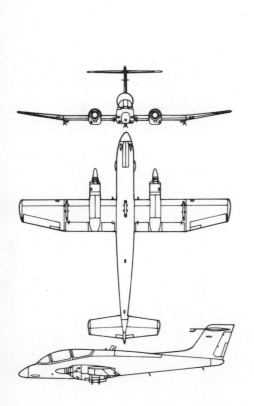

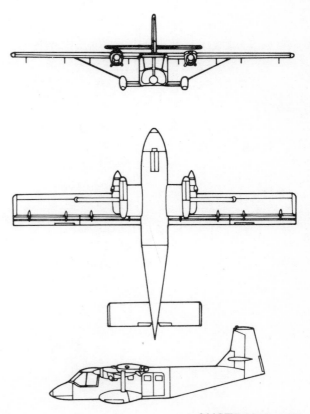

## AEROTEC 122 'UIRAPURU' (T-23)

**Type**
Two-seat trainer
**Weights**
empty 1,190 lb (540 kg)
maximum 1,852 lb (840 kg)
**Performance**
maximum speed at sea level 140 mph (225 km/hr)
maximum cruising speed at 4,987 ft (1,520 m) 115 mph (185 km/hr)
ferry range 497 miles (800 km)
initial rate of climb 13.1 fps (4.0 m/sec)
service ceiling 14,763 ft (4,500 m)
**Dimensions**
wing span 27 ft 10¾ in (8.50 m)
length overall 21 ft 7¾ in (6.60 m)
height overall 8 ft 10¼ in (2.70 m)
wing area 145 sq ft (13.50 sq m)
**Power plant**
One 160 hp Lycoming 0-320-B2B piston engine
**First flights**
Prototype: 2 June 1965
**Production**
Series production from 1968, 110 delivered or on order
**In service**
Brazil, Paraguay

## EMBRAER EMB-110 'BANDEIRANTE'

**Type**
Light transport
**Weights**
empty 6,437 lb (2,920 kg)
maximum 11,243 lb (5,100 kg)
**Performance**
maximum speed at 9,840 ft (3,000 m) 285 mph (458 km/hr)
maximum cruising speed at 9,840 ft (3,000 m) 260 mph (418 km/hr)
ferry range 1,150 miles (1,850 km)
initial rate of climb 32.8 fps (10.0 m/sec)
service ceiling 27,950 ft (8,520 m)
**Dimensions**
wing span 50 ft 2¼ in (15.30 m)
length overall 46 ft 8¼ in (14.22 m)
height overall 15 ft 6 in (4.73 m)
wing area 312.13 sq ft (29.00 sq m)
**Power plant**
Two 680 hp Pratt & Whitney PT6A-27 turboprops
**Payload**
2 man crew and 12 troops or 4 stretcher cases and 2 medics
**First flights**
Prototype: 26 October 1968,
1st production model: 15 August 1972
**Production**
3 Prototypes, series production from 1972, 104 delivered or on order to date, further 70 planned
**In service**
Brazil (C-95)

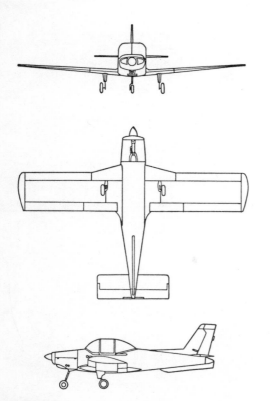

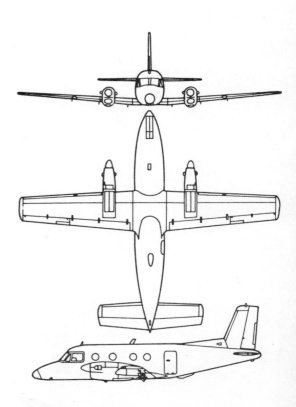

## NEIVA C-42 'REGENTE'

**Type**
Liaison aircraft
**Weights**
empty 1,410 lb (640 kg)
maximum 2,293 lb (1,040 kg)
**Performance**
maximum speed at sea level 137 mph (220 km/hr)
maximum cruising speed at 5,000 ft (1,500 m) 132 mph (212 km/hr)
ferry range 576 miles (928 km)
initial rate of climb 11.5 fps (3.5 m/sec)
service ceiling 11,812 ft (3,600 m)
**Dimensions**
wing span 29 ft 11½ in (9.13 m)
length overall 23 ft 1 in (7.04 m)
height overall 9 ft 7¼ in (2.93 m)
wing area 144.2 sq ft (13.40 sq m)
**Power plant**
One 210 hp Continental IO-360-D piston engine
**Payload**
1 man crew and 3 troops
**First flights**
Prototype: 7 September 1961
C-42: February 1965
**Production**
80 built from 1965-1968
**In service**
Brazil

## NEIVA L-42 'REGENTE'

**Type**
AOP aircraft
Details as for the C-42 with the following exceptions
**Weights**
empty 1,500 lb (680 kg)
**Performance**
maximum speed at sea level 149 mph (240 km/hr)
maximum cruising speed at 5,000 ft (1,500 m) 143 mph (231 km/hr)
ferry range 590 miles (950 km)
initial rate of climb 11.8 fps (3.6 m/sec)
service ceiling 12,009 ft (3,660 m)
**Power plant**
One 180 hp Lycoming O-360-A1D piston engine
**Payload**
2 crew (and 1 casualty)
**First flights**
October 1967
**Production**
40 built from 1967-1970
**In service**
Brazil

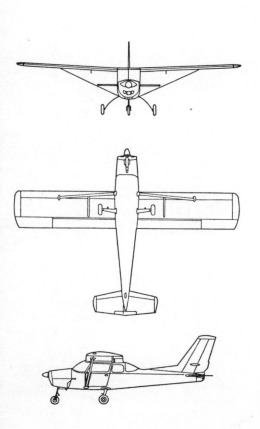

## NEIVA IPD–6201 'UNIVERSAL' (T–25)

**Type**
Two/three-seat trainer
**Weights**
empty 2,425 lb (1,100 kg)
maximum 3,085 lb (1,400 kg)
**Performance**
maximum speed at sea level 201 mph (324 km/hr)
maximum speed at 5000 ft (1,500 m) 190 mph (306 km/hr)
range/radius of action 447 miles (720 km)
ferry range 620 miles (1,000 km)
initial rate of climb 28.9 fps (8.8 m/sec)
service ceiling 26,250 ft (8,000 m)
**Dimensions**
wing span 36 ft 1 in (11.00 m)
length overall 27 ft 10½ in (8.50 m)
height overall 10 ft 2 in (3.10 m)
wing area 183 sq ft (17.00 sq m)
**Power plant**
One 300 hp Lycoming IO–540–K1D5 piston engine
**First flights**
Prototype: 29 April 1966
**Production**
Series production from 1970, 150 planned
**In service**
Brazil (T–25)

## CANADAIR CL–28 'ARGUS' Mk. 2

**Type**
Maritime reconnaissance and ASW aircraft
15 man crew
**Weights**
empty 81,000 lb (36,742 kg)
normal 148,000 lb (67,133 kg)
**Performance**
maximum speed at 20,010 ft (6,100 m) 317 mph (507 km/hr)
patrol speed under 985 ft (300 m) 190 mph (305 km/hr)
maximum cruising speed at 5,000 ft (1,525 m) 230 mph (370 km/hr)
range 4,040 miles (6,500 km)
ferry range 5,900 miles (9,500 km)
initial rate of climb 28.2 fps (8.6 m/sec)
**Dimensions**
wing span 142 ft 3½ in (43.37 m)
length overall 128 ft 2¼ in (39.09 m)
height overall 36 ft 8½ in (11.19 m)
wing area 2,075 sq ft (192.77 sq m)
**Power plant**
Four 3,700 hp Wright R–3350 TC 981–EA–1 piston engines
**Armament**
Max 7,990 lb (3,630 kg) weapon load in two fuselage bays; e.g. depth charges, homing torpedoes and mines plus max 7,600 lb (3,447 kg) weapon load on underwing hard points; e.g. homing torpedoes, rockets and bombs
**Variants**
Argus Mk. 1: Earlier version
**First flights**
Prototype: 28 March 1957
**Production**
Series production from 1958–1960;
Argus Mk. 1: 13 built
Argus Mk. 2: 20 built
**In service**
Canada (CP–107)

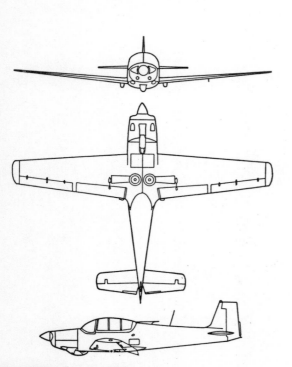

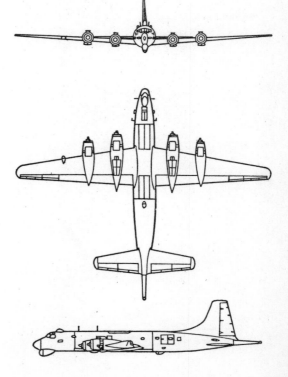

## CANADAIR CL–41A 'TUTOR'

**Type**
Two-seat trainer
**Weights**
empty 4,872 lb (2,210 kg)
normal 7,397 lb (3,355 kg)
**Performance**
maximum speed at 27,500 ft (8,380 m) 486 mph (782 km/hr)
range 945 miles (1,520 km)
ferry range 1,342 miles (2,160 km)
initial rate of climb 70.5 fps (21.5 m/sec)
time to 15,000 ft (4,570 m) 4 min 33 sec
service ceiling 43,000 ft (13,100 m)
**Dimensions**
wing span 36 ft 5½ in (11.11 m)
length overall 32 ft 0¼ in (9.76 m)
height overall 8 ft 9½ in (2.86 m)
wing area 220 sq ft (20.44 sq m)
**Power plant**
One Orenda J85–Can–40 turbojet rated at 2,635 lb
    (1,195 kg) st
**Armament**
CL–41G: Max 3,500 lb (1,588 kg) weapon load on 6 hard
    points, e.g. weapon packs and bombs
**Variants**
*CL–41G*: Trainer and light ground-attack aircraft
*CL–41R*: CL–41A fitted with nose-section of CF–104 strike
    fighter
**First flights**
*CL–41A*: 13 January 1960; *CL–41G*: June 1964;
*CL–41R*: 13 July 1962
**Production**
*CL–41A*: 190 built from 1962–1966;
*CL–41G*: 20 built from 1967–1969
**In service**
*CL–41A*: Canada (CT–114);
*CL–41G*: Malaysia (Tebuan)

## DeHAVILLAND CANADA DHC–1 'CHIPMUNK'

**Type**
Two-seat trainer
**Weights**
empty 1,425 lb (647 kg)
normal 2,015 lb (914 kg)
**Performance**
maximum speed at sea level 125 mph (222 km/hr)
maximum cruising speed 120 mph (192 km/hr)
range 280 miles (451 km)
initial rate of climb 14.1 fps (4.3 m/sec)
service ceiling 15,810 ft (4,820 m)
**Dimensions**
wing span 34 ft 4¼ in (10.47 m)
length overall 25 ft 5 in (7.75 m)
height overall 7 ft 0 in (2.13 m)
wing area 173.2 sq ft (16.10 sq m)
**Power plant**
One 145 hp Bristol Siddeley (D.H.) Gipsy Major 8 piston
    engine
**First flights**
Prototype: 22 May 1946
**Production**
1,292 built from 1946–1959, inc 218 licence-built in Canada
    and 60 Portuguese licence-built by OGMA from
    1955–1959
**In service**
Burma(?), Canada (T.30), Ceylon (Sri Lanka), Denmark
    (T.20), Ghana, Great Britain (T.10, T.20), India, Iraq,
    Ireland, Jordan, Kenya, Lebanon, Malaysia, New
    Zealand, Portugal, Saudi Arabia (?), Thailand, Zambia.

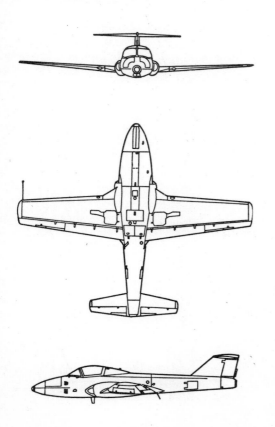

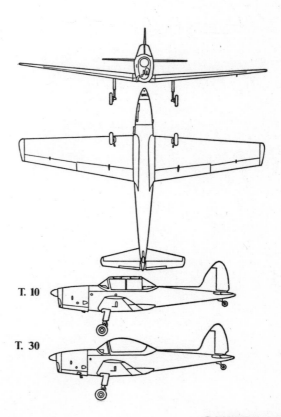

T. 10

T. 30

# DeHAVILLAND CANADA DHC–2 'BEAVER'

**Type**
Liaison aircraft
**Weights**
empty 2,850 lb (1,293 kg)
maximum 5,100 lb (2,313 kg)
**Performance**
maximum speed at sea level 140 mph (225 km/hr)
maximum speed at 5,000 ft (1,530 m) 163 mph (262 km/hr)
maximum cruising speed at 5,000 ft (1,530 m) 143 mph (230 km/hr)
range 453 miles (730 km)
ferry range 733 miles (1,180 km)
initial rate of climb 17.0 fps (5.2 m/sec)
service ceiling 18,000 ft (5,490 m)
**Dimensions**
wing span 47 ft 11½ in (14.63 m)
length overall 30 ft 3 in (9.22 m)
height overall 8 ft 11¾ in (2.74 m)
wing area 250 sq ft (23.20 sq m)
**Power plant**
One 450 hp Pratt & Whitney R–985–AN–1
or—3 Wasp piston engine
Payload 1–2 man crew and 4 troops
**First flights**
Prototype: 16 August 1947
**Production**
1,657 built from 1954–1967
**In service**
Argentine, Austria, Cambodia, Canada, Chile, Colombia, Dominican Republic, Finland, Ghana, Great Britain (Beaver AL.1), Iran, Kenya, Laos, Netherlands, Oman, Pakistan, Peru, South Yemen, Tanzania, Turkey, United States (U–6A), Uruguay, Zambia.

# DeHÅVILLAND CANADA DHC–3 'OTTER'

**Type**
Light transport
**Weights**
empty 4,431 lb (2,010 kg)
maximum 8,000 lb (3,629 kg)
**Performance**
maximum speed at 5,000 ft (1,530 m) 160 mph (257 km/hr)
maximum cruising speed at 5,000 ft (1,530 m) 138 mph (222 km/hr)
range 944 miles (1,520 km)
initial rate of climb 12.1 fps (3.7 m/sec)
service ceiling 18,800 ft (5,730 m)
**Dimensions**
wing span 18 ft 1¼ in (17.69 m)
length overall 41 ft 10 in (12.75 m)
height overall 2 ft 7 in (3.84 m)
wing area 374.5 sq ft (34.80 sq m)
**Power plant**
One 600 hp Pratt & Whitney R–1340–S1H1–G or R–1340–S3H1–G piston engine
**Payload**
2 man crew and 10 troops or 6 stretcher cases and 4 medics
**Variants**
Ski–or floatplane versions
**First flights**
Prototype: 12 December 1951
**Production**
460 built from 1955
**In service**
Australia, Burma, Canada, Chile, Colombia, Ghana, India, Indonesia, Paraguay, United States (U–1A, U–1B)

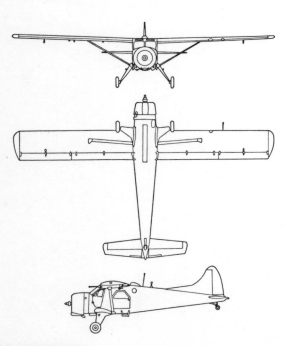

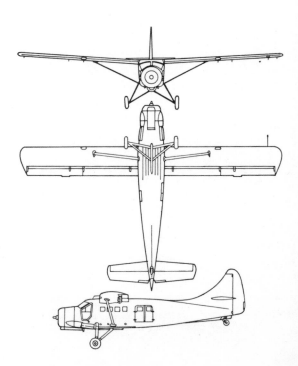

## DeHAVILLAND CANADA DHC–4A 'CARIBOU'

**Type**
Light STOL transport
**Weights**
empty 16,976 lb (7,700 kg)
normal 28,500 lb (12,928 kg)
maximum 31,300 lb (14,197 kg)
**Performance**
maximum speed at 6,500 ft (1,980 m) 216 mph (347 km/hr)
maximum cruising speed at 7,500 ft (2,285 m) 182 mph
  (293 km/hr)
range w.m.p. 242 miles (390 km)
ferry range 1,307 miles (2,103 km)
initial rate of climb 23 fps (7.0 m/sec)
service ceiling 24,800 ft (7,560 m)
**Dimensions**
wing span 95 ft 7½ in (29.15 m)
length overall 72 ft 7 in (22.13 m)
height overall 31 ft 9 in (9.70 m)
wing area 912 sq ft (84.72 sq m)
**Power plant**
Two 1,450 hp Pratt & Whitney R–2000–7M2 piston
  engines
**Payload**
2–3 man crew and 32 troops or 26 paratroops or 22
  stretcher cases and 8 medics or max 8,818 lb (4,000 kg)
  freight
**First flights**
Prototype: 30 July 1958
**Production**
286 built from 1959–1970
**In service**
Abu Dhabi, Australia, Cameroon, China (Taiwan), Ghana,
  India, Kenya, Kuwait, Malaysia, Oman, Spain (T–9),
  Tanzania, Uganda, United States (CV–2A, B), Zambia.

## DeHAVILLAND CANADA DHC–5 'BUFFALO'

**Type**
Medium STOL transport
**Weights**
empty 22,899 lb (10,387 kg)
normal 41,000 lb (18,597 kg)
maximum 45,100 lb (20,457 kg)
**Performance**
maximum speed at 10,000 ft (3,050 m) 282 mph (454 km/hr)
maximum cruising speed 253 mph (407 km/hr)
range w.m.p. 518 miles (834 km)
range with 7,900 lb (3,600 kg) payload 1,600 miles
  (2,575 km)
ferry range 2,218 miles (3,570 km)
initial rate of climb 34.8 fps (10.6 m/sec)
service ceiling 31,500 ft (9,600 m)
**Dimensions**
wing span 96 ft 0 in (29.26 m)
length overall 79 ft 0 in (24.08 m)
height overall 28 ft 8 in (8.73 m)
wing area 945 sq ft (87.80 sq m)
**Power plant**
Two 3,055 hp General Electric CT64–820–1 turboprops
**Payload**
3 man crew and 41 troops or 35 paratroops or 24 stretcher
  cases and 6 medics or max 14,109 lb (6,400 kg) freight
**First flights**
Prototype: 9 April 1964
**Production**
59 built from 1967–1971
**In service**
Brazil, Canada, (CC–115), Peru, Spain, United States
  (C–8A)

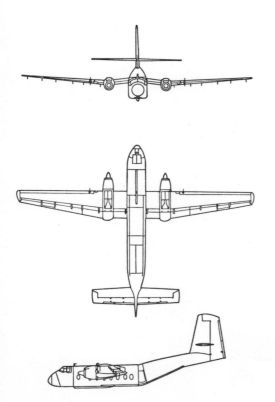

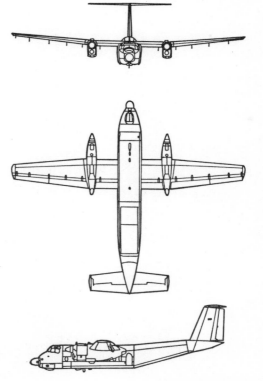

## DeHAVILLAND CANADA DHC–6 'TWIN OTTER' SERIES 300

**Type**
Light transport
**Weights**
empty 7,230 lb (3,180 kg)
maximum 12,500 lb (5,670 kg)
**Performance**
maximum cruising speed at 10,000 ft (3,050 m) 210 mph (338 km/hr)
range with 3,220 lb (1,474 kg) payload 744 miles (1,198 km)
initial rate of climb 26.6 fps (8.1 m/sec)
service ceiling 26,700 ft (8,138 m)
**Dimensions**
wing span 65 ft 0 in (19.81 m)
length overall 51 ft 9 in (15.77 m)
height overall 18 ft 7 in (5.66 m)
wing area 420 sq ft (39.02 sq m)
**Power plant**
Two 652 hp Pratt & Whitney PT6A–27 turboprops
**Payload**
1–2 man crew and 20 troops or 9 stretcher cases and 3 medics
**Variants**
Twin Otter Series 100 and Series 200: Earlier versions, inc floatplane variants
**First flights**
Prototype: 20 May 1965
**Production**
5 prototypes; over 300 built to date, inc only 40 military variants:
*Series 100*: 115 built from 1966–1968; *Series 200*: 115 built from 1968–1969; *Series 300*: over 70 built from 1969.
**In service**
*Series 100*: Chile, Norway, Paraguay, Peru
*Series 300*: Canada (CC–138), Panama (?), Peru

## DeHAVILLAND CANADA DHC–6 'TWIN OTTER' SERIES 200

**Type**
Light transport
Details as for Series 300 with the following exceptions
**Weights**
empty 6,500 lb (2,950 kg)
maximum 11,580 lb (5,252 kg)
**Performance**
maximum cruising speed at 10,000 ft (3,050 m) 190 mph (306 km/hr)
ferry range 945 miles (1,520 km)
initial rate of climb 21.3 fps (6.5 m/sec)
service ceiling 24,300 ft (7,400 m)
**Power plant**
Two 579 hp Pratt & Whitney PT6A–20 turboprops
**Payload**
1–2 man crew and 19 troops or 9 stretcher cases and 3 medics or max 4,000 lb (1,815 kg) freight
**In service**
Series 200: Argentine, Jamaica, Nepal

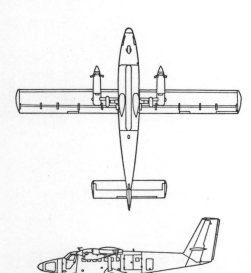

## PAZMANY/CAF PL–1B 'CHIENSHOU'

**Type**
Two-seat trainer
**Weights**
empty 950 lb (431 kg)
maximum 1,437 lb (635 kg)
**Performance**
maximum speed at **sea** level 150 mph (241 km/hr)
Cruising speed at **sea** level 115 mph (185 km/hr)
ferry range 405 miles (651 km)
initial rate of climb 26.9 fps (8.2 m/sec)
service ceiling 18,000 ft (5,500 m)
**Dimensions**
wing span 28 ft 0 in (8.53 m)
length overall 19 ft 7½ in (5.99 m)
height overall 7 ft 4¼ in (2.24 m)
wing area 116 sq ft (10.78 sq m)
**Power plant**
One 150 hp Lycoming 0–320–E2A piston engine
**First flights**
Prototype: PL–1A: 26 October 1968
**Production**
3 prototypes, 50 production models from 1969/70 delivered
  or on order
**In service**
China (Taiwan)

## AERO L–29 'DELFIN' (MAYA)

**Type**
Two-seat trainer
**Weights**
empty 5,027 lb (2,280 kg)
normal 7,231 lb (3,280 kg)
maximum 7,804 lb (3,540 kg)
**Performance**
maximum speed at sea level 382 mph (615 km/hr)
maximum speed at 16,400 ft (5,000 m) 407 mph (655 km/hr)
maximum cruising speed at sea level 359 mph (575 km/hr)
ferry range 592 miles (900 km)
initial rate of climb 45.9 fps (14.0 m/sec)
time to 20,000 ft (6,100 m) 12 min 0 sec
service ceiling 36,100 ft (11,000 m)
**Dimensions**
wing span 33 ft 9 in (10.29 m)
length overall 35 ft 5½ in (10.81 m)
height overall 10 ft 3 in (3.13 m)
wing area 213.1 sq ft (19.80 sq m)
**Power plant**
One M–701 turbojet rated at 1,960 lb (890 kg) st
**Armament**
Two 220 lb (100 kg) bombs or 4 unguided rockets or
  two 7.62 mm machine guns in underwing pods
**Variants**
L–29A Delfin-Akrobat: Aerobatic aircraft
L–39 Super Delfin: Further development and successor to
  L–29, Series production from 1972
**First flights**
Prototype: 5 April 1959
**Production**
Over 2,500 built from 1961–1970
**In service**
Bulgaria, Czechoslovakia (C–29), Egypt (UAR), Germany
  (East), Guinea, Hungary, Indonesia, Iraq, Nigeria,
  Rumania, Soviet Union, Syria, Uganda

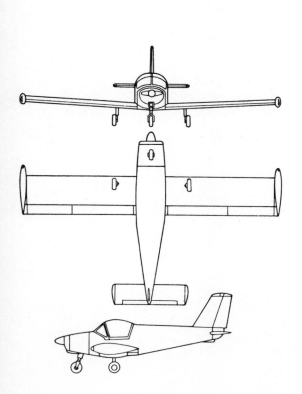

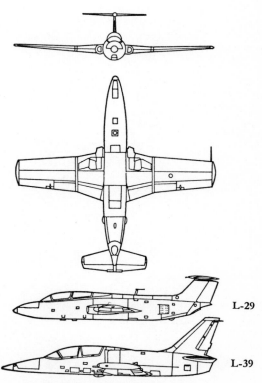

L-29

L-39

CHINA (TAIWAN)/CZECHOSLOVAKIA 65

## L–60 'BRIGADYR'

**Type**
Liaison and AOP aircraft
**Weights**
empty 2,138 lb (970 kg)
normal 3,219 lb (1,460 kg)
maximum 3,439 lb (1,560 kg)
**Performance**
maximum speed 120 mph (193 km/hr)
maximum cruising speed 109 mph (175 km/hr)
range 447 miles (720 km)
initial rate of climb 14.4 fps (4.4 m/sec)
time to 3,280 ft (1,000 m)
service ceiling 13,775 ft (4,200 m)
**Dimensions**
wing span 45 ft 9½ in (13.96 m)
length overall 27 ft 8¼ in (8.45 m)
height overall 8 ft 11 in (2.72 m)
wing area 261.6 sq ft (24.30 sq m)
**Power plant**
One 220 hp Praga Doris M–208B piston engine
**Armament**
One machine-gun optional
**Payload**
1 man crew and 3 troops or 2 stretcher cases
**Variants**
Agricola: Agricultural crop-dusting aircraft
**First flights**
Prototype: 1955
**Production**
Approx 400 built from 1956–1960, majority as civil
crop-dusters
**In service**
Czechoslovakia, Germany (East), Rumania, Yugoslavia.

## ZLIN Z–526 'TRENER'

**Type**
Two-seat trainer
**Weights**
empty 1,499 lb (680 kg)
normal 2,072 lb (940 kg)
**Performance**
maximum speed at sea level 148 mph (238 km/hr)
maximum cruising speed 127 mph (205 km/hr)
range 360 miles (580 km)
ferry range 640 miles (1,030 km)
initial rate of climb 18.0 fps (5.5 m/sec)
service ceiling 15,750 ft (4,800 m)
**Dimensions**
wing span 34 ft 9 in (10.60 m)
length overall 25 ft 8¼ in (7.83 m)
height overall 6 ft 9 in (2.06 m)
wing area 166.3 sq ft (15.45 sq m)
**Power plant**
One 160 hp Walter Minor 6–III piston engine
**Variants**
Z–26, Z–126: earlier versions;
Z–226: Further development of Z–126;
Z–326: Further development of Z–226 with retractable
undercarriage
**First flights**
Prototype: 1947, Z–326: 1957; Z–526: 1965
**Production**
Series production of Zlin–Trener from 1947, over 1,300
of all variants built to date
**In service**
Cuba, Czechoslovakia, Egypt (UAR), Germany (East)

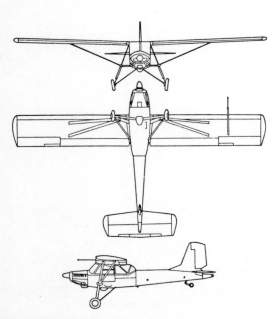

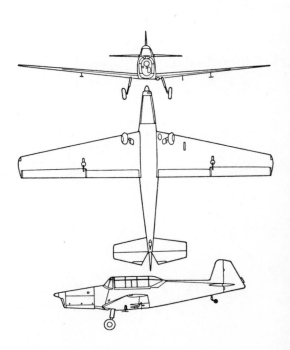

## ZLIN Z–226 'TRENER'

**Type**
Two-seat trainer
Details as for Z–526 'Trener' with the following
    exceptions
**Weights**
empty 1,257 lb (570 kg)
normal 1,786 lb (810 kg)
**Performance**
maximum speed at sea level 146 mph (235 km/hr)
maximum cruising speed 121 mph (195 km/hr)
ferry range 522 miles (840 km)
initial rate of climb 16.4 fps (5.0 m/sec)
hovering ceiling out of ground effect
**Dimensions**
wing span 33 ft 8¾ in (10.28 m)
wing area 160.4 sq ft (14.90 sq m)
**First flights**
Z–226: 1955

## AEROSPATIALE N.262D

**Type**
Light transport
**Weights**
empty 15,287 lb (6,934 kg)
normal 15,873 lb (7,200 kg)
maximum 23,369 lb (10,600 kg)
**Performance**
maximum speed at sea level 260 mph (418 km/hr)
maximum cruising speed 147 mph (397 km/hr)
range w.m.p. 652 miles (1,050 km)
ferry range 1,491 miles (2.400 km)
initial rate of climb 24.9 fps (7.6 m/sec)
service ceiling 26,247 ft (8,000 m)
**Dimensions**
wing span 71 ft 0 in (21.90 m)
length overall 63 ft 3 in (19.28 m)
height overall 20 ft 4 in (6.21 m)
wing area 592 sq ft (55.00 sq m)
**Power plant**
Two 1,360 hp Turboméca Bastan VIIA turboprops
**Payload**
2–3 man crew and 29 troops or 18 paratroops or
    12 stretcher cases and 2 medics or max 6,834 lb
    (3,100 kg) freight
**Variants**
*N.262A.B*: earlier versions, *N.262C*: civil variant of
    N.262D
**First flights**
Prototype: 24 December 1962
**Production**
*N.262A*: 65 built, inc. 21 military, from 1965–1969;
    *N.262B*: 4 built (civil); *N.262C*: 10 built from 1970;
    *N.262D*: 18 built from 1970
**In service**
N.262A,D: France, Gabon

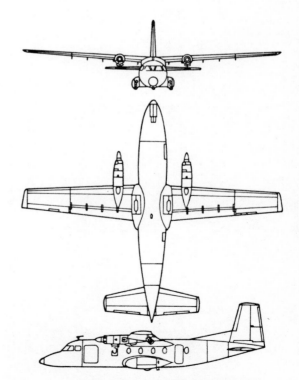

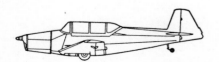

## AEROSPATIALE S.E.313B

**Type**
Light helicopter
**Weights**
empty 1,984 lb (900 kg)
maximum 3,527 lb (1,600 kg)
**Performance**
maximum speed at sea level 115 mph (185 km/hr)
maximum cruising speed 106 mph (170 km/hr)
range with 827 lb (375 kg) payload 186 miles (300 km)
ferry range 351 miles (565 km)
initial rate of climb 14.8 fps (4.5 m/sec)
service ceiling 10,172 ft (3,100 m)
hovering ceiling in ground effect 5,085 ft (1,550 m)
hovering ceiling out of ground effect 2,950 ft (900 m)
**Dimensions**
main rotor diameter 33 ft 5¾ in (10.20 m)
length of fuselage 31 ft 9¾ in (9.70 m)
height 9 ft (2.75 m)
**Power plant**
One 360 hp Turboméca Artouste IIC6 turboshaft
**Armament**
Optional: Two-four A.S.10 or A.S.11 ASMs
**Payload**
1 man crew and 4 troops or max 1,323 lb (600 kg) freight
**Variants**
*S.A.315B Lama*: Uprated engine (870 hp Artouste IIIB)
*S.A.318C* Further development
**First flights**
Prototype: 12 March 1955
**Production**
2 prototypes and 3 pre-production models;
*S.E.313B* 923 built from 1957–1965;
*S.A.315B* 62 built from 1969; 150(?) licence-built in India
   by HAL from 1972
**In service**
*S.E.313B*: Austria, Belgium, Cambodia, Cameroon, Central
   African Republic, Chad, Congo-Brazzaville, Dominican
   Republic, Finland, France, Germany (West), Great
   Britain (*Alouette AH.2*), India, Indonesia, Israel, Ivory
   Coast, Laos, Lebanon, Libya, Madagascar (Malagasy),
   Mexico, Morocco, Nigeria, Peru, Portugal, Senegal,
   South Africa, Sweden (*SKP–2*), Switzerland, Togo,
   Tunisia, Venezuela
S.A.315B: Argentine, India (Cheetah)

## AEROSPATIALE S.A.318C 'ALOUETTE' II

**Type**
Light helicopter
Details as for the S.E.313B with the following exceptions
**Weights**
empty 1,961 lb (890 kg)
maximum 3,630 lb (1,650 kg)
**Performance**
maximum speed at sea level 127 mph (205 km/hr)
maximum cruising speed 112 mph (180 km/hr)
range with 827 lb (375 kg) payload 62 miles (100 km)
ferry range 466 miles (720 km)
initial rate of climb 21.7 fps (6.6 m/sec)
service ceiling 10,800 ft (3,300 m)
**Dimensions**
length of fuselage 31 ft 11¾ in (9.75 m)
**Power plant**
One 523 hp Turboméca Astazou IIA turboshaft
**First flights**
31 January 1961
**Production**
series production from 1964, over 300 delivered or on
   order to date
**In service**
France, Germany (West)

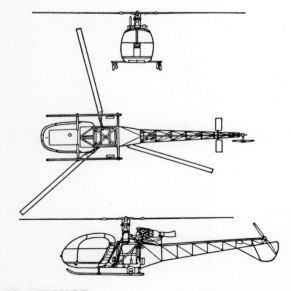

# AEROSPATIALE S.A.316A 'ALOUETTE' III

**Type**
Light transport helicopter
**Weights**
empty 2,447 lb (1,100 kg)
normal 4,189 lb (1,900 kg)
maximum 4,630 lb (2,100 kg)
**Performance**
maximum speed at sea level 131 mph (210 km/hr)
maximum cruising speed 118 mph (190 km/hr)
range 62–310 miles (100–500 km)
ferry range 341 miles (550 km)
initial rate of climb 18.0 fps (5.5 m/sec)
service ceiling 10,670 ft (3,250 m)
hovering ceiling in ground effect 5,578 ft (1,700 m)
hovering ceiling out of ground effect 1,804 ft (550 m)
**Dimensions**
main rotor diameter 36 ft 1 in (11.00 m)
length of fuselage 32 ft 10¾ in (10.03 m)
height 10 ft 1½ in (3.09 m)
**Power plant**
One 550 hp Turboméca Artouste IIIB turboshaft
**Armament**
As armed helicopter: one-two free-mounted 7.62 mm
  machine guns or 20 mm cannon, four A.S.11 or two
  A.S.12 ASMs or two rocket launchers each containing
  either eighteen or thirty-six 37 mm unguided rockets.
**Payload**
1 man crew and 6 troops or 2 stretcher cases and 2 medics
  or max 1,807 lb (820 kg) freight
**Variants**
S.A.316B, S.A.316C, S.A.319: Further developments
**First flights**
Prototype: 28 February 1959
**Production**
2 prototypes and 2 pre-production models:
*S.A.316A*: 981 built from 1961–1971; Licence-built in
  India (by HAL), Switzerland and from 1972 in Rumania;
  *S.A.316B*:—built; *S.A.316C, S.A.319* series—production
  from 1971
**In service**
*S.A.316*: Argentine, Austria, Belgium, Burma, Burundi,
  Chad, Congo, Dahomey, Denmark, Dominican Republic,
  Ecuador, Ethiopia, France, Gabon, India, Ireland, Ivory
  Coast, Jordan, Laos, Lebanon, Libya, Madagascar,
  (Malagasy), Malaysia, Mexico, Morocco, Nepal, Nether-
  lands, Pakistan, Peru, Portugal, Rhodesia, Ruanda,
  Rumania, Saudi Arabia, Singapore, South Africa,
  Switzerland, Tunisia, Venezuela, Yugoslavia
*S.A.319*: Abu Dhabi, France

# AEROSPATIALE S.A.321 'SUPER FRELON'

**Type**
Medium transport helicopter
**Weights**
empty 14,420 lb (6,540 kg)
normal 24,471 lb (11,100 kg)
maximum 27,557 lb (12,500 kg)
**Performance**
maximum speed at sea level 149 mph (240 km/hr)
maximum cruising speed 143 mph (230 km/hr)
range with 5,512 lb (2,500 kg) payload 404 miles (650 km)
ferry range 672 miles (1,080 km)
initial rate of climb 24.9 fps (7.6 m/sec)
service ceiling 11,475 ft (3,500 m)
hovering ceiling in ground effect 7,400 ft (2,250 m)
hovering ceiling out of ground effect 1,822 ft (550 m)
**Dimensions**
main rotor diameter 62 ft 0 in (18.90 m)
length of fuselage 63 ft 7¾ in (19.40 m)
height 21 ft 10¼ in (6.66 m)
**Power plant**
Three 1,550 hp Turboméca Turmo IIIC 6 turboshafts
**Payload**
2 man crew and 27–30 troops or 15 stretcher cases or max
  9,921 lb (4,500 kg) freight
**Variants**
*S.A.321G*: ASW helicopter with up to 4 homing torpedoes
S.A.321F,J: Civil variants
**First flights**
Prototype: 7 December 1962; 1st production model:
  30 November 1965
**Production**
2 prototypes and 4 pre-production models; 57 built from
  1965
**In service**
France (S.A.321G), Iran, Israel (S.A.321K), Libya, South
  Africa (S.A.321L)

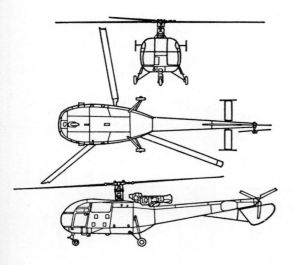

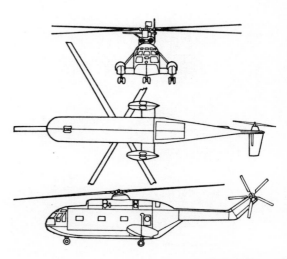

## AEROSPATIALE/WESTLAND S.A.330 'PUMA'

**Type**
Medium transport helicopter
**Weights**
empty 7,562 lb (3,430 kg)
maximum 14,110 lb (6,400 kg)
**Performance**
maximum speed at sea level 174 mph (280 km/hr)
maximum cruising speed 164 mph (265 km/hr)
range 385 miles (620 km)
ferry range 870 miles (1,400 km)
initial rate of climb 23.3 fps (7.1 m/sec)
service ceiling 15,748 ft (4,800 m)
hovering ceiling in ground effect 9,187 ft (2,800 m)
hovering ceiling out of ground effect 6,324 ft (1,900 m)
**Dimensions**
main rotor diameter 49 ft 2½ in (15.00 m)
length of fuselage 46 ft 1½ in (14.06 m)
height 13 ft 8½ in (4.18 m)
**Power plant**
Two 1,320 hp Turboméca Turmo III C4 turboshafts
**Payload**
2 man crew and 16–20 troops or 6 stretcher cases and
  4 medics or max 5,512 lb (2,500 kg) freight
**Variants**
S.A.330F: Civil variant
**First flights**
Prototype: 15 April 1965
**Production**
2 prototypes and 6 pre-production models, series produc-
  tion from 1968, over 280 delivered or on order to date
**In service**
Abu Dhabi, Algeria, Congo, France, Gabon, Great Britain
  (Puma HC. 1), Ivory Coast, Mexico, Portugal, South
  Africa

## AEROSPATIALE/WESTLAND S.A.341 'GAZELLE'

**Type**
Light helicopter
**Weights**
empty 1,875 lb (850 kg)
maximum 3,750 lb (1,700 kg)
**Performance**
maximum speed at sea level 165 mph (265 km/hr)
maximum cruising speed 149 mph (240 km/hr)
range 404 miles (650 km)
initial rate of climb 20.3 fps (6.2 m/sec)
service ceiling 16,730 ft (5,100 m)
hovering ceiling in ground effect 10,170 ft (3,100 m)
hovering ceiling out of ground effect 8,530 ft (2,600 m)
**Dimensions**
main rotor diameter 34 ft 6 in (10.50 m)
length of fuselage 31 ft 3 in (9.52 m)
height 9 ft 8½ in (2.96 m)
**Power plant**
One 592 hp Turboméca Astazou IIISN turboshaft
**Armament**
**Payload**
1 man crew and 4 troops or max 1,323 lb (600 kg) freight
**Variants**
*S.A.341G*: Civil variant
**First flights**
Prototype: 7 April 1967
**Production**
2 prototypes and 6 pre-production models, series produc-
  tion from 1971, 420 currently delivered or on order;
  Licence-built in India (by HAL), in Yugoslavia from
  1972/73 (130 built), and in Brazil by EMB (30 built)
  from 1974(?)
**In service**
France, Great Britain (AH.1, HT.2, HT.3, HCC.4)

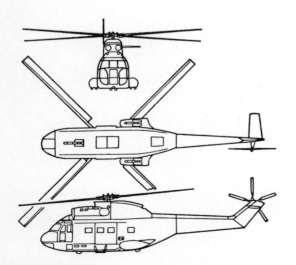

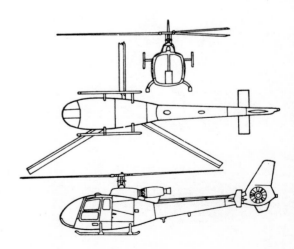

# BREGUET Br.1050 'ALIZE'

**Type**
Shipboard ASW aircraft
**Weights**
empty 12,544 lb (5,690 kg)
normal 18,078 lb (8,200 kg)
**Performance**
maximum speed at 9,840 ft (3,000 m) 292 mph (470 km/hr)
maximum cruising speed 205 mph (330 km/hr)
patrol speed at 1,480 ft (450 m): 143 mph (230 km/hr)
range 745 miles (1,200 km)
ferry range 1,783 miles (2,870 km)
initial rate of climb 22.9 fps (7.0 m/sec)
service ceiling 20,510 ft (6,250 m)
**Dimensions**
wing span 51 ft 2 in (15.60 m)
length overall 45 ft 6 in (13.87 m)
height overall 15 ft 7 in (4.75 m)
wing area 387.5 sq ft (36.00 sq m)
**Power plant**
One 1,950 hp Rolls-Royce Dart R.Da 21 turboprop
**Armament**
Max 2,150 lb (975 kg) weapon load, e.g. one homing
torpedo or three 353 lb (160 kg) depth charges in
fuselage bay and two 330 lb (150 kg) or 385 lb (175 kg)
depth charges and six 127 mm rockets or two A.S. 12
ASMs underwing
**First flights**
Prototype: 6 October 1956
1st production model: 26 March 1959
**Production**
2 prototypes; 3 pre-production and 87 production models
from 1958–1961
**In service**
France, India

# BREGUET Br.1150 'ATLANTIC'

**Type**
Maritime reconnaissance and ASW aircraft 12 man crew
**Weights**
empty 52,911 lb (24,000 kg)
maximum 95,900 lb (43,500 kg)
**Performance**
maximum speed at 19,685 ft (6,000 m) 409 mph (685 km/hr)
patrol speed at 984 ft (300 m) 199 mph (320 km/hr)
maximum cruising speed at 26,247 ft (8,000 m) 311 mph
(500 km/hr)
radius of action 620 miles (1,000 km)
ferry range 5,590 miles (9,000 km)
initial rate of climb 40.7 fps (12.4 m/sec)
service ceiling 32,809 ft (10,000 m)
**Dimensions**
wing span 119 ft 1 in (36.30 m)
length overall 104 ft 2 in (31.75 m)
height overall 37 ft 2 in (11.33 m)
wing area 1,295 sq ft (120.34 sq m)
**Power plant**
Two 6,105 hp Rolls-Royce Tyne Mk. 21 turboprops
**Armament**
Eight 434 lb (197 kg) homing torpedoes or four 1,124 lb
(510 kg) homing torpedoes, plus four A.S. 12 ASMs
**Payload**
**Variants**
Atlantic Mk. 2: Planned further development
**First flights**
Prototype: 21 October 1961
**Production**
3 prototypes and 87 production models from 1965–1973
**In service**
France, Germany (West), Italy, Netherlands (SP–13A)

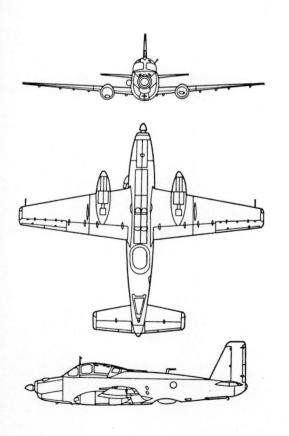

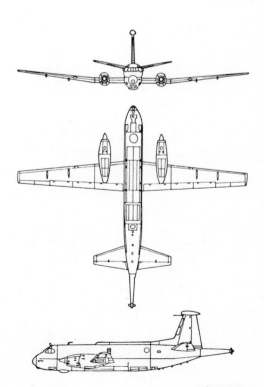

## DASSAULT M.D.315 'FLAMANT'

**Type**
Light transport
**Weights**
empty 9,348 lb (4,240 kg)
normal 12,765 lb (5,790 kg)
**Performance**
maximum speed at 3,450 ft (1,050 m) 236 mph (380 km/hr)
maximum cruising speed 186 mph (300 km/hr)
range 755 miles (1,215 km)
initial rate of climb 16.4 fps (5.0 m/sec)
service ceiling 26,250 ft (8,000 m)
**Dimensions**
wing span 67 ft 10 in (20.68 m)
length overall 41 ft 0 in (12.50 m)
height overall 14 ft 9 in (4.50 m)
wing area 508 sq ft (47.20 sq m)
**Power plant**
Two 580 hp SNECMA-Renault 12S–02–201 piston engines
**Payload**
2 man crew and max 10 troops, casualties or freight
**Variants**
M.D.312: Earlier version
**First flights**
Prototype M.D.303: 10 February 1947;
M.D.315: November 1948
**Production**
M.D.312: 142 built
M.D.315: 137 built
**In service**
Cambodia, France, Madagascar (Malagasy), Tunisia

## DASSAULT 'ETENDARD' IVM

**Type**
Single-seat shipboard strike fighter
**Weights**
empty 12,787 lb (5,800 kg)
normal 19,400 lb (8,800 kg)
maximum 22,650 lb (10,275 kg)
**Performance**
maximum speed at sea level (Mach 0.9) 684 mph
   (1,100 km/hr)
maximum speed at 36,000 ft (11,000 m) (Mach 1.02)
   674 mph (1,085 km/hr)
maximum cruising speed at 36,000 ft (11,000 m) 510 mph
   (820 km/hr)
radius of action 200–435 miles (320–700 km)
ferry range 1,740 miles (2,800 km)
initial rate of climb 328.1 fps (100 m/sec)
time to 42,000 ft (12,800 m) 6 min 0 sec
service ceiling 50,900 ft (15,500 m)
**Dimensions**
wing span 31 ft 6 in (9.60 m)
length overall 47 ft 3 in (14.40 m)
height overall 12 ft 7¾ in (3.85 m)
wing area 312 sq ft (29.00 sq m)
**Power plant**
One SNECMA Atar 8B turbojet rated at 9,700 lb
   (4,400 kg) st
**Armament**
One–two 30 mm DEFA 552 cannon, two Sidewinder
   AAMs or max 3,000 lb (1,350 kg) weapon load, e.g.
   two A.S.30 ASMs and unguided rockets or two 882 lb
   (400 kg) bombs
**Variants**
Etendard IV P: Strike fighter and reconnaissance aircraft
   with 3 cameras
Super Etendard: Planned further development 1973/74
**First flights**
Prototype: 21 May 1958
1st production model: 1 July 1961
**Production**
6 pre-production models; *IV M*: 69 built from 1961–1965;
*IV P*: 21 built from 1962–1965
**In service**
France

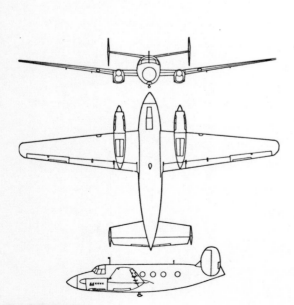

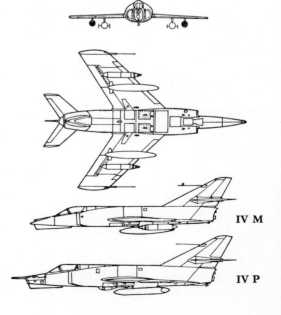

IV M

IV P

## DASSAULT (FAN JET) 'FALCON' 20 ('MYSTERE' 20)

**Type**
Light transport and trainer
**Weights**
empty 15,430 lb (7,000 kg)
normal 22,818 lb (10,350 kg)
maximum 28,660 lb (13,000 kg)
**Performance**
maximum speed at 25,000 ft (7,620 m) 533 mph (859 km/hr)
maximum cruising speed at 40,000 ft (12,200 m) 466 mph (750 km/hr)
range with 1,600 lb (725 kg) payload 1,864 miles (3,000 km)
ferry range 2,274 miles (3,595 km)
service ceiling 42,656 ft (13,000 m)
**Dimensions**
wing span 53 ft 6 in (16.30 m)
length overall 56 ft 3 in (17.15 m)
height overall 17 ft 5 in (5.32 m)
wing area 440 sq ft (41.00 sq m)
**Power plant**
Two General Electric CF-700-2D turbofans each rated at 4,250 lb (1,930 kg) st
**Payload**
2 man crew and 8–14 troops or max 3,042 lb (1,380 kg) freight
**Variants**
Civil variants
*Falcon 10*: Light transport and trainer
**First flights**
Prototype: 4 May 1963
1st production model: 1 January 1965
**Production**
Series production from 1964; 297 ordered of which over 250 delivered to date inc only 17 military variants
**In service**
Australia, Belgium, Canada, Central African Republic, France, Gabon, Ivory Coast, Jordan, Libya, Norway, Pakistan

## DASSAULT 'MIRAGE' IIIC

**Type**
Single-seat fighter and strike fighter
**Weights**
empty 13,820 lb (6,270 kg)
normal 18,636 lb (8,453 kg)
maximum 26,455 lb (12,000 kg)
**Performance**
maximum speed at sea level 926 mph (1,490 km/hr)
maximum speed at 36,000 ft (11,000 m) 1,429 mph (2,300 km/hr)
maximum cruising speed at 36,000 ft (11,000 m) (Mach 0.9) 593 mph (954 km/hr)
radius of action 180–478 miles (290–770 km)
ferry range 1,429 miles (2,300 km)
time to 36,000 ft (11,000 m) 6 min 30 sec
service ceiling 54,100 ft (16,500 m)
**Dimensions**
wing span 27 ft 0 in (8.22 m)
length overall 45 ft 1¼ in (13.75 m)
length overall (IIIB): 45 ft 8¼ in (13.93m)
height overall 13 ft 9¼ in (4.20 m)
wing area 365.9 sq ft (34.0 sq m)
**Power plant**
One SNECMA Atar 09B turbojet rated at 9,370 lb (4,250 kg)/13,228 lb (6,000 kg) st
**Armament**
Two 30 mm DEFA 552 cannon with 125 rpg and (as fighter) two AIM-9 Sidewinder AAMs and one Matra R.530 AAM or (as strike fighter) max 3,968 lb (1,800 kg) weapon load
**Variants**
*Mirage IIIA*: Earlier version
*Mirage IIIB, IIID*: Two-seat strike trainer
**First flights**
Prototype: 17 November 1956
*Mirage IIIC*: 9 October 1960
**Production**
*Mirage IIIB*: 73 built from 1962–1964
*Mirage IIIC*: 244 built from 1961–1964
*Mirage IIID*: Series production from 1966
**In service**
Fighter and strike fighter: France (IIIC), Israel (IICJ), South Africa (IIICZ)
Strike trainer: Argentine (IIIDA), Australia (IIIDO), Brazil (IIIDBR), France (IIIB,BE) Israel (IIIBJ), Lebanon (IIIBL), Pakistan (IIIDP), South Africa (IIIBZ,DZ), Spain (IIIDE=CE-11), Switzerland (IIIBS), Venezuela (IIIDV)

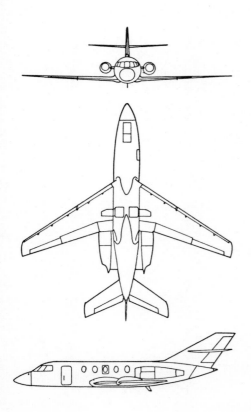

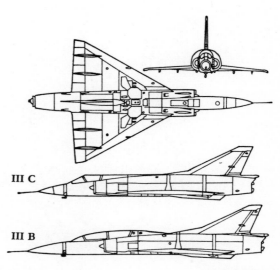

III C

III B

## DASSAULT 'MIRAGE' IIIE

**Type**
Single-seat strike fighter
**Weights**
empty 15,540 lb (7,050 kg)
normal 21,164 lb (9,600 kg)
maximum 29,760 lb (13,500 kg)
**Performance**
maximum speed at sea level 870 mph (1,400 km/hr)
maximum speed at 40,000 ft (12,200 m) (Mach 2.2)
   1,462 mph (2,350 km/hr)
maximum cruising speed at 36,000 ft (11,000 m) (Mach 0.9)
   593 mph (954 km/hr)
radius of action 180–373 miles (290–600 km)
ferry range 1,430 miles (2,300 km)
time to 49,210 ft (15,000 m) 6 min 50 sec
service ceiling 55,773 ft (17,000 m)
**Dimensions**
wing span 27 ft 0 in (8.22 m)
length overall 49 ft 3½ in (15.03 m)
height overall 13 ft 11½ in (4.25 m)
wing area 375 sq ft (34.85 sq m)
**Power plant**
One SNECMA Atar 09C turbojet rated at 9,435 lb
   (4,280 kg)/13,6710 lb (6,200 kg) st, plus optional SEPR
   844 rocket motor rated at 3,307 lb (1,500 kg) st
**Armament**
Two 30 mm DEFA 552 cannon with 125 rpg and (as
   fighter) two AIM–9 Sidewinder AAMs and one Matra
   R.530 AAM or (as strike fighter) max 3,968 lb (1,800 kg)
   weapon Load, e.g. four 882 lb (400 kg) bombs or two
   882 lb (400 kg) bombs plus one A.S.30 ASM
**Variants**
Mirage IIIEA, IIIEBR, IIIEE, IIIEL, IIIEP, IIIEV, IIIEZ:
   Export versions
Mirage IIIO, IIIS: Australian and Swiss licence-built
**First flights**
Mirage IIIE: 5 April 1961
**Production**
Series production from 1963; over 420 delivered to date
**In service**
Argentine (IIIEA), Australia (IIIO), Brazil (IIIEBR),
   France (IIIE), Lebanon (IIIEL), Pakistan (IIIEP), South
   Africa (IIIEZ), Spain (IIIEE=C–11), Switzerland (IIIS)

## DASSAULT 'MIRAGE' IIIR

**Type**
Single-seat reconnaissance aircraft
Details as for 'Mirage' IIIE with the following exceptions
**Weights**
empty 14,550 lb (6,600 kg)
**Dimensions**
length overall 50 ft 10¼ in (15.50 m)
**Variants**
Mirage IIIR, IIIRD: Single-seat reconnaissance aircraft
Mirage IIIRP, IIIRS, IIIRZ: Export versions of IIIR
**First flights**
Mirage IIIR: November 1961
**Production**
Series production from 1963; over 100 delivered to date
**In service**
France (IIIR, IIIRD), Pakistan (IIIRP), South Africa
   (IIIRZ), Switzerland (IIIRS) Venezuela (IIIEV)

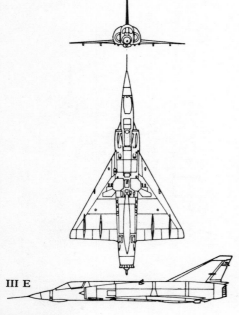

III E

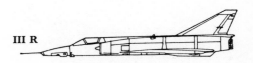

III R

## DASSAULT 'MIRAGE' IVA

**Type**
Two-seat bomber
**Weights**
empty 31,965 lb (14,500 kg)
normal 69,665 lb (31,600 kg)
maximum 73,855 lb (33,500 kg)
**Performance**
maximum speed at 39,375 ft (12,000 m) (Mach 2.2)
   1,454 mph (2,340 km/hr)
maximum cruising speed at 40,000 ft (12,200) (Mach 0.9)
   596 mph (960 km/hr)
radius of action 777–994 miles (1,250–1,600 km)
ferry range 2,485 miles (4,000 km)
time to 36,000 ft (11,000 m) 4 min 15 sec
service ceiling 65,600 ft (20,000 m)
**Dimensions**
wing span 38 ft 10½ in (11.85 m)
length overall 27 ft 1 in (23.50 m)
height overall 18 ft 6½ in (5.65 m)
wing area 840 sq ft (78.00 sq m)
**Power plant**
Two SNECMA Atar 09K turbojets each rated at 10,360 lb
   (4,700 kg)/15,400 lb (7,000 kg) st
**Armament**
Max 14,110 lb (6,400 kg) weapon load, e.g. one 50 kilo-
ton nuclear bomb or sixteen 882 lb (400 kg) bombs or
four A.S.37 Martel ASMs
**First flights**
Prototype: 17 June 1959
1st Production model: 7 December 1963
**Production**
1 prototype, 3 pre-production and 62 production models
   from 1964–1967
**In service**
France

## DASSAULT 'MIRAGE' 5

**Type**
Single-seat strike fighter
**Weights**
empty 14,550 lb (6,600 kg)
maximum 29,752 lb (13,500 kg)
**Performance**
maximum speed at sea level (Mach 1.1) 830 mph
   (1,335 km/hr)
maximum speed at 39,375 ft (12,000 m) (Mach 2.1)
   1,386 mph (2,230 km/hr)
maximum cruising speed at 36,000 ft (11,000 m) 594 mph
   (956 km/hr)
radius of action 400–745 miles (650–1,200 m)
ferry range 2,485 miles (4,000 km)
time to 36,000 ft (11,000 m) 3 min 0 sec
service ceiling 59,060 ft (18,000 m)
**Dimensions**
wing span 27 ft 0 in (8.22 m)
length overall 51 ft 0¼ in (15.55 m)
height overall 13 ft 11½ in (4.25 m)
wing area 375 sq ft (34.85 sq m)
**Power plant**
One SNECMA Atar 9C turbojet rated at 9,436 lb
   (4,280 kg)/13,670 lb (6,200 kg) st
**Armament**
Two 30 mm DEFA 552 cannon with 125 rpg and max
   8,944 lb (4,200 kg) weapon load, e.g. two 882 lb (400 kg)
   bombs, ten 500 lb (227 kg) and two 250 lb (113 kg)
   bombs plus two auxiliary tanks or one R.530 AAM
   and AIM–9 Sidewinder AAMs or rocket launchers and
   one A.S.30 ASM
**Variants**
*Mirage, 5–BR, 5–COR, 5–DR*: single-seat reconnaissance
   aircraft
*Mirage 5–BD, 5–COD, 5–DD, 5–PD*: Two-seat strike
   trainer
*Mirage Milan*: Further development with more powerful
   engine and retractable foreplanes (Moustaches)
**First flights**
Prototype: 19 May 1967; 1st production model: May 1968
**Production**
Series production from 1968. Approx. 340 currently
   delivered or on order, inc 63 Mirage 5–BA, 16 Mirage
   5BD, 27 Mirage 5–BR, 14 Mirage 5–COA, 2 Mirage
   5–COD, 2 Mirage 5–COR, 58 Mirage 5–D, 10 Mirage
   5–DD, 32 Mirage 5–DE, 10 Mirage 5–DR, 50 Mirage
   5–F, 28 Mirage 5–PA, 14 Mirage 5–P, 2 Mirage 5–PD
**In service**
Abu Dhabi, Belgium (5–BA, 5–BD, 5–BR). Colombia
   (5–COA, 5–COD, 5–COR) France (5–F), Libya (5–D,
   5–DD, 5–DE, 5–DR), Pakistan (5–PA), Peru (5–P, 5–PD)

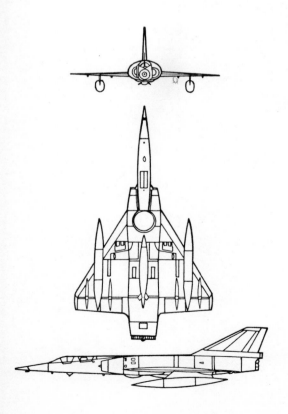

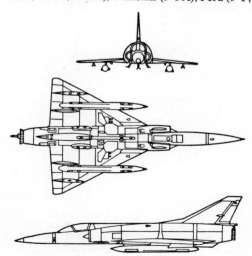

## DASSAULT 'MIRAGE' F1

**Type**
Single-seat fighter and strike fighter
**Weights**
empty 16,314 lb (7,400 kg)
normal 24,030 lb (10,900 kg)
maximum 32,850 lb (14,900 kg)
**Performance**
maximum speed at sea level (Mach 1.2) 905 mph
 (1,472 km/hr)
maximum speed at 39,375 ft (12,000 m) (Mach 2.2)
 1,450 mph (2,335 km/hr)
maximum cruising speed at 29,530 ft (9,000 m) 550 mph
 (885 km/hr)
radius of action 560 miles (900 km)–1,430 miles
 (2,300 km)
range with 4,409 lb (2,000 kg) weapon load 1,430 miles
 (2,300 km)
ferry range 2,050 miles (3,300 km)
initial rate of climb 700 fps (213.0 m/sec)
service ceiling 65,620 ft (20,000 m)
**Dimensions**
wing span 27 ft 6¾ in (8.40 m)
length overall 49 ft 2½ in (15.00 m)
height overall 14 ft 9 in (4.50 m)
wing area 269 sq ft (25.00 sq m)
**Power plant**
One SNECMA Atar 9K–50 turbojet rated at 11,023 lb
 (5,000 kg)/15,873 lb (7,200 kg) st
**Armament**
Two 30 mm DEFA 553 cannon,
*Fighter*: 1–3 Matra 530 AAMs and two A1M–9 Sidewinder AAMS
*Strike fighter*: Max 8,818 lb (4,000 kg) weapon load e.g.
 eight 882 lb (400 kg) bombs or six 80 US gall (300 l)
 napalm tanks or five rocket launchers each containing
 eighteen 70 mm rockets
**Variants**
Planned models: *F–1A*: strike fighter; *F–1B*: Two-seat
 strike trainer; *F–1C*: Fighter, *F–1E*: Fighter and strike
 fighter; *F–1R*: strike fighter and reconnaissance aircraft
 *Mirage F1 International*; planned further devleopment
**First flights**
Prototype: 23 December 1966
1st production model: 15 February 1973
**Production**
4 prototypes, 85 ordered for France and 15 each ordered
 for South Africa and Spain; delivery commencing
 1973; Plans to order a further 20 machines; 50(?) to
 be licence-built in South Africa by Atlas from
 1973/74(?)
**In service**
France, Spain, South Africa

## DASSAULT 'MYSTERE' IVA

**Type**
Single-seat fighter and strike fighter
**Weights**
empty 12,538 lb (5,687 kg)
normal 16,314 lb (7,400 kg)
maximum 18,739 lb (8,500 kg)
**Performance**
maximum speed at sea level (Mach 0.91) 695 mph
 (1,120 km/hr)
maximum speed at 39,375 ft (12,000 m) (Mach 0.94)
 615 mph (990 km/hr)
maximum cruising speed 510 mph (820 km/hr)
ferry range 1,050 miles (1,690 km)
initial rate of climb 147.6 fps (45.0 m/sec)
time to 39,375 ft (12,000 m) 10 min 30 sec
service ceiling 45,000 ft (13,700 m)
**Dimensions**
wing span 36 ft 6 in (11.12 m)
length overall 42 ft 2 in (12.85 m)
height overall 15 ft 1 in (4.60 m)
wing area 344.5 sq ft (32.00 sq m)
**Power plant**
One Hispano-Suiza Verdon 350 turbojet rated at 7,716 lb
 (3,500 kg) st
**Armament**
Two 30 mm cannon with 130 rpg and fuselage rocket
 launcher containing 55 AAMs and max 1,984 lb (900 kg)
 weapon load, e.g. two 882 lb (400 kg) bombs, or Napalm
 tanks or two rocket launchers each containing nineteen
 37 mm rockets or six ASMs
**Variants**
Mystère IVB: Single-seat fighter
**First flights**
Prototype: 28 September 1952
**Production**
IVA: 421 built from 1953–1958
IVB: 16 built in 1953
**In service**
IVA: France, India, Israel

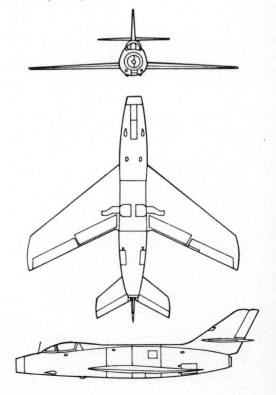

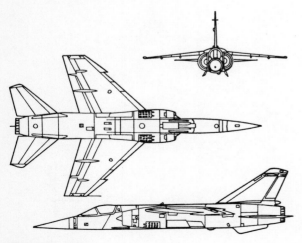

## DASSAULT 'SUPER MYSTERE' B2

**Type**
Single-seat fighter and strike fighter
**Weights**
empty 15,400 lb (6,985 kg)
normal 19,840 lb (9,000 kg)
maximum 22,046 lb (10,000 kg)
**Performance**
maximum speed at sea level (Mach 0.94) 684 mph
  (1,100 km/hr)
maximum speed at 36,000 ft (11,000 m) (Mach 1.13)
  744 mph (1,196 km/hr)
maximum cruising speed at 39,375 ft (12,000 m) 620 mph
  (1,000 km/hr)
radius of action 273 miles (440 km)
ferry range 730 miles (1,175 km)
initial rate of climb 291.3 fps (88.8 m/sec)
time to 40,000 ft (12,200 m) 5 min 0 sec
service ceiling 55,775 ft (17,000 m)
**Dimensions**
wing span 34 ft 5¼ in (10.50 m)
length overall 46 ft 1 in (14.05 m)
height overall 14 ft 10¾ in (4.54 m)
wing area 376.9 sq ft (35.02 sq m)
**Power plant**
One SNECMA Atar 101G–2 turbojet rated at 7,495 lb
  (3,400 kg)/9,700 lb (4,400 kg) st
**Armament**
Two 30 mm cannon and max 2,200 lb (1,000 kg) weapon
  load, e.g. fifty-five 68 mm rockets or two rocket
  launchers each containing 19 rockets, two 1,100 lb
  (500 kg) bombs or Napalm tanks or twelve ASMs
**First flights**
Prototype: 2 March 1955
1st production model: 26 February 1957
**Production**
5 pre-production models; 180 built from 1956–1959
**In service**
France, Israel

## MAX HOLSTE M.H. 1521M 'BROUSSARD'

**Type**
Liaison and AOP aircraft
**Weights**
empty 3,373 lb (1,530 kg)
normal 5,511 lb (2,500 kg)
maximum 5,953 lb (2,700 kg)
**Performance**
maximum speed at 3,280 ft (1,000 m) 168 mph (270 km/hr)
maximum cruising speed at 3,280 ft (1,000 m) 152 mph
  (245 km/hr)
range 746 miles (1,200 km)
initial rate of climb 18.0 fps (5.5 m/sec)
time to 5,500 ft (1,500 m) 5 min
service ceiling 18,050 ft (5,500 m)
**Dimensions**
wing span 45 ft 1 in (13.75 m)
length overall 28 ft 2½ in (8.60 m)
height overall 12 ft 1 in (2.79 m)
wing area 271.3 sq ft (25.20 sq m)
**Power plant**
One 450 hp Pratt & Whitney R–985–AN–1 Wasp piston
  engine
**Payload**
1 man crew and 5 troops or 2 stretcher cases and 2 medics
**First flights**
Prototype: 17 November 1952
1st production model: 16 June 1954
**Production**
2 prototypes; 27 pre-production and 335 production models
  from 1953–1959
**In service**
Cameroon, Central African Republic, Chad, Congo
  (Brazzaville), Dahomey, France, Gabon, Ivory Coast,
  Madagascar (Malagasy), Mali, Mauritania, Niger,
  Portugal, Senegal, Togo, Upper Volta

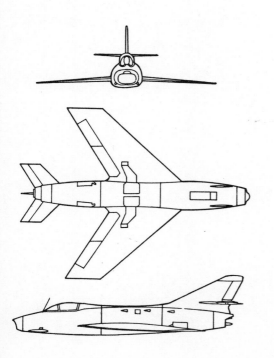

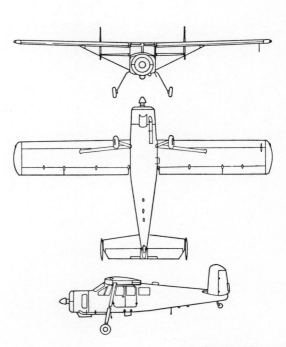

## MORANE-SAULNIER M.S.760A 'PARIS' I

**Type**
Two-seat trainer and four-seat liaison aircraft
**Weights**
empty 4,272 lb (1,941 kg)
normal 7,441 lb (3,375 kg)
maximum 7,658 lb (3,474 kg)
**Performance**
maximum speed at sea level 405 mph (652 km/hr)
maximum speed at 23,016 ft (7,015 m) 345 mph (555 km/hr)
maximum cruising speed at 16,400 ft (5,000 m) 350 mph (563 km/hr)
range 932 miles (1,500 km)
initial rate of climb 38.1 fps (11.6 m/sec)
service ceiling 32,800 ft (10,000 m)
**Dimensions**
wing span 33 ft 3 in (10.13 m)
length overall 32 ft 11 in (10.03)
height overall 8 ft 10 in (2.69 m)
wing area 193.7 sq ft (18.00 sq m)
**Power plant**
Two Turbomeca Marboré IIC turbojets each rated at 880 lb (400 kg) st
**Armament**
Two 7.5 mm machine guns plus (on some aircraft) one 30 mm cannon and max 882 lb (400 kg) weapon load, e.g. eight 110 lb (50 kg) bombs or twelve 75 mm unguided rockets
**Variants**
*M.S.706B*: Trainer and liaison aircraft with more powerful engines (two Marboré II each rated at 1,058 lb (480 kg) st); some converted up from M.S.760A standard
**First flights**
Prototype: 29 July 1954
1st production model: 27 July 1958
**Production**
165 civil and military models built from 1958–1964, inc. 48 assembled by FMA in Argentine, plus 48 M.S.706B assembled in Brazil
**In service**
M.S.760A: Argentine, France, Paraguay
M.S.760B: Brazil, France

## NORD 3202

**Type**
Two-seat trainer
**Weights**
empty 1,896 lb (860 kg)
maximum 2,690 lb (1,220 kg)
**Performance**
maximum speed at sea level 161 mph (260 km/hr)
maximum speed at 4,265 ft (1,300 m) 155 mph (250 km/hr)
maximum cruising speed at 7,960 ft (2,425 m) 146 mph (235 km/hr)
ferry range 620 miles (1,000 km)
initial rate of climb 19.7 fps (6.0 m/sec)
**Dimensions**
wing span 31 ft 2 in (9.50 m)
length overall 26 ft 8 in (8.12 m)
height overall 9 ft 3 in (2.82 m)
wing area 175 sq ft (16.26 sq m)
**Power plant**
One 260 hp Potez 4D 34B piston engine
**First flights**
Prototype: 17 April 1957
**Production**
100 built from 1959–1961
**In service**
France

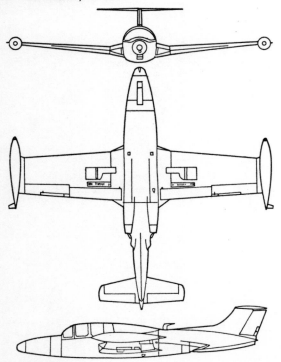

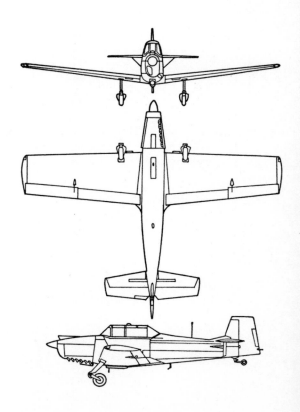

## NORD 3400

**Type**
Liaison and AOP aircraft
**Weights**
empty 2,028 lb (920 kg)
maximum 2,976 lb (1,350 kg)
**Performance**
maximum speed at sea level 147 mph (236 km/hr)
maximum cruising speed at 3,280 ft (1,000 m) 124 mph
    (200 km/hr)
range 620 miles (1,000 km)
initial rate of climb 23 fps (7.0 m/sec)
**Dimensions**
wing span 43 ft 0 in (13.11 m)
length overall 27 ft 8 in (8.42 m)
height overall 7 ft 3 in (2.21 m)
wing area 223.9 sq ft (20.80 sq m)
**Power plant**
One 260 hp Potez 4–D 34 piston engine
**Payload**
2 man crew or 1 man crew and 1 stretcher case
**First flights**
Prototype: 20 January 1958
**Production**
150 built from 1959–1961
**In service**
France

## NORD N.2501 'NORATLAS'

**Type**
Medium transport
**Weights**
empty 29,325 lb (13,302 kg)
maximum 45,423 lb (20,604 kg)
**Performance**
maximum speed at 5,000 ft (1,524 m) 250 mph (402 km/hr)
maximum cruising speed at 4,920 ft (1,500 m) 201 mph
    (324 km/hr)
maximum cruising speed at 9,840 ft (3,000 m): 208 mph
    (335 km/hr)
range w.m.p. 932 miles (1,500 km)
ferry range 2,485 miles (4,000 km)
initial rate of climb 20.67 fps (6.3 m/sec)
service ceiling 23,290 ft (7,100 m)
**Dimensions**
wing span 106 ft 7 in (32.50 m)
length overall 72 ft 0 in (21.96 m)
height overall 19 ft 8 in (6.00 m)
wing area 1,089.3 sq ft (101.20 sq m)
**Power plant**
Two 2,090 hp SNECMA (Bristol) Hercules 738 or 758
    piston engines
**Payload**
5 man crew and 45 troops or 36 paratroops or 18 stretcher
    cases and several medics or max 12,125 lb (5,500 kg)
    payload
**Variants**
Nord N.2504: ASW trainer
**First flights**
Prototype: 27 November 1950
**Production**
*N.2501*: 428 built from 1951–1961, inc 161 German
    licence-built from 1958–1961;
*N.2504*: 5 built
**In service**
N.2501: Chad, France, Greece, Israel, Niger, Portugal,
    Uganda(?)

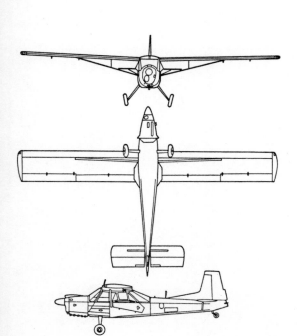

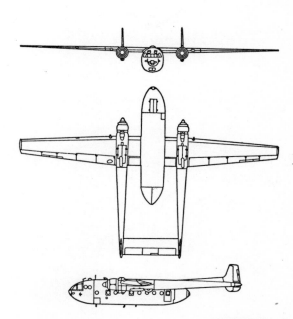

## POTEZ-AIR FOUGA C.M.170 'MAGISTER'

**Type**
Two-seat trainer
**Weights**
empty 4,740 lb (2,150 kg)
normal 6,835 lb (3,100 kg)
**Performance**
maximum speed at sea level 403 mph (648 km/hr)
maximum speed at 30,000 ft (9,140 m) 444 mph (715 km/hr)
ferry range 733 miles (1,180 km)
initial rate of climb 55.8 fps (17.0 m/sec)
service ceiling 36,000 ft (11,000 m)
**Dimensions**
wing span 37 ft 1¼ in (11.30 m)
length overall 33 ft 5½ in (10.20 m)
height overall 9 ft 2 in (2.80 m)
wing area 184.6 sq ft (17.15 sq m)
**Power plant**
Two Turboméca Marboré IIA turbojets each rated at 882 lb (400 kg) st
**Armament**
Two 7.5 or 7.62 mm machine guns, four 55 lb (25 kg) unguided rockets or two rocket launchers each containing either seven 68 mm or eighteen 37 mm rockets or two 110 lb (50 kg) bombs or two A.S.11 ASMs
**Variants**
C.M.175 Zephyr: Naval variant of C.M.170
**First flights**
Prototype: 23 July 1952
1st production model: 29 February 1956
**Production**
6 prototypes and 10 pre-production models;
*C.M.170*: 866 built from 1952–1963, inc. licence-production in Finland, Germany (West) and Israel
*C.M.175*: 32 built from 1959–1961
**In service**
*C.M.170*: Algeria, Belgium, Cambodia, Congo, Finland, France, Germany (West), Israel, Morocco, Netherlands, Nigeria, Ruanda(?), Uganda
*C.M.175*: France

## POTEZ–AIR FOUGA C.M.170–2 'SUPER-MAGISTER'

**Type**
Two-seat trainer
Details as for C.M.170 'Magister' with the following exceptions
**Weights**
empty 5,093 lb (2,310 kg)
normal 7,187 lb (3,260 kg)
**Performance**
maximum speed at sea level 435 mph (700 km/hr)
maximum speed at 463 mph (745 km/hr)
ferry range 870 miles (1,400 km)
initial rate of climb 62.3 fps (19.0 m/sec)
time to 29,500 ft (9,000 m) 14 min 30 sec
service ceiling 39,375 ft (12,000 m)
**Dimensions**
wing span 39 ft (12.15 m)
length overall 32 ft 9¾ in (10.00 m)
wing area 186.1 sq ft (17.30 sq m)
**Power plant**
Two Turboméca Marboré VIC turbojets each rated at 1,058 lb (480 kg) st
**Production**
130 built from 1963–1968
**In service**
Brazil, France, Lebanon

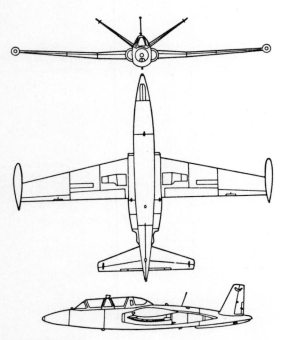

# SEPECAT 'JAGUAR' A

**Type**
Single-seat strike fighter
(A=Appui Tactique)
**Weights**
empty 14,990 lb (6,800 kg)
normal 23,000 lb (10,430 kg)
maximum 32,600 lb (14,790 kg)
**Performance**
maximum speed at 32,800 ft (10,000 m) (Mach 1.6)
   1,057 mph (1,700 km/hr)
maximum speed at 980 ft (300 m) (Mach 1.1) 820 mph
   (1,320 km/hr)
maximum cruising speed at 39,375 ft (12,000 m)
   (Mach 0.65) 429 mph (690 km/hr)
radius of action 373–710 miles (600–1,140 km)
ferry range 2,270 miles (3,650 km)
service ceiling 45,930 ft (14,000 m)
**Dimensions**
wing span 28 ft 6 in (8.69 m)
length overall (A,M,S) 50 ft 11 in (15.52 m)
length overall (B,E): 53 ft 10 in (16.42 m)
height overall 16 ft 0½ in (4.89 m)
wing area 260.3 sq ft (24.18 sq m)
**Power plant**
Two Rolls–Royce/Turbomeca RT.172 Adour 102 turbofans each rated at 4,620 lb (2,095 kg)/7,140 ft (3,240 kg)
st
**Armament**
Two 30 mm DEFA 553 cannon with 150 rpg and max
8,900 lb (4,540 kg) weapon load on 5 hard points, e.g.
2 ASMs or 2 AAMs
**Variants**
*Jaguar S* (=Strike): Single seat strike fighter
*Jaguar B, Jaguar E* (=Ecole): Two-seat strike trainer
**First flights**
Prototype: 8 September 1968
1st production model (Jaguar E): 2 November 1971
**Production**
8 prototypes; *Jaguar A,E*: total 200 to be built from
1971; *Jaguar B*: 35 to be built from 1972; *Jaguar S*:
165 to be built from 1972
**In service**
Jaguar A,E: France
Jaguar B,S: Great Britain (Jaguar GR. 1,T.2)

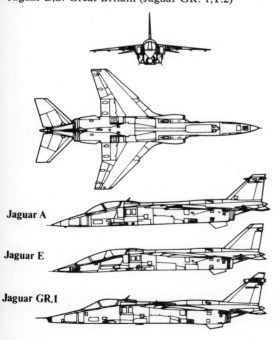

Jaguar A

Jaguar E

Jaguar GR.1

# SUD AVIATION S.O.4050 'VAUTOUR' IIN

**Type**
Two-seat all-weather fighter
**Weights**
empty 23,149 lb (10,500 kg)
normal 33,070 lb (15,000 kg)
maximum 45,635 lb (20,700 kg)
**Performance**
maximum speed at sea level (Mach 0.9) 687 mph
   (1,105 km/hr)
maximum speed at 39,375 ft (12,000 m) 590 mph
   (950 km/hr)
radius of action 745 miles (1,200 km)
ferry range 3,728 miles (6,000 km)
initial rate of climb 196.9 fps (60.0 m/sec)
time to 39,375 ft (12,000 m) 7 min
service ceiling 49,210 ft (15,000 m)
**Dimensions**
wing span 49 ft 6¼ in (15.10 m)
length overall 51 ft 2 in (15.60 m)
height overall 14 ft 1¼ in (4.30 m)
wing area 484.6 sq ft (45.10 sq m)
**Power plant**
Two SNECMA Atar 101E-3 turbojets each rated at
7,716 lb (3,500 kg) st
**Armament**
Four 30 mm DEFA 552 cannon with 100 rpg, four Matra
R.511 AAMs and 232 unguided 68 mm SNEB rockets
**Variants**
Vautour IIA: Heavy strike fighter;
Vautour IIB: Light bomber
**First flights**
Prototype: 16 October 1952
**Production**
Series production from 1955–1959, 14 prototypes and pre-
production models.
*IIA*: 30 built; *IIB*: 40 built; *IIN*: 70 built
**In service**
*IIA, IIN*: Israel, *IIB, IIN*: France

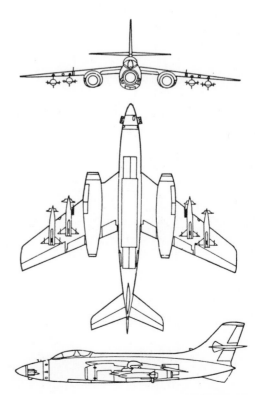

## TRANSALL C.160

**Type**
Medium transport
**Weights**
empty 63,400 lb (28,758 kg)
normal 97,450 lb (44,200 kg)
maximum 108,250 lb (49,100 kg)
**Performance**
maximum speed at 14,760 ft (4,500 m) 333 mph (536 km/hr)
maximum cruising speed at 18,050 ft (5,500 m) 319 mph (513 km/hr)
range with 17,635 lb (8,000 kg) payload 2,832 miles (4,558 km)
ferry range w.m.p. with 35,270 lb (16,000 kg) payload 730 miles (1,175 km)
initial rate of climb 24 fps (7.3 m/sec)
service ceiling 27,900 ft (8,500 m)
**Dimensions**
wing span 131 ft 3 in (40.00 m)
length overall 106 ft 3½ in (32.40 m)
height overall 38 ft 5 in (11.65 m)
wing area 1,722.7 sq ft (160.10 sq m)
**Power plant**
Two 5,665 hp Rolls–Royce Tyne R.Ty. 20 Mk. 22 turbo-props
**Payload**
4 man crew and 93 troops or 81 paratroops or 62 stretcher cases and 4 medics or max 35,270 lb (16,000 kg) freight
**First flights**
Prototype: 25 February 1963
1st production model: 21 May 1965
**Production**
3 prototypes, 6 pre-production and 169 production models (*C.160F*: 50 built, *C.160D*: 110 built, *C.160Z*: 9 built) from 1965–1972: *C.160P*: Conversion· of 4 *C.160F* for the French Postal Service.
**In service**
*C.160D*: Germany (West), Turkey;
*C.160F*: France; *C.160Z*: South Africa

## DORNIER Do–27 A–4

**Type**
Liaison and AOP aircraft
**Weights**
empty 2,368 lb (1,074 kg)
normal 4,070 lb (1,850 kg)
**Performance**
maximum speed at 3,280 ft (1,000 m) 140 mph (227 km/hr)
maximum cruising speed 130 mph (209 km/hr)
ferry range 684 miles (1,100 km)
initial rate of climb 10.8 fps (3.3 m/sec)
service ceiling 10,825 ft (3,300 m)
**Dimensions**
wing span 39 ft 4½ in (12.00 m)
length overall 31 ft 6 in (9.60 m)
height overall 9 ft 2¼ in (2.80 m)
wing area 208.8 sq ft (19.45 sq m)
**Power plant**
One 270 hp Lycoming GO–480–B1A6 piston engine
**Payload**
2 man crew and 4 troops
**Variants**
*Do–25*, *Do–27A–1*, *A–3*: Earlier versions; *Do–27B–1*, *B–2*: Trainers; *Do–27H*: More powerful (340 hp) engine; *Do–27Q*: Civil variant; *CASA C.127*: Spanish licence-built
**First flights**
Prototype: 27 June 1955
Do–27A: 17 October 1956
**Production**
628 of all versions built from 1956–1965; inc 428 Do–27A and 50 Spanish (CASA) licence-built
**In service**
Belgium, Congo, Germany (West), Israel, Nigeria, Portugal, Spain (L–9), Sweden, Switzerland, Turkey

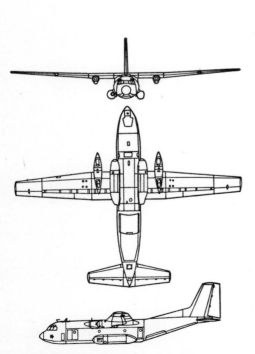

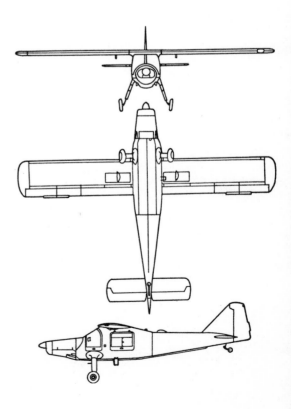

## DORNIER Do-28D 'SKYSERVANT'

**Type**
Light transport and utility aircraft
**Weights**
empty 4,775 lb (2,166 kg)
maximum 8,050 lb (3,650 kg)
**Performance**
maximum speed at 10,000 ft (3,050 m) 199 mph
maximum cruising speed at 10,000 ft (3,050 m) 178 mph
    (286 km/hr)
ferry range 1,142 miles (1,837 km)
initial rate of climb 19.7 fps (6.0 m/sec)
service ceiling 24,300 ft (7,400 m)
**Dimensions**
wing span 50 ft 10¼ in (15.50 m)
length overall 37 ft 5 in (11.40 m)
height overall 12 ft 10 in (3.90 m)
wing area 308 sq ft (28.60 sq m)
**Power plant**
Two 380 hp Lycoming IGSO-540-A1E piston engines
**Payload**
1-2 man crew and 8-12 troops or 5 stretcher cases and
    5 seated wounded
**Variants**
Do-28A, Do-28B: Civil variants
**First flights**
Prototype: 29 April 1959
*Do-28D*: 23 February 1966
**Production**
*Do-28A, B*: Approx 120 built from 1961-1966
*Do-28D*: 3 prototypes, series production since 1967,
    over 200 delivered or on order to date.
**In service**
*Do-28A, B*: Greece, Nigeria, Turkey
*Do-28D*: Germany (West), Thailand, Turkey

## ARMSTRONG WHITWORTH (HAWKER SIDDELEY) 'SEA HAWK' (F.G.A.)Mk.6

**Type**
Single-seat shipboard fighter and strike fighter
**Weights**
empty 9,722 lb (4,410 kg)
normal 13,214 lb (5,994 kg)
maximum 16,202 lb (7,349 kg)
**Performance**
maximum speed at sea level (Mach 0.79) 590 mph
    (949 km/hr)
maximum speed at 20,000 ft (6,100 m) (Mach 0.83)
    587 mph (944 km/hr)
maximum cruising speed 404 mph (650 km/hr)
radius of action 230 miles (370 km)
ferry range 932 miles (1,500 km)
initial rate of climb 95.1 fps (29 m/sec)
time to 35,000 ft (10,600 m) 11 min 50 sec
service ceiling 44,290 ft (13,500 m)
**Dimensions**
wing span 39 ft 0¼ in (11.89 m)
length overall 39 ft 8 in (12.09 m)
height overall 9 ft 0 in (2.64 m)
wing area 276.6 sq ft (25.70 sq m)
**Power plant**
One Rolls-Royce Nene 103 turbojet rated at 5,399 lb
    (2,449 kg) st
**Armament**
Four 20 mm Hispano Mk.V cannon with 200 rpg and
    max 2,000 lb (908 kg) weapon load, e.g. four 500 lb
    (227 kg) bombs or two 500 lb (227 kg) bombs and two
    rocket launchers each containing twenty 76 mm or
    sixteen 127 mm rockets
**Variants**
Sea Hawk F.1, F.2, FB.3, FGA. 4, FB.5: earlier versions
Sea Hawk Mk.50, Mk.100, Mk.101: Export models of the
    FGA.6
**First flights**
Prototype: 2 September 1947
First series production Sea Hawk F.1: 14 November 1951
**Production**
555 of all versions built from 1951-1959, inc. 107 FGA.6,
    36 Mk.50 plus 64 Mk.100 and Mk.101
**In service**
Sea Hawk FGA.6, Mk.100, M.101: India

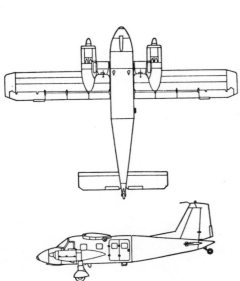
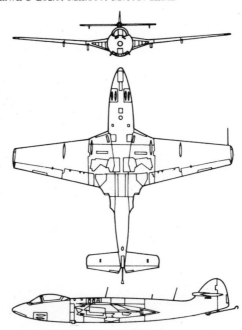

## AUSTER A.O.P.Mk.9

**Type**
Liaison and AOP aircraft
**Weights**
empty 1,590 lb (721 kg)
normal 2,125 lb (964 kg)
maximum 2,330 lb (1,057 kg)
**Performance**
maximum speed 127 mph (204 km/hr)
maximum cruising speed 110 mph (177 km/hr)
range/radius of action 242 miles (390 km)
initial rate of climb 16.1 fps (4.9 m/sec)
service ceiling 19,520 ft (5,950 m)
**Dimensions**
wing span 36 ft 5 in (11.10 m)
length overall 23 ft 8⅛ in (7.23 m)
height overall 8 ft 11 in (2.72 m)
wing area 198 sq ft (18.40 sq m)
**Power plant**
One 173 hp Blackburn Bombardier 203 piston engine
**Payload**
1 man crew and 2 troops
**Variants**
Auster D5/160: Alternative series with Lycoming piston engine
Auster AOP.6: Earlier version
**First flights**
Prototype: 19 March 1954
**Production**
Series production from 1955; 150 Portuguese licence-built by OGMA
**In service**
*AOP.9*: Congo, Great Britain, India, South Africa, Uganda
*D5*: Portugal; *AOP.6*: Libya(?)

## AVRO 'SHACKLETON' M.R.Mk.3, PHASE 3

**Type**
Maritime reconnaissance and ASW aircraft 10 man crew
**Weights**
empty 57,798 lb (26,217 kg)
normal 85,000 lb (38,555 kg)
maximum 100,000 lb (45,359 kg)
**Performance**
maximum speed at 12,000 ft (3,650 m) 302 mph (486 km/hr)
maximum cruising speed at 9,840 ft (3,000 m) 253 mph (407 km/hr)
patrol speed at 1,500 ft (460 m): 200 mph (322 km/hr)
ferry range 4,214 miles (6,783 km)
initial rate of climb 14.1 fps (4.3 m/sec)
service ceiling 19,200 ft (5,850 m)
**Dimensions**
wing span 120 ft 0 in (36.27 m)
length overall 92 ft 6 in (28.19 m)
height overall 23 ft 4 in (7.11 m)
wing area 1,458 sq ft (135.44 sq m)
**Power plant**
Four 2,450 hp Rolls–Royce Griffon 57A piston engines plus two auxiliary Rolls–Royce Bristol Viper 203 turbojets each rated at 2,500 lb (1,134 kg) st
**Armament**
Two 20 mm Hispano Mk. V cannon in nose and max 12,000 lb (5,443 kg) weapon load in fuselage bay; e.g. 3 homing torpedoes and 9 depth charges or twelve 1,000 lb (454 kg) bombs or mines or 29 troops (as auxiliary transport)
**Variants**
*MR.1, MR.2*: Earlier versions
*T.4*: Trainer
*AEW.2*: Early-warning aircraft
**First flights**
Prototype: 9 March 1949
MR.3: 2 September 1955
**Production**
*MR.1*: 77 built from 1950–1952, some converted to T.4
*MR.2*: 69 built from 1952–1955, 12 converted to AEW.2 in 1971/72
*MR.3*: 38(?) built from 1956–1959
**In service**
*AEW.2, MR.2, T.4*: Great Britain
*MR.3*: Great Britain, South Africa

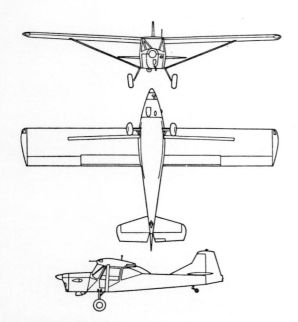

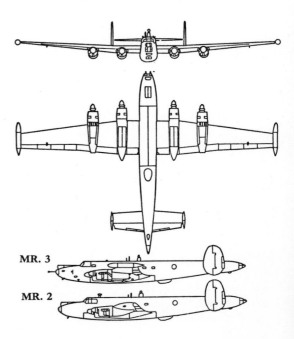

MR. 3

MR. 2

## BAC 145 'JET PROVOST' T.Mk.5

**Type**
Two-seat trainer
**Weights**
empty 5,490 lb (2,490 kg)
normal 7,629 lb (3,460 kg)
maximum 9,200 lb (4,173 kg)
**Performance**
maximum speed at sea level 409 mph (658 km/hr)
maximum speed at 25,00 ft (7,620 m) 440 mph (708 km/hr)
ferry range 900 miles (1,448 km)
initial rate of climb 66.6 fps (20.3 m/sec)
service ceiling 36,750 ft (11,200 m)
**Dimensions**
wing span 35 ft 4 in (10.77 m)
length overall 34 ft 0 in (10.36 m)
height overall 10 ft 2 in (3.10 m)
wing area 213.7 sq ft (19.80 sq m)
**Power plant**
One Rolls–Royce Viper 202 turbojet rated at 2,500 lb
   (1,134 kg) st
**Armament**
Two 7.62 mm FN machine guns with 550 rpg and (T.55)
   max 2,200 lb (1,000 kg) weapon load on 8 hardpoints,
   e.g. two 500 lb (227 kg) and six 200 lb (90.7 kg) bombs
**Variants**
*T.55*: Export version of T.5
*T.3* (Export *T.51*), *T.4* (Export *T.52*): earlier versions
**First flights**
Prototype: 26 June 1954; *T.5*: 28 February 1967
**Production**
*T.3*: *201* built from 1958–1962; *T.51*: 22 built from 1961
*T.4*: 198 built from 1961; *T.52*: 43 built
*T.5*: 110 built from 1968–1972/73; *T.55* 5 built
**In service**
*T.5*: Great Britain; *T.51*: Ceylon (Sri Lanka), Kuwait,
   Sudan
*T.52*: Iraq, Sudan, South Yemen, Venezuela
*T.55*: Sudan

## BAC 167 'STRIKEMASTER'

**Type**
Two-seat trainer and light ground-attack aircraft
**Weights**
empty 5,849 lb (2,760 kg)
normal 8,353 lb (3,615 kg)
maximum 11,500 lb (5,216 kg)
**Performance**
maximum speed at sea level 450 mph (724 km/hr)
maximum speed at 20,000 ft (6,100 m) 472 mph (760 km/hr)
radius of action 145–250 miles (230–400 km)
ferry range 1,680 miles (2,700 km)
initial rate of climb 85.3 fps (26.0 m/sec)
time to 30,000 ft (9,150 m) 8 min 45 sec
service ceiling 40,000 ft (12,200 m)
**Dimensions**
wing span 36 ft 11 in (11.25 m)
length overall 33 ft 8¼ in (10.27 m)
height overall 10 ft 2 in (3.10 m)
wing area 213.7 sq ft (19.80 sq m)
**Power plant**
One Rolls–Royce Viper 535 turbojet rated at 3,420 lb
   (1,547 kg) st
**Armament**
Two 7.62 mm FN machine guns with 550 rpg and max.
   3,000 lb (1,360 kg) weapon load on 8 hard points
**Variants**
*Mk. 80–Mk. 89*: Export versions
**First flights**
Prototype: 26 October 1967
**Production**
Over 101 built from the end of 1968
**In service**
*Mk. 80*: Saudi Arabia, *Mk. 81*: South Yemen
*Mk. 82*: Oman, *Mk. 83*: Kuwait, *Mk. 84*: Singapore
*Mk. 87*: Kenya, *Mk. 88*: New Zealand
*Mk. 89*: Ecuador

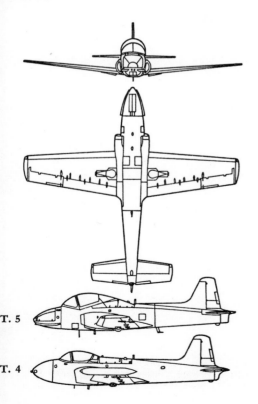

T. 5

T. 4

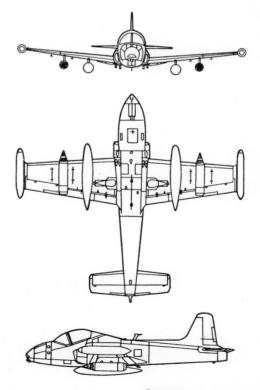

## BAC 'LIGHTNING' F.Mk.6

**Type**
Single-seat all-weather fighter and strike fighter
**Weights**
normal 39,683 lb (18,000 kg) up to 41,888 lb (19,000 kg)
maximum 47,995 lb (21,770 kg)
**Performance**
maximum speed at 36,000 ft (11,000 m) (Mach 2.2)
1,450 mph (2,335 km/hr)
maximum cruising speed at 36,000 ft (11,000 m)—39,000 ft
(12,000 m) 595 mph (957 km/hr)
range 746 miles (1,200 km)
initial rate of climb 833 fps (254.0 m/sec)
time to 40,000 ft (12,200 m) 2 min 30 sec
service ceiling 60,000 ft (18,300 m)
**Dimensions**
wing span 34 ft 10 in (10.61 m)
length overall 55 ft 3 in (16.84 m)
height overall 19 ft 7 in (5.97 m)
wing area 474.4 sq ft (44.08 sq m)
**Power plant**
Two Rolls–Royce RB 146 Avon 301 turbojets each rated
at 12,690 lb (5,756 kg)/16,300 lb (7,393 kg) st
**Armament**
F.6: Two Red Top or Firestreak AAMs or forty-four
51 mm rockets and (F.53) two weapon packs each containing one 30 mm Adem cannon with 120 rpg and two
1,000 lb (454 kg) bombs or eighteen 68 mm SNEB
rockets
**Variants**
*F.1, F.1A, F.2 (Export version F.52), F.3*: earlier versions
*T.4 (Export version T.54), T.5 (Export version T.55)*:
Two-seat strike trainers
**First flights**
Prototype: 4 April 1957
1st production model: April 1958; *F.6*: 16 June 1965
**Production**
5 prototypes, 20 pre-production models; series production
from 1958–1970; *F.1*: 20 built *F.1A*: 28 built; *F.2*:
44 built, of which 30 converted to F.2A and 4 to F.52;
*F.3*: 58 built; *F.6*: 67 built; *F.53*: 46 built; *T.4 and
T.5*: over 20 built; *T.54*: 2 built; *T.55*: 8 built
**In service**
*F.1, F.1A, F.2, F.2A, F.3, F.6, T.4, T.5*: Great Britain
*F.52, T.54*: Saudi Arabia
*F.53, T.55*: Kuwait, Saudi Arabia

## BAC 'VC10' C.Mk. 1

**Type**
Strategic transport
**Weights**
empty 146,979 lb (66,226 kg)
maximum 321,995 lb (146,059 kg)
**Performance**
maximum speed at 30,000 ft (9,140 m) (Mach 0.86)
580 mph (933 km/hr)
maximum cruising speed 38,000 ft (11,600 m) 518 mph
(834 km/hr)
range w.m.p. 3,899 miles (6,275 km)
range with 24,000 lb (10,886 kg) payload 5,370 miles
(8,642 km)
**Dimensions**
wing span 146 ft 2 in (44.55 m)
length overall 165 ft 11½ in (50.60 m)
height overall 40 ft (12.20 m)
wing area 2,932 sq ft (270.40 sq m)
**Power plant**
Four Rolls–Royce Conway R.Co.43 turbofans each rated
at 22,500 lb (10,206 kg) st
**Payload**
4–5 man crew and 150 troops and max 19,057 lb (8,644 kg)
freight or 78 stretcher cases and 8 medics or max
57,386 lb (26,030 kg) payload
**Variants**
VC10 (Series 1100), Super VC10: Civil versions
**First flights**
Prototype: 29 July 1962;
VC10C.1: 26 November 1965
**Production**
VC10C.1: 14 built from 1965–1968
**In service**
Great Britain

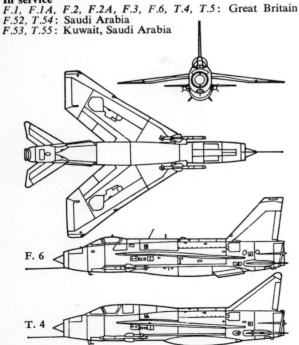

F. 6

T. 4

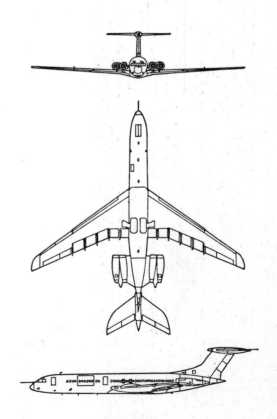

## BEAGLE 'BASSET' C.C.Mk. 1

**Type**
Liaison aircraft
**Weights**
empty 4,620 lb (2,095 kg)
maximum 7,518 lb (3,410 kg)
**Performance**
maximum speed at sea level 220 mph (354 km/hr)
maximum cruising speed at 10,000 ft (3,050 m) 207 mph
   (333 km/hr)
range 990 miles (1,593 km)
ferry range 1,805 miles (2,905 km)
initial rate of climb 19.4 fps (5.9 m/sec)
service ceiling 17,503 ft (5,335 m)
**Dimensions**
wing span 45 ft 9 in (13.95 m)
length overall 33 ft 9½ in (10.29 m)
height overall 11 ft 3 in (3.43 m)
wing area 208.7 sq ft (19.85 sq m)
**power plant**
Two 310 hp Rolls–Royce/Continental GIO–470–A piston
   engines
**Payload**
1 man crew and 7 troops or 2 stretcher cases and 1 medic
**Variants**
B.206: Civil variant
**First flights**
Prototype *B.206X*: 15 August 1961
prototype *Basset*: 24 December 1964
**Production**
Basset: 20 built from 1964–1966
**In service**
Great Britain

## BRISTOL 'BRITANNIA' C.Mk. 1

**Type**
Heavy transport
**Weights**
empty 87,400 lb (39,644 kg)
empty (as freighter) 82,853 lb (37,582 kg)
maximum 180,118 lb (81,700 kg)
**Performance**
maximum speed at 21,000 ft (6,400 m) 397 mph (639 km/hr)
maximum cruising speed 356 mph (574 km/hr)
range w.p.m. 4,310 miles (6,936 km)
range with 23,370 lb (10,602 kg) payload 5,310 miles
   (8,545 km)
initial rate of climb 21.7 fps (6.6 m/sec)
service ceiling 30,000 ft (9.150 m)
**Dimensions**
wing span 142 ft 3½ in (43.38 m)
length overall 124 ft 3 in (37.89 m)
height overall 37 ft 6 in (11.43 m)
wing area 2,074.2 sq ft (192.70 sq m)
**Power plant**
Four 4,445 hp Bristol Siddeley Proteus 765 turboprops
**Payload**
4 man crew and 139 troops or 53 stretcher cases and 6
   medics or max 35,000 lb (15,876 kg) freight
**Variants**
Britannia C.2: Heavy transport
**First flights**
Prototype: 29 December 1958
**Production**
C.1: 20 built from 1959–1960
C.2: 3 built
**In service**
Great Britain

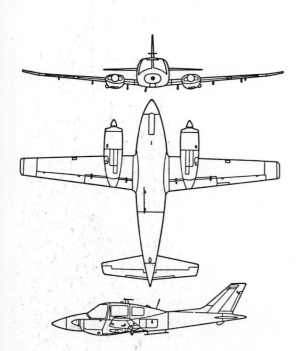

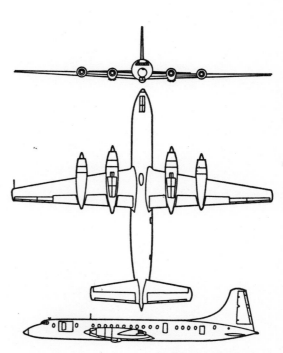

## BRITTEN–NORMAN BN–2A 'ISLANDER'

**Type**
Light transport
**Weights**
empty 3,587 lb (1,627 kg)
normal 6,000 lb (2,722 kg)
maximum 6,300 lb (2,857 kg)
**Performance**
maximum speed at sea level 170 mph (273 km/hr)
maximum cruising speed at 7,000 ft (2,140 m) 160 mph (257 km/hr)
range 717 miles (1,154 km)
ferry range 1,264 miles (2,035 km)
initial rate of climb 17.4 fps (5.3 m/sec)
service ceiling 14,600 ft (4,450 m)
**Dimensions**
wing span 49 ft 0 in (14.94 m)
length overall 35 ft 8 in (10.87 m)
height overall 13 ft 8 in (4.16 m)
wing area 325 sq ft (30.20 sq m)
**Power plant**
Two 260 hp Lycoming 0–540–E4C5 piston engines
**Payload**
1–2 man crew and 8–9 troops or 2 stretcher cases and 2 medics
**Variants**
*Defender*: With weapon hard points and radar
*BN–2A–8S*: With lengthened fuselage
**First flights**
Prototype: 12 June 1965
1st production model: 20 August 1966
**Production**
Over 350 delivered or on order by 1972/73; parts licence-built in Rumania by IRMA
**In service**
Abu Dhabi, Ghana, Guyana, Mexico, Turkey

## DeHAVILLAND (HAWKER SIDDELEY) D.H.104 'DOVE'

**Type**
Light transport and trainer
**Weights**
empty 6,325 lb (2,869 kg)
maximum 8,950 lb (4,060 kg)
**Performance**
maximum speed at 8,500 ft (2,590 m) 230 mph (370 km/hr)
maximum cruising speed at 8,000 ft (2,440 m) 210 mph (338 km/hr)
range 385 miles (620 km)
ferry range 880 miles (1,416 km)
initial rate of climb 18.7 fps (5.7 m/sec)
service ceiling 21,720 ft (6.620 m)
**Dimensions**
wing span 57 ft 0 in (17.37 m)
length overall 39 ft 3 in (11.96 m)
height overall 13 ft 4½ in (4.08 m)
wing area 334.7 sq ft (31.10 sq m)
**Power plant**
Two 400 hp Bristol Siddeley Gipsy Queen 70 Mk. 3 piston engines
**Payload**
2 man crew and 5–11 troops
**Variants**
*Devon C.1 and C.2, Sea Devon C.20*: Military variants of 'Dove' for Great Britain
**First flights**
Prototype: 25 September 1945
**Production**
Over 530 built from 1946–1964, inc over 30 *Devon C.1* and 13 *Sea Devon C.20*. *Devon C.1s* subsequently converted to *Devon C.2* with more powerful engines (Gipsy Queen 175)
**In service**
Argentine, Ceylon, Ethiopia, Great Britain (Devon C.1, C.2, Sea Devon C.20), India (Devon), Ireland, Jordan, Lebanon, Malaysia, New Zealand (Devon C.1)

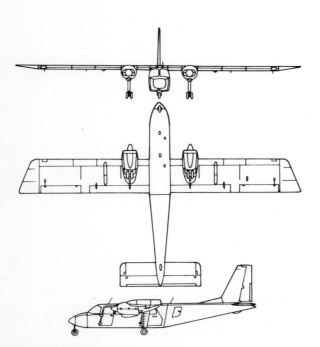

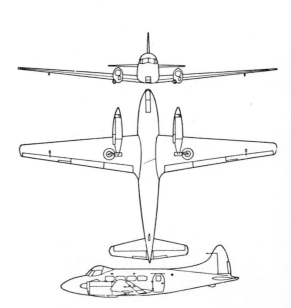

## DeHAVILLAND (HAWKER SIDDELEY) D.H.114 'HERON' SRS.2D

**Type**
Light transport
**Weights**
empty 8,484 lb (3,848 kg)
maximum 13,500 lb (6,124 kg)
**Performance**
maximum cruising speed at 4,000 ft (1,220 m) 191 mph
(306 km/hr)
range/radius of action 500 miles (805 km)
ferry range 1,785 miles (2,873 km)
initial rate of climb 18.7 fps (5.7 m/sec)
service ceiling 17,200 ft (5,240 m)
**Dimensions**
wing span 71 ft 5½ in (21.79 m)
length overall 48 ft 5 in (14.78 m)
height overall 15 ft 7 in (4.75 m)
wing area 4.99 sq ft (46.40 sq m)
**Power plant**
Four 250 hp Bristol Siddeley Gipsy Queen 30 Mk. 2 piston
engines
**Payload**
2 man crew and 14 troops or max 3,053 lb (1,385 kg)
freight
**Variants**
*Heron Srs.1*: Light transport with fixed undercarriage
**First flights**
Prototype: 10 May 1950; *Srs.2*: 14 December 1952
**Production**
Approx 150 of both series built from 1950–1964
**In service**
*Heron Srs.2D*: Ceylon (Sri Lanka), Ghana, Great Britain,
Iraq, Jordan, Malaysia

## DeHAVILLAND D.H.115 'VAMPIRE' T.Mk. 11

**Type**
Two-seat trainer
**Weights**
empty 8,410 lb (3,815 kg)
normal 11,067 lb (5,020 kg)
maximum 13,610 lb (6,170 kg)
**Performance**
maximum speed at sea level (Mach 0.7) 524 mph
(844 km/hr)
maximum speed at 20,000 ft (6,100 m) (Mach 0.71)
540 mph (870 km/hr)
maximum cruising speed at 40,000 ft (12,200 m) 403 mph
(650 km/hr)
ferry range 634 miles (1,020 km)
initial rate of climb 72.5 fps (22.1 m/sec)
service ceiling 40,000 ft (12,200 m)
**Dimensions**
wing span 38 ft 0 in (11.58 m)
length overall 34 ft 5 in (10.49 m)
height overall 6 ft 7 in (2.00 m)
wing area 261.0 sq ft (24.25 sq m)
**Power plant**
One DeHavilland Goblin 35 turbojet rated at 3,450 lb
(1,565 kg) st
**Armament**
*T.11*: Two 20 mm Hispano 404 cannon, two 500 lb (227 kg)
bombs and eight unguided rockets;
*T.55*: Four 20 mm cannon and max 1,477 lb (670 kg)
weapon load
**Variants**
*Vampire T.55*: Export version of T.11;
*Sea Vampire T.22*: Shipboard trainer;
*Vampire T.33, T.34, T.35*: Australian licence-built T.11;
*Vampire F.1, F.3, FB.5, FB.6, FB.9, FB.50*: Single-seat
strike fighters, four 20 mm cannon and max 2,000 lb
(903 kg) weapon load
**First flights**
Prototype: 15 November 1950
**Production**
Series production from 1951–1958, 2 prototypes; *T.11* and
*T.55*: *731* built; *T.22*: 73 built; *T.33, T.34* and *T.35*:
109 built
**In service**
*T.11*: Jordon, Mexico, Rhodesia, South Africa;
*T.22*: Chile; *T.34, T.35*: Australia
*T.55*: Burma, Chile, India, Ireland, South Africa,
Switzerland, Venezuela
*Vampire—strike fighter*: Dominican Republic (F.1, FB.50),
Mexico (F.3), Rhodesia (FB.9), South Africa (FB.5,
FB.9), Venezuela (FB.5)

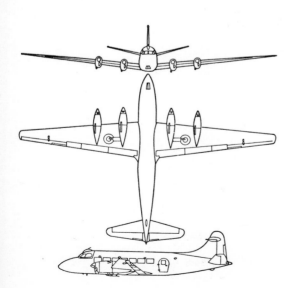

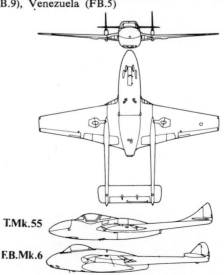

T.Mk.55

F.B.Mk.6

## DeHAVILLAND 'VENOM' F.B.Mk.50

**Type**
Single-seat strike fighter
**Weights**
normal 13,650 lb (6,192 kg)
maximum 15,700 lb (7,122 kg)
**Performance**
maximum speed at sea level 581 mph (936 km/hr)
maximum speed at 20,000 ft (6,100 m) (Mach 0.805)
   565 mph (911 km/hr)
ferry range 1,000 miles (1,610 km)
initial rate of climb 103.3 fps (31.5 m/sec)
service ceiling 37,100 ft (11,300 m)
**Dimensions**
wing span 41 ft 9 in (12.70 m)
length overall 32 ft 11¼ in (10.06 m)
height overall 6 ft 2 in (1.88 m)
wing area 279.8 sq ft (26.00 sq m)
**Power plant**
One DeHavilland Ghost 103 turbojet rated at 4,850 lb
   (2,200 kg) st
**Armament**
Four 20 mm Hispano 804 cannon and max 2,000 lb
   (908 kg) weapon load
**Variants**
*Venom FB.1, FB.4*: Single-seat strike fighters;
*Venom NF.2 and 3*: Two-seat night fighters;
*Sea Venom F.(AW) 20, 21, 22*: Shipboard strike fighters
   (Export version FAW.53)
**First flights**
Prototype Venom: 2 September 1949
**Production**
*Venom*: Series production from 1950–1957
*Venom FB.50*: 250 licence–built in Switzerland;
*Sea Venom*: 206 built
**In service**
*FB.4*: Venezuela
*FB.50*: Switzerland

## ENGLISH ELECTRIC 'CANBERRA' B.(I)Mk.8

**Type**
Two- to three-seat bomber and reconnaissance
   aircraft
**Weights**
empty 23,170 lb (10,510 kg)
normal 47,000 lb (21,319 kg)
maximum 51,000 lb (23,134 kg)
**Performance**
maximum speed at sea level (Mach 0.68) 510 mph
   (821 km/hr)
maximum speed at 40,000 ft (12,200 m) (Mach 0.83)
   560 mph (901 km/hr)
maximum cruising speed 404 mph (650 km/hr)
range 808 miles (1,300 km)
ferry range 3,600 miles (5,792 km)
initial rate of climb 60 fps (18.3 m/sec)
service ceiling 48,000 ft (14,630 m)
**Dimensions**
wing span 63 ft 4¼ in (19.31 m)
length overall 65 ft 5¾ in (19.96 m)
height overall 15 ft 6½ in (4.74 m)
wing area 963.2 sq ft (89.50 sq m)
**Power plant**
Two Rolls–Royce Avon 109 turbojets each rated at
   7,500 lb (3,402 kg) st
**Armament**
*B.8*: Four 20 mm Hispano Mk.V cannon, max 3,000 lb
   (1,362 kg) weapon load in fuselage bay plus 2,000 lb
   (908 kg) weapon load underwing, e.g. five 1,000 lb
   (454 kg) bombs
**Variants**
*B.(I)12, B.(I)58*: Export versions of B.(I)8; *B.2*: Earlier
   version; *B.15*: conversion of B.6; *B.20*: Australian
   licence built B.2; *E.15*: ECM aircraft; *PR.3, 7, 9* and
   *57*: Reconnaissance aircraft; *T.4, 13, 21* and *22*:
   Strike trainers; *T.11* and *17*: Radar trainers, *TT.18*:
   Target-towing aircraft
**First flights**
Prototype: 13 May 1949; B.(I)8: 23 July 1954
**Production**
Series production from 1949–1961; numerous conversions
   by 1971; *B.2*: 424 built; *B.6*: 118 built; *B.8*: 90 built;
   *B.20*: 49 built; *B.58*: 66 built; *PR.3*: 36 built; *PR.7*:
   74 built; *PR.9*: 45 built; *T.4*: 75 built
**In service**
Argentine (B.62, T.64), Ecuador (B.6), Ethiopia (B.52),
   Great Britain (B.2, B.6, B.15, E.15, PR.7, PR.9, T.4, T.11,
   T.17, T.19, T.22, TT.18), India B.(I)58, B.66, PR.57, T.4,
   T.67), Peru (B.72, B(I)78, T.74), Rhodesia (B.2, T.4),
   South Africa (B.(I.)12, T.4), Venezuela (B.82, B.(I)88,
   PR.83, T.84)

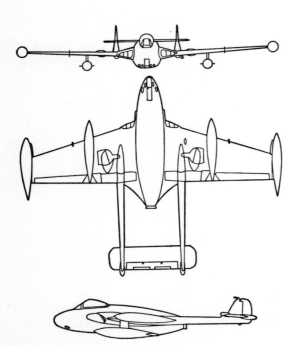

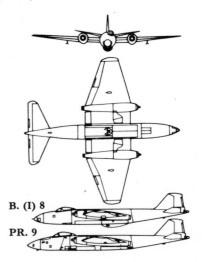

B. (I) 8

PR. 9

## ENGLISH ELECTRIC 'CANBERRA' B.15

**Type**
Light bomber
Details as for B.(I)Mk.8 with the following exceptions
**Weights**
empty 21,760 lb (9,870 kg)
normal 46,000 lb (20,866 kg)
maximum 49,000 lb (22,226 kg)
**Performance**
maximum speed at sea level 518 mph (834 km/hr)
maximum speed at 40,000 ft (12,200 m) 570 mph (917 km/hr)
ferry range 3,100 miles (4,988 km)
initial rate of climb 61.7 fps (18.8 m/sec)
**Armament**
Max 8,000 lb (3,632 kg) weapon load, e.g. eight 1,000 lb
   (454 kg) bombs

## FAIREY 'GANNET' A.E.W.Mk.3

**Type**
Shipboard early-warning aircraft, 3 man crew
**Weights**
normal 21,000 lb (9,525 kg)
maximum 24,967 lb (11,325 kg)
**Performance**
maximum speed at 5,000 ft (1,525 m) 250 mph (402 km/hr)
patrol speed 130–140 mph (210–225 km/hr)
range 800 miles (1,290 km)
service ceiling 25,000 ft (7,620 m)
**Dimensions**
wing span 54 ft 6¾ in (16.61 m)
length overall 44 ft 0 in (13.41 m)
height overall 6 ft 10 in (5.13 m)
wing area 490 sq ft (45.52 sq m)
**Power plant**
One 3,875 hp Bristol Siddeley Double Mamba 102
   turboprop
**Variants**
Gannet COD.4: Shipboard liaison aircraft
**First flights**
Prototype: 20 August 1958
**Production**
AEW.3: 38 built from 1958–1961
COD.4:
**In service**
AEW.3, COD.4: Great Britain

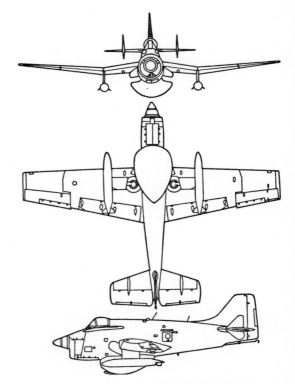

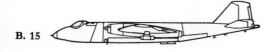

B. 15

# HANDLEY PAGE 'VICTOR' B.(S.R.)Mk.2

**Type**
Strategic reconnaissance aircraft and bomber
5 man crew
**Weights**
maximum 200,180 lb (90,800 kg)
**Performance**
maximum speed at 45,930 ft (14,000 m) (Mach 0.95)
630 mph (1,014 km/hr)
maximum cruising speed at 55,000 ft (16,780 m) 610 mph
(982 km/hr)
radius of action 2,300–2,485 miles (3,700–4,000 km)
(as reconnaissance aircraft)
ferry range 5,965 miles (9,600 km)
service ceiling 60,000 ft (18,300 m)
**Dimensions**
wing span 120 ft 0¼ in (36.58 m)
length overall 114 ft 11 in (35.03 m)
height overall 30 ft 1¼ in (9.18 m)
wing area 2,594.1 sq ft (241.00 sq m)
**Power plant**
Four Rolls–Royce Conway R.Co.17Mk.201 turbofans each
rated at 19,750 lb (8,959 kg) st
**Armament**
As bomber: Max 35,032 lb (15,890 kg) weapon load, e.g.
thirty-five 1,000 lb (454 kg) bombs or one Blue Steel
air-to-surface guided weapon
**Variants**
*B.1, B.1A*: Heavy bombers converted to K.1A tankers
*B.2*: Heavy bomber, 9 converted to B.(SR)2 reconnaissance
aircraft and 17 converted to K.2 tankers
**First flights**
Prototype: 24 December 1952
*B.1*: 1 February 1956
*B.2*: 20 February 1959
**Production**
2 prototypes
*B.1*: 46 built from 1956–1958
*B.2*: 28 built from 1960–1964, conversions to B.(SR) and
K.2 by 1970/71
**In service**
B.(SR)2, K.1A, K.2: Great Britain

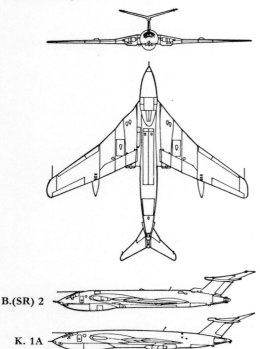

B.(SR) 2

K. 1A

# HAWKER 'HUNTER' F.(G.A.)Mk.9

**Type**
Single-seat fighter and strike fighter
**Weights**
empty 14,400 lb (6,532 kg)
normal 18,386 lb (8,340 kg)
maximum 24,699 lb (11,158 kg)
**Performance**
maximum speed at sea level (Mach 0.94) 714 mph
(1,150 km/hr)
maximum speed at 36,000 ft (11,000 m) (Mach 0.95)
627 mph (1,009 km/hr)
radius of action 217–354 miles (350–570 km)
ferry range 1,864 miles (3,000 km)
initial rate of climb 286.7 fps (87.4 m/sec)
time to 45,930 ft (14,000 m) 6 min 45 sec
service ceiling 55,000 ft (16,760 m)
**Dimensions**
wing span 33 ft 8 in (10.26 m)
length overall 45 ft 10½ in (13.98 m)
height overall 13 ft 1¾ in (4.01 m)
wing area 349 sq ft (32.42 sq m)
**Power plant**
One Rolls–Royce Avon 207 turbojet rated at 10,150 lb
(4,604 kg) st
**Armament**
Four 30 mm Aden cannon and max 3,000 lb (1,816 kg)
weapon load, e.g. two 1,000 lb (454 kg) or 2,000 lb
(908 kg) bombs or twenty-four 76.2 mm rockets
**Variants**
*F.1, F.2, F.4, GA.11, F.5, F.6*: Earlier versions; *F.50,
F.51, F.52*: Export versions of F.4; *F.56, Mk.58*: Export
versions of F.6; *T.7, T.7A, T.8, T.53, T.66, T.66B*: Two-
seat strike trainers; *FGA.9*: Strike fighter, conversion
of F.6; *FR.10*: Strike fighter and reconnaissance aircraft,
conversion of F.6
**First flights**
Prototype: 20 July 1951; *F.6*: 25 March 1955
**Production**
Total of 1,972 built from 1954–1961(?) (inc 445 built in the
Netherlands), over 526 Hunters modernised or con-
verted to date
**In service**
F.6 and FGA.9 strike fighters and T.7 strike trainer: Abu
Dhabi (FGA.76, FR.76A, T.76A), Chile (FGA.71, FR.10,
T.72), Great Britain (F.6, FGA.9, FR.10, GA.11, T.7,
T.7A, T.8), India (F.6, FGA.56, T.66), Iraq, (F.6, FGA.59,
T.69), Jordan (FGA.9, FGA.73, T.66B), Kuwait
(FGA.57, T.67), Lebanon (F.6, FGA.9, T.69), Oman
(FGA.76), Peru (F.52, T.62), Qatar (FGA.78), Rhodesia
(FGA.57, T.52), Singapore (FGA.74, FR.74, T.75),
Switzerland (Mk.58, Mk.58A)

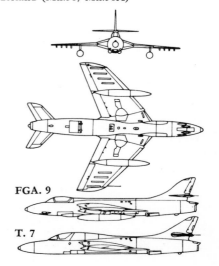

FGA. 9

T. 7

## HAWKER SIDDELEY 'ANDOVER' C.Mk.1

**Type**
Medium transport
**Weights**
empty 26,616 lb (12,073 kg)
maximum 50,001 lb (22,680 kg)
**Performance**
maximum speed at 15,000 ft (4,570 m) 301 mph
   (485 km/hr)
maximum cruising speed at 20,000 ft (6,100 m) 258 mph
   (415 km/hr)
range/w.m.p. 374 miles (602 km)
range with 10,000 lb (4,536 kg) payload 1,186 miles
   (1,909 km)
initial rate of climb 19.7 fps (6.0 m/sec)
service ceiling 24,020 ft (7,320 m)
**Dimensions**
wing span 98 ft 3 in (29.95 m)
length overall 77 ft 11 in (23.75 m)
height overall 30 ft 1 in (9.17 m)
wing area 829 sq ft (77.20 sq m)
**Power Plant**
Two 3,245 hp Rolls–Royce Dart R.Da.12.Mk.201C
   turboprops
**Payload**
4 man crew and 32—44 troops or 26 paratroops and
   2 dispatchers or 18 stretcher cases, 5 seated wounded
   and 3 medics or max 14,750 lb (6,691 kg) freight
**Variants**
*H.S. 748 series 2 and 2A*: Civil airliners and special
   military VIP and command transports
*HS. 748 series 1*: Earlier civil variant
**First flights**
Prototype: 24 June 1960; *Andover C.1*: 9 July 1965
**Production**
*Andover C.1*: 31 built from 1965–1967
*H.S. 748 series 1*: 18 built from 1961–1962
*H.S. 748 series 2 and 2A*: Over 273 built from 1962 (inc
   only a few as military VIP transports) plus 65 Indian
   licence-built by HAL from 1961–1976
**In service**
*Andover C.1*: Great Britain
*H.S. 748 series 2 and 2A*: Argentine, Australia, (C.2, T.4),
   Brazil, Brunei, Chile, Colombia, Ecuador, Great Britain
   (Andover CC.2), India, Thailand, Venezuela, Zambia

## HAWKER SIDDELEY 'ARGOSY' C.Mk.1

**Type**
Medium transport
**Weights**
empty 58,202 lb (26,400 kg)
normal 97,000 lb (43,999 kg)
maximum 47,628 lb (47,628 kg)
**Performance**
maximum cruising speed at 20,000 ft (6,100 m) 269 mph
   (433 km/hr)
range with 20,000 lb (9,072 kg) payload 1,072 miles
   (1,725 km)
ferry range 3,250 miles (5,230 km)
service ceiling 23,000 ft (7,010 m)
**Dimensions**
wing span 115 ft 0 in (35.05 m)
length overall 89 ft 0 in (27.13 m)
height oevrall 27 ft 0 in (8.23 m)
wing area 1,458 sq ft (135.45 sq m)
**Power plant**
Four 2,680 hp Rolls–Royce Dart Mk.101 turboprops
**Armament**
4 man crew and 69 troops or 54 paratroops or 48 stretcher
   cases of max 29,000 lb (13,154 kg)
**Variants**
**First flights**
Argosy 100, 200, 220 and 650: Civil variants
Civil prototype: 8 January 1959
Argosy C.1.: 4 March 1961
Argosy C.1.: 56 built from 1961–1964
**In service**
**Production**
Great Britain

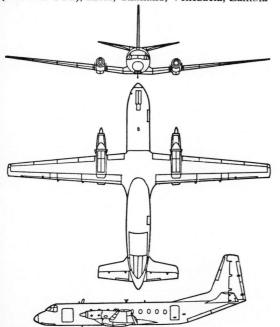

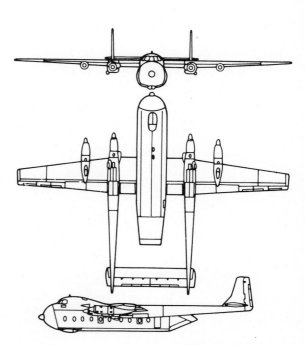

## HAWKER SIDDELEY 'BUCCANEER' S.Mk.2B

**Type**
Two-seat bomber and reconnaissance aircraft
**Weights**
normal 56,000 lb (25,400 kg)
maximum 58,500 lb (26,762 kg)
**Performance**
maximum speed at 29,860 ft (9,100 m) (Mach 0.92)
   620 mph (998 km/hr)
maximum speed at 250 ft (75 m) (Mach 0.85) 646 mph
   (1,040 km/hr)
maximum cruising speed at 3,000 ft (915 m) (Mach 0.75)
   570 mph (917 km/hr)
radius of action 500–600 miles (805–965 km)
ferry range 4,000 miles (6,400 km)
**Dimensions**
wing span 44 ft 0 in (13.41 m)
length overall 63 ft 5 in (19.33 m)
height overall 16 ft 3 in (4.95 m)
wing area 514.7 sq ft (47.82 sq m)
**Power plant**
Two Rolls–Royce RB 168–1A Spey Mk.101 turbofans
   each rated at 11,100 lb (5,035 kg) st
**Armament**
Max 16,000 lb (7,257 kg) weapon load, e.g. four 500 lb
   (227 kg) or 540 lb (245 kg) or 1,000 lb (454 kg) bombs
   in fuselage weapons bay and up to three 1,000 lb
   (454kg) or six 550 lb (227 kg) bombs on each of the
   four hard points
**Variants**
S.1, S.2, S.2A: Earlier versions;
S.50: Export version of S.2.
**First flights**
Prototype: 30 April 1958; S.1: January 1962; S.2: 17 May
   1963; S.2B: 8 January 1970
**Production**
*S.1*: 60 built from 1958–1963; *S.2.*: 84 built from 1963–
   1968, approx. 70 converted to S.2A, S.2B, S.2C and
   S.2D; *S.50*: 16 built; *S.2B*: 26 built from 1970–1972,
   16 repeat orders for 1973–1974
**In service**
*S.2, S.2A, S.2B, S.2C, S2D*: Great Britain; *S.50* South
   Africa

## HAWKER SIDDELEY 'DOMINIE' T.Mk.1

**Type**
Navigation trainer
**Weights**
empty 11,402 lb (5,172 kg)
maximum 21,198 lb (9,615 kg)
**Performance**
maximum speed at 25,000 ft (7,620 m)
maximum speed at 31,000 ft (9,459 m) (Mach 0.735)
   500 mph (805 km/hr)
maximum cruising speed at 38,000 ft (11,600 m) 420 mph
   (676 km/hr)
range 1,330 miles (2,150 km)
ferry range 1,700 miles (2,736 km)
initial rate of climb 76.5 fps (23.3 m/sec)
time to 25,000 ft (7,620 m) 13 min 0 sec
service ceiling 41,000 ft (12,500 m)
**Dimensions**
wing span 47 ft 0 in (14.33 m)
length overall 47 ft 5 in (14.45 m)
height overall 16 ft 6 in (5.03 m)
wing area 353 sq ft (32.79 sq m)
**Power plant**
Two Bristol Siddeley Viper 301 turbojets each rated at
   2,998 lb (1,360 kg) st
**Payload**
2 man crew, 2–3 trainees and 1 instructor
**Variants**
*H.S.125*: Light (6–8 passenger) executive transport
*H.S.125–600*: Further development
**First flights**
*H.S.125*: 13 August 1962;
*Dominie*: 30 December 1964
**Production**
*Dominie*: 20 built from 1965–1966
*H.S.125*: Over 325 built from 1962–1973
**In service**
*Dominie*: Great Britain
*H.S.125*: Argentine, Brazil, Ghana, Great Britain (H.S.125
   C.C.1), Malaysia, South Africa (Mercurius)
*H.S.125–600*: Great Britain

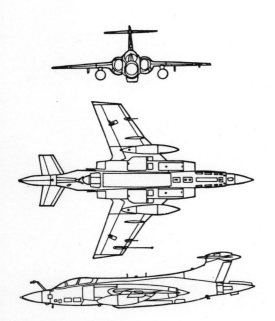

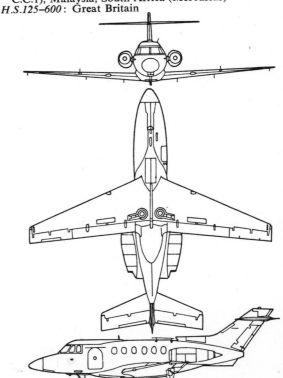

## HAWKER SIDDELEY 'GNAT' Mk.1

**Type**
Single-seat strike fighter
**Weights**
empty 4,850 lb (2,200 kg)
normal 6,650 lb (3,020 kg)
maximum 8,885 lb (4,030 kg)
**Performance**
maximum speed at 20,000 ft (6,100 m) 695 mph
    (1,118 km/hr)
maximum speed at 36,000 ft (11,000 m) 646 mph
    (1,040 km/hr)
maximum cruising speed 400 mph (645 km/hr)
radius of action 500 miles (805 km)
initial rate of climb 334.6 fps (102.0 m/sec)
time to 45,000 ft (13,700 m) 5 min 15 sec
service ceiling 50,000 ft (15,240 m)
**Dimensions**
wing span 22 ft 2 in (6.76 m)
length overall 29 ft 9 in (9.07 m)
height overall 8 ft 10 in (2.69 m)
wing area 136.6 sq ft (12.69 sq m)
**Power plant**
One Bristol Siddeley Orpheus 701 turbojet rated at
    4,700 lb (2,132 kg) st
**Armament**
Two 30 mm Aden cannon with 115 rpg and max 2,000 lb
    (908 kg) weapon load, e.g. two 500 lb (227 kg) or
    1,000 lb (454 kg) bombs or twelve 76 mm rockets
**Variants**
*Gnat T.1*: Two-seat strike trainer
*HAL Gnat*: Indian licence-built Gnat Mk.1;
*Gnat Mk.2*: Indian development
**First flights**
Prototype: 18 July 1955, T.1: 31 August 1959
**Production**
*Mk.1*: 45 built from 1956–1959, plus over 200 (300?)
    Indian licence-built from 1962–1968; *T.1*: 105 built
    from 1962–1964
**In service**
*Mk.1*: India (HAL Gnat);
*T.1*: Great Britain

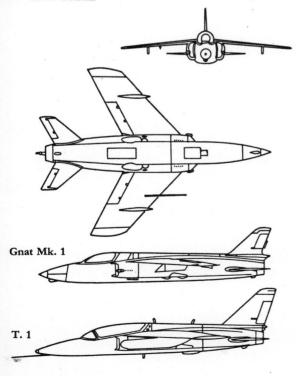

Gnat Mk. 1

T. 1

## HAWKER SIDDELEY 'HARRIER' G.R.Mk.1

**Type**
Single-seat V/STOL strike fighter and reconnaissance
    aircraft
**Weights**
empty 13,550 lb (6,146 kg)
normal 16,000 lb (7,757 kg)
maximum 21,500 lb (9,752 kg)
**Performance**
maximum speed at 980 ft (300 m) (Mach 0.95) 720 mph
    (1,160 km/hr)
maximum speed at 35,000 ft (10,670 m) (Mach 0.93)
    610 mph (980 km/hr)
radius of action with two 100 gal (455 1) auxiliary tanks
    400 miles (644 km)
ferry range 2,250 miles (3,620 km)
initial rate of climb 590.6 fps (180.0 m/sec)
service ceiling 50,000 ft (15,000 m)
**Dimensions**
wing span 25 ft 3 in (7.70 m)
length overall 45 ft 7½ in (13.91 m)
height overall 11 ft 3 in (3.43 m)
wing area 201 sq ft (18.68 sq m)
**Power plant**
One Rolls–Royce Bristol Pegasus 101 turbofan rated at
    19,200 lb (8,710 kg)
**Armament**
Two 30 mm Aden cannon with 130 rpg in central pods
    and max 5,000 lb (2,268 kg) weapon load on 5 hard
    points
**Variants**
*P.1127 Kestrel*: Pre-production model; *Harrier Mk.50*:
    Export version of GR.1; *Harrier GR.3*: Later series,
    strike fighter and reconnaissance aircraft with more
    powerful engine (Pegasus 103 rated at 21,500 lb (9,752
    kg) st); *Harrier T.2., Harrier Mk.51*: Two-seat strike
    trainers
**First flights**
*P.1127 Kestrel*: 31 August 1966; *GR.1*: 28 December
    1967; *T.2*: 24 April 1969; *Mk.50*: 20 November 1970
**Production**
6 pre-production models,
*GR.1*: 77 built from 1968; *GR.3*: 15 built from 1974;
    *T.2*: 13 built from 1969; *Mk.50*: 102 to be built from
    1970–1974; *Mk.51*: 8 to be built from 1973/1974
**In service**
*GR.1, GR.3, T.2*: Great Britain
*Mk.50, Mk.51*: United States (AV–8A, AV–8B)

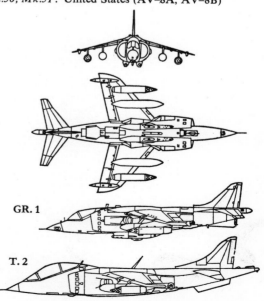

GR. 1

T. 2

## HAWKER SIDDELEY 'NIMROD' M.R.Mk.1

**Type**
Maritime reconnaissance and ASW aircraft
12 man crew
**Weights**
normal 175,500 lb (79,605 kg)
maximum 192,000 lb (87,090 kg)
**Performance**
patrol speed 210 mph (338 km/hr)
maximum speed at 32,800 ft (10,000 m) 575 mph
    (926 km/hr)
maximum cruising speed at 29,530 ft (9,000 m) 547 mph
    (860 km/hr)
ferry range 5,180 miles (8,340 km)
**Dimensions**
wing span 114 ft 10 in (34.99 m)
length overall 126 ft 9 in (38.63 m)
height overall 29 ft 8 in (9.04 m)
wing area 2,121.5 sq ft (197.05 sq m)
**Power plant**
Four Rolls–Royce RB 168–20 Spey Mk.250 turbofans
    each rated at 11,500 lb (5,217 kg) st
**Armament**
Depth charges, torpedoes, bombs. Convertible to transport
    for 45 troops
**Variants**
Nimrod R.1.: Electronic reconnaissance aircraft
**First flights**
Prototype: 23 May 1967
**Production**
2 prototypes; 38 production models from 1968–1971 plus
    3 additional Nimrod R.1. as electronic reconnaissance
    aircraft, 8 further M.R.1 from 1972/73
**In service**
Great Britain

## HAWKER SIDDELEY 'SEA VIXEN' F.(A.W.)Mk.2

**Type**
Two-seat all-weather fighter and strike fighter
**Weights**
empty 31,715 lb (14,380 kg)
maximum 45,123 lb (20,960 kg)
**Performance**
maximum speed at 9,000 ft (3,050 m) (Mach 0.92) 645 mph
    (1,038 km/hr)
maximum speed at 39,375 ft (12,000 m) 610 mph
    (982 km/hr)
maximum cruising speed at 39,375 ft (12,000 m) 497 mph
    (800 km/hr)
range 808 miles (1,300 km)
ferry range 1,609 miles (2,590 km)
time to 39,300 ft ((12,000 m) 6–7 min
service ceiling 48,200 ft (14,700 m)
**Dimensions**
wing span 50 ft 0 in (15.24 m)
length overall 53 ft 7 in (16.33 m)
height overall 11 ft 6 in (3.50 m)
wing area 648 sq ft (60.20 sq m)
**Power plant**
Two Rolls–Royce RA24 Avon Mk.208 turbojets each
    rated at 11,500 lb (5,103 kg) st
**Armament**
Two retractable packs in forward fuselage each with four-
    teen 51 mm rockets and max 4,000 lb (1,816 kg) weapon
    load on 6 hard points, e.g. (fighter) four Firestreak or
    Red Top AAMs or (strike fighter) four 500 lb (227 kg)
    or two 2,000 lb (908 kg) bombs or two Bullpup ASMs
**Variants**
F.(AW)1:Earlier version
**First flights**
Prototype: 20 June 1955; FAW.2: 1 June 1962
**Production**
Series production from 1956–1963;
*FAW.1*: 119 built
*FAW.2*: 29 built plus 67 conversions from FAW.1
**In service**
    Great Britain

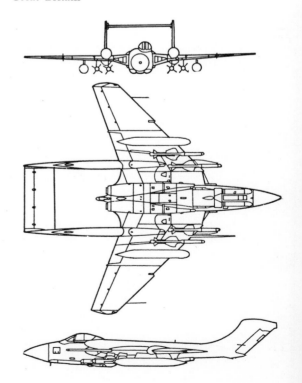

# HAWKER SIDDELEY 'VULCAN' B.Mk.2

**Type**
Heavy bomber
5 man crew
**Weights**
normal 179.898 lb (81,600 kg)
maximum 200,180 lb (90,800 kg)
**Performance**
maximum speed at sea level (Mach 0.75) 528 mph
    (850 km/hr)
maximum speed at 39,375 ft (12,000 m) (Mach 0.96)
    645 mph (1,038 km/hr)
maximum cruising speed at 55,100 ft (16,800 m) (Mach
    0.95) 627 mph (1,009 km/hr)
radius of action 1,710–2,300 miles (2,750–3,700 km)
ferry range 4,750 miles (7,650 km)
service ceiling 65,620 ft (20,000 m)
**Dimensions**
wing span 111 ft 0 in (33.83 m)
length overall 99 ft 11 in (30.45 m)
height overall 27 ft 2 in (8.28 m)
wing area 3,961 sq ft (368.00 sq m)
**Power plant**
Four Bristol Siddeley (RR) Olympus 301 turbojets each
    rated at 20,000 lb (9,072 kg st
**Armament**
One Blue Steel Mk.1 stand-off weapon or twenty-one
    1,000 lb (454 kg) bombs
**Variants**
B.1, B.1A: Earlier versions, some converted to recon-
    naissance aircraft
**First flights**
Prototype: 30 August 1952;
B.1: 4 February 1955; B.2: 19 August 1958
**Production**
2 Prototypes; B.1: 45 built from 1955–1957; B.2: ? built
    from 1958–1964
**In service**
Great Britain

# HUNTING 'PEMBROKE' C.Mk.1

**Type**
Light transport
**Weights**
empty 9,178 lb (4,163 kg)
normal 13,500 lb (6,124 kg)
**Performance**
maximum speed at 2,000 ft (610 m) 224 mph (360 km/hr)
maximum cruising speed at 8,000 ft (2,440 m) 155 mph
    (249 km/hr)
range 1,150 miles (1,850 km)
initial rate of climb 17.7 fps (5.4 m/sec)
service ceiling 21,980 ft (6,700 m)
**Dimensions**
wing span 64 ft 6 in (19.66 m)
length overall 45 ft 11¾ in (14.02 m)
height overall 16 ft 1 in (4.90 m)
wing area 400 sq ft (37.20 sq m)
**Power plant**
Two 540 hp Alvis Leonides 127 piston engines
**Payload**
2 man crew and 8 troops
**Variants**
*Pembroke C.52, C.53, C.54, C.55*: Export Versions of
    C.1; *Sea Prince C.1, C.2*: Light transports *Sea Prince
    T.1*: Radar and navigation trainer
**First flights**
Prototype: 20 November 1952
**Production**
*Pembroke*: ? built from 1953, inc 46 Pembroke (C.1).
    some of which were modernised from 1969–1971; *Sea
    Prince C.1*: 3 built; *C.2*: 4 built; *T.1*: 41 built
**In service**
*Pembroke*: Belgium, Finland (C.53), Great Britain (C.1),
    Malawi, Sudan (C.54), Sweden (C.52, Zambia (C.1)
    *Sea Prince*: Great Britain (C.1, C.2, T.1)

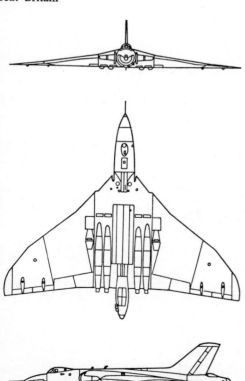

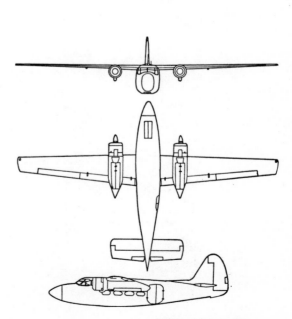

## HUNTING 'PROVOST' T.Mk.1

**Type**
Two-seat trainer
**Weights**
empty 3,353 lb (1,521 kg)
normal 4,250 lb (1,928 kg)
maximum 4,400 lb (1,996 kg)
**Performance**
maximum speed at sea level 195 mph (314 km/hr)
maximum speed at 2,300 ft (700 m) 200 mph (322 km/hr)
maximum cruising speed at 11,520 ft (3,510 m) 177 mph
   (285 km/hr)
ferry range 650 miles (1,046 km)
initial rate of climb 36.7 fps (11.2 m/sec)
service ceiling 22,010 ft (6,710 m)
**Dimensions**
wing span 35 ft 9¼ in (10.90 m)
length overall 28 ft 10½ in (8.80 m)
height overall 12 ft 2½ in (3.72 m)
wing area 213.1 sq ft (19.80 sq m)
**Power plant**
One 550 hp Alvis Leonides 126 piston engine
**Armament**
*T.52, T.53*: Two 7.7 mm machine guns and hard points
   for two 250 lb (113 kg) bombs or eight 25 lb (11.3 kg)
   bombs or eight 60 lb (27.2 kg) unguided rockets
**Variants**
*T.51, T.52, T.53*: Export versions of T.1
**First flights**
Prototype: 23 February 1950
**Production**
461 built from 1952–1960
**In service**
*T.51*: Ceylon, Ireland, Malaysia
*T.52*: Rhodesia
*T.53*: Burma, Iraq, Ireland, Sudan

## SCOTTISH AVIATION 'BULLDOG'

**Type**
Two-seat trainer
**Weights**
empty 1,420 lb (644 kg)
maximum 2,348 lb (1,065 kg)
**Performance**
maximum speed at sea level 150 mph (240 km/hr)
maximum cruising speed at 4,000 ft (1,220 m) 145 mph
   (222 km/hr)
ferry range 627 miles (1,010 km)
initial rate of climb 18.4 fps (5.6 m/sec)
service ceiling 16,404 ft (5,180 m)
**Dimensions**
wing span 33 ft 0 in (10.06 m)
length overall 23 ft 2½ in (7.07 m)
height overall 7 ft 6 in (2.28 m)
wing area 129.4 sq ft (12.02 sq m)
**Power plant**
One 200 hp Lycoming 10–360–A1B6 piston engine
**First flights**
Prototype: 19 May 1969
**Production**
Series production from 1971, over 256 delivered or on
   order
**In service**
Ghana, Great Britain (Bulldog T.1), Kenya, Malaysia,
   Nigeria, Sweden (Sk61), Zambia

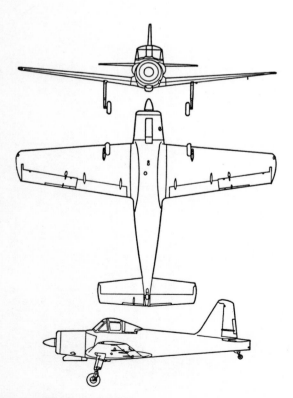

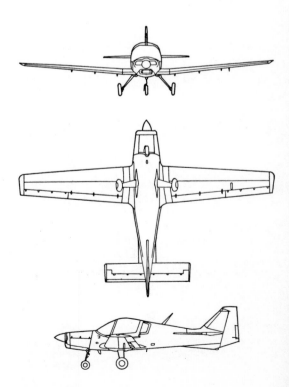

## SCOTTISH AVIATION 'TWIN PIONEER' C.C.Mk.2

**Type**
Light transport
**Weights**
empty 10,062 lb (4,564 kg)
maximum 14,600 lb (6,622 kg)
**Performance**
maximum speed at 2,000 ft (610 m) 163 mph (265 km/hr)
maximum cruising speed at 2,500 ft (750 m) 157 mph (254 km/hr)
range 575 miles (925 km)
ferry range 733 miles (1,180 km)
initial rate of climb 21 fps (6.4 m/sec)
service ceiling 20,000 ft (6,100 m)
**Dimensions**
wing span 76 ft 6 in (23.33 m)
length overall 45 ft 2¾ in (13.79 m)
height overall 12 ft 3 in (3.73 m)
wing area 670 sq ft (62.20 sq m)
**Power plant**
Two 620 hp Alvis Leonides 531/8B piston engines
**Amament**
Max 2,000 lb (907 kg) underwing weapon load, e.g. bombs
**Payload**
1 man crew and 13 troops or 9 stretcher cases and 3 seated wounded or max 3,400 lb (1,542 kg) freight
**Variants**
Twin Pioneer Series 3: Civil variant
**First flights**
Prototype: 28 August 1957
**Production**
*Twin Pioneer CC.1*: 32 built from 1958–1960, converted to CC.2 from 1961; *CC.2*: 4 built from 1961
**In service**
Ceylon (Sri Lanka), Great Britain (CC.2), Indonesia

## SHORT 'BELFAST' C.Mk.1

**Type**
Strategic transport
**Weights**
empty 127,000 lb (57,607 kg)
maximum 230,000 lb (104,330 kg)
**Performance**
maximum cruising speed at 24,000 ft (7,300 m) 338 mph (544 km/hr)
range/w.m.p. 1,000 miles (1,610 km)
ferry range 5,300 miles (8,530 km)
initial rate of climb 17.7 fps (5.4 m/sec)
service ceiling 30,000 ft (9,145 m)
**Dimensions**
wing span 158 ft 9½ in (48.40 m)
length overall 136 ft 5 in (41.58 m)
height overall 47 ft 1½ in (14.33 m)
wing area 2,466 sq ft (229.00 sq m)
**Power plant**
Four 5,730 hp Rolls–Royce Tyne R.Ty 12.Mk.101 turboprops
**Payload**
4–5 man crew and 150–250 troops or max 80,000 lb (36,288 kg) freight
**First flights**
Prototype: 5 January 1964
**Production**
10 built from 1964–1966
**In service**
Great Britain

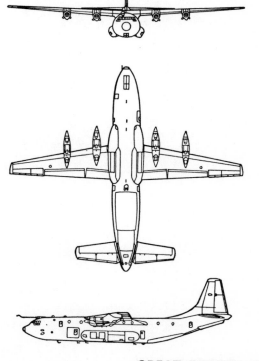

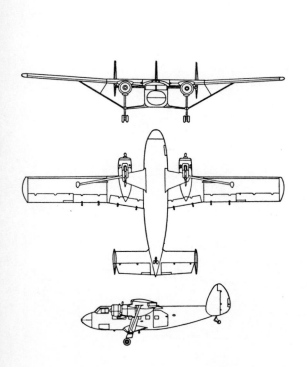

## SHORT 'SKYVAN' 3M

**Type**
Light transport
**Weights**
empty 7,400 lb (3,356 kg)
maximum 14,500 lb (6,577 kg)
**Performance**
maximum speed at 10,000 ft (3,050 m) 200 mph
(323 km/hr)
maximum cruising speed at 10,000 ft (3,050 m) 172 mph
(278 km/hr)
range/w.m.p. 165 miles (267 km)
ferry range 660 miles (1,062 km)
initial rate of climb 24.9 fps (7.6 m/sec)
service ceiling 21,000 ft (6,400 m)
**Dimensions**
wing span 64 ft 11 in (19.79 m)
length overall 41 ft 4 in (12.60 m)
height overall 15 ft 1 in (4.60 m)
wing area 372.9 sq ft (34.65 sq m)
**Power plant**
Two 715 hp Garrett AiResearch TPE 331–201 turboprops
**Payload**
1–2 man crew and 22 troops or 16 paratroops and 1
dispatcher or 12 stretcher cases and 2 medics or max
5,000 lb (2,268 kg) freight
**Variants**
Skyvan Series 3: Civil variant
**First flights**
Prototype 3M: Beginning of 1970
**Production**
Series production from 1970. Over 32 *Skyvan 3M* and
51 *Skyvan 3* delivered or on order by summer of
1973. 1 Skyvan produced per month
**In service**
Argentine, Austria, Ecuador, Indonesia, Nepal, Oman,
Singapore, Thailand

## WESTLAND (S–61B) 'SEA KING' H.A.S.Mk.1

**Type**
Amphibious ASW helicopter
4 man crew
**Weights**
empty 12,975 lb (5,885 kg)
normal 15,474 lb (7,019 kg)
maximum 21,500 lb (9,751 kg)
**Performance**
maximum speed at sea level 143 mph (230 km/hr)
patrol speed 86 mph (138 km/hr)
maximum cruising speed 131 mph (211 km/hr)
range 690 miles (1,110 km)
ferry range 1,012 miles (1,630 km)
initial rate of climb 29.5 fps (9.0 m/sec)
service ceiling 10,000 ft (3,050 m)
hovering ceiling in ground effect 5,000 ft (1,525 m)
**Dimensions**
main rotor diameter 62 ft 0 in (18.89 m)
length of fuselage 54 ft 9 in (16.69 m)
height 15 ft 17 in (4.85 m)
**Power plant**
Two 1,500 hp Rolls–Royce Gnome H.1400 turboshafts
**Armament**
Four homing torpedoes, bombs or four depth charges
**Payload**
As transport: 2 man crew and 25–27 troops or 9–12
stretcher cases and 2 medics or max 6,000 lb (2,720 kg)
freight
**Variants**
SH–3D: Basic American model of Westland Sea King
**First flights**
Prototype: 8 September 1967, *Sea King HAS.1*: 7 May
1969
**Production**
4 prototypes, Series production from 1969: over 116
delivered or on order to date
**In service**
Australia (Sea King Mk.50), Germany (West) (Mk.41),
Great Britain (Sea King HAS.1), India (Mk.42), Norway
(Mk.43), Pakistan (Mk.45)

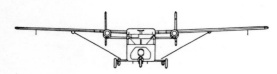

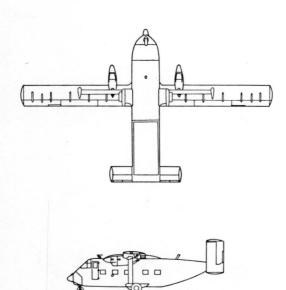

## WESTLAND 'WASP' H.A.S.Mk.1

**Type**
ASW helicopter
**Weights**
empty 3,455 lb (1,567 kg)
maximum 5,500 lb (2,495 kg)
**Performance**
maximum speed at sea level 120 mph (193 km/hr)
maximum cruising speed 109 mph (176 km/hr)
range 270 miles (435 km)
initial rate of climb 23.9 fps (7.3 m/sec)
service ceiling 12,200 ft (3,720 m)
hovering ceiling in ground effect 12,500 ft (3,810 m)
hovering ceiling out of ground effect 8,800 ft (2,682 m)
**Dimensions**
main rotor diameter 32 ft 3 in (9.83 m)
length of fuselage 30 ft 3½ in (9.25 m)
height 8 ft 8 in (2.64 m)
**Power plant**
One 710 hp Rolls–Royce Bristol Nimbus 503 turboshaft
**Armament**
Max 538 lb (244 kg) weapon load, e.g. 2 homing torpedoes or depth charges or bombs
**Payload**
1–2 man crew
**First flights**
Prototype P.531: 9 August 1959; *Wasp*: 28 October 1962
**Production**
Series production from 1963
**In service**
Brazil, Great Britain, Netherlands, New Zealand, South Africa

## WESTLAND 'SCOUT' A.H.Mk.1

**Type**
Light AOP helicopter
Details as for 'Wasp' H.A.S.Mk.1 with the following exceptions
**Weights**
empty 3,084 lb (1,399 kg)
maximum 5,300 lb (2,404 kg)
**Performance**
maximum speed at sea level 131 mph (211 km/hr)
maximum cruising speed 122 mph (196 km/hr)
ferry range 315 miles (507 km)
initial rate of climb 27.6 fps (8.4 m/sec)
service ceiling 13,400 ft (4,085 m)
**Dimensions**
main rotor diameter 32 ft 3 in (9.83 m)
length of fuselage 30 ft 4 in (9.24 m)
height 8 ft 11 in (2.72 m)
**Power plant**
One 685 hp Rolls–Royce Nimbus 101 or 102 turboshaft
**Payload**
2 man crew and 3 troops or 2 stretcher cases and 2 medics
**First flights**
Scout: 4 August 1960
**Production**
Over 150 built from 1961–1970
**In service**
Australia (Mk.31), Bahrein, Great Britain, Uganda

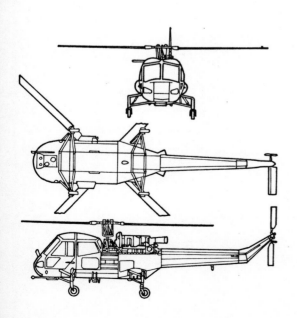

## WESTLAND 'WESSEX' H.A.S.Mk.3

**Type**
ASW helicopter
**Weights**
empty 8,909 lb (4,041 kg)
maximum 14,013 lb (6,356 kg)
**Performance**
maximum speed at sea level 127 mph (204 km/hr)
maximum cruising speed 121 mph (195 km/hr)
range 300 miles (483 km)
initial rate of climb 25.6 fps (7.8 m/sec)
service ceiling 14,100 ft (4,300 m)
hovering ceiling in ground effect 5,500 ft (1,680 m)
hovering ceiling out of ground effect 4,000 ft (1,220 m)
**Dimensions**
main rotor diameter 50 ft 0¼ in (17.08 m)
length of fuselage 48 ft 4½ in (14.74 m)
height 16 ft 2 in (4.93 m)
**Power plant**
One 1,600 hp Rolls–Royce Gazelle 165 turboshaft
**Armament**
2 homing torpedoes
**Payload**
4 man crew
**Variants**
Wessex HAS.1: ASW helicopter;
Wessex HC.2: Transport helicopter;
Wessex Mk.52, Mk.53, Mk.54: Export versions of HC.2;
Wessex HAS.31: ASW helicopter for Australia
**First flights**
Prototype: 17 May 1957
**Production**
376 built of all variants from 1958–1972
**In service**
*HAS.1, HC.2, HAS.3*: Great Britain; *Mk.52*: Iraq; *Mk.53*:
   Ghana; *HAS.31*: Australia

## WESTLAND 'WESSEX' H.U.Mk.5

**Type**
Medium transport helicopter
Details as for H.A.S.Mk.3 with the following exceptions
**Weights**
empty 8,664 lb (3,930 kg)
maximum 13,500 lb (6,124 kg)
**Performance**
maximum speed at sea level 132 mph (212 km/hr)
range 270 miles (435 km)
ferry range 480 miles (770 km)
initial rate of climb 27.6 fps (8.4 m/sec)
**Dimensions**
height 14 ft 5 in (4.39 m)
**Power plant**
Two coupled 1,550 hp Rolls–Royce Gnome 112 and 113
   turboshafts
**Payload**
1–3 man crew and 16 troops or 7 stretcher cases or max
   4,000 lb (1,816 kg) freight
**First flights**
HU.5: 31 May 1963
**In service**
*HU.5*: Bangla Desh, Great Britain

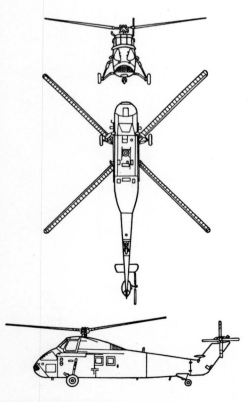

## WESTLAND WG.13 'LYNX' A.H.Mk.1

**Type**
Light transport helicopter
**Weights**
empty 5,299 lb (2,403 kg)
maximum 8,559 lb (3,878 kg)
**Performance**
maximum speed at sea level 184 mph (296 km/hr)
maximum cruising speed 160 mph (259 km/hr)
range 173–497 miles (278–796 km)
ferry range 1,150 miles (1,850 km)
initial rate of climb 41.4 fps (12.7 m/sec)
**Dimensions**
main rotor diameter 42 ft 0 in (12.80 m)
length of fuselage 40 ft 5¾ in (12.34 m)
height 11 ft 3 in (3.43 m)
**Power plant**
Two 900 hp Rolls–Royce B.S.360–07–26 turboshafts
**Armament**
*HAS.2* (ASW version): Two homing torpedoes, or depth
  charges and rockets
**Payload**
2 man crew and 12 troops or max 2,738 lb (1,242 kg)
  freight
**Variants**
*Lynx HAS.2*: ASW helicopter;
*Lynx HC.4*: Light helicopter;
*Lynx HT.3*: Training helicopter
**First flights**
Prototype: 21 March 1971
**Production**
12 prototypes; series production from 1972/73, approx
  360 on order to date
**In service**
*Lynx AH.1, HC.4, HT.3*: Great Britain
*Lynx HAS.2*: Argentine, France, Great Britain

## HAL HAOP–27 'KRISHAK' Mk.2

**Type**
Liaison and AOP aircraft
**Weights**
empty 1,971 lb (894 kg)
maximum 2,800 lb (1,270 kg)
**Performance**
maximum speed at sea level 130 mph (209 km/hr)
maximum speed at 5,000 ft (1,530 m) 116 mph
  (187 km/hr)
maximum cruising speed 110 mph (177 km/hr)
ferry range 293 miles (471 km)
initial rate of climb 15.1 fps (4.6 m/sec)
service ceiling 19,500 ft (5,940 m)
**Dimensions**
wing span 37 ft 6 in (11.43 m)
length overall 27 ft 7 in (8.41 m)
height overall 10 ft 9½ in (3.29 m)
wing area 200.7 sq ft (18.65 sq m)
**Power plant**
One 225 hp Continental 0–470–J piston engine
**Payload**
1 man crew and 2 troops or 1 stretcher case
**First flights**
Prototype: November 1959
Krishak Mk.2: 1965
**Production**
2 prototypes; 68 built from 1965–1969
**In service**
India

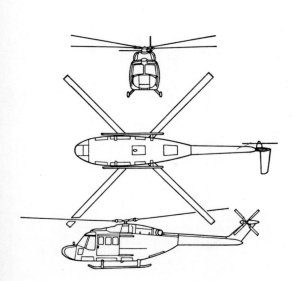

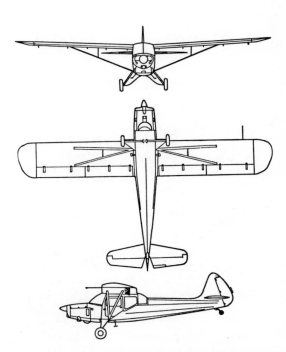

## HAL HF–24 'MARUT' Mk.1A

**Type**
Single-seat fighter and strike fighter
**Weights**
empty 13,658 lb (6,195 kg)
normal 19,734 lb (8,951 kg)
maximum 24,048 lb (10,908 kg)
**Performance**
maximum speed at 40,000 ft (12,200 m) (Mach 1.02)
  673 mph (1,083 km/hr)
maximum speed at 3,280 ft (1,000 m) 745 mph (1,200
  km/hr)
maximum cruising speed at 36,000 ft (11,000 m) 559 mph
  (900 km/hr)
radius of action 373–423 miles (600–680 km)
ferry range 870 miles (1,400 km)
time to 39,375 ft (12,000 m) 7 min 9 sec
service ceiling 45,932 ft (14,000 m)
**Dimensions**
wing span 29 ft 6¼ in (9.00 m)
length overall 52 ft 0¾ in (15.87 m)
height overall 11 ft 9¾ in (3.60 m)
wing area 306.8 sq ft (28.50 sq m)
**Power plant**
Two Rolls–Royce Bristol Orpheus 703 turbojets each rated
  at 4,850 lb (2,200 kg) st
**Armament**
Four 30 mm Aden Mk.2 cannon with 130 rpg, 50
  unguided 68 mm rockets or four 1,000 lb (454 kg)
  bombs.
**Variants**
HF–24 'Marut' Mk.1T: Two-seat fighter trainer
HF–24 'Marut' Mk.1A, Mk.1R, Mk.2, Mk.3: Later
  series with more powerful engines
**First flights**
Prototype: 17 June 1961; 1st production model: March
  1963
Prototype HF–24 Mk.1T: 30 April 1970
**Production**
18 prototypes and pre-production models
*Marut*: Series production from 1965, 100 (124 ?)
  ordered of which only 80 delivered by 1973
*Marut 1T*: 2 prototypes, 10 ordered, delivery from 1971,
  plans for 78–85 aircraft
**In service**
India

## HAL HJT–16 Mk.2 'KIRAN'

**Type**
Two-seat trainer
**Weights**
empty 5,362 lb (2,432 kg)
normal 7,712 lb (3,498 kg)
maximum 8,660 lb (3,928 kg)
**Performance**
maximum speed at sea level 494 mph (795 km/hr)
maximum speed at 30,000 ft (9,100 m) 457 mph
  (735 km/hr)
maximum cruising speed 391 mph (630 km/hr)
range 497 miles (800 km)
ferry range 876 miles (1,410 km)
initial rate of climb 79.4 fps (24.2 m/sec)
time to 30,200 ft (9,200 m) 10 min 30 sec
service ceiling 42,196 ft (12,800 m)
**Dimensions**
wing span 35 ft 1¾ in (10.71 m)
length overall 34 ft 9 in (10.60 m)
height overall 11 ft 11¼ in (3.65 m)
wing area 204.5 sq ft (19.00 sq m)
**Power plant**
One Hindustan Aeronautics HJE–2500 turbojet rated at
  2,500 lb (1,134 kg) st
**Armament**
Machine guns and practice bombs
**First flights**
Prototype: 4 September 1964
**Production**
Pre-production series: 24 built from 1965–1969, 60 built
  from 1969, further 100 planned
**In service**
India

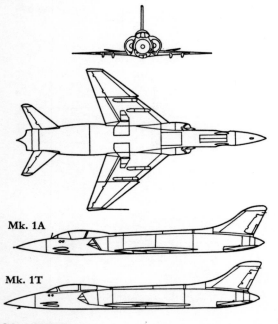

Mk. 1A

Mk. 1T

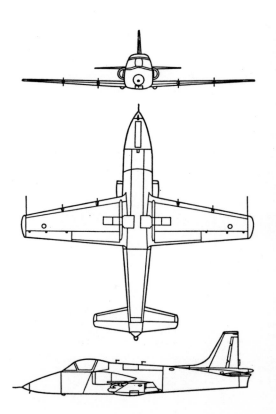

## HAL HT-2

**Type**
Two-seat trainer
**Weights**
empty 1,533 lb (699 kg)
normal 2,236 lb (1,016 kg)
**Performance**
maximum speed 130 mph (209 km/hr)
maximum cruising speed 115 mph (185 km/hr)
range 350 miles (563 km)
initial rate of climb 13.1 fps (4.0 m/sec)
service ceiling 14,500 ft (4,420 m)
**Dimensions**
wing span 35 ft 3 in (10.74 m)
length overall 24 ft 8½ in (7.53 m)
height overall 8 ft 11 in (2.72 m)
wing area 173.3 sq ft (16.10 sq m)
**Power plant**
One 155 hp Blackburn Cirrus Major III piston engine
**First flights**
Prototype: 13 August 1951
**Production**
160 built from 1953–1964
**In service**
Ghana, India

## AERFER–AERMACCHI AM.3C

**Type**
Liaison and AOP aircraft
**Weights**
empty 2,549 lb (1,156 kg)
normal 3,307 lb (1,500 kg)
maximum 3,858 lb (1,750 kg)
**Performance**
maximum speed at sea level 162 mph (260 km/hr)
maximum speed at 8,000 ft (2,440 m) 173 mph (278 km/hr)
maximum cruising speed at 8,000 ft (2,440 m) 153 mph (246 km/hr)
ferry range 615 miles (990 km)
initial rate of climb 22.9 fps (7.0 m/sec)
time to 9,840 ft (3,000 m) 7 min 30 sec
service ceiling 27,560 ft (8,400 m)
**Dimensions**
wing span 41 ft 5¾ in (12.64 m)
length overall 29 ft 5½ in (8.98 m)
height overall 8 ft 11 in (2.72 m)
wing area 219.1 sq ft (20.36 sq m)
**Power plant**
One 340 hp Lycoming GSO–480–B1B6 piston engine
**Armament**
Max 1,150 lb (522 kg) weapon load, e.g. two weapon packs each containing two 7.62 mm machine guns with 1,000 rpg or two Matra rocket launchers each containing six 70 mm rockets or two 250 lb (113 kg) or 200 lb (91 kg) bombs
**Payload**
1 man crew and 2 troops
**First flights**
Prototype: 12 May 1967
**Production**
2 Prototypes, series production from 1972, 63 delivered or on order to date
**In service**
Italy, Ruanda, South Africa

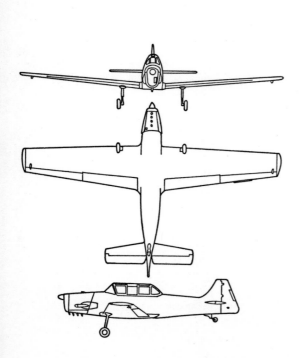

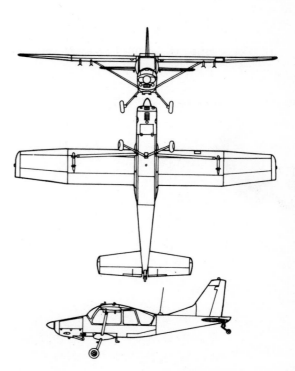

## AERMACCHI MB.326G

**Type**
Two-seat trainer
**Weights**
empty 5,920 lb (2,685 kg)
maximum 10,090 lb (4,577 kg)
**Performance**
maximum speed at 20,000 ft (6,100 m) (Mach 0.82)
   524 mph (843 km/hr)
maximum cruising speed 495 mph (797 km/hr)
ferry range 1,520 miles (2,445 km)
initial rate of climb 101 fps (30.8 m/sec)
time to 20,000 ft (6,100 m) 4 min 10 sec
service ceiling 47,000 ft (14,325 m)
**Dimensions**
wing span 33 ft 3¾ in (10.15 m)
length overall 34 ft 11¼ in (10.65 m)
height overall 12 ft 2½ in (3.72 m)
wing area 208.3 sq ft (19.35 sq m)
**Power plant**
One Rolls–Royce Viper 20 Mk.540 turbojet rated at
   3,410 lb (1,547 kg) st
**Armament**
Max 4,004 lb (1,816 kg) weapon load on 6 hardpoints
**Variants**
*MB.326, MB326B, MB.326F*: Earlier versions;
*MB.326GB*: Export version of MB.326G, licence-built in
   Brazil by Embraer;
*MB.326H, MB.326M*: Australian and South African
   licence-built versions of MB.326G by GAF resp. by
   Atlas.
*MB.326K*: Single-seat light ground-attack aircraft
**First flights**
Prototype *MB.326*: 10 December 1957;
MB.326G: 9 May 1967
*MB.326K*: 22 August 1970
**Production**
Series production from 1959,
*MB.326*: 100 built; *MB.326B*: 8 built; *MB.326F*: 7 built;
   *MB.326G*: 100 (?) built; *MB.326GB*: 165 built;
   *MB.326H*: 108 built; *MB.326K*: 40 built; *MB.326M*:
   200 (?) built
**In service**
*MB.326, MB.326G*: Italy; *MB.326B*: Tunisia; *MB.326F*:
   Ghana; *MB.326GB*: Argentine, Brazil (TF–26 Xavante),
   Bolivia, Congo, Zambia; *MB.326H*: Australia;
   *MB.326K*: Argentine, South Africa (?); *MB.326M*:
   South Africa (Impala)

## AERMACCHI MB.326K

**Type**
Light ground-attack aircraft
Details as for trainer with the following exceptions
**Weights**
empty 5,920 lb (2,558 kg)
maximum 11,500 lb (5,216 kg)
**Performance**
maximum speed at 20,000 ft (6,100 m) (Mach 0.75)
   483 mph (778 km/hr)
radius of action 80–404 miles (130–650 km)

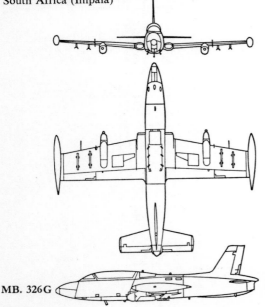

MB. 326G

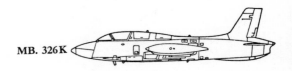

MB. 326K

## FIAT G.91R.1 and R.3

**Type**
single–seat strike fighter and reconnaissance aircraft
**Weights**
empty 6,834 lb (3,100 kg)
normal 11,750 lb (5,330 kg)
maximum 12,522 lb (5,680 kg)
**Performance**
maximum speed at sea level (Mach 0.88) 667 mph
(1,075 km/hr)
maximum speed at 5,000 ft (1.500 m) (Mach 0.9)
radius of action 195–373 miles (215–600 km)
ferry range 1,150 miles (1,850 km)
initial rate of climb 98.4 fps (30.0 m/sec)
service ceiling 39,375 ft (12,000 m)
**Dimensions**
wing span 28 ft 1 in (8.56 m)
length overall 33 ft 9½ in (10.30 m)
height overall 31 ft 1 in (4.00 m)
wing area 176.6 sq ft (16.43 sp m)
**Power Plant**
One Bristol Siddeley Orpheus 803 turbojet rated at
5,000 lb (2,270 kg) st
**Armament**
*R.1, R.4*: Four 12.7 mm machine guns with 300 rpg and
max 1,000 lb (454 kg) weapon load
*R.3*: Two 30 mm DEFA 552 cannon with 125 rpg and
max 1,000 lb (454 kg) weapon load, e.g. two 500 lb
(227 kg) bombs or two A.S.20 ASMs or rocket
launchers
**Variants**
*G.91T.1, T.4*: Two-seat strike trainer
*G.91PAN*: Aerobatic machine
**First flights**
Prototype: 9 August 1956; *G.91T*: 31 May 1960;
First G.91 completed in Germany: 20 July 1961
**Production**
Series production from 1958–1966; 3 prototypes and 27
pre-production models inc 16 converted to G.91PAN;
*G.91R.1*: 98 built; *G.91R.3*: 344 built, inc 294 licence-
built by Dornier; *G.91R.4*: 50 built; *G.91T.1*: 76 built,
plus 25 (?) repeat orders from 1971; *G.91T.3*: 44 built,
plus 22 repeat orders from 1969–1971
**In service**
*G.91R.1, G.91T.1, G.91PAN*: Italy
*G.91R.3, G.91T.3*: Germany (West)
*G.91R.4*: Portugal

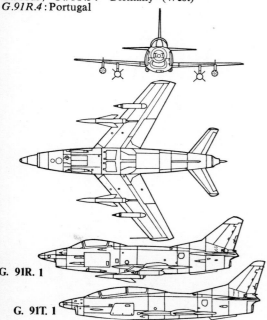

G. 91R. 1

G. 91T. 1

## FIAT G.91Y

**Type**
single-seat strike fighter and reconnaissance aircraft
**Weights**
empty 8,598 lb (3,900 kg)
normal 17,196 lb (7,800 kg)
maximum 19,180 lb (8,700 kg)
**Performance**
maximum speed at sea level (Mach 0.9) 690 mph
(1,110 km/hr)
maximum speed at 32.810 ft (10,000 m) (Mach 0.95)
671 mph (1,080 km/hr)
maximum cruising speed at 492 ft (150 m) 391 mph
(630 km/hr)
radius of action 239–466 miles (385–750 km)
ferry range 2,112 miles (3,400 km)
initial rate of climb 283.5 fps (86.4 m/sec)
time to 40.000 ft (12,200 m) 4 min 30 sec
service ceiling 41,000 ft (12,500 m)
**Dimensions**
wing span 29 ft 6½ in (9.01 m)
length overall 38 ft 3½ in (11.67 m)
height overall 14 ft 6 in (4.43 m)
wing area 195.15 sq ft (18.13 sq m)
**Power Plant**
Two general Electric J85–GE–13A turbojets each rated
at 2,720 lb (1,236 kg)/4,080 lb (1,850 kg) st
**Armament**
Two 30 mm DEFA 552 cannon and max 4,000 lb
(1,814 kg) weapon load on 4 hard points
**Variants**
G.91YT: Planned two–seat strike trainer
**First flights**
Prototype: 27 December 1966
**Production**
2 prototypes
20 pre-production models from 1968–1971,
delivery of 55 production models from 1971–1973
**In service**
Italy

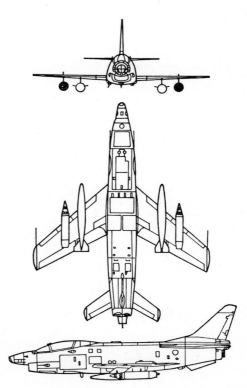

## FIAT G.222

**Type**
medium transport
**Weights**
empty 29,321 lb (13,300 kg)
maximum 57,320 lb (26,000 kg)
**Performance**
maximum speed at sea level 329 mph (530 km/hr)
maximum cruising speed at 14,750 ft (4,500 m)
   273 mph (440 km/hr)
range/w.m.p. 2,029 miles (3,250 km)
ferry range 3,262 miles (5,250 km)
initial rate of climb 31.5 fps (9.6 m/sec)
service ceiling 29,500 ft (9,000 m)
**Dimensions**
wing span 94 ft 6¼ in (28.80 m)
length overall 74 ft 5½ in (22.70 m)
height overall 32 ft 1¾ in (9.80 m)
wing area 970.9 sq ft (90.20 sq m)
**Power Plant**
Two 3,400 hp General Electric T64–P4D turboprops
**Payload**
3–4 man crew and 44 troops or 40 paratroops or 36
   stretcher cases or max 11,023 lb (5,000 kg) freight
**First flights**
Prototype: 18 July 1970
**Production**
2 prototypes, 6 (?) pre-production models, series
   production from 1972/73; 44 delivered or on order to
   date
**In service**
Italy

## PIAGGIO P.148

**Type**
two-seat trainer
**Weights**
empty 1,929 lb (875 kg)
normal 2,646 lb (1,200 kg)
**Performance**
maximum speed at sea level 145 mph (233 km/hr)
maximum speed at 3,280 ft (1000 m) 143 mph
   (230 km/hr)
maximum cruising speed at 2,950 ft (900 m) 126 mph
   (204 km/hr)
ferry range 572 miles (920 km)
initial rate of climb 14.7 fps (4.5 m/sec)
time to 65.620 ft (2,000 m) 8 min 10 sec
service ceiling 16,404 ft (5,000 m)
**Dimensions**
wing span 36 ft 6 in (11.12 m)
length overall 27 ft 8¼ in (8.44 m)
height overall 7 ft 10½ in (2.40 m)
wing area 203 sq ft (18.80 sq m)
**Power Plant**
One 190 hp Lycoming 0–435–A piston engine
**First flights**
Prototype: 12 February 1951
**Production**
100 built from 1952–1955
**In service**
Congo, Italy, Somali

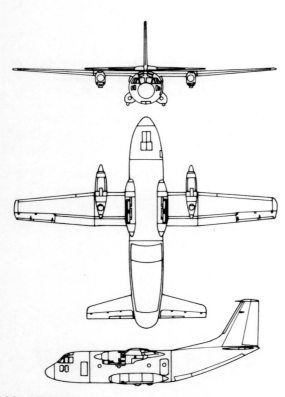
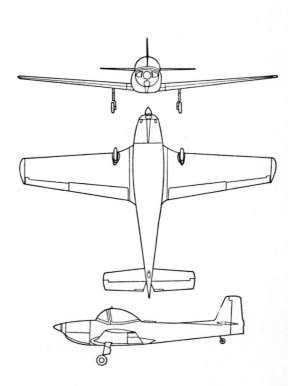

**PIAGGO P.149D**

**Type**
two–seat trainer and four–seat liaison aircraft
**Weights**
empty 2,557 lb (1,160 kg)
normal 3,704 lb (1,680 kg)
**Performance**
maximum speed at sea level 192 mph (309 km/hr)
maximum speed at 6,560 ft (2,000 m) 177 mph
  (285 km/hr)
maximum cruising speed at 10,800 ft (3,300 m)
  145 mph (233 km/hr)
ferry range 686 miles (1,100 km)
initial rate of climb 16.1 fps (4.9 m/sec)
service ceiling 16,400 ft (5,000 m)
**Dimensions**
wing span 36 ft 6¼ in (11.13 m)
length overall 28 ft 10 in (8.78 m)
height overall 9 ft 6 in (2.90 m)
wing area 203 sq ft (18.90 sq m)
**Power Plant**
One 270 hp Piaggio-Lycoming GO–480–B1A6 piston
  engine
**First flights**
Prototype: 19 June 1953
**Production**
268 built from 1956–1959, inc 190 licence-built in
  Germany (West)
**In service**
Germany (West), Nigeria, Tanzania, Uganda

**PIAGGIO P.166M**

**Type**
light transport
**Weights**
empty 5,181 lb (2,350 kg)
maximum 8,115 lb (3,681 kg)
**Performance**
maximum speed at 9,500 ft (2,900 m) 222 mph
  (357 km/hr)
maximum cruising speed at 12,800 ft (3,900 m) 207 mph
  (333 km/hr)
range 801 miles (1,290 km)
ferry range 1,199 miles (1,930 km)
initial rate of climb 20.7 fps (6.3 m/sec)
service ceiling 25,527 ft (7,780 m)
**Dimensions**
wing span 45 ft 9 in (14.25 m)
length overall 38 ft 1 in (11.61 m)
height overall 16 ft 5 in (5.00 m)
wing area 285.9 sq ft (26.56 sq m)
**Power Plant**
Two 340 hp Lycoming GSO–480–B–1C6 piston engines
**Payload**
1 man crew and max 10 troops
**Variants**
*P.166, P.166B Portofino, P.166C*: Civil variants
*P.166S*: Maritime reconnaissance variant for South
  Africa
**First flights**
Prototype: 26 November 1957
**Production**
P.166M: 60 (94?) built;
P.166S: 9 built
**In service**
P.166M: Italy
P.166S: South Africa (Albatross)

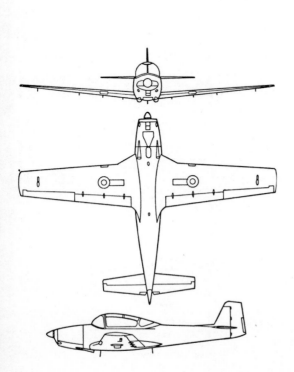

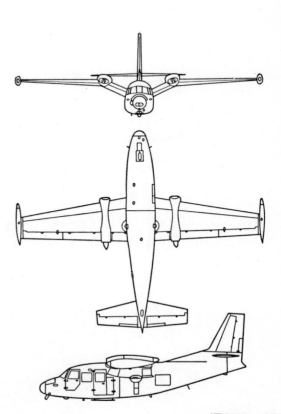

## SIAI–MARCHETTI S.208M

**Type**
Liaison aircraft
**Weights**
empty 1,823 lb (827 kg)
maximum 3,310 lb (1,502 kg)
**Performance**
maximum speed at sea level 177 mph (285 km/hr)
maximum cruising speed at 6,560 ft (2,000 m) 161 mph
  (260 km/hr)
range 746 miles (1,200 km)
ferry range 1,118 miles (1,800 km)
service ceiling 17,716 ft (5,400 m)
**Dimensions**
wing span 34 ft 8½ in (10.88 m)
length overall 26 ft 7 in (8.09 m)
height overall 9ft 5¾ in (2.89 m)
wing area 173 sq ft (16.09 sq m)
**Power Plant**
One 260 hp Lycoming O–540–E4A5 piston engine
**Payload**
2 man crew and 3 troops
**Variants**
S.205 and S.208: Light civil aircraft
**First flights**
Prototype: 22 May 1967
**Production**
24 built from 1968–1970, 20 more ordered?
**In service**
Italy

## SIAI–MARCHETTI SF.260MX

**Type**
two-seat trainer
**Weights**
empty 1,587 lb (720 kg)
normal 2,205 lb (1,000 kg)
maximum 2,645 lb (1,200 kg)
**Performance**
maximum speed at sea level 211 mph (340 km/hr)
maximum cruising speed at 10,000 ft (3,050 m) 186 mph
  (300 km/hr)
ferry range 895 miles (1,440 km)
initial rate of climb 26.3 fps (8.0 m/sec)
service ceiling 16,400 ft (5,000 m)
**Dimensions**
wing span 26 ft 11¾ in (8.25 m)
length overall 23 ft 3½ in (7.10 m)
height overall 7 ft 11 in (2.41 m)
wing area 108.5 sq ft (10.10 sq m)
**Power Plant**
One 260 hp Lycoming O–540–E4A5 piston engine
**Armament**
*SF.260W*: Max 661 lb (300 kg) weapon load, e.g. two
  110 lb (50 kg) practice bombs, or two weapon packs
  each containing two 7.62 mm machine guns or 2 rocket
  launchers each containing 14 rockets
**Variants**
*SF.260*: Civil variant
*SF.260W Warrior*: Light trainer and ground-attack
  aircraft
**First flights**
Prototype: 1966; prototype *SF.206W*: May 1972
**Production**
Series production of *SF.260MX* military export variant
  from 1969, 102 delivered or on order
**In service**
Belgium (260MB), Congo (260MC), Philippines (260MP),
  Singapore (260MS), Thailand (260MT), Zambia
  (260MZ)

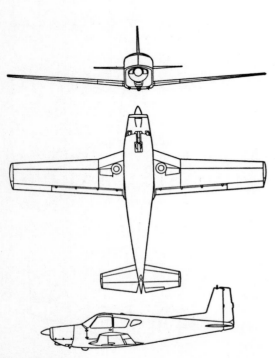

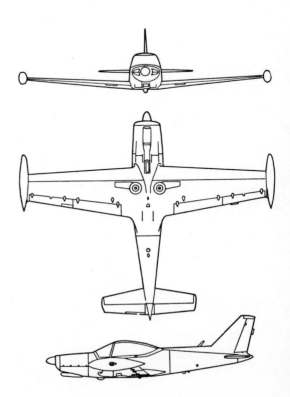

## SIAI–MARCHETTI SM.1019A

**Type**
liaison and AOP aircraft
**Weights**
empty 1,480 lb (672 kg)
maximum 2,513 lb (1,140 kg)
**Performance**
maximum speed at 6,000 ft (1,830 m) 237 mph
  (400 km/hr)
maximum cruising speed at 6,000 ft (1,830 m) 173 mph
  (278 km/hr)
range 320 miles (515 km)
ferry range 764 miles (1,230 km)
initial rate of climb 27.2 fps (8.3 m/sec)
service ceiling 30,000 ft (9,150 m)
**Dimensions**
wing span 36 ft 0 in (10.97 m)
length overall 27 ft 7¼ in (8.43 m)
height overall 7 ft 9¾ in (2.38 m)
wing area 174 sq ft (16.16 sq m)
**Power Plant**
One 317 hp Allison 250–B15G turboprop
**Armament**
Max 500 lb (227 kg) weapon load on 2 hard points, e.g.
  weapon pack containing 7.62 mm Minigun or two
  rocket launchers
**First flights**
Prototype: 24 May 1969
**Production**
Two prototypes, series production from 1972/73, 100
  delivered or on order to date
**In service**
Italy

## FUJI KM–2

**Type**
two-seat trainer
**Weights**
empty 2,386 lb (1,083 kg)
maximum 3,286 lb (1,495 kg)
**Performance**
maximum speed at sea level 201 mph (323 km/hr)
maximum speed at 16,400 ft (5,000 m) 227 mph
  (365 km/hr)
maximum cruising speed 183 mph (295 km/hr)
ferry range 767 miles (1,235 km)
initial rate of climb 25.9 fps (7.9 m/sec)
service ceiling 29,200 ft (8,900 m)
**Dimensions**
wing span 32 ft 10 in (10.00 m)
length overall 26 ft 1 in (7.95 m)
height overall 9 ft 7 in (2.92 m)
wing area 177.6 sq ft (16.49 sq m)
**Power Plant**
One 340 hp Lycoming IGSO–480–A1C6 piston engine
**Variants**
Fuji LM–1 and LM–2 Nikko: Four-seat liaison aircraft
  and trainers
**First flights**
LM–1: 6 June 1955
**Production**
*LM–1*: 27 built 1956/57, some converted to LM–2 with
  more powerful engine;
*LM–2*: ? built; *KM–2*: 28 built from 1963–1969.
**In service**
Japan

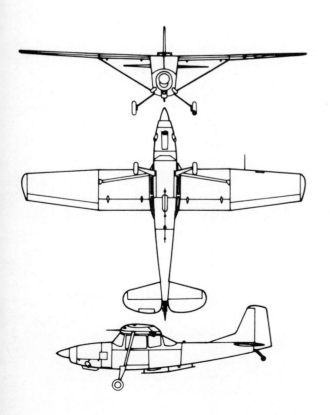

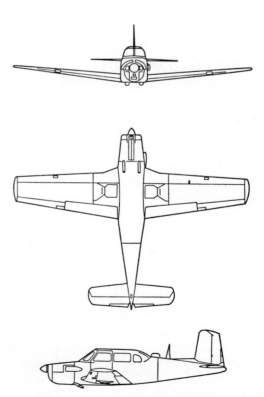

**FUJI T–1A 'HATSUTAKA'**

**Type**
two-seat trainer
**Weights**
empty 6,088 lb (2,757 kg)
normal 11,000 lb (4,993 kg)
**Performance**
maximum speed at 21,650 ft (6,600 m) 576 mph
    (927 km/hr)
maximum cruising speed 404 mph (650 km/hr)
range 652 miles (1,050 km)
ferry range 1,050 miles (1,690 km)
initial rate of climb 110.9 fps (33.8 m/sec)
service ceiling 47,200 ft ( 14,400 m)
**Dimensions**
wing span 34 ft 5 in (10.50 m)
length overall 39 ft 9 in (12.12 m)
height overall 13 ft 4½ in (4.07 m)
wing area 239.2 sq ft (22.22 sq m)
**Power Plant**
One Bristol Siddeley Orpheus 80506 turbojet rated at
    4,000 lb (1,810 kg) st
**Armament**
One 12.7 mm machine gun and max 1,500 lb (680 kg)
    weapon load, e.g. two 12.7 mm machine guns in
    weapon packs, two Sidewinder AAMs, two rocket
    launchers or two bombs
**Variants**
*T–1B*: Japanese power plant
**First flights**
Prototype: 19 January 1958
**Production**
*T–1A*: 42 built from 1959–1962;
*T–1B*: 22 built from 1961–1963
**In service**
Japan

**KAWASAKI (NAMC) C–1A**

**Type**
medium transport
**Weights**
empty 50,706 lb (23,000 kg)
maximum 85,980 lb (39,000 kg)
**Performance**
maximum speed at 23,200 ft (7,600 m)
    507 mph (815 km/hr)
maximum cruising speed at 35,100 ft (10,700 m)
    438 mph (704 km/hr)
range with 17,640 lb (8,000 kg) payload 866 miles
    (1,297 km)
ferry range 2,072 miles (3,335 km)
initial rate of climb 63.3 fps (19.3 m/sec)
service ceiling 39,375 ft (12,000 m)
**Dimensions**
wing span 10 ft 8½ in (31.00 m)
length overall 95 ft 1¾ in (29.00 m)
height overall 32 ft 9¾ in (10.00 m)
wing area 1,291.7 sq ft (120.00 sq m)
**Power Plant**
Two Pratt & Whitney JT8D–9 turbofans each rated at
    14,500 lb (6,575 kg) st
**Payload**
5 man crew and 60 troops or 45 paratroops or 36
    stretcher cases
**First flights**
Prototype: 12 November 1970
**Production**
2 prototypes, series production from 1972/1973,
    25 delivered or on order to date
**In service**
Japan

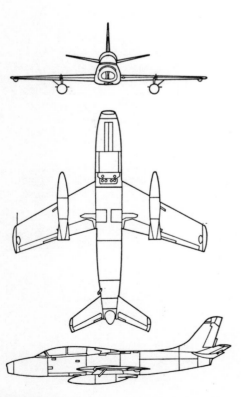

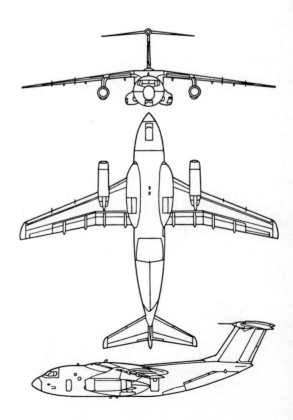

## MITSUBISHI MU–2C

**Type**
liaison and reconnaissance aircraft
**Weights**
empty 5,340 lb (2,422 kg)
maximum 8,929 lb (4,050 kg)
**Performance**
maximum cruising speed at 10,000 ft (3,050 m) 310 mph
(500 km/hr)
ferry range 1,200 miles (1,930 km)
initial rate of climb 35.4 fps (10.8 m/sec)
service ceiling 26,080 ft (7,950 m)
**Dimensions**
wing span 39 ft 2 in (11.94 m)
length overall 33 ft 2¾ in (10.13 m)
height overall 12 ft 11¼ in (3.94 m)
wing area 177.6 sq ft (16.50 sq m)
**Power Plant**
Two 575 hp Garrett AiResearch TPE–331–25A
turboprops
**Armament**
Two 12.7 mm machine guns, practice bombs, rockets,
2 cameras
**Payload**
1 man crew and 6–8 troops
**Variants**
*MU–2E*: ASR aircraft;
*MU–2G*; *MU–2J*: Further development
**First Flights**
Prototype: 14 September 1963
**Production**
Series production from 1966, over 197 delivered or on
order by beginning of 1973, inc 33 military variants:
(10 MU–2C, 19 MU–2E, 4 MU–2G)
**In service**
*MU–2C*: Japan (LR–1); *MU–2E*: Japan (MU–2S);
*MU–2G*: Japan, *MU–2J*: Mexico

## MITSUBISHI T–2

**Type**
two-seat strike trainer
**Weights**
maximum 20,833 lb (9,450 kg)
**Performance**
maximum speed at 40,000 ft (12,200 m) (Mach 1.6)
1,056 mph (1,700 km/hr)
ferry range 1,600 miles (2,575 km)
service ceiling 52,490 ft (16,000 m)
**Dimensions**
wing span 25 ft 11 in (7.90 m)
length overall 58 ft 4¾ in (17.80 m)
height overall 14 ft 9¼ in (4.50 m)
wing area 228.2 sq ft (21.20 sq m)
**Power Plant**
Two Rolls–Royce Turbomeca RB.172–T.260 Adour
turbofans each rated at 4,598 lb (2,086 kg)/6,945 lb
(3,150 kg) st
**Armament**
One 20 mm M–61A–1 cannon and max 6,000 lb (2,722 kg)
weapon load, e.g. eight 500 lb (227 kg) bombs
**Variants**
*Mitsubishi FS–T2 kai*: Planned single-seat strike fighter
(original designation F–1)
**First flights**
Prototype: 20 July 1971
**Production**
4 prototypes, series production from 1973, 59 *T–2*
delivered or on order to date
*FS–T2 kai*: 68 aircraft planned
**In service**
Japan

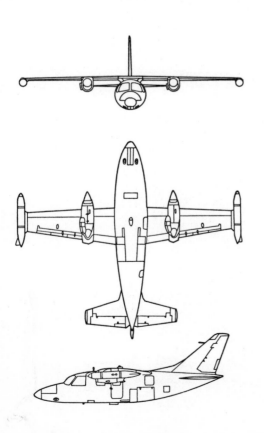

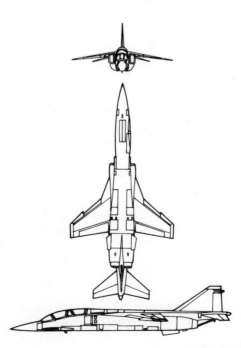

## NAMC YS–11A

**Type**
medium transport
**Weights**
empty 33,942 lb (15,396 kg)
maximum 54,010 lb (24,500 kg)
**Performance**
maximum speed at 15,000 ft (4,575 m)
   291 mph (469 km/hr)
maximum cruising speed at 20,000 ft (6,100 m)
   281 mph (452 km/hr)
range/w.m.p. 680 miles (1,090 km)
ferry range 1,998 miles (3,215 km)
initial rate of climb 20.3 fps (6.2 m/sec)
service ceiling 22,900 ft (6,980 m)
**Dimensions**
wing span 104 ft 11¾ in (32.00 m)
length overall 86 ft 3½ in (26.30 m)
height overall 29 ft 6¼ in (9.00 m)
wing area 1,020.4 sq ft (94.80 sq m)
**Power Plant**
Two 3,060 hp Rolls–Royce Dart Mk.542–10K turboprops
**Payload**
2 man crew and 32–48 troops or max 13,228 lb (6,000 kg)
   payload
**Variants**
*YS–11A–206*: ASW trainer: *YS–11A–207*: ASR aircraft
**First flights**
Prototype: 30 August 1962
**Production**
182 built from 1963–1972, 20 of which delivered to
   Japanese air arms (16 as transports and 4 as ASW
   trainers)
**In service**
Gabon, Japan, Philippines

## SHIN MEIWA PS–1

**Type**
amphibious maritime reconnaissance and ASW aircraft
9 man crew
**Weights**
empty 58,000 lb (26,300 kg)
normal 79,366 lb (36,000 kg)
maximum 99,208 lb (45,000 kg)
**Performance**
maximum speed at 5,000 ft (1,520 m) 340 mph (547 km/hr)
maximum cruising speed at 5,000 ft (1,520 m) 265 mph
   (426 km/hr)
range 1,346 miles (2,167 km)
ferry range 2,948 miles (4,745 km)
initial rate of climb 37.7 fps (6.9 m/sec)
time to 10,000 ft (3,000 m) 5 min 0 sec
service ceiling 29,500 ft (9,000 m)
**Dimensions**
wing span 108 ft 8¾ in (33.14 m)
length overall 109 ft 10¼ in (33.48 m)
height overall 31 ft 10 in (9.70 m)
wing area 1,453.1 sq ft (135.80 sq m)
**Power Plant**
Four 3,060 hp Ishikawajima–Harima (General Electric)
   T64–IHI–10 turboprops
**Armament**
Max 8,820 lb (4,000 kg) weapon load, e.g. four 330 lb
   (150 kg) depth charges in weapons bay, two underwing
   pods mounted between each pair of engine nacelles
   and each containing 2 homing torpedoes, and one
   launcher beneath each wingtip each containing three
   127 mm rockets
**Variants**
*SS–2*: Further development as ASR aircraft (US–1)
**First flights**
Prototype: 5 October 1967
**Production**
2 Prototypes; 2 pre-production models 1972; 14 production
   models from 1972–1976, another 3 SS–2 ordered for
   delivery by 1976
**In service**
Japan

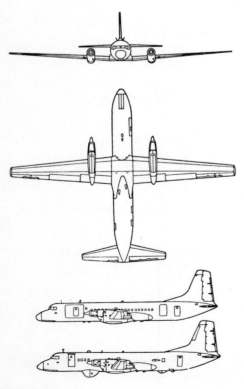

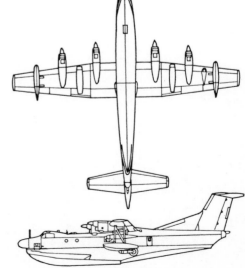

## FOKKER S.11 'INSTRUCTOR'

**Type**
Two-seat trainer
**Weights**
empty 1,808 lb (820 kg)
maximum 2,425 lb (1,100 kg)
**Performance**
maximum speed at sea level 130 mph (209 km/hr)
maximum cruising speed 102 mph (164 km/hr)
ferry range 400 miles (644 km)
time to 9,840 ft (3,000 m) 19 min 30 sec
service ceiling 13,120 ft (4,000 m)
**Dimensions**
wing span 36 ft 1 in (11.00 m)
length overall 26 ft 8 in (8.13 m)
height overall 7 ft 5 in (2.26 m)
wing area 199.1 sq ft (18.50 sq m)
**Power plant**
One 190 hp Lycoming 0–435–A piston engine
**Variants**
*S.12*: trainer similar to S.11 but with fixed tricycle :
    undercarriage
**First flights**
Prototype: 1947
**Production**
*S.11*: 291 built from 1948–, inc 150 licence-built in Italy
    (Macchi M.416) and 100 Brazilian licence-built; *S.12;*
    70 built from 1954
**In service**
*S.11*: Brazil, Israel (?), Italy, Netherlands;
*S.12*: Brazil

## FOKKER–VFW F.27M 'TROOPSHIP'

**Type**
Medium transport
**Weights**
empty 23,200 lb (10,524 kg)
maximum 42,000 lb (19,051 kg)
**Performance**
maximum speed at 20,000 ft (6,100 m)
maximum cruising speed 282 mph (454 km/hr)
range/w.m.p. 656 miles (1,056 km)
ferry range 1,285 miles (2,068 km)
initial rate of climb 23.3 fps (7.1 m /sec)
service ceiling 30,184 ft (9,200 m)
**Dimensions**
wing span 95 ft 2 in (29.00 m)
length overall 17 ft 3½ in (23.56 m)
height overall 27 ft 6¾ in (8.40 m)
wing area 754 sq ft (70.00 sq m)
**Power plant**
Two 2,210 hp Rolls–Royce Dart R.Da. 7 Mk.532–7
    turboprops
**Payload**
2–3 man crew and 45 paratroops or 24 stretcher cases
    and 7 medics or max 10,000 lb (4,536 kg) freight
**Variants**
*F.27* Friendship: Civil airliner for 40–56 passengers
**First flights**
Prototype: 24 November 1955
**Production**
*F.27M*: 38 built from 1958–1971;
*F.27*: Over 596 delivered or on order to date
**In service**
*F.27M*: Iran, Ivory Coast, Netherlands, Sudan (?),
    Uruguay;
*F.27*: Argentine, Iceland, Iran, Netherlands, New Zealand
    Nigeria, Pakistan, Philippines

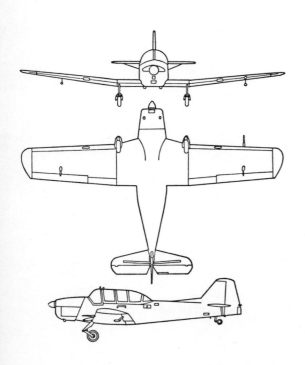

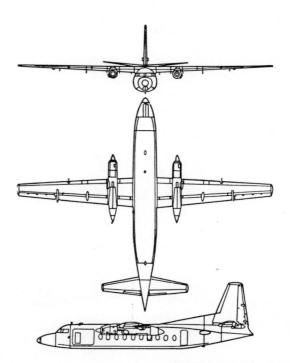

## AESL 'AIRTRAINER' CT.4

**Type**
Two-three seat trainer
**Weights**
empty 1,521 lb (690 kg)
maximum 2,358 lb (1,070 kg)
**Performance**
maximum speed at sea level 180 mph (290 km/hr)
maximum speed at 5,265 ft (1,605 m) 172 mph (278 km/hr)
maximum cruising speed at sea level 155 mph (250 km/hr)
range 808 (?) miles (1,300 (?) km)
initial rate of climb 22.3 fps (6.8 m/sec)
**Dimensions**
wing span 26 ft 0 in (7.92 m)
length overall 23 ft 5½ in (7.15 m)
height overall 8 ft 6 in (2.59 m)
wing area 129.0 sq ft (12.00 sq m)
**Power plant**
One 210 hp Continental 10–360–D piston engine
**Variants**
*Airtourer T.6*: Earlier version
**First flights**
Prototype: 21 February 1972
**Production**
Series production from 1973, over 200 delivered or on
  order to date
**In service**
*Airtrainer CT.4*: Australia, Thailand
*Airtrainer T.6*: New Zealand, Singapore, Thailand

## PZL–104 'WILGA' 35AD

**Type**
Liaison and AOP aircraft
**Weights**
empty 1,874 lb (850 kg)
maximum 2,711 lb (1,230 kg)
**Performance**
maximum speed 130 mph (210 km/hr)
maximum cruising speed 120 mph (193 km/hr)
ferry range 422 miles (680 km)
initial rate of climb 21.0 fps (8.0 m/sec)
service ceiling 15,025 ft (4,580 m)
**Dimensions**
wing span 36 ft 6 in (11.12 m)
length overall 26 ft 6¾ in (8.10 m)
height overall 9 ft 4¼ in (2.85 m)
wing area 166.8 sq ft (15.50 sq m)
**Power Plant**
One 260 hp Ivchenko AI–14R piston engine
**Payload**
1 man crew and 3 troops or 1 stretcher case and 1 medic
**First flights**
Prototype: 24 April 1962
**Production**
Series production from 1963, 56 Indonesian licence-built
  by Lipnur
**In service**
Bulgaria, Germany (East), Indonesia (Gelatik), Korea
  (North), Mongolian Peoples Republic, Poland, Soviet
  Union.

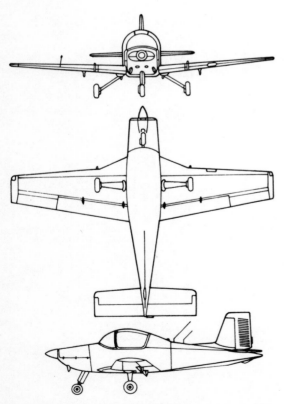

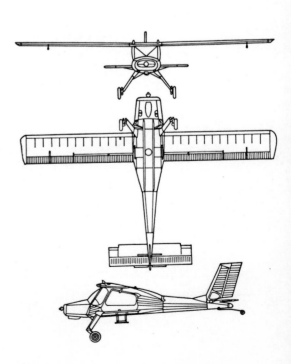

## WSK SM–2

**Type**
Light helicopter
**Weights**
empty 4,167 lb (1,890 kg)
maximum 5,500 lb (2,495 kg)
**Performance**
maximum speed at 6,560 ft (2,000 m) 105 mph
   (170 km/hr)
maximum cruising speed 81 mph (130 km/hr)
range 190 miles (305 km)
ferry range 310 miles (500 km)
initial rate of climb 14.8 fps (4.5 m/sec)
service ceiling 13,120 ft (4,000 m)
hovering ceiling in ground effect 6,103 ft (1,860 m)
**Dimensions**
main rotor diameter 47 ft 1 in (14.35 m)
length of fuselage 39 ft 8½ in (12.09 m)
height 10 ft 10 in (3.30 m)
**Power Plant**
One 575 hp LiT–3 piston engine
**Payload**
1 man crew and 4 troops or 3 stretcher cases or max
   705 lb (320 kg) freight
**First flights**
Prototype: 1960
**Production**
Series production from 1961
**In service**
Hungary, Poland, Rumania

## WSK TS–11 'ISKRA'

**Type**
Two-seat trainer
**Weights**
empty 5,390 lb (2,445 kg)
normal 6,834 lb (3,100 kg)
maximum 8,378 lb (3,800 kg)
**Performance**
maximum speed at 26,250 ft (8,000 m) 491 mph
   (790 km/hr)
maximum cruising speed 342 mph (550 km/hr)
ferry range 907 miles (1,460 km)
initial rate of climb 75.5 fps (23.0 m/sec)
time to 20,000 ft (6,000 m) 9 min 36 sec
service ceiling 41,010 ft (12,500 m)
**Dimensions**
wing span 33 ft 0½ in (10.07 m)
length overall 36 ft 11 in (11.25 m)
height overall 11 ft 0½ in (3.37 m)
wing area 188.4 sq ft (17.50 sq m)
**Power Plant**
One OKL S0–1 turbojet rated at 2,205 lb (1,000 kg) st
**Armament**
Machine guns or cannon, bombs or unguided rockets
**First flights**
Prototype: 5 February 1960
**Production**
Series production from 1963
**In service**
Poland

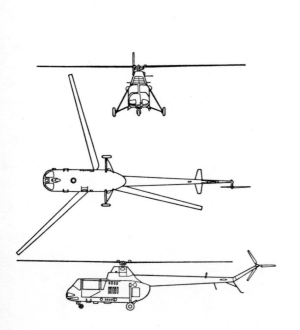

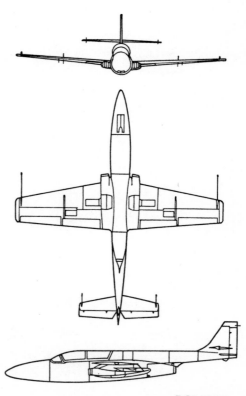

## ANTONOV AN-2 (COLT)

**Type**
Light transport
**Weights**
empty 7,496 lb (3,400 kg)
normal 11,574 lb (5,250 kg)
maximum 12,125 lb (5,500 kg)
**Performance**
maximum speed at 5,750 ft (1,750 m) 159 mph
    (256 km/hr)
maximum cruising speed at 3,820 ft (1,000 m) 118 mph
    (190 km/hr)
range/w.m.p. 559 miles (900 km)
initial rate of climb 9.2 fps (2.8 m/sec)
time to 6,560 ft (2,000 m) 8 min 6 sec
service ceiling 14,750 ft (4,500 m)
**Dimensions**
wing span (Upper) 59 ft 8½ in (18.18 m)
wing span (Lower) 46 ft 8½ in (14.24 m)
length overall 41 ft 9½ in (12.74 m)
height overall 13 ft 7¾ in (4.16 m)
wing area 767.5 sq ft (71.31 sq m)
**Power Plant**
One 1,000 hp Shvetsov ASh–62–IR piston engine
**Payload**
2 man crew and 10–12 troops or 14 paratroops or 6
    stretcher cases and 2 medics or max 2,634 lb (1,240 kg)
    freight
**Variants**
Over 18 variants, inc An-2NAK, An-2P, An-2S, An-2Sa
    and An-2W
*Fongshu 2*: Chinese licence-built An-2;
*An-2M*: Further development
**First flights**
Prototype: 1947
**Production**
*An-2*: Series production from 1949, over 5,000 delivered
    up to 1962
Licence-built in Poland by PZL (from 1960) and China
    from 1957),
*An-2M*: Series production from 1964
**In service**
Afghanistan, Albania, Bulgaria, Cambodia (?), China
    (Fongshu 2), Cuba, Czechoslovakia, Germany (East),
    Hungary, Iraq, Korea (North), Mali (?), Mongolian
    People's Republic, Poland, Rumania, Somali, Soviet
    Union (SS-1), Tanzania, Vietnam (North)

## ANTONOV AN-12 (Cub)

**Type**
Medium transport
**Weights**
empty 61,700 lb (28,000 kg)
normal 119,000 lb (54,000 kg)
maximum 134,500 lb (61,000 kg)
**Performance**
maximum speed 416 mph (670 km/hr)
maximum cruising speed 360 mph (580 km/hr)
range with 22,000 lb (10,000 kg) payload 2,110 miles
    (3,400 km)
ferry range 3,542 miles (5,700 km)
initial rate of climb 32.8 fps (10.0 m/sec)
service ceiling 33,465 ft (10,200 m)
**Dimensions**
wing span 124 ft 8 in (38.00 m)
length overall 121 ft 4¾ in (37.00 m)
height overall 32 ft 1 in (9.78 m)
wing area 1,286.3 sq ft (119.50 sq m)
**Power Plant**
Four 4,000 hp Ivchenko AI–20K turboprops
**Armament**
One 20 mm cannon or two 23 mm NR–23 cannon in
    tail position
**Payload**
3–5 man crew and 120 troops or 100 paratroops or max
    35,270 lb (16,000 kg) freight
**Variants**
*An–10A(CAT)*: Civil airliner
**First flights**
Prototype: 1957
**Production**
Series production from 1958, over 1,000 built to date
**In service**
Algeria, Egypt (UAR), India, Indonesia, Iraq, Poland,
    Soviet Union, Sudan

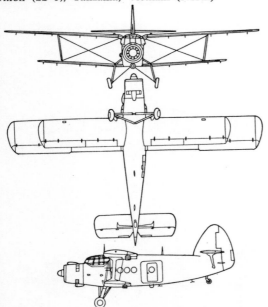

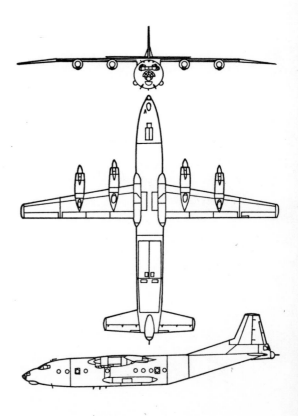

## ANTONOV AN–14 'PCHELKA' (Clod)

**Type**
Light transport and liaison aircraft
**Weights**
empty 5,730 lb (2,600 kg)
maximum 7,935 lb (3,600 kg)
**Performance**
maximum speed at 3,280 ft (1,000 m) 137 mph
 (220 km/hr)
maximum cruising speed at 6,560 ft (2,000 m) 109 mph
 (175 km/hr)
range/w.m.p. 292 miles (470 km)
range with 1,290 lb (630 kg) payload 422 miles (680 km)
initial rate of climb 16.7 fps (5.1 m/sec)
time to 6,560 ft (2,000 m) 8 min 0 sec
service ceiling 16,400 ft (5,000 m)
**Dimensions**
wing span 72 ft 2½ in (22.00 m)
length overall 37 ft 1½ in (11.32 m)
height overall 15 ft 2½ in (4.63 m)
wing area 441 sq ft (41.00 sq m)
**Power Plant**
Two 300 hp Ivchenko AI–14RF piston engines
**Payload**
1 man crew and 7–9 troops or 8 paratroops or 6 stretcher
 cases and 2 medics or max 1,590 lb (720 kg) freight
**Variants**
Also civil versions; *An–14A*: further development for
 11–15 passengers
*Capital No. 1 Shat–Tu*: Scaled-down Chinese version
 of An–14 licence-built from 1958–1959
**First flights**
Prototype: 15 March 1958
**Production**
Series production from 1965
**In service**
China, Germany (East), Guinea, Soviet Union

## ANTONOV AN–22 'ANTHEUS' (Cock)

**Type**
Strategic transport
**Weights**
empty 251,300 lb (114,000 kg)
maximum 551,200 lb (250,000 kg)
**Performance**
maximum speed at 26,250 ft (8,000 m)–32,800 ft
 (10,000 m) 460 mph (740 km/hr)
maximum cruising speed at 26,250 ft (8,000 m)–32,800 ft
 (10,000 m) 423 mph (679 km/hr)
range with 99,200 lb (45,000 kg) payload 6,835 miles
 (11,000 km)
service ceiling 26,250–32,800 ft (8,000–10,000 m)
**Dimensions**
wing span 211 ft 4 in (64.40 m)
length overall 189 ft 7 in (57.80 m)
height overall 41 ft 1½ in (12.53 m)
wing area 3,713 sq ft (345.00 sq m)
**Power Plant**
Four 15,000 hp Kusnetsov NK–12MA turboprops
**Payload**
5–6 man crew and 28–29 troops plus max 176,350 lb
 (80,000 kg) freight
**Variants**
Civil version for 300–350 passengers
**First flights**
Prototype: 27 February 1965;
production model: 1967
**Production**
Series production from 1967
**In service**
Soviet Union

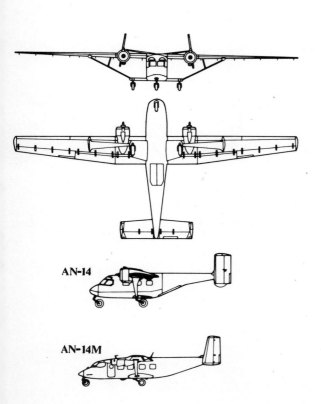

AN–14

AN–14M

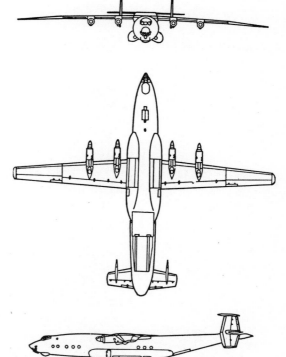

## ANTONOV AN–26 (Curl)

**Type**
Medium transport

**Weights**
empty 37,300 lb (16,914 kg)
maximum 52,910 lb (24,000 kg)

**Performance**
maximum speed at 19,700 ft (6,000 m) 335 mph
   (540 km/hr)
maximum cruising speed at 19,700 ft (6,000 m) 280 mph
   (450 km/hr)
range with 3,300 lb (1,500 kg) payload 1,550 miles
   (2,500 km)
range/w.m.p. 800 miles (1,300 km)
service ceiling 24,935 ft (7,600 m)

**Dimensions**
wing span 95 ft 9½ in (29.20 m)
length overall 77 ft 2½ in (23.53 m)
height overall 27 ft 3½ in (8.32 m)
wing area 780 sq ft (72.46 sq m)

**Power Plant**
Two 2,820 hp Ivchenko AI–24T turboprops plus one
   Tumansky RU–19–300 auxiliary turbojet rated at
   1,985 lb (900 kg) st in starboard nacelle

**Payload**
5 man crew and 38 troops or max 11,000 lb (5,000 kg)
   freight

**Variants**
*An–24 (Coke)*: Civil airliner

**First flights**
Prototype An–24: 1959
*An–24*: series production since 1961, over 320 (?) built;
*An–26*: series production since 1969

**In service**
*An–24, An–26*: Congo (Brazzaville) (?), Cuba, Czecho-
slovakia, Egypt (UAR), Iraq, Mongolian People's
Republic, Somali, Soviet Union, Sudan, Vietnam
(North)

## BERIEV BE–6 (Madge)

**Type**
Maritime reconnaissance and ASW flying boat

**Weights**
empty 41,505 lb (18,827 kg)
normal 51,590 lb (23,400 kg)
maximum 55,120 lb (25,000 kg)

**Performance**
maximum speed at sea level 234 mph (377 km/hr)
maximum speed at 8,200 ft (2,500 m) 258 mph
   (415 km/hr)
maximum cruising speed 211 mph (340 km/hr)
ferry range 3,040 miles (4,900 km)

**Dimensions**
wing span 108 ft 3¼ in (33.00 m)
length overall 77 ft 3½ in (23.56 m)
height overall 225 ft 0¾ in (7.64 m)
wing area 1,291.7 sq ft (120.00 sq m)

**Power plant**
Two 2,400 hp Shvetsov ASh–73TK piston engines

**Armament**
Three–four 23 mm cannon, mines, bombs and torpedoes
   in fuselage bay, rockets and bombs underwing

**Variants**
4 variants: Maritime reconnaissance aircraft with tail
   armament; ASW aircraft with MAD (magnetic anom-
   aly detection) search equipment in tail 'sting'; ASW
   aircraft with ECM direction finding equipment; rescue
   and transport aircraft

**First flights**
Prototype: 1947

**Production**
Series production from 1949

**In service**
China, Soviet Union

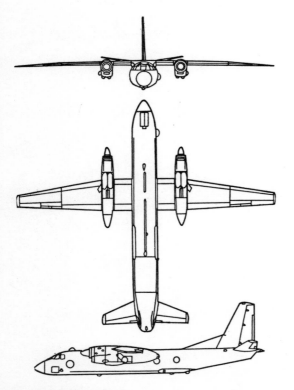

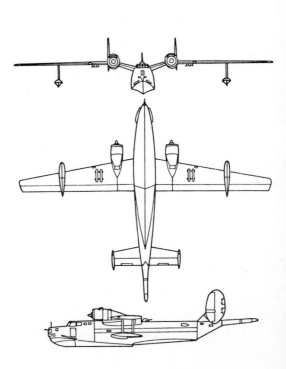

**BERIEV BE-10 (Mallow)**

**Type**
Maritime reconnaissance and ASW flying boat
**Weights**
empty 53,131 lb (24,100 kg)
normal 90,390 lb (41,000 kg)
maximum 105,515 lb (46,500 kg)
**Performance**
maximum speed at 5,000 ft (1,500 m) (Mach 0.75)
    565 mph (910 km/hr)
maximum speed at 36,000 ft (11,000 m) 500 mph
    (815 km/hr)
maximum cruising speed 348–398 mph (560–640 km/hr)
radius of action w.m.p. 1,305 miles (2,100 km)
ferry range 2,982 miles (4,800 km)
service ceiling 45,930 ft (14,000 m)
**Dimensions**
wing span 73 ft 1¾ in (22.30 m)
length overall 102 ft 0¼ in (31.10 m)
height overall 32 ft 11¾ in (10.08 m)
wing area 1,203.4 sq ft (111.80 sq m)
**Power plant**
Two Lyulka AL-7PB turbojets each rated at 14,330 lb
    (6,500 kg) st
**Armament**
Two fixed 23 mm cannon in nose, two 23 mm cannon
    in manned tail position and max 4,410 lb (2,000 kg)
    weapon load, e.g. rockets, bombs and mines
**First flights**
Prototype: 1959
**Production**
Series production from 1960
**In service**
Soviet Union (M-10)

**BERIEV BE-12 'TCHAIKA' (Mail)**

**Type**
Maritime reconnaissance amphibian 6–10 man crew
**Weights**
maximum 59,525–65,035 lb (27,000–29,500 kg)
**Performance**
maximum speed at 10,000 ft (3,050 m) 379 mph
    (610 km/hr)
maximum cruising speed at 15,000 ft (4,570 m) 340 mph
    (547 km/hr)
patrol speed at 5,000 ft (1,500 m): 199–249 mph
    (320–400 km/hr)
ferry range 2,500 miles (4,025 km)
initial rate of climb 49.9 fps (15.2 m/sec)
service ceiling 37,075 ft (11,300 m)
**Dimensions**
wing span 107 ft 11½ in (32.90 m)
length overall 96 ft 1½ in (29.30 m)
height overall 22 ft 11½ in (7.00 m)
wing area 1027.9 sq ft (95.70 sq m)
**Power plant**
Two 4,190 hp Ivchenko A1-20D turboprops
**Armament**
Homing torpedoes, depth charges, mines, rockets, bombs
**First flights**
Prototype: 1960
**Production**
Series production from 1964
**In service**
Soviet Union (M-12)

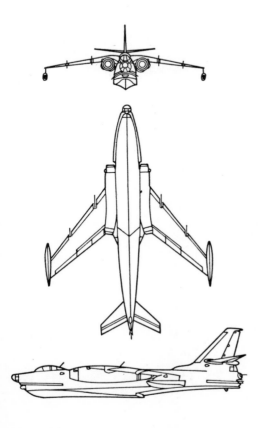

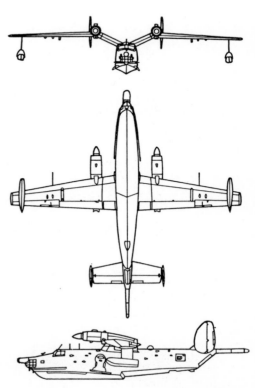

## ILYUSHIN IL-14M (CRATE)

**Type**
Medium transport
**Weights**
empty 27,998 lb (12,700 kg)
maximum 38,580 lb (17,500 kg)
**Performance**
maximum speed at 7,875 ft (2,400 m) 268 mph
(431 km/hr)
maximum cruising speed 8,200–9,850 ft (2,500–3,000 m)
199 mph (320 km/hr)
range with 3,527 lb (1,600 kg) payload 1,087 miles
(1,750 km)
initial rate of climb 20.0 fps (6.1 m/sec)
service ceiling 24,280 ft (7,400 m)
**Dimensions**
wing span 104 ft 0½ in (31.70 m)
length overall 73 ft 2½ in (22.31 m)
height overall 25 ft 7¼ in (7.80 m)
wing area 1,076 sq ft (100 sq m)
**Power plant**
Two 1,900 hp Shvetsov ASh–82T–7 piston engines
**Payload**
3 man crew and 30–32 troops or 24 paratroops or max
7,275 lb (3,300 kg) freight
**First flights**
Il–14: 1953
Il–14M: 1956
**Production**
*Il–14*: Approx 3,500 built from 1954; licence-built in
East Germany as Il–14P from 1956–1959; Czech licence-
built as Avia–14
**In service**
Afghanistan, Albania, Bulgaria, Cambodia (?), China,
Congo Brazzaville (?), Cuba, Czechoslovakia, Egypt,
Ethiopia, Germany (East), Guinea, Hungary, India,
Indonesia, Iraq, Korea (North), Mongolia, People's
Republic, Poland, Rumania, Soviet Union, Syria,
Vietnam (North), Yemen, Yugoslavia

## ILYUSHIN IL-12 (COACH)

**Type**
Medium transport
Details as for Il–14M with the following exceptions
**Weights**
empty 808 lb (12,000 kg)
maximum 38,030 lb (17,250 kg)
**Performance**
maximum speed at 8,200 ft (2,500 m) 253 mph
(407 km/hr)
maximum cruising speed at 8,200–9,850 ft (2,500–3,000 m)
205 mph (330 km/hr)
range with 3,527 lb (1,600 kg) payload 777 miles
(1,250 km)
ferry range 1,243 miles (2,000 km)
initial rate of climb 15.1 fps (4.6 m/sec)
service ceiling 21,980 ft (6,700 m)
**Dimensions**
length overall 69 ft 11 in (21.30 m)
height overall 26 ft (8.07 m)
**Power plant**
Two 1,775 hp Shvetsov ASh–82FNV piston engines
**Payload**
4 man crew and 26 troops or 20 paratroops or max
6,614 lb (3,000 kg) freight
**Variants**
**First flights**
*Il–12*: 1945
**Production**
*Il–12*: Approx 3,000 built from 1947
**In service**
Bulgaria, China, Korea (North), Mongolian People's
Republic, Poland, Rumania, Soviet Union, Vietnam
(North)

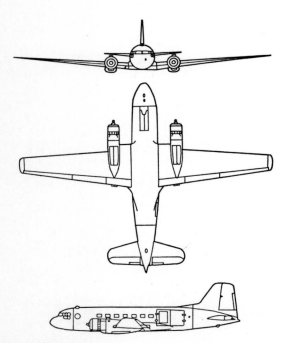

## ILYUSHIN IL-18 (COOT)

**Type**
Medium transport
**Weights**
empty 77,162 lb (35,000 kg)
maximum 141,100 lb (64,000 kg)
**Performance**
maximum speed 400 mph (675 km/hr)
maximum cruising speed at 26,250 ft (8,000 m)
   388 mph (625 km/hr)
range with 29,760 lb (13,500 kg) payload 2,300 miles
   (3,700 km)
ferry range 4,038 miles (6,500 km)
service ceiling 35,470 ft (10,750 m)
**Dimensions**
wing span 122 ft 9 in (37.40 m)
length overall 117 ft 9¾ in (35.90 m)
height overall 33 ft 3¾ in (10.16 m)
wing area 1,507 sq ft (140.00 sq m)
**Power plant**
Four 4,250 hp Ivchenko AI-20M turboprops
**Payload**
5 man crew and max 29,760 lb (13,500 kg) freight
**Variants**
Il-38 (May): Conversion of Il-18 to maritime
   reconnaissance and ASW aircraft with 12 man crew
**First flights**
Prototype *Il-18*: 4 July 1957
**Production**
*Il-18*: 541 (?) built from 1957-1967
**In service**
Afghanistan, Algeria, Bulgaria (?), China, Czechoslovakia,
   Germany (East), Guinea, Poland, Rumania, Soviet
   Union, Syria (?), Yugoslavia

## ILYUSHIN IL-38 (MAY)

**Type**
Maritime reconnaissance and ASW aircraft
Details as for Il-18 with the following exceptions
**Weights**
empty 80,000 lb (36,287 kg)
maximum 140,000 lb (63,500 kg)
**Performance**
maximum speed 400 mph (645 km/hr)
patrol speed at 2,000 ft (610 m) 250 mph (400 km/hr)
ferry range 4,500 miles (7,240 km)
**Dimensions**
length overall 131 ft 0 in (39.92 m)
**Payload**
12 man crew
**First flights**
Prototype Il-38: 1968
**Production**
From 1969
**In service**
Soviet Union

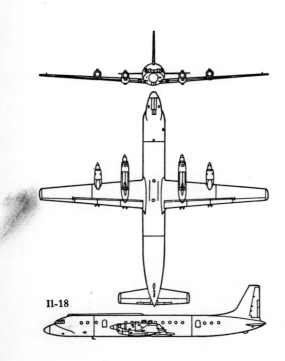

Il-18

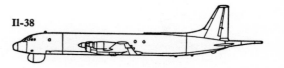

Il-38

## ILYUSHIN IL-28 (BEAGLE)

**Type**
Three-seat light bomber
**Weights**
empty 28,417 lb (12,890 kg)
normal 40,565 lb (18,400 kg)
maximum 51,148 lb (23,200 kg)
**Performance**
maximum speed at sea level 497 mph (800 km/hr)
maximum speed at 14,765 ft (4,500 m) 559 mph
  (900 km/hr)
maximum cruising speed at 32,800 ft (10,000 m)
  478 mph (770 km/hr)
radius of action 590 miles (950 km)
ferry range 2,144 miles (3,450 km)
initial rate of climb 49.2 fps (15.0 m/sec)
time to 41,300 ft (12,600 m) 45 min
service ceiling 40,355 ft (12,300 m)
**Dimensions**
wing span 70 ft 4¾ in (21.45 m)
length overall 57 ft 10¾ in (17.65 m)
height overall 20 ft 4¼ in (6.20 m)
wing area 654.44 sq ft (60.80 sq m)
**Power plant**
Two Klimov VK–1 turbojets each rated at
  5,952 lb (2,700 kg) st
**Armament**
Two 23 mm NR–23 cannon with 85 rpg in fuselage
  nose and two 23 mm NR–23 cannon with 225 rpg
  in tail position; max 6,614 lb (3,000 kg) weapon load,
  e.g., bombs, torpedoes, mines
**Variants**
*Il–28T*: Torpedo bomber; *Il–28R*: Reconnaissance
  aircraft with 3–5 cameras
*Il–28U* (*Mascot*): Bomber trainer
*Il–20*: Civil transport version
**First flights**
Prototype: 8 August 1948
**Production**
Several thousand built from 1949–1961; licence-built in
  Czechoslovakia, version also built in China. Conversion
  from ECM aircraft from 1965/1966
**In service**
Afghanistan, Algeria, Bulgaria, China, Czechoslovakia,
  Egypt (UAR), Finland, Germany (East), Hungary,
  Indonsesia, Iraq, Korea (North), Morocco, Nigeria,
  Poland, Rumania, Somali (?) Soviet Union, Vietnam
  (North), Yemen

## KAMOV Ka-15 (HEN)

**Type**
Light AOP helicopter
**Weights**
empty 1,764 lb (800 kg)
normal 2,588 lb (1,174 kg)
**Performance**
maximum speed at sea level 93 mph (150 km/hr)
maximum cruising speed 75 mph (120 km/hr)
range 180 miles (290 km)
ferry range 292 miles (470 km)
service ceiling 9,845 ft (3,000 m)
**Dimensions**
main rotor diameter 32 ft 8 in (9.96 m)
length of fuselage 19 ft 6¼ in (5.95 m)
height 10 ft 10 in (3.30 m)
**Power plant**
One 255 hp Ivchenko AI–14V piston engine
**Payload**
1 man crew and 1 observer or max 661 lb (300 kg) freight
**Variants**
*Ka–15M*: Civil variant
*Ka–18* (*Hog*): Further development
**First flights**
Prototype: 1952
**Production**
Series production from 1953–1965
**In service**
Soviet Union

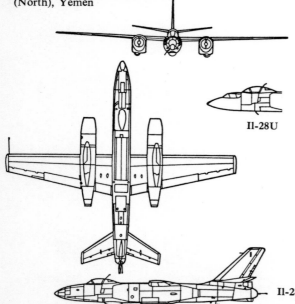

Il-28U

Il-28

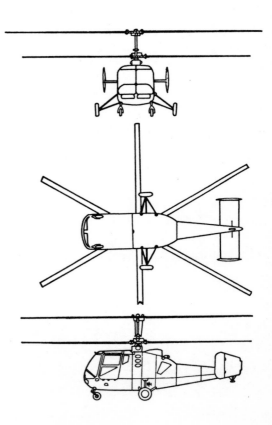

## KAMOV Ka-25 (HORMONE-A)

**Type**
Shipboard ASW helicopter
3–4 man crew
**Weights**
empty 9,700 lb (4,400 kg)
maximum 16,100 lb (7,300 kg)
**Performance**
maximum speed at sea level 135 mph (220 km/hr)
maximum cruising speed 120 mph (195 km/hr)
range 250 miles (400 km)
ferry range 405 miles (650 km)
service ceiling 11,500 ft (3,500 m)
**Dimensions**
main rotor diameter 51 ft 8 in (15.73 m)
length of fuselage 32 ft 11 in (9.83 m)
height 17 ft 8 in (5.73 m)
**Power plant**
Two 900 hp Glushenkov GTD–3 turboshafts
**Armament**
Two homing torpedoes or bombs and mines
**Variants**
*Ka–20 (HARP)*: Earlier version
*Ka–25K (HORMONE–A)*: Civil version
**First flights**
Prototype 1961; Ka–25K: 1965
**Production**
Series production from 1962
**In service**
Soviet Union

## MIKOYAN–GUREVICH MiG–15UTI (MIDGET)

**Type**
Two-seat trainer
**Weights**
empty 8,818 lb (4,000 kg)
normal 10,692 bl (4,850 kg)
maximum 11,905 lb (5,400 kg)
**Performance**
maximum speed at sea level 628 mph (1,010 km/hr)
maximum cruising speed at 16,400 ft (5,000 m)
    423 mph (680 km/hr)
ferry range with two 55 gall (2501) auxiliary tanks
    833 miles (1,340 km)
initial rate of climb 126.3 fps (38.5 m/sec)
service ceiling 48,637 ft (14,825 m)
**Dimensions**
wing span 36 ft 1 in (11.00 m)
length overall 33 ft 1¾ in (10.10 m)
height overall 12 ft 2 in (3.70 m)
wing area 222.8 sq ft (20.70 sq m)
**Power plant**
One RD–45F turbojet rated at 5,005 lb (2,270 kg) st
**Armament**
One 12.7 mm UBK–E machine-gun with 150 rpg; one
    23 mm NR–23 cannon with 80 rpg; two 220 lb (100 kg)
    bombs
**Variants**
*CS–102*: Czechoslovakian licence-built; *LIM–3*: Polish
    licence-built; *MiG–15 and MiG–15 bis (FAGOT)*:
    Single-seat strike fighters; *Shenyang F–2*: Chinese
    licence-built MiG–15
**First flights**
Prototype *MiG–15*: 30 December 1947
*MiG–15 UTI*: 1949/50 (?)
**Production**
Series production from 1950–1958 (1960?)
**In service**
Afghanistan, Albania, Algeria, Bulgaria, Ceylon (Sri
    Lanka), China, Cuba, Czechoslovakia, Egypt (UAR),
    Finland, Germany (East), Hungary, Indonesia, Iraq,
    Korea (North), Mali, Mongolian People's Republic,
    Morocco, Nigeria (?), Pakistan, Poland, Rumania,
    Somali, Soviet Union, Syria, Uganda (?), Vietnam
    (North)

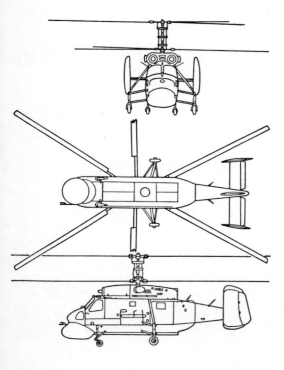

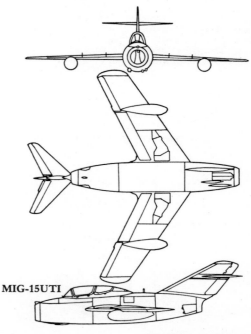

MIG-15UTI

## MIKOYAN–GUREVICH MiG–17
### ('FRESCO–A, B and C')

**Type**
Single-seat fighter and strike fighter
**Weights**
normal 12,566 lb (5,700 kg)
maximum 14,330 lb (6,500 kg)
**Performance**
maximum speed at sea level (Mach 0.92) 699 mph
  (1,125 km/hr)
maximum speed at 34,400 ft (10,500 m) (Mach 0.98)
  655 mph (1,055 km/hr)
maximum cruising speed at 32,830 ft (10,000 m)
  485 mph (780 km/hr)
radius of action 360 miles (580 km)
ferry range 1,398 miles (2,250 km)
initial rate of climb 164.0 fps (50.0 m/sec)
time to 39,375 ft (12,000 m) 7 min 54 sec
service ceiling 54,100 ft (16,500 m)
**Dimensions**
wing span 31 ft 7 in (9.63 m)
length overall 36 ft 4½ in (11.09 m)
height overall 12 ft 5¾ in (3.80 m)
wing area 243.3 sq ft (22.60 sq m)
**Power plant**
One Klimov VK–1A turbojet rated at 5,953 lb
  (2,700 kg)/7,055 lb (3,200 kg) st
**Armament**
*FRESCO–A and B*: Two 23 mm NR–23 cannon with
  80 rpg, one 37 mm NS–37 cannon with 40 rpg
*FRESCO–C*: Three 23 mm NR–23 cannon, two 550 lb
  (250 kg) bombs or 4 rocket launchers each containing
  eight 55 mm rockets or four unguided rockets
**Variants**
*LIM–5, S–104*: Polish and Czechoslovakian licence-built
  FRESCO–C; *Shenyang F–4*; Chinese licence-built
  MiG–17
*LIM–6*: Polish single–seat ground-attack aircraft
**First flights**
Prototype: January 1950
**Production**
Series production from 1952/53; licence-built in China,
  Czechoslovakia, Poland
**In service**
*MiG–17*: Afghanistan, Albania, Algeria, Bulgaria, Ceylon
  (Sri Lanka), China, Cuba, Czechoslovakia, Egypt
  (UAR), Guinea, Hungary, Indonesia, Iraq, Korea
  (North), Mali, Morocco, Nigeria, Poland, Rumania,
  Somali, South Yemen, Soviet Union, Syria, Uganda,
  Vietnam (North), Yemen
*F–4*: Albania, China, Korea (North), Sudan, Tanzania

## MIKOYAN–GUREVICH MiG–17
### ('Fresco–D, E and F')

**Type**
Single-seat all-weather fighter
(Details as for 'Fresco–A, B and C' with the following
  exceptions)
**Weights**
normal 12,897 lb (5,850 kg)
maximum 14,705 lb (6,670 kg)
**Performance**
maximum speed at 34,450 ft (10,500 m) (Mach 0.93)
  634 mph (1,020 km/hr)
time to 39,370 ft (12,000 m) 8 min 12 sec
**Dimensions**
length overall 38 ft 4¾in (11.70 m)
**Power plant**
One Klimov VK–1FA turbojet rated at 5,953 lb
  (2,700 kg)/7,456 lb (3,380 kg) st
**Armament**
*FRESCO–D, E and F*: Details as for FRESCO–C
*FRESCO–D, E*: Alternative): 4 ALKALI AAMs

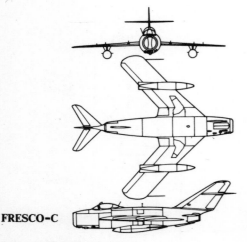

FRESCO-C

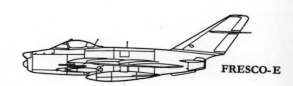

FRESCO-E

## MIKOYAN MiG-19 (FARMER-C)

**Type**
Single-seat fighter and strike fighter
**Weights**
empty 12,125 lb (5,500 kg)
normal 18,628 lb (8,450 kg)
maximum 20,503 lb (9,300 kg)
**Performance**
maximum speed at sea level (Mach 0.95) 684 mph
    (1,100 km/hr)
maximum speed at 32,800 ft (10,000 m) (Mach 1.33)
    900 mph (1,450 km/hr)
maximum cruising speed 590 mph (950 km/hr)
radius of action 280–425 miles (450–685 km)
ferry range 1,367 miles (2,200 km)
initial rate of climb 377 fps (115.0 m/sec)
time to 32,800 ft (10,000 m) 1 min 6 sec
service ceiling 55,770 ft (17,000 m)
**Dimensions**
wing span 29 ft 6¼ in (9.00 m)
length overall 41 ft 4½ in (12.61 m)
height overall 12 ft 5½ in (3.80 m)
wing area 269 sq ft (25.00 sq m)
**Power plant**
Two Klimov VK-9 turbojets each rated at 6,172 lb
    (2,800 kg)/7,848 lb (3,560 kg) st
**Armament**
Three 30 mm NR-30 cannon and two Atoll AAMs or
    four rocket launchers each containing eight 55 mm
    rockets or two 550 lb (250 kg) bombs
**Variants**
*Farmer-A*: Pre-production model, two 23 mm and one
    37 mm cannon
*Farmer-B*: First production model with limited all-
    weather capability, two 23 mm and one 37 mm cannon;
    *Shenyang F-6*: Chinese licence-built MiG-19
**First flights**
Prototype: 1953
**Production**
Series production from 1955–1960, licence-built in China
    and Czechoslovakia (?)
**In service**
*MiG-19*: Afghanistan, Bulgaria, Cuba, Czechoslovakia,
    Egypt (UAR), Germany (East), Hungary, Indonesia,
    Korea (North), Poland, Rumania, Soviet Union; *F-6*:
    Albania, China, Pakistan, Tanzania (?), Vietnam (North)

## MIKOYAN MiG-19 (FARMER-D)

**Type**
Limited all-weather fighter
Details as for Farmer-C with the following exceptions
**Weights**
maximum 21,936 lb (9,950 kg)
**Dimensions**
length overall 43 ft 3¾ in (13.20 m)
**Power plant**
Two Klimov RD-9B turbojets
**Armament**
Four Alkali AAMs

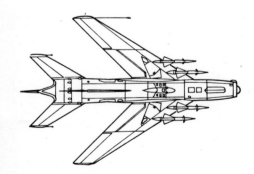

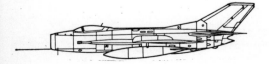

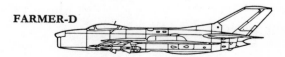

FARMER-D

## MIKOYAN MiG–21F (FISHBED–C)

**Type**
Single-seat fighter and strike fighter
**Weights**
empty 12,015 lb (5,450 kg)
normal 15,543 lb (7,050 kg)
maximum 17,086 lb (7,750 kg)
**Performance**
maximum speed at 36,000 ft (11,000 m) (Mach 2.0)
  1,317 mph (2,120 km/hr)
radius of action 375 miles (600 km)
ferry range 1,150 miles (1,850 km)
initial rate of climb 492.1 fps (150.0 m/sec)
time to 39,375 ft (12,000 m) 4 min 30 sec
service ceiling 59,420 ft (17,500 m)
**Dimensions**
wing span 23 ft 5½ in (7.15 m)
length overall 44 ft 2 in (13.46 m)
height overall 14 ft 9 in (4.50 m)
wing area 347.57 sq ft (23.00 sq m)
**Power plant**
One Tumansky R–37F turbojet rated at 9,920 lb
  (4,500 kg)/13,228 lb (6,000 kg) st
**Armament**
One (or two) 30 mm cannon NR–30 and two Atoll AAMs
  or two rocket launchers each containing nineteen 55 mm
  rockets or two 550 lb (250 kg) bombs
**Variants**
*MiG–21FL*: Export version; *MiG–21* (Fishbed–A and B):
  Earlier versions; *MiG–21* (Fishbed–G): Single-seat
  VTOL strike fighter, experimental model only, two lift-
  jet engines in fuselage; *MiG–21UTI* (Mongol–A): Two-
  seat strike trainer; *Shenyang F–8*: Chinese built
  MiG–21
**First flights**
Prototype: 1955
**Production**
Series production from 1959, licence–built in China,
  Czechoslovakia and India (200 built by HAL from
  1966/67–1973)
**In service**
*MiG–21F, PF and UTI*: Afghanistan, Algeria, Bangla
  Desh, Cuba, Czechoslovakia, Egypt (UAR), Finland,
  Germany (East), Hungary, India, (Type 74, Type 77,
  Type 66), Indonesia, Iraq, Korea (North), Vietnam
  (North), Yugoslavia;
*F–8*: Albania, China

## MIKOYAN MiG–21PF (FISHBED–D)

**Type**
Single-seat fighter and strike fighter
Details as for MiG–21F with the following exceptions
**Weights**
normal 17,637 lb (8,000 kg)
maximum 19,511 lb (8,850 kg)
**Dimensions**
length overall 45 ft 11 in (14.00 m)
**Armament**
Details as for MiG–21F excluding the cannon

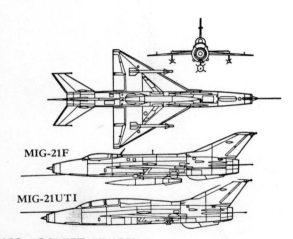

MIG-21F

MIG-21UTI

MIG-21PF

## MIKOYAN MiG–21MF (FISHBED–J)

**Type**
Single-seat fighter and strike fighter
**Weights**
normal 19,731 lb (8,950 kg)
maximum 20,723 lb (9,400 kg)
**Performance**
maximum speed at sea level (Mach 1.06) 808 mph
(1,300 km/hr)
maximum speed at 39,375 ft (12,000 m) (Mach 2.1)
1,386 mph (2,230 km/hr)
radius of action 311 miles (500 km)
ferry range 1,118 miles (1,800 km)
service ceiling 59,055 ft (18,000 m)
**Dimensions**
wing span 23 ft 5¼ in (7.15 m)
length overall 45 ft 11 in (14.00 m)
height overall 14 ft 9 in (4.50 m)
wing area 247.3 sq ft (23.00 sq m)
**Power plant**
One Tumansky R–11 turbojet rated at 11,244 lb
(5,100 kg)/14,550 lb (6,600 kg) st
**Armament**
Two 23 mm cannon with 100 rpg and (as fighter) two–
four Atoll AAMs or (as strike fighter) max 2,200 lb
(?) (1,000 kg (?)) weapon load, e.g. four 550 lb (250 kg)
bombs or four rocket launchers each containing sixteen
55 mm rockets or four 220 mm or 325 mm rockets
**Variants**
*MiG–21* (*Fishbed–F*): Single-seat fighter and strike fighter
*MiG–21* (*Fishbed–H*): Single–seat reconnaissance aircraft
**First flights**
*MiG–21MF*: 1968
**Production**
Series production from 1968; Licence-built in India by
HAL (60 from 1973?)
**In service**
*MiG–21* (*Fishbed–F*): Czechoslovakia (MiG–21SPS), Ger-
many (East), India, (Type 88), Poland, Rumania, Soviet
Union;
*MiG–21MF*: Soviet Union

## MIKOYAN MiG–25 (FOXBAT)

**Type**
Single-seat all-weather strike fighter and reconnaissance
aircraft
**Weights**
empty 34,000 lb (15,420 kg)
normal 50,000–55,000 lb (22,680–24,950 kg)
maximum 64,200 lb (29,120 kg)
**Performance**
maximum speed at 39,375 ft (12,000 m) (Mach 3.2)
2,100 mph (3,380 km/hr)
maximum speed at 5,000 ft (1,500 m) (Mach 1.3) 975 mph
(1,570 km/hr)
radius of action 698 miles (1,125 km) range: 1,865 miles
(3,000 km)
time to 36,000 ft (11,000 m) 2 min 30 sec
service ceiling 73,820 ft (22,500m)
**Dimensions**
wing span 41 ft 0¼ in (12.50 m)
length overall 69 ft 11¾ in (21.33 m)
height overall 19 ft 8¼ in (6.00 m)
wing area 645.1 sq ft (60.00 sq m)
**Power plant**
Two Tumansky RD–31 turbojets each rated at 17,637 lb
(8.000 kg)/24,250 lb (11,000 kg) st
**Armament**
*All–weather fighter*: One 30 mm cannon, four ASH or
ATOLL AAMs
*Strike fighter*: Underwing weapon load, e.g. bombs and
rockets
**Variants**
*E–266*: Record-breaking aircraft
*MiG–25R* (*Foxbat — B*): Fighter and reconnaissance
aircraft
**First flights**
Prototype: 1964
**Production**
Series production from 1968 (?), monthly output three
aircraft
**In service**
Soviet Union

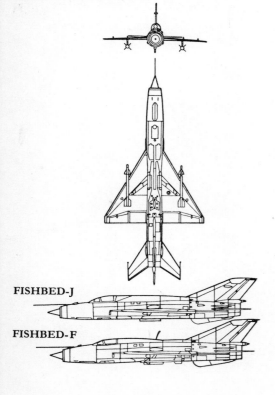

FISHBED-J

FISHBED-F

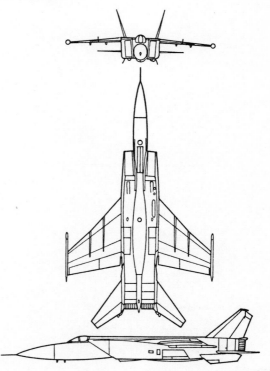

## MIL MI-4 (HOUND)

**Type**
Medium transport and ASW helicopter
**Weights**
empty 10,803 lb (4,900 kg)
normal 15,763 lb (7,150 kg)
maximum 16,645 lb (7,550 kg)
**Performance**
maximum speed at sea level 115 mph (185 km/hr)
maximum cruising speed at 1,640 ft (500 m) 3,280 ft
   (1,000 m) 99 mph (160 km/hr)
range w.m.p. 124 miles (200 km)
ferry range 255 miles (410 km)
initial rate of climb 16.4 fps (5.0 m/sec)
service ceiling 16,400 ft (5,000 m)
hovering ceiling in ground effect 5,578 ft (1,700 m)
**Dimensions**
main rotor diameter 68 ft 11 in (21.00 m)
length of fuselage 55 ft 1 in (16.79 m)
height 17 ft (5.18 m)
**Power plant**
One 1,700 hp Shvetsov ASh–82V piston engine
**Armament**
Optional: One 12.7 mm TKB machine gun in
   under-fuselage gondola
**Payload**
2–3 man crew and 8–14 troops or 8 stretcher cases and 1
   medic or max 2,650 lb (1,200 kg) freight
**Variants**
*Mi-4A, Mi-4P, Mi-4S*: Civil versions
**First flights**
Prototype: August 1952
**Production**
Over 3,000 built from 1953–1964, licence-built in China
**In service**
Afghanistan, Albania, Algeria, Bulgaria, Burma, China,
   Cuba, Czechoslovakia, Egypt (UAR), Finland, Germany
   (East), Hungary, India, Indonesia, Iraq, Korea (North),
   Mali, Mongolian People's Republic, Poland, Rumania,
   Soviet Union, Sudan, Syria, Vietnam (North), Yemen,
   Yugoslavia

## MIL MI-1 and MI-3 (HARE)

**Type**
Light AOP and transport helicopter
**Weights**
empty 4,107 lb (1,863 kg)
normal 5,200 lb (2,358 kg)
maximum 5,622 lb (2,550 kg)
**Performance**
maximum speed at sea level 105 mph (170 km/hr)
maximum speed at 6,560 ft (2,000 m) 96 mph (155 km/hr)
maximum cruising speed up to 3,280 ft (1,000 m) 84 mph
   (135 km/hr)
range 217 miles (350 km)
ferry range 360 miles (580 km)
initial rate of climb 21.3 fps (6.5 m/sec)
service ceiling 14,765 ft (4,500 m)
hovering ceiling in ground effect 10,830 ft (3,300 m)
hovering ceiling out of ground effect 6,560 ft (2,000 m)
**Dimensions**
main rotor diameter 46 ft 0½ in (14.34 m)
length of fuselage 39 ft 9 in (12.11 m)
height 10 ft 9¾ in (3.30 m)
**Power plant**
One 575 hp Ivchenko AI–26V piston engine
**Payload**
1 man crew and 3 troops or 2 stretcher cases and 1 medic
   or max 397 lb (180 kg) freight
**Variants**
*Mi-1U*: Training helicopter;
*Mi-1T, Mi-1NCH* and *Mi-1 Moskvich*: Civil variants;
*Mi-3*: Further development of Mi-1;
*SM-1*: Polish licence-built Mi-1;
*SM-2*: Polish further development
**First flights**
Prototype: September 1948
**Production**
*Mi-1*: Series production from 1950–1963;
*SM-1*: Series production from 1957–1963;
*SM-2*: Series production from 1964–
**In service**
Afghanistan, Albania, Bulgaria, China, Cuba, Czechoslo-
   vakia, Egypt (UAR), Germany (East), Hungary, Iraq,
   Korea (North), Mongolian People's Republic, Poland
   (also SM-1, SM-2), Rumania, Soviet Union, Syria,
   Vietnam (North), Yemen

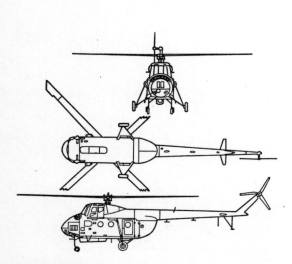

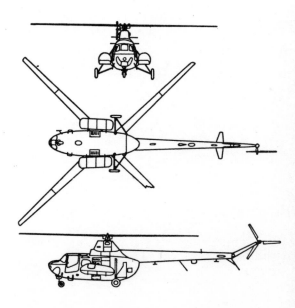

## MIL MI–2 (HOPLITE)

**Type**
Light transport helicopter
**Weights**
empty 5,180 lb (2,350 kg)
normal 7,826 lb (3,550 kg)
maximum 8,157 lb (3,700 kg)
**Performance**
maximum speed at 1,640 ft (500 m) 130 mph (210 km/hr)
maximum cruising speed 124 mph (200 km/hr)
range w.m.p. 105 miles (170 km)
ferry range 360 miles (580 km)
initial rate of climb 14.8 fps (4.5 m/sec)
service ceiling 13,120 ft (4,000 m)
hovering ceiling in ground effect 6,560 ft (2,000 m)
hovering ceiling out of ground effect 3,280 ft (1,000 m)
**Dimensions**
main rotor diameter 47 ft 6¾ in (14.50 m)
length of fuselage 37 ft 4¾ in (11.40 m)
height 11 ft 4 in (3.45 m)
**Power plant**
Two 437 hp Isotov GTD–350 turboshafts
**Payload**
1 man crew and 6–8 troops or 4 stretcher cases and 1
    medic or max 1,543 lb (700 kg) freight
**Variants**
Civil versions
**First flights**
Prototype: 1961
**Production**
Series production from 1963; licence-built in Poland
    (WSK/Mil Mi–2)
**In service**
Bulgaria, Hungary, Poland, Rumania, Soviet Union

## MIL MI–6 (HOOK)

**Type**
Heavy transport helicopter
**Weights**
empty 60,055 lb (27,240 kg)
normal 85,675 lb (40,500 kg)
maximum 93,500 lb (42,500 kg)
**Performance**
maximum speed at 3,280 ft (1,000 m) 186 mph (300 km/hr)
maximum cruising speed 155 mph (250 km/hr)
range with 17,640 lb (8,000 kg) payload 385 miles (620 km)
range with 9,920 lb (4,500 kg) payload: 620 miles 1,000 km
ferry range 900 miles (1,450 km)
service ceiling 14,750 ft (4,500 m)
**Dimensions**
main rotor diameter 114 ft 10 in (35.00 m)
length of fuselage 108 ft 9½ in (33.16 m)
height 32 ft 4 in (9.86 m)
**Power plant**
Two 5,500 hp Soloview D–25V turboshafts
**Payload**
5 man crew and 65–70 troops or 41 stretcher cases and
    2 medics or max 26,450 lb (12,000 kg) freight
**Variants**
*Mi–6P*: Civil version
**First flights**
Prototype: 1957
**Production**
5 prototypes and 30 pre-production models, over 500(?)
    production models built from 1959/1960
**In service**
Egypt (UAR), Indonesia, Soviet Union, Vietnam (North)

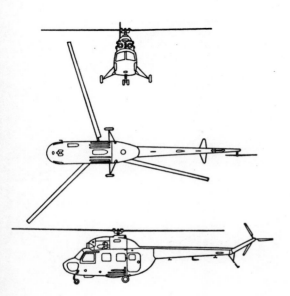

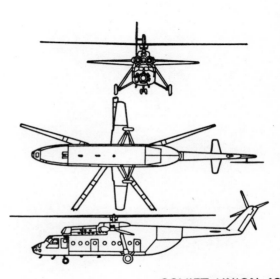

## MIL MI–8 (HIP)

**Type**
Medium transport helicopter
**Weights**
empty 15,829 lb (7,180 kg)
normal 24,470 lb (11,100 kg)
maximum 26, 455 lb (12,000 kg)
**Performance**
maximum speed at sea level 155 mph (250 km/hr)
maximum cruising speed 140 mph (225 km/hr)
range with 6,615 lb (3,000 kg) payload 264 miles (425 km)
ferry range 590 miles (950 km)
service ceiling 14,760 ft (4,500 m)
hovering ceiling in ground effect 5,900 ft (1,800 m)
hovering ceiling out of ground effect 2,625 ft (800 m)
**Dimensions**
main rotor diameter 69 ft 10½ in (21.29 m)
length of fuselage 60 ft 0¾ in (18.31 m)
height 18 ft 4½ in (5.60 m)
**Power plant**
Two 1,500 hp Isotov TB–2–117A turboshafts
**Payload**
2–3 man crew and 28 troops or 12 stretcher cases and
    1 medic or max 8,820 lb (4,000 kg) freight
**Variants**
Civil versions
**First flights**
Prototype: 1961 (only one power plant!)
**Production**
Series production from 1964
**In service**
Czechoslovakia, Bulgaria(?), Egypt (UAR), Finland,
    Germany (East), Hungary, Iraq, Pakistan, Peru(?),
    Poland, Rumania, Soviet Union, Sudan, Syria,
    Yugoslavia

## MIL MI–10 (HARKE)

**Type**
Heavy flying-crane helicopter
**Weights**
empty 60,186 lb (27,300 kg)
maximum 95,790 lb (43,450 kg)
**Performance**
maximum speed at sea level 124 mph (200 km/hr)
maximum cruising speed 112 mph (180 km/hr)
range with 26,455 lb (12,000 kg) payload 155 miles
    (250 km)
ferry range 391 miles (630 km)
service ceiling 9,850 ft (3,000 m)
**Dimensions**
main rotor diameter 114 ft 10 in (35.00 m)
length of fuselage 10 ft 9¾ in (32.86 m)
height 32 ft 6 in (9.90 m)
**Power plant**
Two 5,500 hp Soloview D–25V turboshafts
**Payload**
2–3 man crew and 28 troops or max 33,070 lb (15,000 kg)
    external freight
**Variants**
*Mi–10K*: Further development
**First flights**
Prototype: 1960
**Production**
*Mi–10*: Series production from 1960/1961
**In service**
Soviet Union

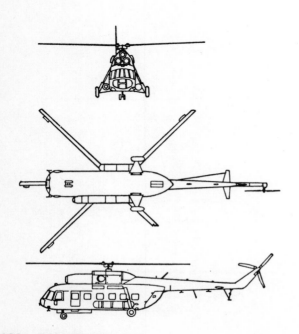

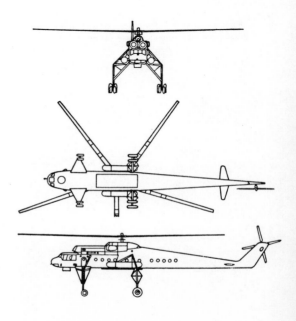

## MIL MI–10K (HARKE)

**Type**
Heavy flying-crane helicopter
Details as for Mi–10 (Harke) with the following
   exceptions
**Weights**
empty 54,410 lb (24,680 kg)
maximum 83,776 lb (38,000 kg)
**Performance**
maximum speed at sea level 155 mph (250 km/hr)
maximum cruising speed 124 mph (200 km/hr)
ferry range 494 miles (795 [?] km)
**Dimensions**
height overall 25 ft 7 in (7.80 m)
**Payload**
2–3 man crew and 28 troops or max 24,250 lb (11,000 kg)
   external freight
**First flights**
*Mi–10K*: 1965
**Production**
Series production from 1969

## MYASISHCHEV MYA–4 'MOLOT' (BISON)

**Type**
Strategic heavy bomber and reconnaissance aircraft
   6–8 man crew
**Weights**
empty 176,370 lb (80,000 kg)
normal 363,762 lb (165,000 kg)
maximum 407,855 lb (185,000 kg)
**Performance**
maximum speed at 10,000 ft (3,050 m) (Mach 0.85)
   621 mph (1,000 km/hr)
maximum speed at 39,375 ft (12,000 m) 559 mph
   (900 km/hr)
maximum cruising speed at 36,000 ft (11,000 m) 478 mph
   (770 km/hr)
range 6,990 miles (11,250 km)
service ceiling 51,800 ft (15,800 m)
**Dimensions**
wing span 167 ft 3¾ in (51.00 m)
length overall 159 ft 1¼ in (48.50 m)
height overall 42 ft 0 in (12.80 m)
wing area 3,229.2 sq ft (300.00 sq m)
**Power plant**
Four Mikulin AM–3D turbojets each rated at 19,180 lb
   (8,700 kg) st
**Armament**
Six 23 mm NR–23 cannon set in pairs, max 26,455 lb
   (12,000 kg) weapon load, e.g. bombs, rockets or ASMs
**Variants**
*201–M Molot*: Further development with more powerful
   engines (each of 28,660 lb [13,000 kg] st)
**First flights**
Prototype: 1953
**Production**
*Mya–4*: Approx 150 built from 1954–1956;
*201–M*: Only a limited number built?
**In service**
*Mya–4, 201–M*: Soviet Union

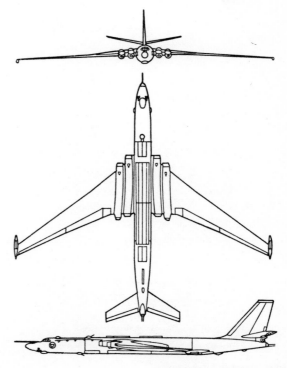

## SUKHOI SU–7MF (FITTER)

**Type**
Single-seat strike fighter
**Weights**
empty 19,004 lb (8,620 kg)
normal 26,450 lb (12,000 kg)
maximum 29,797 lb (13,425 kg)
**Performance**
maximum speed at 39,375 ft (12,000 m) (Mach 1.7)
  (1,700 km/hr)
maximum speed at 980 ft (300 m) (Mach 0.95) 720 mph
  (1,160 km/hr)
radius of action 120–285 miles (320–460 km)
ferry range 900 miles (1,450 km)
initial rate of climb 492.1 fps (150.0 m/sec)
service ceiling 49,210 ft (15,000 m)
**Dimensions**
wing span 31 ft 2 in (9.50 m)
length overall 56 ft 0 in (17.00 m)
height overall 15 ft 5 in (4.70 m)
**Power plant**
One Lyulka AL–7F–1 turbojet rated at 14,198 lb
  (6,440 kg)/22,046 lb (10,000 kg) st
**Armament**
Two 30 mm NR–30 cannon with 70 rpg and max 2,200 lb
  (1,000 kg) weapon load on four hard points e.g. two
  1,100 lb (500 kg) or 550 lb (250 kg) bombs and 2 rocket
  launchers each containing sixteen 55 mm unguided
  rockets
**Variants**
SU–7UTI (Moujik): Two-seat strike fighter
**First flights**
Prototype: 1955
**Production**
Series production from 1958
**In service**
Afghanistan, Cuba, Czechoslovakia, Egypt (UAR),
  Germany (East), Hungary, India, Iraq, Korea (North),
  Poland, Rumania, Soviet Union, Syria

## SUKHOI SU–9 (FISHPOT)

**Type**
Single-seat all-weather fighter
**Weights**
normal 25,353 lb (11,500 kg)
maximum 28,660–29,983 lb (13,000–13,600 kg)
**Performance**
maximum speed at 39,375 ft (12,000 m) (Mach 1.8)
  1,190 mph (1,915 km/hr)
maximum cruising speed at 36,000 ft (11,000 m) 571 mph
  (920 km/hr)
radius of action 310 miles (500 km)
initial rate of climb 449.4 fps (137.0 m/sec)
time to 39,375 ft (12,000 m) 4 min 30 sec
service ceiling 55,770 ft (17,000 m)
**Dimensions**
wing span 27 ft 8¾ in (9.45 m)
length overall 54 ft 11¾ in (16.76 m)
height overall 16 ft 0¼ in (4.88 m)
wing area 425.1 sq ft (39.50 sq m)
**Power plant**
One Tumansky TRD–31 turbojet rated at 15,432 lb
  (7,000 kg)/22,046 lb (10,000 kg) st
**Armament**
Four ALKALI AAMs or two ANAB AAMs
**Variants**
SU–9UTI (Maiden): Two-seat strike trainer
**First flights**
Prototype: 1955
**Production**
Series production from 1959, several series
**In service**
Soviet Union

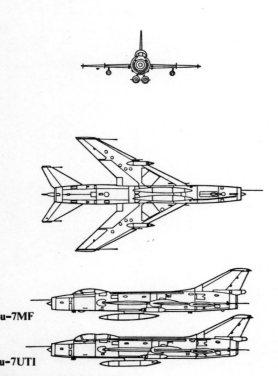

Su-7MF

Su-7UTI

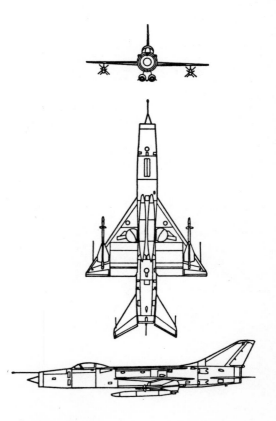

## SUKHOI SU–11 (FLAGON–A)

**Type**
Single-seat all-weather fighter
**Weights**
normal 35,000 lb (15,875 kg)
maximum 40,000 lb (18,145 kg)
**Performance**
maximum speed at 39,375 ft (12,000 m) (Mach 2.5)
   (1,650 mph) (2,655 km/hr)
maximum speed at 980 ft (300 m) (Mach 1.2) 910 mph
   (1,465 km/hr)
ferry range 1,490 miles (2,400 km)
**Dimensions**
wing span 31 ft 2 in (9.50 m)
length overall 70 ft 6¼ in (21.50 m)
height overall 16 ft 5 in (5.00 m)
**Power plant**
Two Lyulka AL–9 turbojets each rated at 25,000 lb
   (11,340 kg)
**Armament**
Two Anab AAMs
**Variants**
*Flagon–B*: STOL fighter with three additional lift-jet
   engines in fuselage (experimental model?)
**First flights**
Prototype: 1964–1965
**Production**
Series production from 1969, over 400(?) delivered to
   date, monthly production of 15(?) aircraft
**In service**
Soviet Union

## TUPOLEV TU–16 (BADGER–A)

**Type**
Medium bomber and reconnaissance aircraft
   7 man crew
**Weights**
empty 88,185 lb (40,000 kg)
normal 115,713 lb (52,500 kg)
maximum 169,757 lb (77,000 kg)
**Performance**
maximum speed at 35,000 ft (10,700 m) (Mach 0.87)
   587 mph (945 km/hr)
maximum cruising speed at 32,800 ft (10,000 m) 490 mph
   (790 km/hr)
range with 6,600 lb (3,000 kg) payload 4,000 miles
   (6,400 km)
range w.m.p. 3,000 miles (4,800 km)
service ceiling 42,650 ft (13,000 m)
**Dimensions**
wing span 110 ft 0 in (33.50 m)
length overall 120 ft 11½ in (36.87 m)
height overall 35 ft 6in (10.80 m)
wing area 1,814.8 sq ft (168.60 sq m)
**Power plant**
Two Mikulin AM–3M turbojets each rated at 20,950 lb
   (9,500 kg) st
**Armament**
*BADGER–A*: Seven 23 mm cannon and max 19,800 lb
   (9,000 kg) weapon load; e.g. bombs
*BADGER–B*: Two Kennel or Kelt ASMs underwing;
*BADGER–C*: One Kipper ASM stand-off bomb mounted
   beneath the fuselage
**Variants**
*BADGER–B and BADGER–C*: with ASMs;
*BADGER–D, E, F*: with additional electronic equipment,
   mounted partly in underwing pods
**First flights**
Prototype: 1954
**Production**
Over 2,000 built from 1955; manufactured in China(?)
**In service**
China, Egypt (UAR), Indonesia, Iraq, Soviet Union

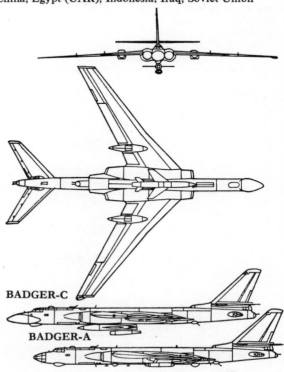

BADGER-C

BADGER-A

## TUPOLEV TU–20 (BEAR–A)

**Type**
Strategic heavy bomber and reconnaissance aircraft 6–8 man crew
**Weights**
empty 198,416 lb (90,000 kg)
normal 370,376 lb (168,000 kg)
maximum 414,469 lb (188,000 kg)
**Performance**
maximum speed at 41,000 ft (12,500 m) (Mach 0.76) 500 mph (805 km/hr)
maximum speed at 11,480 ft (3,500 m) (Mach 0.83) 540 mph (870 km/hr)
maximum cruising speed at 32,800 ft (10,000 m) 470 mph (756 km/hr)
range 7,800 miles (12,550 km)
ferry range 9,320 miles (15,000 km)
initial rate of climb 137.8 fps (42.0 m/sec)
service ceiling 44,300 ft (13,500 m)
**Dimensions**
wing span 167 ft 8 in (51.10 m)
length overall 162 ft 4¾ in (49.50 m)
height overall 44 ft 0 in (13.50 m)
wing area 3,349 sq ft (311.10 sq m)
**Power plant**
Four 14,750 hp Kusnetsov NK–12M turboprops
**Armament**
*Bear–A*: One fixed 23 mm cannon in starboard nose, two fuselage turrets and one tail position each with two 23 mm NR–23 cannon and max 26,500 lb (12,000 kg) weapon load
**Variants**
*Bear–B*: Strategic bomber with one Kangaroo ASM;
*Bear–C, Bear–D*: Strategic maritime reconnaissance aircraft;
*Tu–114 (Cleat)*: Airliner
**First flights**
Prototype: 1954
**Production**
*Bear–A*: Approx 300 built from 1956–1960, from 1961 conversions to *Bear–B*, from 1964 to *Bear–C* and from 1966/67 to *Bear–D*
**In service**
Soviet Union

## TUPOLEV TU–20 (MOSS)

**Type**
Early warning and reconnaissance aircraft over 20 man crew
**Weights**
empty 253,532 lb (115,000 kg)
normal 360,000 lb (163,290 kg)
**Performance**
maximum speed at sea level 528 mph (850 km/hr)
maximum cruising speed at 25,000 ft (7,620 m) 460 mph (740 km/hr)
patrol speed: 310 mph (500 km/hr)
ferry range 4,000 miles (6,440 km)
service ceiling 39,000 ft (11,890 m)
**Dimensions**
wing span 168 ft 0 in (51.20 m)
length overall 188 ft 0 in (57.30 m)
height overall 51 ft 0 in (15.50 m)
wing area 3,349 sq ft (311.10 sq m)
**Power plant**
Four 14,795 hp Kuznetsov NK–12MV turboprops
**First flights**
Prototype: 1966(?)
**Production**
Series production from 1968(?)
**In service**
Soviet Union

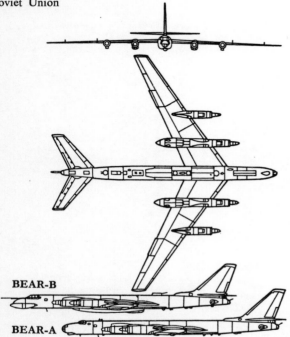

BEAR-B

BEAR-A

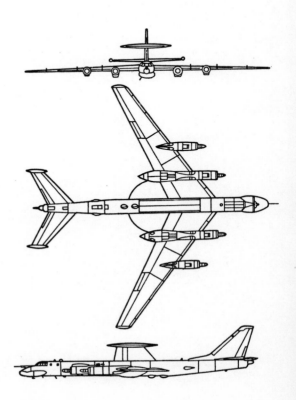

## TUPOLEV TU–22 (BLINDER–A)

**Type**
Medium bomber and reconnaissance aircraft 3–4 man crew
**Weights**
maximum 185,188 lb (84,000 kg)
**Performance**
maximum speed at 39,375 ft (12,000 m) (Mach 1.5)
  988 mph (1,590 km/hr)
maximum speed at 1,000 ft (300 m) (Mach 0.95) 720 mph
  (1,160 km/hr)
maximum cruising speed at 39,375 ft (12,000 m) (Mach 0.9)
  596 mph (960 km/hr)
radius of action 696 miles (1,120 km)
ferry range 4,850 miles (7,800 km)
service ceiling 60,000 ft (18,300 m)
**Dimensions**
wing span 91 ft 0 in (27.74 m)
length overall 132 ft 10¼ in (40.50 m)
height overall 17 ft 0 in (5.18 m)
wing area 2,030 sq ft (188.60 sq m)
**Power Plant**
Two turbojets each rated at 27,006 lb (12,250 kg) st
**Armament**
One 23 mm cannon in tail position, bombs and ASMs
**Variants**
*Blinder-B*: Bomber with Kitchen ASMs
*Tu–22U* (*Blinder-C*): Bomber trainer
**First flights**
Prototype: 1960
**Production**
175–200 built from 1961
**In service**
Soviet Union (from 1965)

## TUPOLEV TU–28P (FIDDLER)

**Type**
Two-seat all-weather fighter and reconnaissance aircraft
**Weights**
normal 78,044 lb (35,400 kg)
maximum 96,011 lb (43,550 kg)
**Performance**
maximum speed at 39,375 ft (12,000 m) (Mach 1.65)
  1,084 mph (1,745 km/hr)
radius of action 900–1,100 miles (1,450–1,770 km)
ferry range 3,107 miles (5,000 km)
service ceiling 65,620 ft (20,000 m)
**Dimensions**
wing span 64 ft 11½ in (19.80 m)
length overall 90 ft 0 in (27.43 m)
height overall 22 ft 11½ in (7.00 m)
wing area 807.3 sq ft (75.00 sq m)
**Power plant**
Two turbojets each rated at 24,251 lb (11,000 kg) st
**Armament**
Four Ash AAMs
**First flights**
Prototype: 1957
**Production**
Series production from 1960
**In service**
Soviet Union

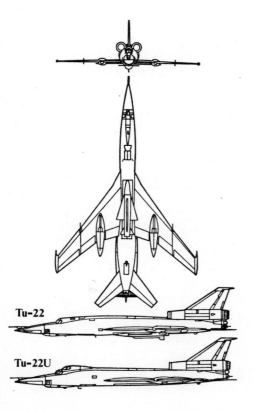

Tu–22

Tu–22U

## TUPOLEV TU–124 (COOKPOT)

**Type**
Medium transport
**Weights**
empty 49,600 lb (22,500 kg)
normal 80,470 lb (36,500 kg)
maximum 83,775 lb (38,000 kg)
**Performance**
maximum speed at 26,250 ft (8,000 m) 603 mph
(970 km/hr)
maximum cruising speed at 32,800 ft (10,000 m) 540 mph
(870 km/hr)
range/w.m.p. 746 miles (1,200 km)
ferry range 1,305 miles (2,100 km)
service ceiling 38,390 ft (11,700 m)
**Dimensions**
wing span 83 ft 9½ in (25.55 m)
length overall 100 ft 4 in (30.58 m)
height overall 26 ft 6 in (8.08 m)
wing area 1,281 sq ft (119.00 sq m)
**Power plant**
Two Soloviev D–20P turbojets each rated at 11,905 lb
(5,400 kg) st
**Payload**
3–4 man crew and 44–56 troops or max 13,290 lb
(6,000 kg) freight
**Variants**
Civil versions
**First flights**
Prototype: June 1960
**Production**
Approx 100 built from 1961–1966, nearly all as civil
versions
**In service**
Germany (East), India, Iraq, Soviet Union

## YAKOVLEV YAK–11 (MOOSE)

**Type**
Two-seat trainer
**Weights**
empty 4,409 lb (2,000 kg)
normal 5,512 lb (2,500 kg)
**Performance**
maximum speed at sea level 262 mph (423 km/hr)
maximum speed at 7,380 ft (2,250 m) 286 mph (430 km/hr)
maximum cruising speed 205 mph (330 km/hr)
ferry range 795 miles (1,280 km)
service ceiling 23,300 ft (7,100 m)
**Dimensions**
wing span 30 ft 10 in (9.40 m)
length overall 27 ft 10¼ in (8.50 m)
height overall 10 ft 9¼ in (3.28 m)
wing area 166 sq ft (15.40 sq m)
**Power plant**
One 730 hp Shvetsov ASh–21 piston engine
**Armament**
One 7.62 mm machine gun
**Variants**
*C–11*: Czechoslovakian licence-built
**First flights**
Prototype: 1946
**Production**
Series production from 1946, licence-built in Czechoslo-
vakia
**In service**
Afghanistan, Albania, Algeria, Bulgaria, China, Czecho-
slovakia (C.11), Egypt (UAR), Germany (East),
Hungary, Indonesia, Korea (North), Mongolian People's
Republic, Poland, Rumania, Somali, Soviet Union,
Syria, Vietnam (North), Yemen

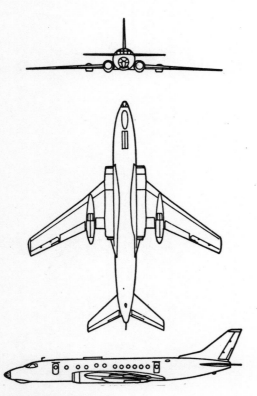

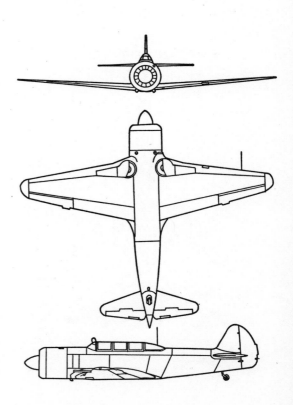

## YAKOVLEV YAK-12A (CREEK-D)

**Type**
Liaison and AOP aircraft
**Weights**
empty 2,330 lb (1,059 kg)
maximum 3,494 lb (1,588 kg)
**Performance**
maximum speed 133 mph (214 km/hr)
maximum cruising speed 112 mph (180 km/hr)
range 472 miles (760 km)
ferry range 688 miles (1,070 km)
initial rate of climb 11.8 fps (3.6 m/sec)
service ceiling 15,090 ft (4,600 m)
**Dimensions**
wing span 41 ft 4 in (12.60 m)
length overall 29 ft 6 in (9.00 m)
height overall 10 ft 3 in (3.12 m)
wing area 233.6 sq ft (21.70 sq m)
**Power plant**
One 240 hp Ivchenko AI-14R piston engine
**Payload**
1 man crew and 2–3 troops or 1 stretcher case and 1
    seated casualty plus 1 medic or max 660 lb (300 kg)
    freight
**Variants**
*Yak-12 (CREEK-A), Yak-12R (CREEK-B), Yak-12M
(CREEK-C):* Earlier versions
PZL-101 'Cawron': further development in Poland
**First flights**
Prototype *Yak-12*: 1944
*Yak-12A*: 1957
Prototype PZL-101: 1958
**Production**
Series production from 1946–1961, licence-built in Poland
    by PZL from 1959–1961
*PZL-101*: series production from 1962
**In service**
Germany (East), Mali (?), Soviet Union, Yugoslavia (?)

## YAKOVLEV YAK-18A

**Type**
Two-seat trainer
**Weights**
empty 2,259 lb (1,025 kg)
normal 2,910 lb (1,316 kg)
**Performance**
maximum speed 162 mph (260 km/hr)
ferry range 466 miles (750 km)
initial rate of climb 17.4 fps (5.3 m/sec)
service ceiling 16,601 ft (5,060 m)
**Dimensions**
wing span 34 ft 9¼ in (10.60 m)
length overall 27 ft 4¼ in (8.53 m)
height overall 11 ft 0 in (3.35 m)
wing area 183 sq ft (17.00 sq m)
**Power plant**
One 260 hp Ivchenko AI-14R piston engine
**Variants**
*Yak-18(Max), Yak-18U:* Earlier versions;
*Yak-18 P and PM:* Single-seat aerobatic versions
**First flights**
Prototype *Yak-18*: 1945
**Production**
*Yak-18:* from 1946–1955; *Yak-18U:* from 1955-1957;
*Yak-18A:* from 1957–; *Yak-18P:* from 1961–
**In service**
Afghanistan, Albania, Algeria, Bulgaria, China, Czecho-
    slovakia (?), Egypt (UAR), Germany (East), Guinea,
    Hungary, Iraq, Korea (North), Mali (?), Mongolian
    People's Republic, Poland, Rumania, Somali, Soviet
    Union, Syria, Vietnam (North)

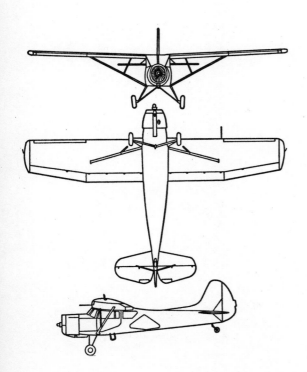

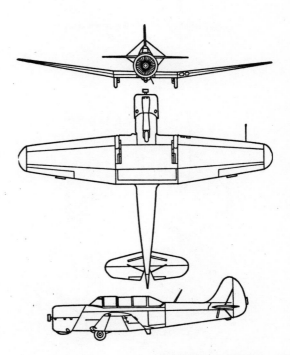

## YAKOVLEV YAK–25 (FLASHLIGHT–A)

**Type**
Two-seat all-weather fighter
**Weights**
normal 20,723–22,046 lb (9,400–10,000 kg)
maximum 25,000 lb (11,340 kg)
**Performance**
maximum speed at sea level (Mach 0.83) 630 mph
   (1,015 km/hr)
maximum speed at 36,000 ft (11,000 m) (Mach 0.9)
   593 mph (955 km/hr)
maximum cruising speed at 36,000 ft (11,000 m) 497 mph
   (800 km/hr)
ferry range 1,864 miles (3,000 km)
initial rate of climb 164.0 fps (50.0 m/sec)
service ceiling 50,900 ft (15,500 m)
**Dimensions**
wing span 36 ft 9 in (11.20 m)
length overall 51 ft 10 in (15.80 m)
height overall 12 ft 5¾ in (3.80 m)
wing area 322.9 sq ft (30.00 sq m)
**Power plant**
Two Klimov RD–9 turbojets each rated at 6,173 lb
   (2,800 kg) st
**Armament**
Two 37 mm cannon and two-four AAMs or four rocket
   launchers containing 55 mm rockets
**Variants**
*Yak–27C (Flashlight–C)*: Further development, limited
   production;
*Yak–25R*: Two-seat reconnaissance aircraft
**First flights**
Prototype: 1952
**Production**
Series production from 1954–.
**In service**
Soviet Union

## YAKOVLEV YAK–28 (BREWER)

**Type**
Two-seat light bomber and reconnaissance aircraft
**Weights**
normal 37,479 lb (17,000 kg)
maximum 41,888 lb (19,000 kg)
**Performance**
maximum speed at sea level (Mach 0.95) 720 mph
   (1,160 km/hr)
maximum speed at 39,375 ft (12,000 m) (Mach 1.1)
   730 mph (1,175 km/hr)
maximum cruising speed at 32,800 ft (10,000 m) 578 mph
   (930 km/hr)
radius of action 248–490 miles (400–790 km)
ferry range 1,500–1,600 miles (2,415–2,575 km)
initial rate of climb 466 fps (142.0 m/sec)
service ceiling 55,770 ft (17,000 m)
**Dimensions**
wing span 44 ft 5¾ in (13.56 m)
length overall 64 ft 6 in (19.66 m)
height overall 15 ft 0 in (4.57 m)
wing area 403.6 sq ft (37.50 sq m)
**Power plant**
Two Tumansky RD–11 turbojets each rated at 10,141 lb
   (4,600 kg)/13,669 lb (6,200 kg) st
**Armament**
One 30 mm NR–30 cannon, max 4,410 lb (2,000 kg)
   weapon load, e.g. two ASMs
**Variants**
*Yak–28U (Maestro)*: Two-seat bomber trainer
**First flights**
Prototype: 1959 or 1960
**Production**
Series production from 1961/62
**In service**
Soviet Union

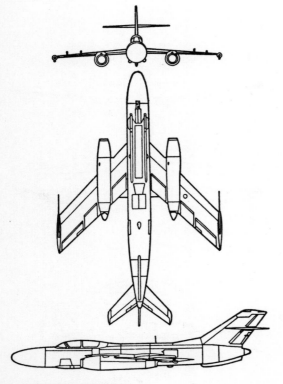

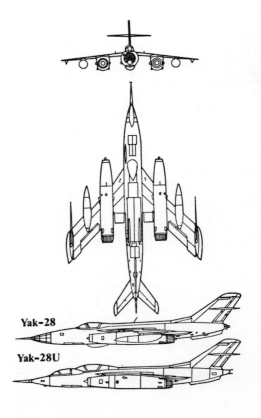

Yak-28

Yak-28U

## YAKOVLEV YAK–28P (FIREBAR)

**Type**
Two-seat all-weather fighter
**Weights**
normal 37,480 lb (17,000 kg)
maximum 40,786 lb (18,500 kg)
**Performance**
maximum speed at 39,375 ft (12,000 m) (Mach 1.15)
   761 mph (1,225 km/hr)
maximum cruising speed (Mach 0.9) 559 mph
   (900 km/hr)
radius of action 550 miles (885 km)
initial rate of climb 466.5 fps (142.2 m/sec)
service ceiling 55,000 ft (16,765 m)
**Dimensions**
wing span 43 ft 11¾ in (13.56 m)
length overall 66 ft 11¾ in (20.42 m)
height overall 14 ft 11¾ in (4.57 m)
**Power plant**
Two Tumansky RD–11 turbojets each rated at 10,141 lb
   (4,600 kg)/13,669 lb (6,200 kg) st
**Armament**
Two ANAB AAMs and (on some aircraft) two ATOLL
   AAMs
**First flights**
Prototype: 1960
**Production**
Series production from 1963–1964
**In service**
Soviet Union

## AISA I–11B 'PEQUE'

**Type**
Two-seat liaison aircraft and trainer
**Weights**
empty 926 lb (421 kg)
normal 1,417 lb (644 kg)
maximum 1,474 lb (670 kg)
**Performance**
maximum speed 124 mph (200 km/hr)
maximum cruising speed 177 mph (110 km/hr)
ferry range 403 miles (650 km)
initial rate of climb 10.8 fps (3.3 m/sec)
service ceiling 15,415 ft (4,700 m)
**Dimensions**
wing span 30 ft 7 in (9.34 m)
length overall 21 ft 3¼ in (6.48 m)
height overall 6 ft 3 in (1.90 m)
wing area 144 sq ft (13.40 sq m)
**Power plant**
One 90 hp Continental C90–12F piston engine
**First flights**
Prototype: 1950; *I–11B*: 16 October 1953
**Production**
Approx 450 built from 1953
**In service**
Spain (L–8C)

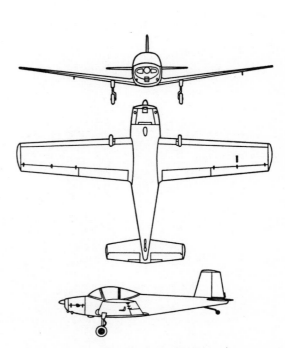

## AISA I–115

**Type**
Two-seat trainer
**Weights**
empty 2,001 lb (610 kg)
normal 1,980 lb (900 kg)
maximum 2,183 lb (990 kg)
**Performance**
maximum speed 143 mph (230 km/hr)
maximum cruising speed 126 mph (204 km/hr)
initial rate of climb 12.5 fps (3.8 m/sec)
service ceiling 14,042 ft (4,280 m)
**Dimensions**
wing span 31 ft 3¼ in (9.53 m)
length overall 24 ft 1 in (7.34 m)
height overall 6 ft 10 in (2.08 m)
wing area 150.6 sq ft (14.00 sq m)
**Power plant**
One 150 hp ENMA Tigre G–IV–B piston engine
**First flights**
Prototype: 16 July 1952
**Production**
Approx 450 built from 1954
**In service**
Spain (E–9)

## CASA C.207 'AZOR'

**Type**
Medium transport
**Weights**
empty 21,716 lb (9,850 kg)
maximum 34,502 lb (15,650 kg)
**Performance**
maximum speed at 6,100 ft (1,860 m) 285 mph (458 km/hr)
maximum cruising speed at 12,340 ft (3,760 m) 265 mph (427 km/hr)
range 683 miles (1,100 km)
ferry range 1,830 miles (2,960 km)
service ceiling 28,215 ft (8,600 m)
**Dimensions**
wing span 91 ft 2½ in (27.80 m)
length overall 68 ft 5 in (20.85 m)
height overall 25 ft 5 in (7.75 m)
wing area 923.2 sq ft (85.80 sq m)
**Power plant**
Two 2,040 hp Bristol Hercules 730 piston engines
**Payload**
4 man crew and 36 troops
**First flights**
Prototype: 28 September 1955
**Production**
20 built from 1956–1968
**In service**
Spain (T–7)

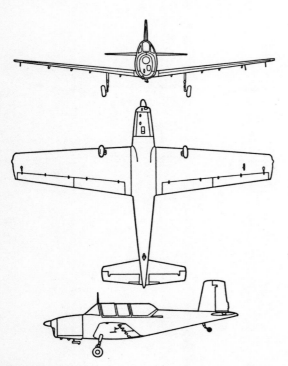

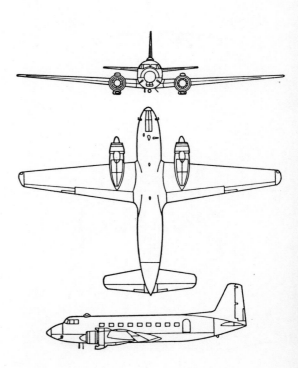

## CASA C.212 'AVIOCAR'

**Type**
Light transport
**Weights**
empty 8,045 lb (3,650 kg)
maximum 13,890 lb (6,300 kg)
**Performance**
maximum speed at 12,000 ft (3,660 m) 249 mph
  (400 km/hr)
maximum cruising speed at 12,000 ft (3,660 m) 227 mph
  (365 km/hr)
range 445 miles (720 km)
ferry range 1,198 miles (1,927 km)
initial rate of climb 27.9 fps (8.5 m/sec)
service ceiling 24,606 ft (7,500 m)
**Dimensions**
wing span 62 ft 4 in (19.00 m)
length overall 49 ft 10½ in (15.20 m)
height overall 20 ft 8 in (6.30 m)
wing area 430.56 sq ft (40.00 sq m)
**Power plant**
Two 766 hp Garrett–AiResearch TPE–331–5–251C
  turboprops
**Payload**
2 man crew and 18–21 troops or 10 stretcher cases and
  3 medics or 15 paratroops and 1 dispatcher or max
  4,410 lb (2,000 kg) freight
**First flights**
Prototype: 26 March 1971
**Production**
2 prototypes, 8 pre-production models series production
  from 1973/74, 32 delivered or on order to date
**In service**
Spain

## HISPANO HA–100 'TRIANA'

**Type**
Two-seat trainer
**Weights**
empty 4,343 lb (1,970 kg)
normal 6,459 lb (2,930 kg)
**Performance**
maximum speed at 9,500 ft (2,900 m) 276 mph (444 km/hr)
maximum cruising speed 237 mph (381 km/hr)
ferry range 821 miles (1,323 km)
initial rate of climb 35.4 fps (10.8 m/sec)
service ceiling 33,620 ft (10,250 m)
**Dimensions**
wing span 34 ft 1 in (10.40 m)
length overall 29 ft 5 in (8.99 m)
height overall 9 ft 9¾ in (2.99 m)
wing area 187.2 sq ft (17.40 sq m)
**Power plant**
One 755 hp ENMA Beta B–4 piston engine
**Armament**
Two 12.7 mm machine guns and four 110 lb (50 kg)
  bombs or four practice rockets
**First flights**
Prototype: 10 December 1954
**Production**
4 Prototypes and 40 production models built from 1958–.
**In service**
Spain (E–12)

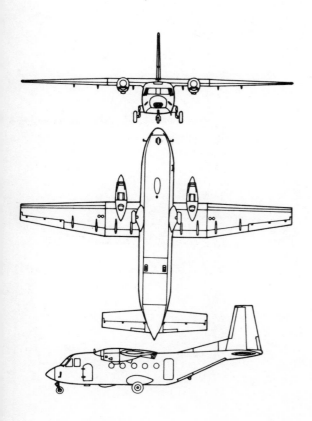

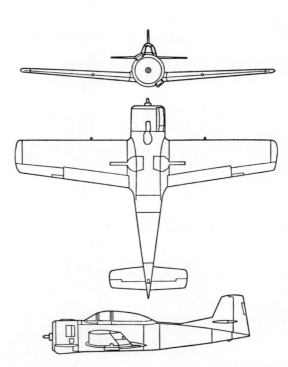

## HISPANO HA–200D 'SAETA'

**Type**
Two-seat trainer and light ground-attack aircraft
**Weights**
empty 4,233 lb (1,920 kg)
normal 5,842 lb (2,650 kg)
maximum 8,047 lb (3,650 kg)
**Performance**
maximum speed at sea level 405 mph (652 km/hr)
maximum speed at 29,500 ft (9,000 m) 435 mph
  (700 km/hr)
maximum cruising speed at 9,840 ft (3,000 m) 323 mph
  (520 km/hr)
ferry range 932 miles (1,500 km)
initial rate of climb 47.6 fps (14.5 m/sec)
service ceiling 39,370 ft (12,000 m)
**Dimensions**
wing span 35 ft 10¼ in (10.93 m)
length overall 29 ft 5 in (8.97 m)
height overall 10 ft 8¼ in (3.26 m)
wing area 187.4 sq ft (17.42 sq m)
**Power plant**
Two Turbomeca Marboré IIA turbojets each rated at
  882 lb (400 kg) st
**Armament**
Two 7.7 mm machine guns, four 110 lb (50 kg) bombs or
  four 22 lb (10 kg) unguided rockets
**Variants**
*HA–200A*: Earlier version; *HA–2008B*: Egyptian licence-
  built; *HA–200E 'Super Saeta'*: Further development;
  *HA–220*: Single-seat light ground–attack aircraft
**First flights**
Prototype HA–200: 12 August 1955; 1st production
  model: 30 October 1962
**Production**
*HA–200A*: 35 built from 1962; *HA–200B*: 100 built;
  *HA–200D*: 55 built; *HA–220*: 25 built 1970/71
**In service**
*HA–200A*, D: Spain (E-14);
*HA–200B*: Egypt (UAR) (Al Kahira);
*HA–220*: Spain

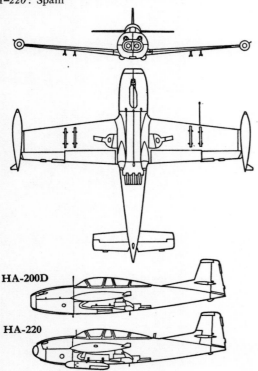

HA-200D

HA-220

## SAAB 32 'LANSEN' (A 32A)

**Type**
Two-seat strike fighter
**Weights**
empty 16,402 lb (7,440 kg)
normal 22,950 lb (10,410 kg)
maximum 28,660 lb (13,000 kg)
**Performance**
maximum speed at sea level (Mach 0.9) 700 mph
  (1,125 km/hr)
maximum speed at 36,000 ft (11,000 m) 627 mph
  (1,009 km/hr)
maximum cruising speed at 36,000 ft (11,000 m) 528 mph
  (850 km/hr)
radius of action 404–746 miles (650–1,200 km)
ferry range 2,000 miles (3,220 km)
initial rate of climb 196.9 fps (60.0 m/sec)
service ceiling 49,200 ft (15,000 m)
**Dimensions**
wing span 42 ft 8 in (13.00 m)
length overall 48 ft 0 in (14.65 m)
height overall 15 ft 6 in (4.75 m)
wing area 402.6 sq ft (37.40 sq m)
**Power plant**
One Svenska Flygmotor RM5A2 turbojet rated at 7,937 lb
  (3,600 kg)/9,921 lb (4,500 kg) st
**Armament**
Four 20 mm Hispano cannon, max 2,645 lb (1,200 kg)
  weapon load, e.g. two Rb 04C ASMs or four 550 lb
  (250 kg) or two 1,100 lb (500 kg) or twelve 220 lb
  (100 kg) bombs or max twenty-four 135 mm or 150 mm
  rockets
**Variants**
*J 32B*: Two seat all-weather fighter (four 30 mm cannon
  and 24 sidewinder AAMs)
*S 32C*: Two seat reconnaissance aircraft
**First flights**
Prototype: 3 November 1952
**Production**
*A 32A*: Approx 280 built from 1955–1958;
*J 32B*: Approx 150 built from 1958–1960;
*S 32C*: Approx 35 built from 1958–1960
**In service**
*A 32A, J 32B, S 32C*: Sweden

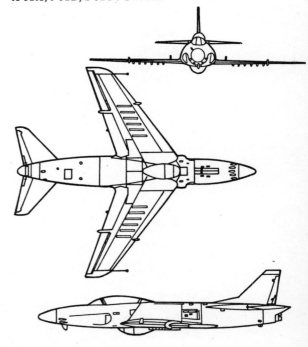

## SAAB 35 'DRAKEN' (J 35F)

**Type**
Single-seat fighter and strike fighter
**Weights**
empty 16,815 lb (7,627 kg)
normal 25,130 lb (11,400 kg)
maximum 33,070 lb (15,000 kg)
**Performance**
maximum speed at 36,000 ft (11,000 m) (Mach 2.0)
  1,320 mph (2,125 km/hr)
maximum speed with 4 AAMs at 36,000 ft (11,000 m)
  (Mach 1.4) 926 mph (1,490 km/hr)
maximum cruising speed 590 mph (950 km/hr)
radius of action 348–684 miles (560–1,100 km)
ferry range 1,760 miles (2,840 km)
initial rate of climb 574 fps (175 m/sec)
time to 36,000 ft (11,000 m) 2 min 36 sec
service ceiling 60,040 ft (18,300 m)
**Dimensions**
wing span 30 ft 9¼ in (9.38 m)
length overall 46 ft 10¼ in (14.28 m)
height overall 12 ft 9 in (3.89 m)
wing area 529.6 sq ft (49.20 sq m)
**Power plant**
One Svenska Flygmotor RM6C turbojet rated at 12,710 lb
  (5,765 kg)/17,262 lb (7,830 kg) st
**Armament**
One 30 mm Aden M/55 cannon with 90 rpg;
*Fighter*: Two Rb27 and two Rb28 (Falcon) AAMs;
*Strike Fighter*: Max 2,205 lb (1,000 kg) weapon load;
  e.g. twelve 135 mm Bofors unguided rockets or two
  1,102 lb (500 kg) bombs or nine 220 lb (100 kg) bombs
  or two rocket launchers each containing nineteen 75
  mm rockets
**Variants**
*J 35A, J 35B, J 35D*: Earlier versions;
*S 35E*: Single-seat reconnaissance aircraft
*Sk 35C*: Two-seat strike trainer;
*Saab 35X*: Export version of J 35F;
*Saab 35XT*: Two-seat strike trainer
**First flights**
Prototype: 25 October 1955
*J 35F*: 1961; *S 35E*: 27 June 1963, *Saab 35X*: 29 January
  1970
**Production**
Approx 550 of all versions for Sweden built from 1958–
  1970; 58 export versions built from 1970–1974
**In service**
*J 35A, J 35B, J 35D, J 35F, S 35E, Sk 35C*: Sweden;
*Saab 35D and XT*: Denmark (F–35, TF–35);
*Saab 35BS, Saab 35XS*: Finland

## SAAB 37 'VIGGEN' (AJ 37)

**Type**
Single-seat strike fighter and all-weather fighter
**Weights**
normal 35,275 lb (16,000 kg)
**Performance**
maximum speed at 36,000 ft (11,000 m) (Mach 2.0)
  1,320 mph (2,125 km/hr)
maximum speed at 360 ft (100 m) (Mach 1.15) 876 mph
  (1,410 km/hr)
radius of action 310–620 miles (500–1,000 km)
time to 36,000 ft (11,000 m) 2 min 0 sec
service ceiling 60,000 ft (18,300 m)
**Dimensions**
wing span 34 ft 9¼ in (10.60 m)
length overall 50 ft 8¼ in (15.45 m)
height overall 18 ft 4½ in (5.60 m)
**Power plant**
One Svenska Flygmotor RM8 turbofan rated at 14,705 lb
  (6,670 kg)/26,455 lb (12,000 kg) st
**Armament**
Weapon load on 7 hard points;
*Strike Fighter*: Bombs, rockets and Rb 04C or Rb 05A
  ASMs;
*Fighter*: Rb 24 (Sidewinder) or Rb 27 and Rb 28 (Falcon)
  AAMs
**Variants**
*Sk 37*: Two-seat strike trainer; *JA 37*: Planned single-
  seat interceptor with one 30 mm Oerlikon KCA cannon
  and AAMs
*S 37, SF 37, SH 37*: Single-seat reconnaissance aircraft
**First flights**
Prototype *AJ 37*: 8 February 1967
*Sk 37*: 2 July 1970
**Production**
7 prototypes and pre-production models;
*AJ 37*: 150 on order for delivery from 1971;
*Sk 37*: 25 on order
**In service**
Sweden

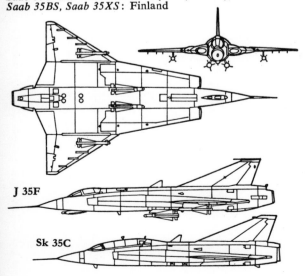

J 35F

Sk 35C

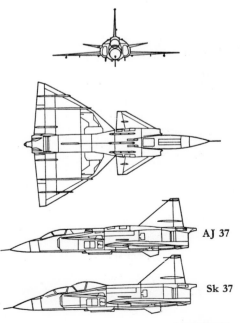

AJ 37

Sk 37

## SAAB 91D 'SAFIR'

**Type**
Two to four-seat trainer and liaison aircraft
**Weights**
empty 1,565 lb (710 kg)
maximum 2,657 lb (1,205 kg)
**Performance**
maximum speed at sea level 165 mph (265 km/hr)
maximum cruising speed 136 mph (220 km/hr)
ferry range 660 miles (1.060 km)
initial rate of climb 13.4 fps (4.1 m/sec)
service ceiling 16,400 ft (5,000 m)
**Dimensions**
wing span 34 ft 9 in (10.60 m)
length overall 26 ft 4 in (8.03 m)
height overall 7 ft 2 in (2.20 m)
wing area 146.3 sq ft (13.60 sq m)
**Power plant**
One 180 hp Lycoming 0–360–A1A piston engine
**Variants**
*Saab 91A, 91B*: Two to three-seat trainers
*Saab 91C*: Two to four-seat trainer and liaison aircraft
**First flights**
*Prototype Saab 91*: 20 November 1945
*Saab 91D*: 1957
**Production**
*Saab 91A*: 49 built from 1946;
*Saab 91B*: 135 built from 1951;
*Saab 91C*: 39 built; *Saab 91D*: 100 built
**In service**
*Saab 91B*: Ethiopia, Norway, Sweden (Sk 50B, Tp91):
*Saab 91C*: Ethiopia, Sweden (Sk 50C);
*Saab 91D*: Austria, Finland, Tunisia

## SAAB 105 (Sk 60)

**Type**
Two-seat trainer and light ground-attack aircraft
**Weights**
empty 5,534 lb (2,510 kg)
normal 8,930 lb (4,050 kg)
maximum 9,920 lb (4,500 kg)
**Performance**
maximum speed at sea level 447 mph (720 km/hr)
maximum speed at 20,000 ft (6,000 m) 478 mph
(770 km/hr)
maximum cruising speed at 20,000 ft (6,000 m) 441 mph
(710 km/hr)
radius of action with 1,543 lb (700 kg) weapon load
196 miles (315 km)
ferry range 680 miles (1,940 km)
initial rate of climb 65.6 fps (20.0 m/sec)
time to 32,800 ft (10,000 m) 17 min 30 sec
service ceiling 41,667 ft (12,700 m)
**Dimensions**
wing span 31 ft 2 in (9.50 m)
length overall 34 ft 5 in (10.50 m)
height overall 8ft 10¼ in (2.70 m)
wing area 175.45 sq ft (16.30 sq m)
**Power plant**
Two Turbomeca Aubisque turbojets each rated at
1,638 lb (743 kg) st
**Armament**
Max 1,653 lb (750 kg) weapon load on 6 hard points
**Variants**
*Sk 60B*: Two-seat trainer and light ground-attack
aircraft;
*Sk 60C*: Two-seat trainer and light reconnaissance
aircraft;
*Saab 105XT*: Export version of Saab 105 with more
powerful engines
*Saab 105G*: Light ground-attack aircraft
**First flights**
Prototype: 29 June 1963
*Saab 105G*: 26 May 1972
**Production**
150 built from 1965–1970
**In service**
Sweden (Sk 60A, Sk 60B, Sk 60C)

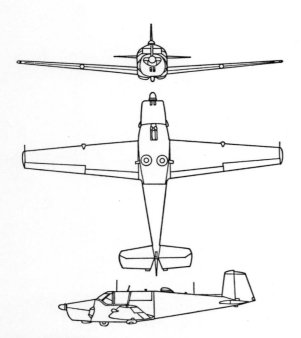

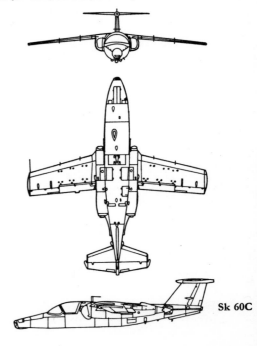

Sk 60C

## SAAB 105XT

**Type**
Two-seat trainer and light ground-attack aircraft
Details as for Saab 105 (Sk 60) with the following
  exceptions
**Weights**
empty 5,988 lb (2,720 kg)
normal 10,258 lb (4,653 kg)
maximum 14,330 lb (6,500 kg)
**Performance**
maximum speed at sea level 603 mph (970 km/hr)
maximum speed at 32,800 ft (10,000 m) 543 mph
  (875 km/hr)
maximum cruising speed at 42,650 ft (13,000 m) 435 mph
  (700 km/hr)
radius of action 528 miles (850 km)
ferry range 1,373 miles (2,225 km)
initial rate of climb 213.3 fps (65.0 m/sec)
time to 32,800 ft (10,000 m) 4 min 30 sec
service ceiling 44,950 ft (13,700 m)
**Power plant**
Two General Electric J85–GE–17B turbojets each rated
  at 2,850 lb (1,293 kg) st
**Armament**
Max 4,400 lb (2,000 kg) weapon load on 6 hard points,
  e.g. six 500 lb (227 kg) bombs or two Sidewinder AAMs
**First flights**
29 April 1967
**Production**
40 built from 1970–1972
**In service**
Austria (Saab 105OE)

## PILATUS P–3

**Type**
Two-seat trainer
**Weights**
empty 2,447 lb (1,110 kg)
normal 3,303 lb (1,498 kg)
**Performance**
maximum speed at sea level 192 mph (309 km/hr)
maximum cruising speed 156 mph (251 km/hr)
ferry range 466 miles (750 km)
initial rate of climb 23.3 fps (7.1 m/sec)
service ceiling 18,011 ft (5,490 m)
**Dimensions**
wing span 34 ft 1 in (10.40 m)
length overall 28 ft 8 in (8.75 m)
height overall 10 ft 0 in (3.05 m)
wing area 177.1 sq ft (16.45 sq m)
**Power plant**
One 260 hp Lycoming GO–435–C2A
**Armament**
One weapon pack containing one 7.92 mm machine gun
  plus two 50 mm rockets or four 25 lb (12 kg) practice
  bombs
**First flights**
Prototype: 3 September 1953
**Production**
78 built from 1956
**In service**
Brazil, Switzerland

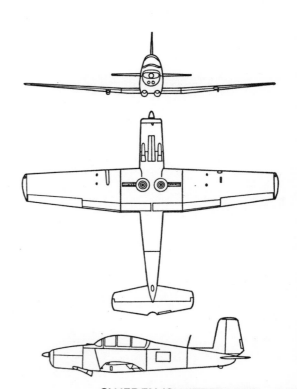

Saab 105

## PILATUS PC–6 'PORTER'

**Type**
Liaison aircraft
**Weights**
empty 2,359 lb (1,070 kg)
maximum 4,321 lb (1,960 kg)
**Performance**
maximum speed 144 mph (233 km/hr)
maximum cruising speed 135 mph (217 km/hr)
range 398 miles (640 km)
ferry range 746 miles (1,200 km)
initial rate of climb 17.1 fps (5.2 m/sec)
service ceiling 23,950 ft (7,300 m)
**Dimensions**
wing span 49 ft 10½ in (15.20 m)
length overall 33 ft 5½ in (10.20 m)
height overall 10 ft 6 in (3.20 m)
wing area 310 sq ft (28.80 sq m)
**Power plant**
One 340 hp Lycoming G.SO–480–B1AG/piston engine
**Payload**
1 man crew and 7 troops
**Variants**
*PC–6A*: Variant with one 523 hp Turboméca Astazou
    IIE or IIG turboprop
*PC–6C*: Variant with one 575 hp Garret-Research
    TPE 331–25D turboprop
Fairchild–Hiller Porter: American licence-built PC–6B
    and PC–6C by Fairchild–Hiller; Fairchild AU–23A
    'Peacemaker': light night ground support aircraft
**First flights**
Prototype *PC–6*: May 1959;
Prototype *PC–6A*: 2 May 1961
**Production**
*PC–6*: 59 built from 1959–1968
*FH Porter*: Approx 100 built from 1964
*AU–23A*: 17 (22?) built 1972/73
**In service**
Brazil, Colombia, Switzerland

## PILATUS PC–6A, B, C 'TURBO-PORTER'

**Type**
Liaison aircraft
Details as for PC–6 with the following exceptions
    (N.B.: Figures below refer specifically to *PC–6B*)
**Weights**
empty 2,401 lb (1,089 kg)
maximum 4,850 lb (2,205 kg)
**Performance**
maximum speed 175 mph (282 km/hr)
maximum cruising speed at 10,000 ft (3,050 m) 158 mph
    (254 km/hr)
ferry range 584 miles (940 km)
initial rate of climb 23.6 fps (7.2 m/sec)
service ceiling 25,918 ft (7,900 m)
**Dimensions**
length overall 36 ft 1½ in (11.00 m)
**Power plant**
One 550 hp Pratt & Whitney PTA6A–6 or PT6A–20
    turboprop
**First flights**
*PC–6B*: 1 May 1964
**Production**
*PC–6A, B, C*: Series production from 1961, over 200
    delivered or on order to date
**In service**
*PC–6A, B, C*: Australia, Colombia, Ecuador, Peru, Sudan,
    Switzerland; AU–23A: Thailand

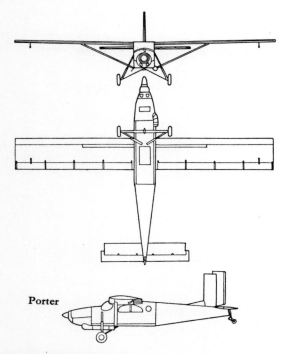

Porter

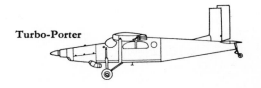

Turbo-Porter

## BEECHCRAFT C–45G 'EXPEDITOR'

**Type**
Light transport
**Weights**
empty 5,795 lb (2,624 kg)
normal 9,000 lb (4,082 kg)
**Performance**
maximum speed at sea level 225 mph (362 km/hr)
maximum cruising speed at 5,000 ft (1,520 m) 211 mph
(340 km/hr)
range 1,200 miles (1,930 km)
initial rate of climb 20.0 fps (6.1 m/sec)
service ceiling 26,250 ft (8,000 m)
**Dimensions**
wing span 47 ft 6¾ in (14.50 m)
length overall 43 ft 11½ in (13.40 m)
height overall 9 ft 2½ in (2.81 m)
wing area 345 sq ft (32.50 sq m)
**Power plant**
Two 450 hp Pratt & Whitney R–985–AN–3 or –B5 piston
engines
**Payload**
2 man crew and 6 troops
**Variants**
*C–45H*: Later series; *RC–45H*: Photographic aircraft;
*TC–45H*: Trainer; *T–7;* Navigation trainer;
*T–11 Kansan*: Trainer; *Super 18* and *Model 18*:
Civil series
**First flights**
Civil prototype: 15 January 1937;
Military variant: 1941
**Production**
5,204 military variants built from 1941–1945;
1,030 civil variants built (C–18 and D–18) up to 1954
**In service**
*C–45*: Argentine, Bolivia, Brazil, Burma, Canada, Chile,
Colombia, Ecuador, Haiti, Iran, Italy(?), Mexico,
Netherlands, Nicaragua, Paraguay, Portugal, Somali,
Thailand, Turkey, United States, Uruguay
*T–11*: Argentine, Dominican Republic, El Salvador,
Honduras, Mexico, Nicaragua, Venezuela

## BEECHCRAFT 'MUSKETEER SPORT'

**Type**
Two-seat trainer
**Weights**
empty 1,349 lb (612 kg)
maximum 2,249 lb (1,020 kg)
**Performance**
maximum speed at sea level 140 mph (225 km/hr)
maximum cruising speed at 7,000 ft (2,135 m) 131 mph
(211 km/hr)
ferry range 767 miles (1,235 km)
initial rate of climb 11.5 fps (3.5 m/sec)
service ceiling 11,100 ft (3,380 m)
**Dimensions**
wing span 32 ft 9 in (9.98 m)
length overall 25 ft 0 in (7.62 m)
height overall 8 ft 3 in (2.51 m)
wing area 146 sq ft (13.57 sq m)
**Power plant**
One 150 hp Lycoming 0–320–E2C piston engine
**Payload**
As liaison aircraft: 1 man crew and 3 troops
**Variants**
*Musketeer Custom, Musketeer Super, Musketeer Super R*:
Other series
**First flights**
Prototype: 23 October 1961
**Production**
Series production from 1962, over 2,000 delivered to date,
almost all as civil models
**In service**
Canada, Mexico

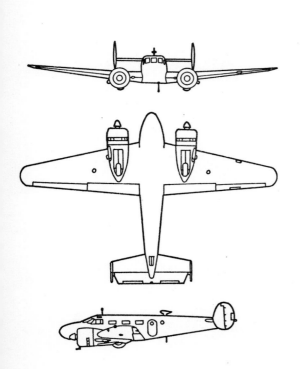

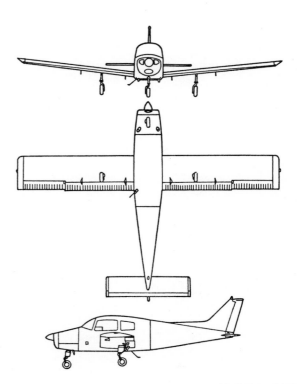

## BEECHCRAFT T–34A 'MENTOR'

**Type**
Two-seat trainer
**Weights**
empty 2,155 lb (978 kg)
maximum 2,950 lb (1,338 kg)
**Performance**
maximum speed at sea level 189 mph (304 km/hr)
maximum speed at 7,550 ft (2,300 m) 184 mph
  (297 km/hr)
maximum cruising speed at 10,000 ft (3,050 m) 173 mph
  (278 km/hr)
range 735 miles (1,183 km)
initial rate of climb 18.7 fps (5.7 m/sec)
time to 5,020 ft (1,530 m) 4 min 54 sec
service ceiling 18,210 ft (5,550 m)
**Dimensions**
wing span 32 ft 10 in (10.00 m)
length overall 25 ft 1¼ in (7.91 m)
height overall 9 ft 7 in (2.92 m)
wing area 177.6 sq ft (16.49 sq m)
**Power plant**
One 225 hp Continental 0–470–13 piston engine
**Variants**
*T–34B*: Naval version of T–34A
*Beech Bonanza*: Civil predecessor
**First flights**
Prototype: 2 December 1948
**Production**
3 prototypes, 1,149 built from 1953–1957, inc 475 *T–34A*,
  423 *T–34B*, 75 Argentinian and 167 Japanese licence–
  built from 1955–1962
**In service**
Argentine, Chile, Colombia, El Salvador, Iran, Japan,
  Mexico, Peru, Philippines, Saudi Arabia, Spain, Turkey,
  United States (T–34A, T–34B), Uruguay, Venezuela

## BEECHCRAFT T–42A 'COCHISE'

**Type**
Four–to six-seat trainer and liaison aircraft
**Weights**
empty 3,071 lb (1,393 kg)
maximum 5,100 lb (2,313 kg)
**Performance**
maximum speed at sea level 236 mph (380 km/hr)
maximum cruising speed at 10,000 ft (3,050 m) 195 mph
  (314 km/hr)
ferry range 1,225 miles (1,970 km)
initial rate of climb 27.9 fps (8.5 m/sec)
service ceiling 19,700 ft (6,000 m)
**Dimensions**
wing span 37 ft 10 in (11.53 m)
length overall 27 ft 3 in (8.31 m)
height overall 9 ft 7 in (2.92 m)
wing area 199.2 sq ft (18.50 sq m)
**Power plant**
Two 260 hp Continental I0–470–L piston engines
**Variants**
Beechcraft Baron: Civil variant
**First flights**
Prototype: 24 February 1960
**Production**
2,242 built from 1960–1969, inc only 65 T–42A models
  from 1965–1966
**In service**
*T–42A*: Turkey, United States;
*Baron*: Rhodesia, Spain

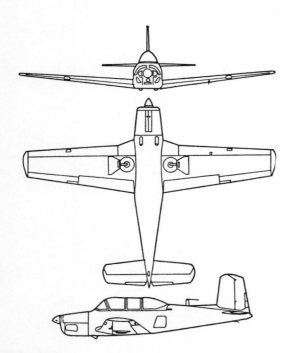

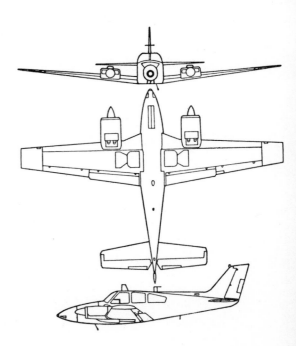

## BEECHCRAFT U–8F 'SEMINOLE'

**Type**
Liaison aircraft
**Weights**
empty 4,641 lb (2,105 kg)
maximum 7,700 lb (3,493 kg)
**Performance**
maximum speed at 12,000 ft (3,600 m) 239 mph
 (385 km/hr)
maximum cruising speed at 15,000 ft (4,600 m) 214 mph
 (344 km/hr)
ferry range 1,590 miles (2,558 km)
initial rate of climb 21.7 fps (6.6 m/sec)
service ceiling 31,300 ft (9,540 m)
**Dimensions**
wing span 45 ft 10½ in (13.98 m)
length overall 33 ft 4½ in (10.17 m)
height overall 14 ft 2 in (4.32 m)
wing area 277.06 sq ft (25.73 sq m)
**Power plant**
Two 340 hp Lycoming IGS0–480–A1A6 piston engines
**Payload**
1–2 man crew and 6 troops
**Variants**
*Queen Air*: *King Air*; Civil light aircraft
*U–8D, E*: Earlier versions
*Model 150 Twin–Bonanza*: Earlier (civil) version
**First flights**
Prototype Queen Air: 28 August 1958; Prototype King
 Air: 20 January 1964
**Production**
Series production from 1959; *U–8F*: pre-production and
 68 production models;
*Queen Air*: Over 330 of all versions delivered or on order
 up to 1969
King Air: Series production from 1964, over 700 delivered
 or on order to date
**In serivce**
*U–8D, U–8F*: United States; *Queen Air*: Japan, Peru,
 Uruguay, Venezuela, King Air: Japan
*Twin–Bonanza*: Chile, Morocco, Pakistan, Switzerland

## BEECHCRAFT U–21A 'UTE'

**Type**
Liaison aircraft
**Weights**
empty 5,335 lb (2,420 kg)
maximum 9,661 lb (4,382 kg)
**Performance**
maximum speed at 21,000 ft (6,400 m) 272 mph
 (483 km/hr)
maximum cruising speed at 14,760 ft (4,500 m) 254 mph
 (409 km/hr)
range 1,220 miles (1,963 km)
ferry range 1,676 miles (2,697 km)
initial rate of climb 36.1 fps (11.0 m/sec)
service ceiling 26,150 ft (7,970 m)
**Dimensions**
wing span 45 ft 10½ in (13.98 m)
length overall 35 ft 6¾ in (10.84 m)
height overall 14 ft 1¼ in (4.30 m)
wing area 279.7 sq ft (25.98 sq m)
**Power plant**
Two 550 hp Pratt & Whitney (VACL) PT6A–20
 turboprops
**Payload**
2 man crew and 6–10 troops or 3 stretcher cases and 3
 seated wounded or max 3,000 lb (1,360 kg) freight
**Variants**
*RU–21A, B, C, D, E, F*: Electronic reconnaissance
 aircraft
*VC–6A*: Command and VIP transport
**First flights**
Prototype: March 1967
**Production**
167 built from 1967–1970;
*RU–21E*: built from 1971
**In service**
*U–21A*: Korea (South)
*RU–21, VC–6A*: United States

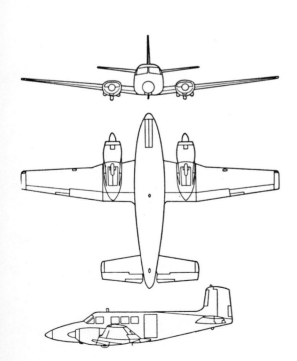

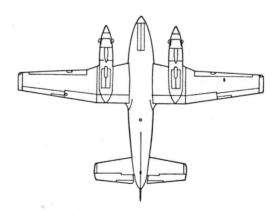

## BELL 47G–3B–2 'TROOPER' (OH–13H 'SIOUX')

**Type**
Light helicopter
**Weights**
empty 1,794 lb (814 kg)
maximum 2,950 lb (1,338 kg)
**Performance**
maximum speed at sea level 105 mph (169 km/hr)
maximum cruising speed 87 mph (140 km/hr)
range 315 miles (507 km)
initial rate of climb 22.6 fps (6.9 m/sec)
service ceiling 20,000 ft (6,100 m)
hovering ceiling in ground effect 18,000 ft (5,486 m)
hovering ceiling out of ground effect 15,000 ft (4,572 m)
**Dimensions**
main rotor diameter 37 ft 2 in (11.32 m)
length of fuselage 31 ft 7 in (9.63 m)
height 9 ft 2¾ in (2.83 m)
**Power plant**
One 240 hp Lycoming TV0–435–A1B piston engine
**Payload**
1 man crew and 1–2 troops or 2 stretcher cases
**Variants**
*Bell 47D*: Earlier version: *Bell 47G–3B* (*OH–13S*): Later
   and more powerful (260 hp) series; *AB.47G*: Italian
   licence-built by Agusta; *KH–4*: Japanese licence-built
   by Kawasaki; *Westland Sioux*: British licence–built;
   *TH–13M, TH–13T*: Helicopter trainers
**First flights**
Prototype: 8 December 1945
**Production**
Series production from 1947, model *47G* from 1953; over
   3,500 delivered to date. licence-built in Great Britain,
   Italy and Japan; *AB.47*: Over 1,000 built; *KH–4*: 423
   built from 1954; *Sioux*: 250 built
**In service**
*Bell 47D*: Argentine, Chile, Colombia, Spain;
*Bell 47G*: Argentine, Australia, Brazil, Burma, Ceylon
   (Sri Lanka), Chile, China (Taiwan), Colombia, Congo,
   Ecuador, France, Germany (West), Greece, Guinea,
   India, Indonesia, Israel, Jamaica, Kenya, Madagascar
   (Malagasy), Malta, Mexico, Morocco, New Zealand,
   Pakistan, Paraguay, Peru, Turkey(?), United States
   (OH–13G, OH–13H, OH–13S, TH–13M, TH–13S),
   Uruguay, Venezuela;
*AB.47G*: Italy, Libya, Senegal, Spain;
*KH–4*: China (Taiwan), Japan, Korea (South), Thailand
*Sioux*: Great Britain (AH.1, HT.2), South Yeman (AH.1)

## BELL 47J–2 'RANGER' (UH–13)

**Type**
Light helicopter
**Weights**
empty 1,731 lb (785 kg)
normal 2,851 lb (1,293 kg)
maximum 2,950 lb (1,338 kg)
**Performance**
maximum speed at sea level 105 mph (169 km/hr)
maximum cruising speed 93 mph (150 km/hr)
range 258 miles (415 km)
initial rate of climb 13.5 fps (4.1 m/sec)
service ceiling 10,982 ft (3,353 m)
hovering ceiling in ground effect 9,203 ft (2,805 m)
**Dimensions**
main rotor diameter 37 ft 2 in (11.32 m)
length of fuselage 32 ft 5 in (9.87 m)
height 9 ft 2¾ in (2.83 m)
**Power plant**
One 260 hp Lycoming VO–540–B1B piston engine
**Payload**
1 man crew and 3–4 troops or 2 stretcher cases
**Variants**
*AB.47J*: Italian licence-built by Agusta; some with uprated
   power plants
*AB.47J–3*: ASW helicopter
**First flights**
Prototype: 1954, *Bell 47J–2*: 1960
**Production**
Series production from 1955–1966, majority as civil
   models; licence-built in Italy and Japan (122 built by
   Kawasaki)
**In service**
*Bell 47J*: Argentine, Brazil, Chile, Colombia, Iceland,
   Mexico, United States (UH–13J, UH–13P), Venezuela(?)
*AB 47J*: Cyprus, Italy

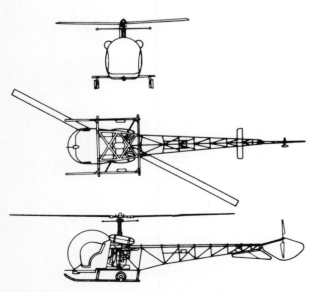

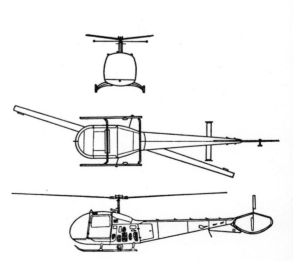

## BELL 204B (UH–1B 'IROQUOIS')

**Type**
Transport helicopter
**Weights**
empty 4,599 lb (2,086 kg)
normal 8,499 lb (3,855 kg)
maximum 9,500 lb (4,309 kg)
**Performance**
maximum speed at sea level 120 mph (193 km/hr)
maximum cruising speed 110 mph (177 km/hr)
ferry range 390 miles (630 km)
initial rate of climb 23.3 fps (7.1 m/sec)
service ceiling 15,810 ft (4,820 m)
hovering ceiling in ground effect 10,000 ft (3,050 m)
hovering ceiling out of ground effect 4,300 ft (1,370 m)
**Dimensions**
main rotor diameter 48 ft 0 in (14.63 m)
length of fuselage 40 ft 4¾ in (12.31 m)
height 12 ft 8½ in (3.87 m)
**Power plant**
One 1,100 hp Lycoming T53–L–11A turboshaft
**Armament**
Optional
**Payload**
2 man crew and 7 troops or 3 stretcher cases and 1 medic
or max 3,000 lb (1,360 kg) freight
**Variants**
*AB.204B*: Italian licence-built UH–1B by Agusta;
*UH–1C, E, F, L*: Later series, majority with uprated
power plants;
*HH–1K*: ASR helicopter;
*TH–1F, TH–1L Seawolf*: Helicopter trainers;
*AB.204ASW*: ASW helicopter, 3 man crew, 2 homing
torpedoes
**First flights**
Prototype: 22 October 1956
**Production**
Series production from 1961, several thousand delivered
or on order to date; licence-built in Italy (Agusta) and
Japan (102 built by Fuji from 1962–1971)
**In service**
*Bell 204B*: Argentine, Australia, Colombia, Indonesia,
Japan, Peru, Spain, Thailand, United States (UH–1B,
C, E, F, L; HH–1K; TH–1F, L), Vietnam (South);
*AB.204B*: Austria, Finland, Italy, Netherlands, Norway,
Saudi-Arabia, Sweden (HKP–3), Spain, Turkey;
*AB.204ASW*: Italy, Spain

## BELL 205A (UH–1D 'IROQUOIS')

**Type**
Transport helicopter
**Weights**
empty 4,722 lb (2,142 kg)
take-off
normal 8,801 lb (3,992 kg)
maximum 9,500 lb (4,309 kg)
**Performance**
maximum speed at sea level 127 mph (204 km/hr)
maximum cruising speed 111 mph (179 km/hr)
range 323 miles (520 km)
ferry range 404 miles (650 km)
initial rate of climb 28.2 fps (8.6 m/sec)
service ceiling 21,980 ft (6,700 m)
hovering ceiling in ground effect 10,400 ft (3,170 m)
hovering ceiling out of ground effect 6,000 ft (1,830 m)
**Dimensions**
main rotor diameter 48 ft 0 in (14.63 m)
length of fuselage 41 ft 6 in (12.65 m)
height 14 ft 7¼ in (4.45 m)
**Power plant**
One 1,100 hp Lycoming T53–L–11 turboshaft
**Armament**
Optional
**Payload**
2 man crew and 1 troops or 6 stretcher cases and 1 medic
or max 4,000 lb (1,816 kg) freight
**Variants**
*AB.205*: Italian licence-built *UH–1D* by Agusta;
*UH–1H*: Later series with more powerful (1,400 hp) engine
*Bell 212 (UH–1N)*: Further development, Italian licence-
built *AB.212*
**First flights**
Prototype: 16 August 1961
**Production**
Series production from 1963, over 4,000 delivered or on
order to date;
Licence-built in China (Taiwan), Germany (West), Italy
and Japan (81 *UH–1H* by Fuji from 1972)
**In service**
*UH–1D*: Australia, Brazil, Brunei, Cambodia, Chile,
Colombia(?), Germany (West), Guatemala, Israel, Korea
(South), Laos, New Zealand, Phillipines, Thailand,
Uganda, United States, Venezuela(?), Vietnam (South);
*AB.205*: Greece, Iran, Italy, Kuwait, Morocco, Oman,
Saudi Arabia, Turkey, Uganda, Zambia;
*UH–1H*: Brazil, Canada (CUH–1H), China (Taiwan),
Ethiopia, Japan, New Zealand, Panama, Peru, Spain,
Thailand, United States, Vietnam (South);
*UH–1N*: Canada (CUH–1N), United States;
*Bell 212*: Brunei, Colombia, Ghana, Iran, Korea (South),
Mexico, Peru, Uganda, Zambia

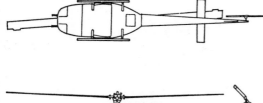

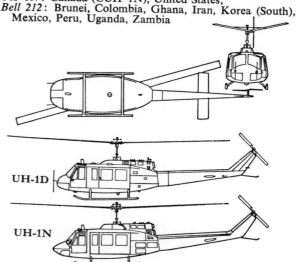

UH-1D

UH-1N

## BELL 206A 'JETRANGER' (OH–58A 'KIOWA')

**Type**
Light helicopter
**Weights**
empty 1,424 lb (646 kg)
normal 2,000 lb (953 kg)
maximum 3,000 lb (1,360 kg)
**Performance**
maximum speed at sea level 150 mph (241 km/hr)
maximum cruising speed 131 mph (211 km/hr)
range 392 miles (630 km)
ferry range 460 miles (740 km)
initial rate of climb 24.3 fps (7.4 m/sec)
service ceiling 17,700 ft (5,395 m)
hovering ceiling in ground effect 9,700 ft (2,410 m)
hovering ceiling out of ground effect 3,350 ft (1,020 m)
**Dimensions**
main rotor diameter 33 ft 4 in (10.16 m)
length of fuselage 31 ft 2 in (9.50 m)
height 9 ft 6½ in (2.91 m)
**Power plant**
One 317 hp Allison 250–C18A turboshaft
**Payload**
1 man crew and 4 troops or max 250 lb (113 kg)(?) freight
**Variants**
*TH–57A Sea Ranger*: Training helicopter
*AB.206A, AN.206A–1*: Italian licence-built by Agusta
**First flights**
Prototype: 10 January 1966
**Production**
Series production from 1967, over 3,000 delivered or on
  order to date inc *OH–58A*: over 2,200 built from
  1967–1972; *TH–57A*: 40 built, Licence-built in Australia,
  Italy and Japan
**In service**
*Bell 206A*: Australia, Brazil, Brunei, Canada (COH–58A),
  Ceylon (Sri Lanka), Chile, Jamaica, Japan, Malta,
  Mexico, Spain, Thailand, Uganda, United States
  (OH–58A, TH–57A);
*AB.206A*: Austria, Finland, Greece, Iran, Italy, Libya,
  Oman, Saudi Arabia, Sweden (HKP–6), Spain, Turkey

## BELL AH–1G 'HUEYCOBRA'

**Type**
Two-seat attack helicopter
**Weights**
empty 6,096 lb (2,765 kg)
maximum 9,500 lb (4,309 kg)
**Performance**
maximum speed at sea level 219 mph (352 km/hr)
radius of action 230 miles (370 km)
range 386 miles (622 km)
initial rate of climb 26.5 fps (8.0 m/sec)
service ceiling 12,697 ft (3,870 m)
hovering ceiling in ground effect 9,892 ft (3,015 m)
**Dimensions**
main rotor diameter 44 ft 0 in (13.41 m)
length of fuselage 44 ft 5 in (13.54 m)
height 13 ft 5¾ in (4.10 m)
**Power plant**
One 1,400 hp Lycoming T53–L–13 turboshaft
**Armament**
Two 7.62 mm Miniguns with 4,000 rpg or two 40 mm
  grenade launchers, each with 300 rounds, or one
  Minigun and one 40 mm grenade launcher in rotating
  turret and max 1,653 lb (750 kg) weapon load on 4 hard
  points, e.g. 2–4 rocket launchers each containing nineteen
  70 mm FFAR rockets or 2 rocket launchers each con-
  taining seven 70 mm FFAR rockets plus 2 weapon
  packs each containing one 7.62 mm Minigun with 1,500
  rpg
**Variants**
*KingCobra*: Further development
*AH–1Q*: Conversion of about 300 AH–1G to anti-tank
  helicopters with six Tow ASM's
**First flights**
Prototype: 7 September 1965,
*KingCobra*: 10 September 1971
**Production**
1 prototype and 2 pre-production models;
*AH–1G*: Series production from 1966, 1,200 delivered or
  on order to date
**In service**
Spain, United States

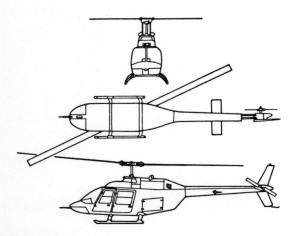

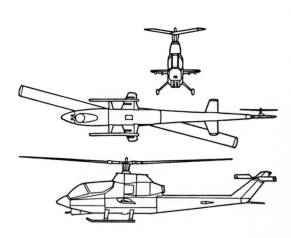

## BELL AH-1J 'SEACOBRA'

**Type**
Two–seat attack helicopter
Details as for AH-1G with the following exceptions
**Weights**
empty 6,618 lb (3,002 kg)
normal 6,825 lb (3,096 kg)
maximum 10,000 lb (4,535 kg)
**Performance**
maximum speed at sea level 208 mph (333 km/hr)
maximum cruising speed 185 mph (298 km/hr)
range 358 miles (577 km)
initial rate of climb 18.0 fps (5.5 m/sec)
service ceiling 10,548 ft (3,215 m)
hovering ceiling in ground effect 9,892 ft (3,794 m)
hovering ceiling out of ground effect 3,498 ft (1,066 m)
**Dimensions**
main rotor diameter 44 ft 0 in (13.41 m)
length of fuselage 44 ft 7 in (13.59 m)
height 13 ft 7½ in (4.15 m)
**Power plant**
One 1,800 hp Pratt & Whitney T400–CP–400 coupled
   turboshaft
**Armament**
One three-barrel 20 mm cannon in rotating turret and max
   1,653 lb (750 kg) weapon load on 4 hard points
**Production**
49 built from 1969–1971; an additional 222 to be built
   from 1973
**In service**
Iran, United States

## BOEING 707–320C

**Type**
Long-range transport
**Weights**
empty 138,323 lb (62,742 kg)
maximum 328,000 lb (148,780 kg)
**Performance**
maximum speed 627 mph (1,010 km/hr)
maximum cruising speed at 25,000 ft (7,620 m) 600 mph
   (966 km/hr)
range w.m.p. 3,400 miles (5,470 km)
ferry range 7,510 miles (12,086 km)
initial rate of climb 48.9 fps (14.9 m/sec)
**Dimensions**
wing span 145 ft 9 in (44.42 m)
length overall 152 ft 11 in (46.61 m)
height overall 42 ft 4¾ in (12.94 m)
wing area 3,010 sq ft (279.64 sq m)
**Power plant**
Four Pratt & Whitney JT4A–11 turbojets each rated at
   18,000 lb (8,165 kg) st
**Payload**
4 man crew and up to 199 troops or max 80,000 lb
   (36,285 kg) freight
**Variants**
*Boeing 707, Boeing 720:* Civil airliners and freighters,
   numerous series:
*E–3A;* Airborne HQ command post (original designation
   EC–137D)
**First flights**
Prototype: 15 July 1954
**Production**
Series production from 1958, 886 aircraft of all variants
   delivered by mid 1973
*E–3A;* 2 prototypes, 5 pre-production and 42 series
   production models planned from 1973
**In service**
*707–120, 707–320B:* United States (VC–137B, C);
*707–320C:* Canada (CC–137), Germany (West), Iran,
   Portugal;
*E–3A:* United States

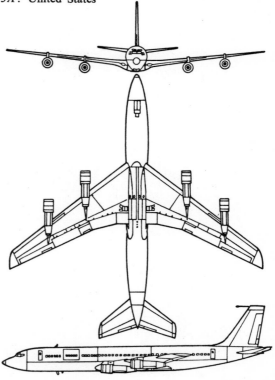

# BOEING B–52H 'STRATOFORTRESS'

**Type**
Strategic heavy bomber 6 man crew
**Weights**
empty 225,484 lb (111,350 kg)
maximum 488,000 lb (221,357 kg)
**Performance**
maximum speed at 39,375 ft (12,000 m) (Mach 0.95)
630 mph (1,014 km/hr)
maximum speed at 20,000 ft (6,100 m) (Mach 0.95)
665 mph (1,070 km/hr)
maximum cruising speed at 36,000 ft (11,000 m) 565 mph
(909 km/hr)
ferry range 11,992 miles (19,300 km)
service ceiling 55,100 ft (16,800 m)
**Dimensions**
wing span 185 ft 0 in (56.39 m)
length overall 157 ft 7 in (48.03 m)
height overall 40 ft 8¼ in (12.40 m)
wing area 4,000 sq ft (371.60 sq m)
**Power plant**
Eight Pratt & Whitney TF 33–P–3 turbofans each rated
at 17,000 lb (7,711 kg) st
**Armament**
One 20 mm ASG–21 cannon in tail position, max 60,000 lb
(27,216 kg) weapon load, e.g. two AGM–28B Hound
Dog ASMs and diversionary missile launchers underwing, bombs and ADM–20C Qual diversionary missile
in fuselage bay or max twenty AGM–69A SRAM ASMs
underwing and sixty–six 750 lb (340 kg) bombs in
fuselage bay
**Variants**
*B–52B, C, D, E, F, G*: Earlier versions
**First flights**
Prototype: 2 October 1952; *B–52H*: 6 March 1961
**Production**
3 prototypes; series production from 1954–1962, *B–52B*:
50 built; *B–52C*: 35 built; *B–52D*: 170 built; *B–52E*:
100 built; *B–52F*: 88 built; *B–52G*: 193 built; *B–52H*:
102 built
**In service**
B–52D, F, G, H: United States

# BOEING KC–97G 'STRATOFREIGHTER'

**Type**
Heavy tanker and transport
**Weights**
empty 58,410 lb (38,741 kg)
normal 153,132 lb (69,460 kg)
maximum 175,157 lb (79,450 kg)
**Performance**
maximum speed at 25,000 ft (7,625 m) 375 mph
(603 km/hr)
maximum cruising speed at 23,000 ft (7,010 m) 298 mph
(479 km/hr)
ferry range 4,300 miles (6,920 km)
initial rate of climb 18.4 fps (5.6 m/sec)
**Dimensions**
wing span 141 ft 2¾ in (43.05 m)
length overall 110 ft 4 in (33.63 m)
height overall 38 ft 3 in (11.66 m)
wing area 1,765.3 sq ft (164.2 sq m)
**Power plant**
Four 3,500 hp Pratt & Whitney R–4360–59B piston
engines
**Payload**
As transport: 5 man crew and 96 troops or 69 stretcher
cases or max 68,500 lb (31,072 kg) freight
**Variants**
*KC–97L*: Tanker with two auxiliary J47 turbojets
underwing;
*C–97G, C–97K*: Freight and passenger transports
respectively;
*HC–97C*: Search and rescue aircraft
**First flights**
Prototype: 15 November 1944
**Production**
888 built from 1945–1956, inc 592 KC–97G;
various conversions of *KC–97G*: to *KC–97L*, to
*C–97G* (135 built), to
*C–97K* (26 built) and to *HC–97G*
**In service**
Israel (KC–97G only), Spain (KC–97L only),
United states

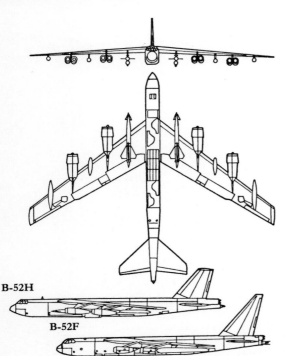

B-52H

B-52F

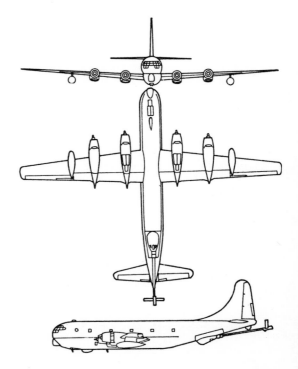

# BOEING KC-135A 'STRATOTANKER'

**Type**
Heavy tanker-transport
**Weights**
empty 98,465 lb (44,664 kg)
normal 245,000 lb (111,123 kg)
maximum 297,000 lb (134,719 kg)
**Performance**
maximum speed at 25,000 ft (7,600 m) 624 mph
  (1,004 km/hr)
maximum cruising speed at 35,000 ft (10,700 m) 592 mph
  (953 km/hr)
radius of action 1,150 miles (1,850 km)
initial rate of climb 21.6 fps (6.6 m/sec)
**Dimensions**
wing span 130 ft 10 in (39.88 m)
length overall 136 ft 3 in (41.53 m)
height overall 38 ft 4 in (11.68 m)
wing area 2,433.1 sq ft (226.04 sq m)
**Power plant**
Four Pratt & Whitney J57–P–59W turbojets each rated at
  13,750 lb (6,237 kg) st
**Payload**
4 man crew, 26,060 gal (118,470 l) transferable fuel cap-
  acity or 80 troops or max 50,000 lb (22,680 kg) freight
**Variants**
*KC–135F*: Tanker for France;
*EC–135C, G, H, J, K, L, N, P*: Flying command posts;
*RC–135A, B, C, D, E, U*: Electronic reconnaissance
  aircraft;
*VC–135B*: VIP and command transport;
*WC–135B*: Weather-reconnaissance aircraft
**First flights**
*KC–135A*: 31 August 1956
*C–135A*: 19 May 1961
**Production**
*KC–135A*: 732 built from 1957–1965, inc a number
  converted to EC–135, RC–135 and WC–135;
*KC–135B* (later *EC–135B*): 17 built; *KC–135F*: 12 built;
*C–135A*: 15 built; *RC–135A*: 4 built; *RC–135B*: 10 built
**In service**
*KC–135A, C–135B, EC–135, RC–135, VC–135, WC–135*:
  United States
*KC–135F*: France

# BOEING C-135B 'STRATOLIFTER'

**Type**
Heavy transport
Details as for KC–135A with the following exceptions
**Weights**
empty 106,472 lb (48,295 kg)
normal 275,500 lb (124,967 kg)
maximum 292,000 lb (132,451 kg)
**Performance**
maximum speed at 36,000 ft (11,000 m) 638 mph
  (1,027 km/hr)
maximum cruising speed at 40,000 ft (12,200 m) 604 mph
  (972 km/hr)
range 2,993 miles (4,817 km)
**Dimensions**
length overall 134 ft 6 in (41.00 m)
height overall 41 ft 8 in (12.70 m)
**Power plant**
Four Pratt & Whitney TF33–P–5 turbofans each rated
  at 18,000 lb (8,165 kg) st
**Payload**
6 man crew and 126 troops or 44 stretcher cases and 54
  seated wounded or max 87,100 lb (39,545 kg) freight
**Production**
30 built

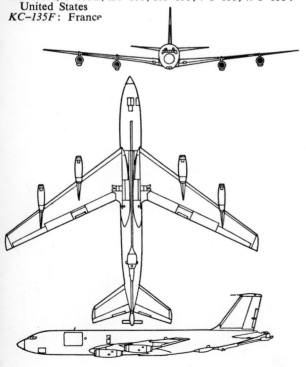

## BOEING VERTOL 107–II
### (CH–46D 'SEAKNIGHT')

**Type**
Medium transport helicopter
**Weights**
empty 13,067 lb (5,927 kg)
maximum 23,000 lb (10,433 kg)
**Performance**
maximum speed at sea level 166 mph (267 km/hr)
maximum cruising speed 143–161 mph (246–259 km/hr)
range 239 miles (385 km)
initial rate of climb 21.0 fps (6.4 m/sec)
service ceiling 14,000 ft (4,265 m)
hovering ceiling in ground effect 9,500 ft (2,895 m)
hovering ceiling out of ground effect 5,750 ft (1,753 m)
**Dimensions**
main rotor diameter 51 ft 0¼ in (15.55 m)
length of fuselage 44 ft 9½ in (13.67 m)
height 16 ft 11¾ in (5.18 m)
**Power plant**
Two 1,400 hp General Electric T58–GE–10 turboshafts
**Armament**
Optional
**Payload**
2–3 man crew and 25 troops or 15 stretcher cases and
2 medics or freight
**Variants**
*CH–46A, UH–46A*: Earlier versions with less powerful
engines, modified up to CH–46D, UH–46D standard;
*CH–46E, CH–46F*: Later series; *Kawasaki-Vertol KV–107*
Japanese licence-built version by Kawasaki
**First flights**
Prototype: 22 April 1958; *CH–46D*: September 1966
**Production**
Series production from 1961, over 640 delivered or on
order to date, plus over 77 Japanese licence-built
**In service**
Burma (KV–107), Canada (CH–113 Labrador, CH–113A
Voyageur), Japan (KV–107/II–3, –4, –5), Sweden
(HKP–4 and HKP–7 = KV–107), Thailand (KV–107),
United States (CH–46D, CH–46E, CH–46F, UH–46D)

## BOEING VERTOL CH–47C 'CHINOOK'

**Type**
Medium transport helicopter
**Weights**
empty 20,377 lb (9,243 kg)
normal 33,070 lb (15,000 kg)
maximum 46,000 lb (20,865 kg)
**Performance**
maximum speed at sea level 190 mph (306 km/hr)
maximum cruising speed 158 mph (254 km/hr)
radius of action 115 miles (185 km)
ferry range 311 miles (500 km)
initial rate of climb 47.9 fps (14.6 m/sec)
service ceiling 19,521 ft (5,950 m)
hovering ceiling out of ground effect 9,596 ft (2,925 m)
**Dimensions**
main rotor diameter 60 ft 0 in (18.29 m)
length of fuselage 51 ft 0 in (15.54 m)
height 18 ft 6½ in (5.65 m)
**Power plant**
Two 3,750 Lycoming T55–L–11 turboshafts
**Payload**
2 man crew and 33–44 troops or 27 paratroops or 24
stretcher cases and 2 medics or max 22,000 lb (10,000
kg) freight
**Variants**
*C–47A, CH–47B*: Earlier versions, from 1973 conversions
to CH–47C.
**First flights**
Prototype: 21 September 1961, *CH–47C*: 14 October 1967
**Production**
Series production from 1962, over 680 delivered or on
order to date, plus 46 Italian licence-built by Agusta
(Elicotteri Meridionali)
**In service**
*CH–47A*: United States, Vietnam (South);
*CH–47B*: United States;
*CH–47C*: Australia, Iran, Italy, Spain, United States,
Vietnam (South)

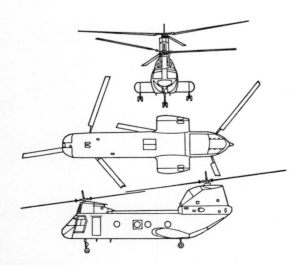
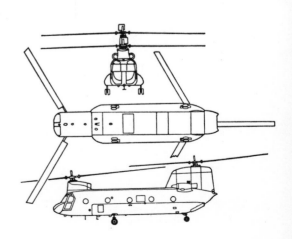

## CESSNA A–37B 'DRAGONFLY'

**Type**
Two-seat light ground-attack aircraft
**Weights**
empty 5,843 lb (2,650 kg)
maximum 14,000 lb (6,350 kg)
**Performance**
maximum speed at sea level 475 mph (769 km/hr)
maximum speed at 16,000 ft (4,875 m) 507 mph
  (816 km/hr)
radius of action with 3,700 lb (1,680 kg) weapon load
  249 miles (400 km)
ferry range 1,012 miles (1,628 km)
initial rate of climb 116.5 fps (35.5 m/sec)
service ceiling 41,765 ft (12,730 m)
**Dimensions**
wing span 35 ft 10½ in (10.93 m)
length overall 29 ft 3½ in (8.93 m)
height overall 9 ft 2 in (2.79 m)
wing area 183.9 sq ft (17.09 sq m)
**Power plant**
Two General Electric J85–GE–17A turbojets each rated
  at 2,850 lb (1,293 kg) st
**Armament**
One 7.62 mm GAU–2B/A Minigun with 1,500 rpg and
  max 5,392 lb (2,446 kg) weapon load on 8 hard points
**Variants**
*T–37A, T–37B, T–37C*: Two-seat trainers
**First flights**
*YAT–37D*: 22 October 1963; *A–37B*: May 1968
**Production**
*A–37A*: 3 prototypes and 37 production models built
  from May–September 1967;
*A–37B*: Series production from 1968, about 400 delivered
  or on order to date
**In service**
*A–37A*: Vietnam (South)
*A–37B*: Guatemala, United States, Vietnam (South)

## CESSNA O–1E 'BIRDDOG'

**Type**
Liaison and AOP aircraft
**Weights**
empty 1,613 lb (732 kg)
normal 2,429 lb (1,102 kg)
**Performance**
maximum speed at sea level 115 mph (185 km/hr)
maximum cruising speed at 5,000 ft (1,530 m) 104 mph
  (167 km/hr)
ferry range 530 miles (853 km)
initial rate of climb 19.4 fps (5.9 m/sec)
service ceiling 18,500 ft (5,640 m)
**Dimensions**
wing span 36 ft 0 in (10.97 m)
length overall 25 ft 10 in (7.87 m)
height overall 7 ft 4½ in (2.25 m)
wing area 173.5 sq ft (16.15 sq m)
**Power plant**
One 213 hp Continental O–470–11 piston engine
**Payload**
2 man crew
**Variants**
*O–1A, O–1B, O–1C*: Earlier versions (original
  designation L–19);
*O–1F, O–1G*: Conversions of previous series;
*TO–1D*: Instrument trainer
**First flights**
Prototype: January 1950; *O–1A*: November 1950
**Production**
Series production from 1950–1964;
*O–1A*: 2,554 built; *O–1B*: 60 built; *O–1C*: 25 built;
*O–1E*: 485 built, plus 50 Japanese licence-built by Fuji
  and under production in Pakistan; *TO–1D*: 307 built
**In service**
Austria, Brazil, Cambodia, Canada, Chile, France, Italy,
  Japan, Korea (South), Laos, Norway, Pakistan, Spain
  (L–12), Thailand, United States (0–1E, F, G, TO–1D),
  Vietnam (South)

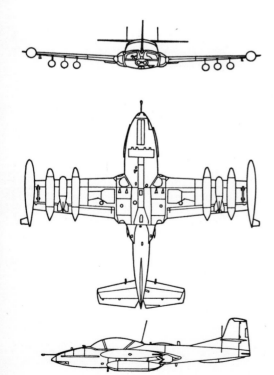

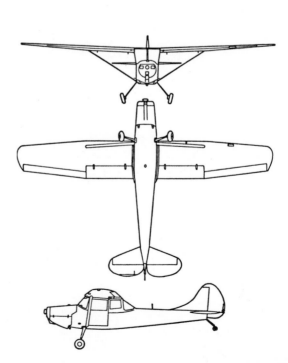

## CESSNA O-2A

**Type**
AOP aircraft
**Weights**
empty 2,848 lb (1,292 kg)
normal 4,299 lb (1,950 kg)
maximum 4,629 lb (2,100 kg)
**Performance**
maximum speed at sea level 200 mph (322 km/hr)
maximum cruising speed at 5,480 ft (1,670 m) 192 mph
  (309 km/hr)
range 985 miles (1,585 km)
ferry range 1,300 miles (2,092 km)
initial rate of climb 19.7 fps (6.0 m/sec)
service ceiling 19,300 ft (5,880 m)
**Dimensions**
wing span 38 ft 0 in (11.58 m)
length overall 29 ft 9½ in (9.08 m)
height overall 9 ft 4¼ in (2.85 m)
wing area 201 sq ft ( 18.67 sq m)
**Power plant**
Two 210 hp Continental IO–360–D piston engines
**Armament**
Max 1,400 lb (635 kg) weapon load on 4 hard points,
  e.g. Two 7.62 mm Minigun machine guns and two
  rocket launchers each containing seven 70 mm rockets
**Payload**
1 man crew and 3 troops
**Variants**
*O–2B*: Special loudspeaker-equipped version for
  psychological warfare duties;
*Cessna 337 Super Skymaster*: Civil variant, licence-built
  in France by Reims-Aviation (F.337)
**First flights**
Prototype Super Skymaster: 28 February 1961
*O–2*: 1967
**Production**
*O–2A*: Approx 480 built from 1967–1970;
*O–2B*: 31 built from 1967
*Super Skymaster*; Series production from 1961, over 1500
  delivered or on order to date
**In service**
*O–2A*: Iran, United States (also *O–2B*), Vietnam (South);
*Super Skymaster*: Ghana, Gabon (?), Ivory Coast, Niger,
  Upper Volta, Trinidad

## CESSNA T-37B

**Type**
Two-seat trainer
**Weights**
empty 3,800 lb (1,724 kg)
normal 6,400 lb (2,903 kg)
**Performance**
maximum speed at 20,000 ft (6,100 m) 425 mph
  (686 km/hr)
maximum cruising speed at 35,000 ft (10,700 m) 360 mph
  (580 km/hr)
range 932 miles (1,500 km)
ferry range 1,324 miles (2,130 km)
initial rate of climb 56.1 fps (17.1 m/sec)
service ceiling 38,700 ft (11,800 m)
**Dimensions**
wing span 33 ft 9¼ in (10.30 m)
length overall 29 ft 3 in (8.93 m)
height overall 9 ft 4¼ in (2.85 m)
wing area 183.9 sq ft (17.09 sq m)
**Power plant**
Two Continental J69–T–25 turbojets each rated at
  1,025 lb (465 kg) st
**Armament**
*T–37C*: Max 500 lb (226 kg) weapon load on 2 hard
  points, e.g. two weapon packs each containing one 12.7
  mm machine gun or four Sidewinder AAMs or four
  70 mm rockets or two 250 lb (113 kg) bombs
**Variants**
*T–37C*: Two-seat trainer and light ground-attack aircraft
*A–37B*: Light ground-attack aircraft
**First flights**
Prototype: 12 October 1954;
*T–37A*: 27 September 1955
**Production**
*T–37A*: 416 built from 1954–1959, all converted to T–37B;
*T–37B*: Over 400 built from 1959–1967;
*T–37C*: Over 60 built from 1964–1966
**In service**
*T–37B*: Cambodia, Chile, Germany (West), Greece,
  Pakistan, Peru, Thailand, Turkey, United States,
  Vietnam (South);
*T–37C*: Brazil, Cambodia, Chile, Colombia, Portugal,
  United States, Vietnam (South)

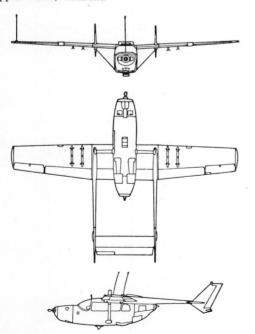

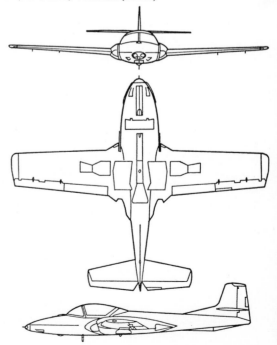

## CESSNA T–41A

**Type**
Two-seat trainer
**Weights**
empty 1,245 lb (565 kg)
maximum 2,300 lb (1,043 kg)
**Performance**
maximum speed at sea level 139 mph (224 km/hr)
maximum cruising speed at 10,000 ft (3,050 m) 117 mph (188 km/hr)
ferry range 640 miles (1,030 km)
initial rate of climb 10.5 fps (3.2 m/sec)
service ceiling 13,120 ft (4,000 m)
**Dimensions**
wing span 36 ft 2 in (11.02 m)
length overall 26 ft 6 in (8.08 m)
height overall 8 ft 9½ in (2.68 m)
wing area 174 sq ft (16.16 sq m)
**Power plant**
One 145 hp Lycoming O–300C piston engine
**Variants**
*Cessna 172 and Cessna Skyhawk*: Civil variants; Cessna 172 licence-built in France by Reims-Aviation (F.172, FR.172)
*Cessna 180 Skywagon, Cessna 182*: Further developments
**First flights**
Prototype: 1955
**Production**
*Cessna 172*: Over 16,350 built from 1955–1967,
*T–41A*: 204 built from 1964–1967;
*T–41B*: 255 built from 1966–1967;
*T–41C*: 45 built from 1967–1968;
*T–41D*: — built
**In service**
*T–41A*: Ecuador, Greece, Peru (Mescalero), Saudi Arabia, United States;
*T–41B*: Laos, United States; *T–41C*: United States;
*T–41D*: Colombia, Greece, Laos, Turkey;
*Cessna 172*: Bolivia, Canada, Iran, Ireland, Pakistan, Saudi Arabia, Singapore;
*Cessna 180*: Argentine, Australia, Burma, Chile, Ecuador, Guatemala, Honduras, Iran, Mexico, Nicaragua, Uganda, Venezuela;
*Cessna 182*: Canada (L–19L), Uruguay, Venezuela

## CESSNA U–3A 'BLUE CANOE'

**Type**
Liaison aircraft
**Weights**
empty 3,065 lb (1,381 kg)
normal 4,751 lb (2,155 kg)
maximum 4,989 lb (2,263 kg)
**Performance**
maximum speed at sea level 240 mph (386 km/hr)
maximum cruising speed at 6,500 ft (1,980 m) 223 mph (359 km/hr)
range 963 miles (1,550 km)
ferry range 1,725 miles (2,780 km)
initial rate of climb 28.9 fps (8.8 m/sec)
service ceiling 21,500 ft (6,500 m)
**Dimensions**
wing span 36 ft 11 in (11.25 m)
length overall 29 ft 7 in (9.02 m)
height overall 9 ft 11 in (3.02 m)
wing area 181.1 sq ft (16.83 sq m)
**Power plant**
Two 260 hp Continental IO–470–D piston engines
**Payload**
1 man crew and 5 troops or max 595 lb (270 kg) freight
**Variants**
*U–3B*: All-weather version;
*Cessna 310, 320 Skynight*: Civil variants, some with different powerplants;
*Cessna 411*: Different series
**First flights**
Prototype: 3 January 1953
**Production**
Over 3,000 civil and military variants built from 1954–1971, inc 160 *U–3A* and 35 *U–3B*
**In service**
France, Iran, Tanzania, United States (U–3A, U–3B)

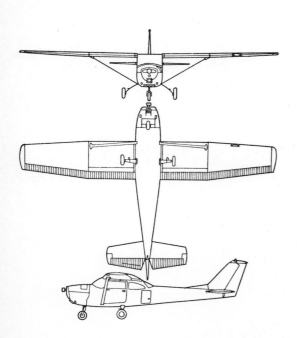

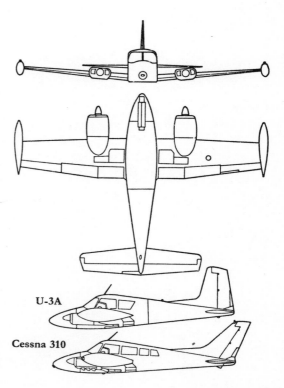

U-3A

Cessna 310

# CESSNA U-17A and B

**Type**
Liaison aircraft
**Weights**
empty 1,550 lb (708 kg)
maximum 3,201 lb (1,452 kg)
**Performance**
maximum speed at sea level 178 mph (286 km/hr)
maximum cruising speed at 6,890 ft (2,100 m) 167 mph (269 km/hr)
ferry range 1,233 miles (1,985 km)
initial rate of climb 16.7 fps (5.1 m/sec)
service ceiling 17,306 ft (5,275 m)
**Dimensions**
wing span 36 ft 2 in (11.02 m)
length overall 25 ft 8¾ in (7.84 m)
height overall 7 ft 9 in (2.36 m)
wing area 174 sq ft (16.16 sq m)
**Power plant**
One 260 hp Continental IO–470–F piston engine
**Payload**
1 man crew and 5 troops or max 397 lb (180 kg) (?) freight
**Variants**
*Cessna 185 Skywagon*: Civil variant
*Cessna 207 Turbo-Skywagon*: Further development
**First flights**
Prototype: July 1960
**Production**
Series production from 1961, by 1970 a total of 1,612 delivered or on order, inc 169 *U–17A* and 136 *U–17B*
**In service**
*U–17*: Argentine, Costa Rica, Greece, Laos, Nicaragua, Turkey, Uruguay, Vietnam (South);
*Skywagon*: Bolivia, Honduras, Iran, Jamaica, Peru, Rhodesia, South Africa;
*Turbo-Skywagon*: Indonesia, Israel

# CONVAIR C-131B 'SAMARITAN'

**Type**
Transport and aeromedical transport aircraft
**Weights**
empty 29,000 lb (13,154 kg)
normal 47,000 lb (21,319 kg)
**Performance**
maximum speed at 15,940 ft (4,860 m) 305 mph (491 km/hr)
maximum cruising speed at 18,640 ft (5,680 m) 275 mph (444 km/hr)
ferry range 1,900 miles (3,060 km)
initial rate of climb 21.0 fps (6.4 m/sec)
**Dimensions**
wing span 105 ft 4¼ in (32.11 m)
length overall 79 ft 0 in (24.13 m)
height overall 28 ft 1¼ in (8.58 m)
wing area 963.2 sq ft (89.50 sq m)
**Power plant**
Two 2,500 hp Pratt & Whitney R–2800–103W piston engines
**Payload**
3 man crew and 48 troops or 27 stretcher cases or 37 seated wounded
**Variants**
*C–131D, F, G*: Later series; *CC–109 Cosmopolitan*: Variant for Canada; *C–131E*: Electronic trainer, converted to RC–131F and G calibration aircraft;
*T–29A, B, C, D*: Navigation and radar trainers;
*Convair 240, 340, 440*: Civil airliners
**First flights**
Civil prototype: 16 March 1947;
*T–29A*: 22 September 1949
**Production**
508 military variants built from 1950–, inc 48 *T–29A*, 105 *T–29B*, 119 *T–29C*, 93 *T–29D*, 26 *C–131A*, 36 *C–131B*, 33 *C–131D*, 10 *C–131E*, 36 *C–131F*
Numerous conversions
**In service**
*C–131, T–29, VC–131, VT–29*: United States;
*CC–109*: Canada; *Convair 240*: Paraguay;
*Convair 440*: Bolivia, Italy, Spain

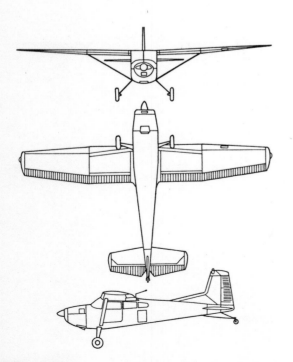

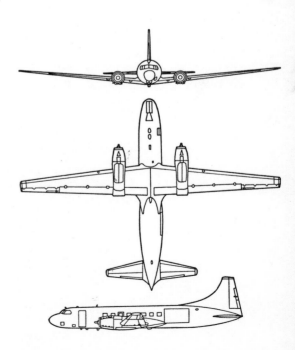

## CONVAIR F–102A 'DELTA DAGGER'

**Type**
Single-seat all-weather fighter
**Weights**
normal 27,701 lb (12,565 kg)
maximum 31,526 lb (14,300 kg)
**Performance**
maximum speed at 39,375 ft (12,000 m) (Mach 1.25)
   825 mph (1,328 km/hr) *TF–102A*: Maximum speed at
   39,375 ft (12,000 m) 645 mph (1,038 km/hr)
maximum speed at 36,000 ft (11,000 m) with two auxiliary
   tanks (Mach 0.95): 631 mph (1,015 km/hr)
maximum cruising speed at 34,400 ft (10,500 m) 540 mph
   (869 km/hr)
radius of action 497 miles (800 km)
ferry range 1,352 miles (2,175 km)
initial rate of climb 216.9 fps (66.1 m/sec)
time to 32,808 ft (10,000 m) 4 min 15 sec
service ceiling 54,000 ft (16,460 m)
**Dimensions**
wing span 38 ft 1½ in (11.62 m)
length overall 68 ft 4½ in (20.84 m)
height overall 21 ft 2½ in (6.46 m)
wing area 695 sq ft (64.57 sq m)
**Power plant**
One Pratt & Whitney J57–P–23 turbojet rated at 11,700 lb
   (5,307 kg)/17,200 lb (7,802 kg) st
**Armament**
Six AIM–4A or AIM–4C Falcon AAMs
**Variants**
*TF–102A*: Two-seat strike trainer
*QF–102A*: Conversion to drone aircraft, initially only 2
   machines rebuilt, later up to 200 ?
**First flights**
*YF–102*: 24 October 1953
*YF–102A*: 20 December 1954
*TF–102A*: 8 November 1955
**Production**
*F–102A*: 975 built from 1954–1958
*TF–102A*: 63 (111?) built
**In service**
Greece, Turkey, United States

## CONVAIR F–106A 'DELTA DART'

**Type**
Single-seat all-weather fighter
**Weights**
empty 23,655 lb (10,730 kg)
normal 35,500 lb (16,103 kg)
maximum 38,250 lb (17,350 kg)
**Performance**
maximum speed at 41,000 ft (12,500 m) (Mach 2.31)
   1,525 mph (2,455 km/hr)
maximum cruising speed at 41,000 ft (12,500 m)
   (Mach 0.92) 609 mph (980 km/hr)
radius of action 575 miles (925 km)
ferry range 1,500 miles (2,415 km)
service ceiling 57,100 ft (17,400 m)
**Dimensions**
wing span 38 ft 3½ in (11.67 m)
length overall 70 ft 3¾ in (21.56 m)
height overall 20 ft 3¼ in (6.18 m)
wing area 687 sq ft (63.83 sq m)
**Power plant**
One Pratt & Whitney J75–P–17 turbojet rated at 17,200 lb
   (7,802 kg)/24,500 lb (11,113 kg) st
**Armament**
Four AIM–4E or –4F Super Falcon AAMs and one
   AIR–2A or –2B Genie AAM with nuclear warhead
**Variants**
*F–106B*: Two-seat strike trainer
**First flights**
*F–106A*: 26 December 1956
*F–106B*: 9 April 1958
**Production**
*F–106A*: 257 built from 1956–1960;
*F–106B*: 63 built
**In service**
United States

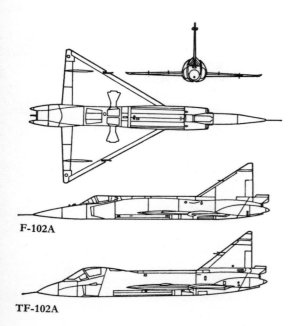

F-102A

TF-102A

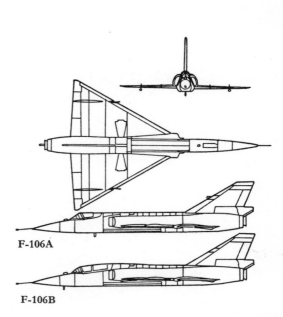

F-106A

F-106B

## CONVAIR PBY–5A 'CATALINA'

**Type**
Maritime reconnaissance and ASW amphibian
7–9 man crew
**Weights**
empty 17,564 lb (7,967 kg)
normal 34,000 lb (15,422 kg)
maximum 35,453 lb (16,081 kg)
**Performance**
maximum speed at sea level 169 mph (272 km/hr)
maximum speed at 6,560 ft (2,000 m) 195 mph (315 km/hr)
ferry range 2,520 miles (4,055 km)
time to 10,000 ft (3,050 m) 19 min 20 sec
service ceiling 14,700 ft (4,480 m)
**Dimensions**
wing span 104 ft 0 in (31.70 m)
length overall 63 ft 10¼ in (19.46 m)
height overall 18 ft 10 in (5.74 m)
wing area 1,400 sq ft (130.06 sq m)
**Power plant**
Two 1,200 hp Pratt & Whitney R–1930–92 piston engines
**Armament**
Two 7.62 mm machine guns in nose turret, one 7.62 mm machine gun in dorsal position, one 7.62 mm machine gun in each side blister, max 3,993 lb (1,816 kg) weapon load, e.g. four 1,000 lb (454 kg) bombs or twelve 100 lb (45 kg) bombs and four 650 lb (295 kg) depth charges or two torpedoes
**Variants**
*PBY–6A*: Further development;
*GST (Mop)*: Soviet licence-built
**First flights**
Prototype XPBY–5A: 22 November 1939
**Production**
3,290 of all variants built from 1939–1945, excluding Soviet licence-built
**In service**
Brazil, China (Taiwan), Colombia, Dominican Republic, Ecuador, Indonesia, Mexico

## CURTISS–WRIGHT C–46D 'COMMANDO'

**Type**
Medium transport
**Weights**
empty 27,480 lb (13,372 kg)
maximum 45,000 lb (20,412 kg)
**Performance**
maximum speed at 13,120 ft (4,000 m) 140 mph (388 km/hr)
maximum cruising speed 226 mph (365 km/hr)
radius of action 900 miles (1,450 km)
ferry range 2,995 miles (4,820 km)
initial rate of climb 21.6 fps (6.6 m/sec)
service ceiling 27,560 ft (8,400 m)
**Dimensions**
wing span 108 ft 1 in (32.94 m)
length overall 76 ft 4 in (23.27 m)
height overall 21 ft 9 in (6.63 m)
wing area 1,361.6 sq ft (126.50 sq m)
**Power plant**
Two 2,000 hp Pratt & Whitney R–2800–51 or –75 piston engines
**Payload**
4 man crew and 50 troops or max 16,000 lb (7,258 kg) freight
**Variants**
*C–46A, C–46E, C–46F*: Other series
**First flights**
Prototype: 26 March 1940
**Production**
3,180 built from 1941–1945, inc *C–46A*: 1,491 built, *C–46D*: 1,410 built, *C–46F*: 234 built
**In service**
China (Taiwan), Dominican Republic, Japan, Korea (South), Peru, United States (?), Uruguay

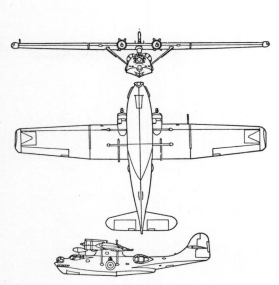

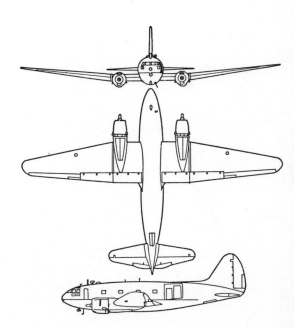

## DOUGLAS A–1J 'SKYRAIDER'

**Type**
Single-seat ground-attack aircraft
**Weights**
empty 12,549 lb (5,692 kg)
normal 19,000 lb (8,618 kg)
maximum 25,000 lb (11,340 kg)
**Performance**
maximum speed at 18,370 ft (5,600 m) 318 mph
  (512 km/hr)
maximum cruising speed 188 mph (303 km/hr)
radius of action 404 miles (650 km)
ferry range 3,000 miles (4,830 km)
initial rate of climb 39.7 fps (12.1 m/sec)
service ceiling 31,170 ft (9,500 m)
**Dimensions**
wing span 50 ft 9 in (15.47 m)
length overall 38 ft 10¼ in (11.84 m)
height overall 15 ft 8 in (4.78 m)
wing area 402.5 sq ft (37.40 sq m)
**Power plant**
One 3,050 hp Wright R–3350–WB piston engine
**Armament**
Four 20 mm cannon, max 8,000 lb (3,630 kg) weapon load
**Variants**
*A–1D, A–1H*: Single-seat ground-attack aircraft
**First flights**
Prototype: 6 July 1944
*A–1J*: August 1966
**Production**
3,180 built in 28 variants from 1944–1957, inc 670 *A–1E*
  (inc *EA–1F* and *A–1G* sub-variants), 713 *A–1H* and
  72 *A–1J*
**In service**
*A–1D*: Chad
*A–1E, H, J*: Cambodia, United States, Vietnam (South)

## DOUGLAS A–1E 'SKYRAIDER'

**Type**
Two-seat ground-attack aircraft
Details as for A–1J with the following exceptions
**Weights**
empty 12,092 lb (5,485 kg)
normal 18,800 lb (8,527 kg)
maximum 25,000 lb (11,340 kg)
**Performance**
maximum speed at 18,370 ft (5,600 m) 310 mph
  (500 km/hr)
maximum cruising speed at 5,900 ft (1,800 m) 200 mph
  (322 km/hr)
ferry range 2,750 miles (4,425 km)
initial rate of climb 38.4 fps (11.7 m/sec)
service ceiling 25,000 ft (7,620 m)
**Dimensions**
length overall 40 ft 1 in (12.22 m)
height overall 15 ft 10 in (4.83 m)
**Power plant**
One 3,020 hp Wright R–3350–26WA piston engine
**First flights**
17 August 1951

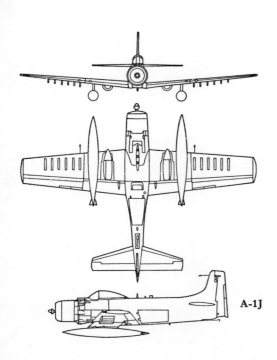

A-1J

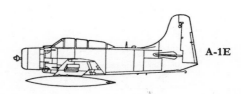

A-1E

## DOUGLAS A–3B 'SKYWARRIOR'

**Type**
Three-seat shipboard bomber
**Weights**
empty 39,408 lb (17,875 kg)
normal 73,000 lb (33,113 kg)
maximum 81,000 lb (37,195 kg)
**Performance**
maximum speed at 10,000 ft (3,050 m) (Mach 0.83)
   610 mph (982 km/hr)
maximum speed at 36,000 ft (11,000 m) (Mach 0.85)
   560 mph (901 km/hr)
maximum cruising speed at 36,000 ft (11,000 m)
   (Mach 0.72) 475 mph (765 km/hr)
radius of action 1,050 miles (1,690 km)
ferry range 2,900 miles (4,666 km)
time to 20,000 ft (6,000 m) 5 min 0 sec
service ceiling 41,000 ft (12,500 m)
**Dimensions**
wing span 72 ft 6 in (22.10 m)
length overall 76 ft 4½ in (23.27 m)
height overall 22 ft 9¾ in (6.95 m)
wing area 815.9 sq ft (75.80 sq m)
**Power plant**
Two Pratt & Whitney J57–P–10 turbojets each rated at
   10,500 lb (4,763 kg)/12,400 lb (5,624 kg) st
**Armament**
Max 12,000 lb (5,443 kg) weapon load plus (some aircraft)
   two 20 mm cannon in tail barbette
**Variants**
*A–3A*: Earlier version, *RA–3B*: Photo-reconnaissance
aircraft, *EA–3B*: ECM aircraft, *TA–3B*: Radar trainer,
*KA–3B*, *EKA–3B*: Tankers, *B–66* Destroyer: Bomber,
*RB–66A*, *B*, *C*: Photo- and electronic reconnaissance
aircraft, *EB–66B*, *C*, *F*: Reconnaissance and ECM air-
craft
**First flights**
Prototype: 28 October 1952
*A–3A*: 16 September 1953
**Production**
Series production from 1953–1961;
*A–3A*: 45 built, *EA–3B*: 5 built, *A–3B*: 164 built,
*RA–3B*: 30 built, *EA–3B*: 25 built, *TA–3B*: 12 built;
aircraft of various series converted to 50 *KA–3B* and
31 *EKA–3B*
**In service**
*A–3B*, *RA–3B*, *EA–3B*, *TA–3B*, *KA–3B*, *EKA–3B*,
*EB–66*: U.S.A.

## DOUGLAS (ONMARK) B–26K 'COUNTER-INVADER'

**Type**
Three-seat light bomber
**Weights**
maximum 43,409 lb (19,690 kg)
**Performance**
maximum speed at sea level 397 mph (639 km/hr)
range 1,150 miles (1,850 km)
service ceiling 30,020 ft (9,150 m)
**Dimensions**
wing span 71 ft 5¼ in (21.79 m)
length overall 50 ft 0 in (15.24 m)
height overall 18 ft 6 in (5.64 m)
**Power plant**
Two 2,500 hp Pratt & Whitney R–2800–103W piston
   engines
**Armament**
Fourteen 12.7 mm machine guns, weapon load in fuselage
   bay and max 8,000 lb (3,630 kg) underwing weapon load
**Variants**
*B–26B*, *B–26C Invader*: Light bombers, some converted
   to *B–26K*
**First flights**
Prototype *B–26*: 10 July 1942;
Prototype *YB–26K*: Beginning of 1963
**Production**
5 prototypes;
*B–26B*: 1,355 built from 1942–1945;
*B–26C*: 1,091 built from 1945–., conversion by OnMark
   from 1964–1967
**In service**
*B–26B*, *C*: Chile, Colombia, Dominican Republic,
   Honduras (?), Indonesia, Nicaragua, Portugal;
*B–26K*: Brazil, United States (A–26A)

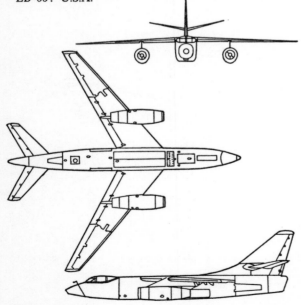

## DOUGLAS C–47 'SKYTRAIN' (DAKOTA)

**Type**
Transport
**Weights**
empty 16,971 lb (7,698 kg)
maximum 26,000 lb (11,794 kg)
**Performance**
maximum speed at 7,550 ft (2,300 m) 228 mph (368 km/hr)
maximum cruising speed at 9,840 ft (3,000 m) 185 mph
   (298 km/hr)
range 1,500 miles (2,414 km)
initial rate of climb 18.7 fps (5.7 m/sec)
service ceiling 23,950 ft (7,300 m)
**Dimensions**
wing span 95 ft 0½ in (28.96 m)
length overall 64 ft 5½ in (19.65 m)
height overall 16 ft 11¾ in (5.18 m)
wing area 977 sq ft (91.70 sq m)
**Power plant**
Two 1,200 hp Pratt & Whitney R–1830–90C piston
   engines
**Payload**
2 man crew and 28 troops or max 7,495 lb (3,400 kg)
   freight
**Variants**
*Li–2 (Cab)*: Soviet licence-built; *DC–3*: Airliner; *AC–47*:
   Night ground-support aircraft with three 7.62 mm
   Miniguns; *EC–47*: Electronic reconnaissance aircraft;
   *C–117D*: Further development
**First flights**
Prototype DC–3: 22 December 1935
**Production**
C–47: 10,926 built from 1941–1945; numerous conversions;
   approx 2,000 Soviet licence-built by Lisunov
**In service**
Argentine, Australia, Belgium, Bolivia, Brazil, Burma,
   Cambodia, Cameroon, Canada, Central African Republic,
   Chad, Chile, China (Taiwan), Congo, Congo (Brazza-
   ville), Dahomey, Denmark, Dominican Republic,
   Ecuadoar, El Salvador, Ethiopia, Finland, Gabon(?),
   Germany (West), Greece, Guatemala, Haiti, Honduras,
   India, Indonesia, Iran, Israel, Italy, Ivory Coast, Jordan,
   Korea (South), Laos, Libya, Madagascar (Malagasy),
   Malawi, Mali, Mauritania, Mexico, Morocco, New
   Zealand, Nicaragua, Niger, Nigeria, Norway, Pakistan,
   Paraguay, Peru, Philippines, Portugal, Rhodesia,
   Ruanda, Senegal, Somali, South Africa, South Yemen,
   Spain (T–3), Sweden, Syria, Thailand, Togo, Turkey,
   Uganda, United States, Upper Volta, Uruguay,
   Venezuela, Vietnam (South), Yemen, Yugoslavia,
   Zambia;
*C–117D*: United States;
*Li–2*: Bulgaria, China, Czechoslovakia, Germany (East),
   Hungary, Korea (North), Poland, Rumania, Syria(?),
   Vietnam (North), Yugoslavia;
*AC–47*: Cambodia, Laos, Thailand, United States,
   Vietnam (South);
*EC–47*: United States, Vietnam (South)

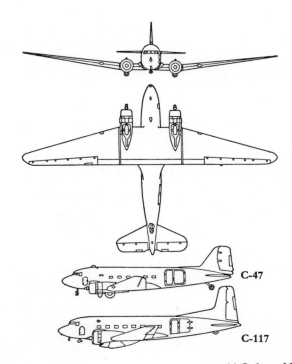

C-47

C-117

## DOUGLAS C-54 'SKYMASTER'

**Type**
Medium transport
**Weights (Applicable for C-54D)**
empty 38,201 lb (17,328 kg)
maximum 73,000 lb (33,113 kg)
**Performance**
maximum speed at 14,100 ft (4,300 m) 275 mph
 (441 km/hr)
maximum cruising speed at 15,160 ft (4,620 m) 239 mph
 (385 km/hr)
range 1,500 miles (2,414 km)
ferry range 3,900 miles (6,275 km)
initial rate of climb 17.7 fps (5.4 m/sec)
**Dimensions**
wing span 117 ft 6 in (35.81 m)
length overall 93 ft 11½ in (28.63 m)
height overall 27 ft 6¼ in (8.39 m)
wing area 1,463.9 sq ft (136.00 sq m)
**Power plant**
Four 1,350 hp Pratt & Whitney R-2000-7 or -11 piston
 engines
**Payload**
4-5 man crew and 50 troops or max 32,000 lb (14,515 kg)
 freight
**Variants**
*C-54A, B, E, G*: Other series;
*DC-4*: Airliner
*HC-54D*: Rescue aircraft
**First flights**
Prototype: 26 March 1942
**Production**
1,088 of all military variants built from 1942-1945, inc
 350 *C-54D*
**In service**
Argentine, Bolivia, Brazil, Cambodia, Colombia, Congo,
 Denmark, El Salvador, Ethiopia, Guatemala, Honduras,
 Mexico, Paraguay, Peru, Portugal, Rhodesia, South
 Africa, Spain (T-4), Thailand, Turkey, United States,
 Venezuela

## DOUGLAS C-118A 'LIFTMASTER'

**Type**
Long-range transport
**Weights**
empty 49,763 lb (22,572 kg)
maximum 107,000 lb (48,535 kg)
**Performance**
maximum speed at 17,880 ft (5,450 m) 370 mph (598 km/hr)
maximum cruising speed at 22,300 ft (6,800 m) 307 mph
 (494 km/hr)
range 3,859 miles (6,211 km)
ferry range 4,909 miles (7,900 km)
initial rate of climb 18.7 fps (5.7 m/sec)
**Dimensions**
wing span 117 ft 6 in (35.81 m)
length overall 105 ft 7 in (32.18 m)
height overall 28 ft 5 in (8.66 m)
wing area 1,463.9 sq ft (136.00 sq m)
**Power plant**
Four 2,500 hp Pratt & Whitney R-2800-52W piston
 engines
**Payload**
5 man crew and 76 troops or 60 stretcher cases or max
 27,000 lb (12,247 kg) freight
**Variants**
*C-118B*: Transport; *VC-118A, B*: VIP and command
 transports;
*DC-6A, B, C*: Civil airliners
**First flights**
Prototype *DC-6*: 15 February 1946;
*C-118A*: September 1949
**Production**
Series production of military variants from 1950-1955;
*C-118A*: 100 built; *C-118B*: 61 built; *VC-118*: 1 built;
 *VC-118B*: 4 built
**In service**
*C-118A, B*: Mexico, Saudi-Arabia, United States;
*DC-6*: Argentine, Belgium (A, C), Brazil (B), Chile,
 China (Taiwan), Congo, Ecuador (B), France, Gabon (B),
 Germany (West) (B), Italy, Portugal (A, B), Yugosalvia

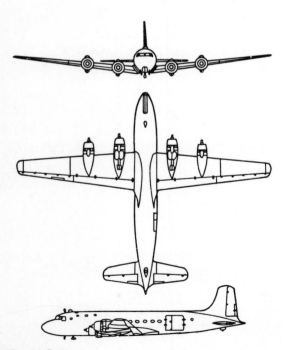

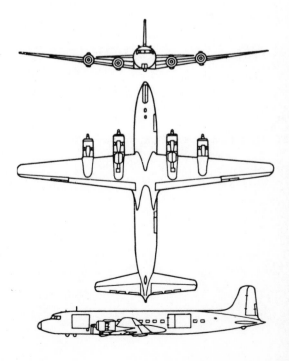

## DOUGLAS C-124C 'GLOBEMASTER' II

**Type**
Strategic transport
**Weights**
empty 101,163 lb (45,887 kg)
normal 185,000 lb (83,915 kg)
maximum 190,085 lb (86,221 kg)
**Performance**
maximum speed at sea level 271 mph (436 km/hr)
maximum speed at 20,670 ft (6,300 m) 304 mph
  (489 km/hr)
maximum cruising speed 272 mph (438 km/hr)
range with 56,000 lb (25,400 kg) payload 1,232 miles
  (1,983 km)
ferry range 6,820 miles (10,975 km)
initial rate of climb 12.8 fps (3.9 m/sec)
service ceiling 22,100 ft (6,736 m)
**Dimensions**
wing span 174 ft 1½ in (53.07 m)
length overall 130 ft 5 in (39.77 m)
height overall 48 ft 3½ in (14.72 m)
wing area 2,497.2 sq ft (232.80 sq m)
**Power plant**
Four 3,800 hp Pratt & Whitney R-4360-63A piston
  engines
**Payload**
5–8 man crew and 200 troops or 127 stretcher cases and
  25 medics or max 74,000 lb (33,566 kg) freight
**Variants**
C-124A: Earlier version
**First flights**
Prototype: 27 November 1949
**Production**
C-124A: 204 built from 1950, majority converted to
  C-124C;
C-124C: 243 built from 1955
**In service**
United States

## FAIRCHILD C-119G 'FLYING BOXCAR'

**Type**
Medium transport
**Weights**
empty 39,983 lb (18,136 kg)
normal 46,000 lb (29,030 kg)
maximum 74,470 lb (33,778 kg)
**Performance**
maximum speed at 17,000 ft (5,200 m) 295 mph
  (476 km/hr)
maximum cruising speed at 14,760 ft (4,500 m) 200 mph
  (322 km/hr)
range with 10,000 lb (4,536 kg) payload 2,000 miles
  (3,220 km)
ferry range 2,267 miles (3,648 km)
initial rate of climb 10.8 fps (3.3 m/sec)
service ceiling 21,980 ft (6,700 m)
**Dimensions**
wing span 109 ft 3¼ in (33.32 m)
length overall 86 ft 6½ in (26.38 m)
height overall 26 ft 3 in (8.00 m)
wing area 1,446.7 sq ft (134.40 sq m)
**Power plant**
Two 2,500 hp Wright R-3350-89A piston engines
**Payload**
4–5 man crew and 62 troops or 35 stretcher cases or max
  30,000 lb (13,608 kg) freight
**Variants**
C-119B, C, F: Earlier versions; C-119J: Conversions of
  C-119F or G, new designations; C-119K: C-119G with
  two auxiliary underwing J85 turbojets; AC-119G,
  K Shadow: Conversions to night ground-support air-
  craft with four 7.62 mm Minigun machine guns and (K)
  two 20 mm cannons
**First flights**
Prototype: November 1947;
C-119G: 28 October 1952
**Production**
1,112 of all series built from 1948–1955; C-119B: 55 built
  C-119C: 347 built; C-119F: 210 built; C-119G:
  480 built, inc 26 each converted to AC-119G and
  AC-119K
**In service**
C-119C: United States
C-119F, G: Belgium, Brazil, China (Taiwan), Ethiopia,
  India (some with additional turbojet mounted above
  fuselage), Italy, Morocco, United States, Vietnam
  (South);
C-119J: Italy, United States;
C-119K: Ethiopia, United States;
AC-119G, K: United States, Vietnam (South)

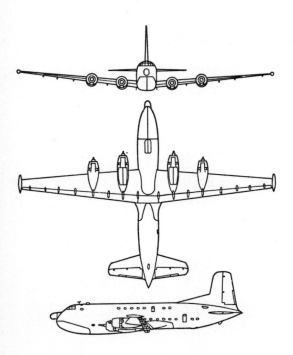

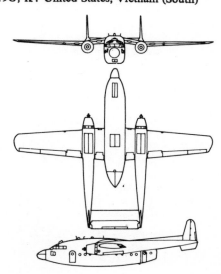

## FAIRCHILD C–123B 'PROVIDER'

**Type**
Medium transport
**Weights**
empty 31,378 lb (14,233 kg)
normal 56,500 lb (25,628 kg)
maximum 60,000 lb (27,216 kg)
**Performance**
maximum speed at 9,840 ft (3,000 m) 253 mph (407 km/hr)
maximum cruising speed 186 mph (299 km/hr)
range with 19,000 lb (8,618 kg) payload 1,350 miles (2,156 km)
range with 4,753 lb (2,156 kg) payload 2,440 miles (3,927 km)
initial rate of climb 19.0 fps (5.8 m/sec)
service ceiling 23,000 ft (7,000 m)
**Dimensions**
wing span 110 ft 0 in (33.55 m)
length overall 75 ft 3 in (23.24 m)
height overall 34 ft 1 in (10.38 m)
wing area 1,223.2 sq ft (113.64 sq m)
**Power plant**
Two 2,500 lb Pratt & Whitney R–2800–99W piston engines
**Payload**
Two man crew and 60 troops or 50 stretcher cases and 12 medics or max 24,000 lb (10,886 kg) freight
**Variants**
*C–123K*: With two auxiliary underwing J85–GE–17 turbojets each rated at 2,850 lb (1,293 kg) st, max 26,900 lb (12,200 kg) freight
**First flights**
Prototype: 14 October 1949;
*C–123B*: 1 September 1954;
*C–123K*: 27 May 1966
**Production**
5 pre-production and 300 production models built from 1954–1958, inc 183 converted to C–123K from 1966–1969
**In service**
*C–123B*: Thailand, Venezuela, United States;
*C–123K*: United States

## FAIRCHILD A–10A

**Type**
Single-seat ground-attack aircraft
**Weights**
empty 21,300 lb (9,661 kg)
normal 41,945 lb (19,026 kg)
maximum 45,825 lb (20,786 kg)
**Performance**
maximum speed 460 mph (740 km/hr)
maximum speed at sea level 500 mph (805 km/hr)
range/radius of action with 9,500 lb (4,309 kg) weapon load 288–560 miles (463–900 km)
**Dimensions**
wing span 55 ft 0 in (16.76 m)
length overall 52 ft 7 in (16.03 m)
height overall 14 ft 5½ in (4.41 m)
wing area 488 sq ft (45.13 sq m)
**Power plant**
Two General Electric TF34–GE–2 turbofans each rated at 9,275 lb (4,207 kg) st
**Armament**
One 30 mm cannon GAU–8/A with 1,350 rpg and max 16,000 lb (7,257 kg) (18,500 lb (8,392 kg)?) weapon load on 11 hard points, e.g. twenty-four 500 lb (227 kg) bombs or sixteen 750 lb (340 kg) bombs or four 2,000 lb (907 kg) bombs or nine AGM–65 Maverick ASMs
**First flights**
Prototype: 10 May 1972
**Production**
2 prototypes, 10 pre-production models delivered or on order to date, production of 720 aircraft planned
**In service**
United States

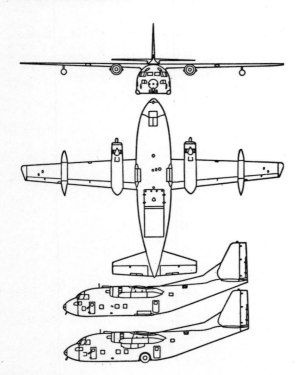

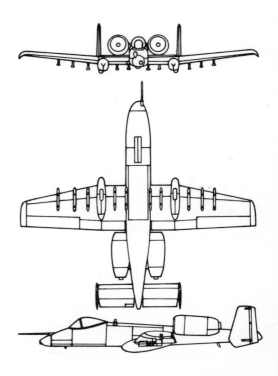

# FAIRCHILD HILLER FH–1100

**Type**
Light helicopter
**Weights**
empty 1,396 lb (633 kg)
maximum 2,750 lb (1,247 kg)
**Performance**
maximum speed at sea level 127 mph (204 km/hr)
maximum cruising speed 122 mph (196 km/hr)
range 348 miles (560 km)
initial rate of climb 26.6 fps (8.1 m/sec)
service ceiling 14,200 ft (4,325 m)
hovering ceiling in ground effect 13,400 ft (4,085 m)
hovering ceiling out of ground effect 8,400 ft (2,560 m)
**Dimensions**
main rotor diameter 35 ft 4¼ in (10.79 m)
length of fuselage 29 ft 9½ in (9.08 m)
height 9 ft 3½ in (2.83 m)
**Power plant**
One 317 hp Allison 250–C18 turboshaft
**Payload**
1 man crew and 4 troops
**First flights**
Prototype: 26 January 1963;
1st production model: 3 June 1966
**Production**
Series production from 1965, over 250 delivered or on order to date, approx only 30 as military variants
**In service**
Argentine, Brazil, Cyprus, Ecuador, El Salvador, Panama, Philippines, Thailand

# GENERAL DYNAMICS F–111E

**Type**
Two-seat strike fighter
**Weights**
empty 51,864 lb (23,525 kg)
normal 74,000 lb (33,566 kg)
maximum 91,501 lb (41,504 kg)
**Performance**
maximum speed at sea level (Mach 1.2) 864 mph
  (1,390 km/hr)
maximum speed at 40,000 ft (12,200 m) (Mach 2.5)
  1,650 mph (2,655 km/hr)
radius of action with 16,000 lb (7,257 kg) weapon load
  1,500 miles (2,415 km)
ferry range 3,800 miles (6,115 km)
initial rate of climb 666.7 fps (203.2 m/sec)
service ceiling 60,000 ft (18,300 m)
**Dimensions**
(Spread) 63 ft 0 in (19.20 m)
wing span (fully swept) 31 ft 11½ in (9.74 m)
length overall 73 ft 6 in (22.40 m)
height overall 17 ft 1½ in (5.22 m)
**Power plant**
Two Pratt & Whitney TF30–P–9 turbofans each rated at
  11,993 lb (5,440 kg)/19,600 lb (8,890 kg) st
**Armament**
One 20 mm M–61A cannon with 2,000 rpg or two 750 lb
  (340 kg) bombs in fuselage weapon-bay and max
  30,000 lb (13,608 kg) weapon load on 8 hard points
**Variants**
*F–111A*: Earlier version; *F–111C*: 24 built for Australia;
*F–111D*: Strike fighter with improved avionics;
*F–111F*: Strike fighter with more powerful (24,912 lb
  (11,300 kg) st) engines and simplified avionics;
*RF–111A*: Reconnaissance and strike fighter under
  development
**First flights**
*F–111A*: 21 December 1964
**Production**
28 evaluation aircraft; *F–111A*: 141 built from
  1965–1973;
*F–111C*: 24 built; *F–111E*: 94 built from 1969–1970;
*F–111D*: 96 built from 1970/71–1973;
*F–111F*: 82 built from 1971/72–1973
**In service**
*F–111A, E, D, F*: United States;
*F–111C*: Australia

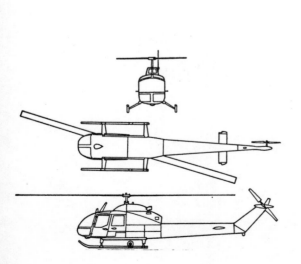

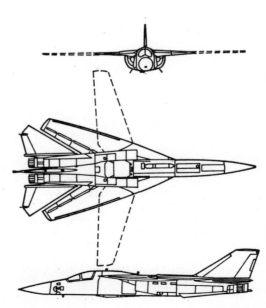

## GENERAL DYNAMICS FB-111A

**Type**
Two-seat strategic bomber
**Weights**
maximum 100,002 lb (45,360 kg)
**Performance**
maximum speed at sea level (Mach 1.1) 839 mph
  (1,350 km/hr)
maximum speed at 40,000 ft (12,200 m) (Mach 2.2)
  1,450 mph (2,334 km/hr)
radius of action with four SRAM ASMs 1,200 miles
  (1,930 km)
ferry range 4,101 miles (6,600 km)
service ceiling 65,000 ft (19,810 m)
**Dimensions**
(Spread) 70 ft 0 in (21.34 m)
wing span (fully swept) 33 ft 11 in (10.34 m)
length overall 73 ft 6 in (22.40 m)
height overall 17 ft 1½ in (5.22 m)
**Power plant**
Two Pratt & Whitney TF30-P-7 turbofans each rated at
  20,496 lb (9,297 kg) st
**Armament**
*Strategic operations*: max six 2,200 lb (998 kg) Boeing
  AGM-69A SRAM missiles;
*Conventional operations*: max 37,480 lb (17,000 kg)
  weapon load, e.g. fifty 750 lb (340 kg) bombs with wings
  spread, reducing to twenty 750 lb (340 kg) bombs with
  wings fully swept
**First flights**
Prototype: 30 July 1967
**Production**
77 built from 1968–1971
**In service**
United States

## GRUMMAN A-6A 'INTRUDER'

**Type**
Two-seat shipboard bomber
**Weights**
empty 25,684 lb (11,650 kg)
normal 37,147 lb (16,836 kg)
maximum 60,281 lb (27,343 kg)
**Performance**
maximum speed at sea level (Mach 0.9) 685 mph
  (1,102 km/hr)
maximum speed at 36,000 ft (11,000 m) (Mach 0.94)
  625 mph (1,006 km/hr)
maximum cruising speed at 32,800 ft (10,000 m) 479 mph
  (772 km/hr)
range with four Bullpup ASMs 1,920 miles (3,090 km)
ferry range 2,989 miles (4,890 km)
**Dimensions**
wing span 13 ft 0 in (16.15 m)
length overall 54 ft 7 in (16.64 m)
height overall 15 ft 7 in (4.75 m)
wing area 529 sq ft (49.15 sq m)
**Power plant**
Two Pratt & Whitney J52-P-8A turbojets each rated at
  9,300 lb (4,218 kg) st
**Armament**
Max 15,000 lb (6,804 kg) weapon load on 5 hard points,
  e.g. thirty 500 lb (227 kg) bombs or four AGM-12
  Bullpup ASMs or two 1,000 lb (454 kg) bombs and
  three 300 gal (1,364 l) auxiliary tanks
**Variants**
*A-6C*: Conversion of 12 A-6A
*A-6B*: Conversion of 19 A-6A to provide AGM-78A
  anti-radar missile (ARM) capability;
*A-6E*: Further developments;
*EA-6A*: Conversion of 27 A-6A to ECM aircraft
*EA-6B*: *'Prowler'*: Four-seat ECM aircraft;
*KA-6D*: Conversion of 51 A-6A to flight-refuelling
  tanker aircraft
**First flights**
Prototype: 19 April 1960,
1st production model: delivered 1963
**Production**
8 evaluation aircraft;
Series production from 1963, *A-6A*: 488 built from 1963–
  1970; *A-6E*: 57 built from 1971; *EA-6B*: 44 built
**In service**
United States

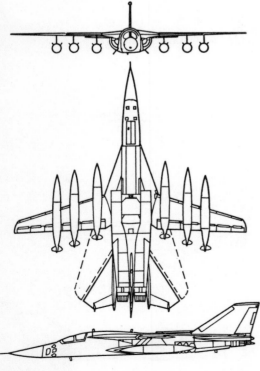

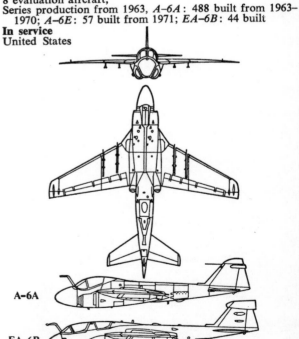

A-6A

EA-6B

## GRUMMAN C-2A 'GREYHOUND'

**Type**
Shipboard transport
**Weights**
empty 31,674 lb (14,367 kg)
maximum 54,807 lb (24,860 kg)
**Performance**
maximum speed at 11,500 ft (3,500 m) 352 mph (567 km/hr)
maximum cruising speed at 27,300 ft (8,320 m) 297 mph (478 km/hr)
range with 10,000 lb (4,536 kg) payload 1,500 miles (2,414 km)
initial rate of climb 38.7 fps (11.8 m/sec)
service ceiling 28,800 ft (8,780 m)
**Dimensions**
wing span 80 ft 7 in (24.56 m)
length overall 55 ft 6 in (17.22 m)
height overall 15 ft 11 in (4.85 m)
wing area 700 sq ft (65.03 sq m)
**Power plant**
Two 4,050 hp Allison T-56-A-8A turboprops
**Payload**
2 man crew and 39-42 troops or 20 stretcher cases and 4 medics or max 15,000 lb (6,804 kg) freight
**First flights**
Prototype: 18 November 1964
**Production**
19 built from 1966-1968, plus 8 further C-2A built from 1970
**In service**
United States

## GRUMMAN E-1B 'TRACER'

**Type**
Ship-board early warning and maritime patrol aircraft
4 man crew
**Weights**
empty 21,025 lb (9,537 kg)
normal 26,967 lb (12,232 kg)
**Performance**
maximum speed at sea level 265 mph (426 km/hr)
maximum speed at 4,000 ft (1,220 m) 227 mph (365 km/hr)
patrol speed at 10,000-15,000 ft (3,050-4,570 m) 180-220 mph (290-355 km/hr)
service ceiling 20,000 ft (6,095 m)
**Dimensions**
wing span 72 ft 4 in (22.05 m)
length overall 45 ft 4 in (13.82 m)
height overall 16 ft 10 in (5.13 m)
wing area 506 sq ft (47.01 sq m)
**Power plant**
Two 1,525 hp Wright R-1820-82 piston engines
**Variants**
*EC-1A*: Earlier version of *E-1B*
**First flights**
*EC-1A*: 26 November 1955
*E-1B*: 17 December 1956
**Production**
*EC-1A*: 4 built 1956
*E-1B*: 88 built from 1958-1960
**In service**
*C-1A, E-1B*: United States

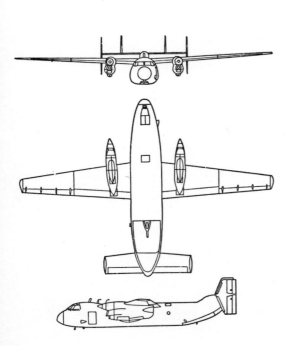

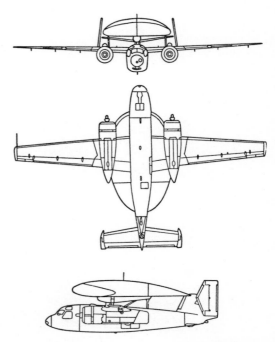

## GRUMMAN C-1A 'TRADER'

**Type**
Shipboard transport
Details as for E-1B with the following exceptions
**Weights**
normal 24,650 lb (11,180 kg)
maximum 27,000 lb (12,250 kg)
**Performance**
maximum speed at 4,000 ft (1,220 m) 280 mph (452 km/hr)
maximum cruising speed 250 mph (402 km/hr)
range 800 miles (1,290 km)
ferry range 1,110 miles (1,785 km)
initial rate of climb 33.1 fps (10.1 m/sec)
service ceiling 20,000 ft (6,095 m)
**Dimensions**
wing span 72 ft 6¼ in (22.13 m)
length overall 42 ft 6 in (13.26 m)
height overall 16 ft 7 in (5.05 m)
wing area 499 sq ft (46.36 sq m)
**Payload**
4 man crew and 9 troops or max 3,500 lb (1,588 kg)
  freight
**First flights**
19 January 1955
**Production**
87 built from 1955–1958

## GRUMMAN E-2B 'HAWKEYE'

**Type**
Shipboard early-warning and maritime patrol aircraft
  5 man crew
**Weights**
empty 37,948 lb (17,213 kg)
maximum 49,079 lb (22,262 kg)
**Performance**
maximum speed at sea level 397 mph (639 km/hr)
maximum cruising speed 315 mph (507 km/hr)
ferry range 1,901 miles (3,060 km)
initial rate of climb 69.9 fps (21.3 m/sec)
service ceiling 31,700 ft (9,660 m)
**Dimensions**
wing span 80 ft 7½ in (24.57 m)
length overall 56 ft 4 in (17.17 m)
height overall 16 ft 5 in (5.00 m)
wing area 700 sq ft (65.03 sq m)
**Power plant**
Two 4,050 hp Allison T56–A–8 turboprops
**Variants**
*E-2B*: 52 E-2As with new electronic computer installation;
*E-2C*: Further development
*TE-2A*: Trainer
**First flights**
Prototype: 21 October 1960
*E-2C*: 20 January 1971
**Production**
*E-2A*: 50 built from 1964–1967; *TE-2A*: 2 built;
*E-2C*: 13 built from 1971
**In service**
United States

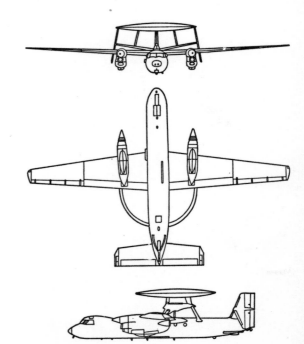

C-1A

# GRUMMAN F-14A 'TOMCAT'

**Type**
Two-seat shipboard strike fighter
**Weights** (Estimated)
empty 37,501 lb (17,010 kg)
normal 57,301 lb (25,991 kg)
maximum 66,200 lb (30,028 kg)
**Performance** (Estimated)
maximum speed at sea level (Mach 1.2) 915 mph
(1,470 km/hr)
maximum speed at 40,000 ft (12,200 m) (Mach 2.34)
1,565 mph (2,517 km/hr)
radius of action 580 miles (930 km)
service ceiling 60,000 ft (18,290 m)
**Dimensions** (Estimated)
wing span spread 62 ft 10 in (19.15 m)
wing span fully swept: 37 ft 7 in (11.45 m)
length overall 61 ft 10½ in (18.86 m)
height overall 16 ft 0 in (4.88 m)
**Power plant**
Two Pratt & Whitney TF30-P-412 turbofans each rated
20,600 lb (9,344 kg) st
**Armament**
One 20 mm M61A1 cannon, four AIM-7 Sparrow and
four AIM-9 Sidewinder AAMs or six AIM-54 Phoenix
and two AIM-9 Sidewinder AAMs
**Variants**
*F-14B, F-14C*: Planned further development with uprated
engines (2 Pratt & Whitney F401-PW-401 each rated at
30,000 [13,610 kg] st) and more sophisticated avionics
**First flights**
Prototype: 21 December 1970
**Production**
12 pre-production models
*F-14A*: 122 on order, delivery from 1973;
*F-14B*: 179 on order
**In service**
United States

# GRUMMAN HU-16B 'ALBATROSS'

**Type**
Maritime reconnaissance, ASW and ASR amphibian
3-6 man crew
**Weights**
empty 22,883 lb (10,379 kg)
normal 29,500 lb (13,381 kg)
maximum 37,500 lb (17,010 kg)
**Performance**
maximum speed at sea level 236 mph (380 km/hr)
maximum speed at 18,700 ft (5,700 m) 259 mph (416 km/hr)
maximum cruising speed 224 mph (361 km/hr)
range 1,770 miles (2,850 km)
ferry range 3,280 miles (5,280 km)
initial rate of climb 24.3 fps (7.4 m/sec)
service ceiling 21,500 ft (6,550 m)
**Dimensions**
wing span 96 ft 8 in (29.46 m)
length overall 62 ft 10 in (19.15 m)
height overall 25 ft 10 in (7.87 m)
wing area 1,035 sq ft (96.20 sq m)
**Power plant**
Two 1,425 hp Wright R-1820-76A piston engines
**Armament**
ASW version: Max 5,200 lb (2,358 kg) weapon load
underwing and in fuselage bay, e.g. four homing
torpedoes, depth charges, rockets or mines
**Payload**
3 man crew and 10-22 troops or 12 stretcher cases or
max 6,610 lb (3,000 kg) freight
**Variants**
*HU-16A*: Basic model; *HU-16C*: Naval version;
*HU-16E*: Version for United States Coast Guard;
*TU-16C*: Trainer
**First flights**
Prototype: 24 October 1947;
*HU-16B*: 16 January 1956
**Production**
Series production from 1949-1954; *HU-16A*: 305 built,
majority converted to HU-16B from 1957; *HU-16C*:
112 built, converted to HU-16D; *HU-16E*: approx 35
built, plus 37 converted from HU-16A; *TU-16C*: 5
built
**In service**
*HU-16A, B*: Argentine, Brazil, Canada (CSR-110), Chile,
China (Taiwan), Greece (ASW), Italy, Japan, Norway,
Pakistan, Peru, Philippines, Spain (ASW, AD-1),
Thailand, United States;
*HU-16C, D*: Indonesia, United States, Venezuela(?)

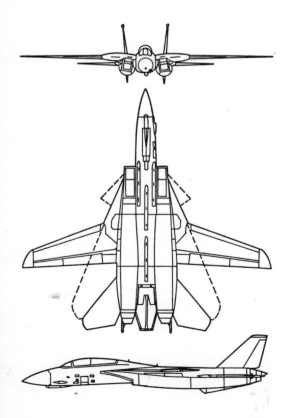

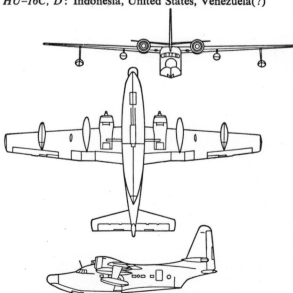

# GRUMMAN OV–1C 'MOHAWK'

**Type**
Two-seat AOP and reconnaissance aircraft with infra-red
 surveillance equipment
**Weights**
empty 10,311 lb (4,704 kg)
normal 13,040 lb (5,915 kg)
maximum 15,400 lb (6,985 kg)
**Performance**
maximum speed at 5,000 ft (1,520 m) 308 mph (496 km/hr)
maximum cruising speed 279 mph (478 km/hr)
range 441 miles (710 km)
ferry range 1,330 miles (2,140 km)
initial rate of climb 44.6 fps (13.6 m/sec)
service ceiling 30,000 ft (9,150 m)
**Dimensions**
wing span 42 ft 0 in (12.80 m)
length overall 41 ft 0 in (12.50 m)
height overall 12 ft 8 in (3.86 m)
wing area 330 sq ft (30.65 sq m)
**Power plant**
Two 1,150 hp Lycoming T–53–L–7 or L–15 turboprops
**Armament**
Max 4,000 lb (1,816 kg) weapon load on 6 hard points,
 e.g. rocket launchers containing unguided 70 mm rockets
 and weapon pods containing 12.7 mm machine guns
**Variants**
*OV–1A*: Photographic-reconnaissance aircraft;
*OV–1B*: and *OV–1D*: Electronic reconnaissance aircraft
 with SLAR (Side-looking Airborne Radar)
**First flights**
Prototype: 14 April 1959
**Production**
365 of all variants built from 1959–1971; 270 additional
 aircraft planned.
**In service**
United States

# GRUMMAN OV–1B

**Type**
Electronic reconnaissance aircraft with SLAR (Side-
looking Airborne Radar)
(Details as for OV–1C with the following exceptions)
**Dimensions**
wing span 48 ft 0 in (14.63 m)
length overall 43 ft 8 in (13.31 m)
height overall 12 ft 8 in (3.86 m)
wing area 360.6 sq ft (33.50 sq m)

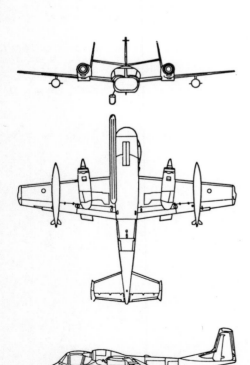

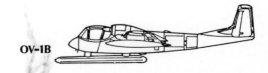

OV–1B

## GRUMMAN S-2E 'TRACKER'

**Type**
Shipboard ASW aircraft
4 man crew
**Weights**
empty 18,750 lb (8,505 kg)
normal 26,147 lb (11,860 kg)
maximum 29,150 lb (13,222 kg)
**Performance**
maximum speed at sea level 268 mph (431 km/hr)
maximum speed 265 mph (426 km/hr)
maximum cruising speed at 5,000 ft (1,524 m) 170 mph
    (273 km/hr)
patrol speed at 1,500 ft (457 m) 150 mph (241 km/hr)
ferry range 1,300 miles (2,095 km)
service ceiling 21,000 ft (6,400 m)
**Dimensions**
wing span 72 ft 7 in (22.13 m)
length overall 43 ft 6 in (13.26 m)
height overall 16 ft 7 in (5.06 m)
wing area 496 sq ft (46.08 sq m)
**Power plant**
Two 1,525 hp Wright R-1820-82WA piston engines
**Armament**
Fuselage bay: 2 homing torpedoes, 2 nuclear depth charges
    or four 386 lb (174.5 kg) depth charges. Underwing
    attachments for six 250 lb (113.4 kg) bombs or 6
    unguided 127 mm rockets or Zuni rockets or torpedoes
**Variants**
*S-2A, S-2C, S-2D*: Earlier versions;
*S-2B, S-2F*: Conversions of S-2A;
*S-2G, S-2N*: Conversions of S-2E;
*CS2F-1* and *-2*: Canadian licence-built S-2A;
*TS-2A*: Trainer, 209 converted from S-2A
**First flights**
Prototype: 4 December 1952;
*S-2D*: 20 May 1959
**Production**
Series production from 1953–1968; *S-2A*: 755 built;
    *S-2C*: 60 built; *S-2D*: 100 built; *S-2E*: 252 built from
    1962–1968; *CS2F-1* and *-2*: 100 built
**In service**
*S-2A*: Argentine, Brazil, China (Taiwan), Uruguay;
*S-2D*: Turkey;
*S-2E*: Australia, Turkey, United States;
*S-2F*: Italy, Japan, Thailand;
*S-2G*: United States; *S-2N*: Netherlands;
*CS2F-1* and *-2*: Brazil, Canada, Netherlands;
*TS-2A*: Turkey, United States

## GRUMMAN TF-9J 'COUGAR'

**Type**
Two-seat shipboard strike trainer
**Weights**
normal 20,618 lb (9,352 kg)
**Performance**
maximum speed at sea level 705 mph (1,134 km/hr)
maximum speed at 36,000 ft (11,000 m) 550 mph
    (885 km/hr)
radius of action 280 miles (450 km)
ferry range 1,000 miles (1,610 km)
time to 40,000 ft (12,200 m) 8 min 30 sec
service ceiling 42,000 ft (12,800 m)
**Dimensions**
wing span 34 ft 6 in (10.52 m)
length overall 44 ft 5 in (13.54 m)
height overall 12 ft 3 in (3.73 m)
**Power plant**
One Pratt & Whitney J48-P-8A turbojet rated at 7,200 lb
    (3,266 kg)/8,500 lb (3,856 kg) st
**Armament**
Two 20 mm cannon and max 2,000 lb (908 kg) weapon
    load, e.g. four Sidewinder AAMs
**First flights**
Prototype: 4 April 1956
**Production**
399 built from 1956–1960
**In service**
Argentine, United States

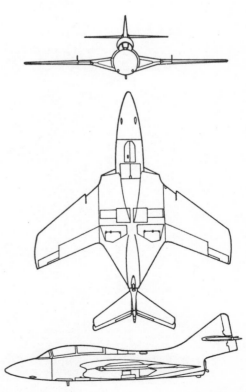

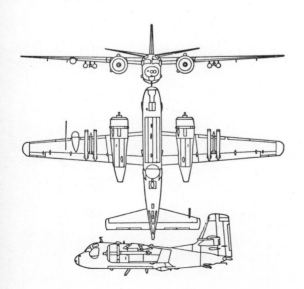

## HELIO U–10A 'COURIER'

**Type**
Liaison aircraft
**Weights**
empty 2,037 lb (924 kg)
normal 3,000 lb (1,360 kg)
maximum 3,820 lb (1,778 kg)
**Performance**
maximum speed at sea leevl 176 mph (283 km/hr)
maximum cruising speed 170 mph (274 km/hr)
range 800 miles (1,285 km)
ferry range 1,035 miles (1,667 km?)
initial rate of climb 22.9 fps (6.9 m/sec)
service ceiling 20,510 ft (6,250 m)
**Dimensions**
wing span 39 ft 0 in (11.89 m)
length overall 30 ft 8¾ in (9.37 m)
height overall 8 ft 10 in (2.69 m)
wing area 231 sq ft (21.46 sq m)
**Power plant**
One 295 hp Lycoming GO–480–G1D6 piston engine
**Payload**
1 man crew and 4 troops
**Variants**
*U–10B, U–10D*: Further developments;
*H–295 Super Courier*: Civil variant
**First flights**
Civil prototype: 1958
*U–10*: 1962
**Production**
Over 300 built, inc. civil variants from 1958
**In service**
*U–10A, B, D*: United States
*H–295 Super Courier*: Guyana
*Courier*: Somali

## HILLER 12E (OH–23G 'RAVEN')

**Type**
Light AOP helicopter
**Weights**
empty 1,755 lb (796 kg)
normal 2,800 lb (1,270 kg)
maximum 3,303 lb (1,498 kg)
**Performance**
maximum speed at sea level 96 mph (154 km/hr)
maximum cruising speed 90 mph (145 km/hr)
range 250 miles (400 km)
ferry range 500 miles (805 km)
initial rate of climb 21.3 fps (6.5 m/sec)
service ceiling 15,200 ft (4,640 m)
**Dimensions**
main rotor diameter 35 ft 0¼ in (10.67 m)
length of fuselage 28 ft 6 in (8.69 m)
height 9 ft 3½ in (2.83 m)
**Power plant**
One 305 hp Lycoming VO–540–A1B piston engine
**Payload**
1 man crew and 2 troops
**Variants**
*Hiller 12*: Civil variant;
*OH–23A, B, C, D*: Earlier versions;
*OH–23F*: Four-seat further development
**First flights**
Prototype: 1949; *OH–23G*: 1958;
*OH–23F*: 1960
**Production**
Over 2,000 built of all versions from 1950–1966, inc
  *OH–23A*: 82 built; *OH–23B*: 289 built; *OH–23C*: 143
  built; *OH–23D*: 484 built; *OH–23F*: 22 built; *OH–23G*
  347 (?) built
**In service**
*OH–23D*: Bolivia; *OH–23F*: United States;
*OH–23G*: Argentine, Chile, Colombia, Guatemala,
  Mexico, Netherlands, Paraguay, Peru, Thailand,
  Uruguay, United States;
*Hiller 12E*: Great Britain (HT.2)

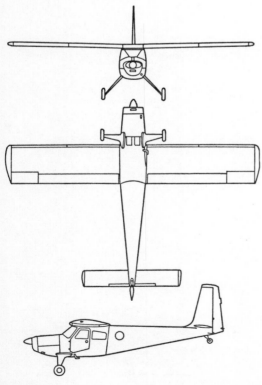

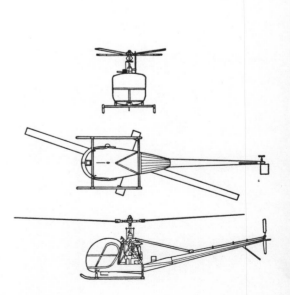

## HUGHES 269A (TH–55A 'OSAGE')

**Type**
Training helicopter
**Weights**
empty 1,010 lb (458 kg)
normal 1,598 lb (725 kg)
**Performance**
maximum at sea level 86 mph (138 km/hr)
maximum cruising speed 70 mph (113 km/hr)
range 198 miles (320 km)
initial rate of climb 19.0 fps (5.8 m/sec)
service ceiling 11,900 ft (3,625 m)
hovering ceiling in ground effect 5,500 ft (1,675 m)
hovering ceiling out of ground effect 3,750 ft (1,145 m)
**Dimensions**
main rotor diameter 25 ft 3½ in (7.71 m)
length of fuselage 21 ft 11 in (6.67 m)
height 8 ft 3 in (2.51 m)
**Power plant**
One 180 hp Lycoming HIO–360–B1A piston engine
**Payload**
2 man crew
**Variants**
*Hughes 300*: Three-seat civil variant
**First flights**
Prototype: October 1956; 1st production model:
    October 1961
**Production**
Series production from 1961, over 1,175 civil variants
    built by mid–1968;
*TH–55A*: 792 built from 1964–1968;
*TH–55J*: 48 Japanese licence-built by Kawasaki
**In service**
*Hughes 269*: Brazil, Ghana, Nicaragua, Sweden;
*TH–55A*: Colombia, United States;
*TH–55J*: Japan;
*Hughes 300*: India

## HUGHES OH–6A 'CAYUSE'

**Type**
Light helicopter
**Weights**
empty 1,157 lb (525 kg)
normal 2,400 lb (1,089 kg)
maximum 2,700 lb (1,225 kg)
**Performance**
maximum speed at sea level 150 mph (241 km/hr)
maximum cruising speed at 5,000 ft (1,500 m) 134 mph
    (216 km/hr)
range/radius of action 379 miles (610 km)
initial rate of climb 25.9 fps (7.9 m/sec)
service ceiling 15,800 ft (4,815 m)
hovering ceiling in ground effect 11,800 ft (3,595 m)
hovering ceiling out of ground effect 7,300 ft (2,225 m)
**Dimensions**
main rotor diameter 26 ft 3 in (8.00 m)
length of fuselage 23 ft 0 in (7.01 m)
height 8 ft 1½ in (2.48 m)
**Power plant**
One 252 hp Allison T63–A–5A turboshaft
**Armament**
As armed helicopter: weapon pack with machine guns or
    two XM–75 automatic grenade-launchers
**Payload**
2 man crew and 4 troops or max 950 lb (431 kg) freight
**Variants**
*Hughes 500*: Civil variant;
*Hughes 500M*: Export version of OH–6A;
*KH–369*: Japanese licence-built by Kawasaki (OH–6J);
*Hughes 500 ASW*: ASW helicopter with 2 homing
    torpedoes
**First flights**
Prototype: 27 February 1963
**Production**
Series production from 1965, over 1,500 delivered or on
    order to date; licence-built in Italy (by Nardi) and
    Japan (49 built from 1969); *Hughes 500 ASW*: Series
    production from 1972
**In service**
OH–6A: Argentine, Brazil, Denmark, Dominican
    Republic, United States; *OH–6J*: Japan;
*Hughes 500M*: Argentine, Bolivia, China (Taiwan),
    Colombia, Italy, Nicaragua;
*Hughes 500ASW*: Spain

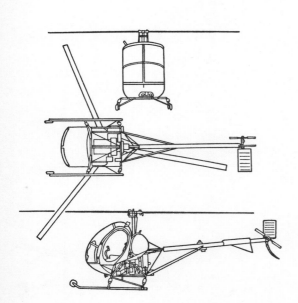

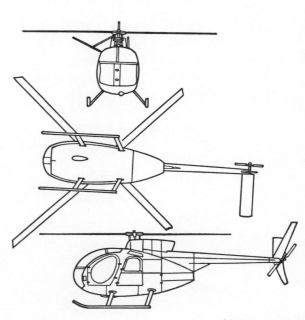

## KAMAN HH–43B 'HUSKIE'

**Type**
Fire-fighting and transport helicopter
**Weights**
empty 4,469 lb (2,027 kg)
normal 5,969 lb (2,707 kg)
maximum 9,150 lb (4,155 kg)
**Performance**
maximum speed at sea level 120 mph (193 km/hr)
maximum cruising speed 110 mph (177 km/hr)
range 236 miles (380 km)
ferry range 277 miles (445 km)
initial rate of climb 33.1 fps (10.1 m/sec)
service ceiling 25,000 ft (7,620 m)
hovering ceiling in ground effect 21,650 ft (6,600 m)
hovering ceiling out of ground effect 18,000 ft (5,500 m)
**Dimensions**
main rotor diameter 47 ft 0 in (14.33 m)
length of fuselage 25 ft 2 in (7.67 m)
height 12 ft 7 in (3.84 m)
**Power plant**
One 860 hp Lycoming T53–L–1.. turboshaft
**Payload**
1 man crew and 8 troops or 2 fire-fighters and 1,000 lb
(454 kg) fire-fighting equipment
**Variants**
*HH–43A*: Earlier version
*UH–43C, OH–43D*: Transport helicopters
**First flights**
Prototype: 27 September 1956;
*HH–43B*: 13 December 1958
**Production**
Series production from 1958–1965; *HH–43A*: 18 built;
*HH–43B*: 193 built; *UH–43C*: 24 built; *OH–43D*: 81
built
**In service**
*HH–43B*: Burma, Colombia, Pakistan, Thailand, United
States;
*UH–43C*: United States

## KAMAN HH–43F 'HUSKIE'

**Type**
Fire-fighting and transport helicopter
Details as for HH–43B with the following exceptions
**Weights**
empty 4,620 lb (2,096 kg)
normal 6,500 lb (2,948 kg)
**Performance**
ferry range 504 miles (810 km)
initial rate of climb 30.2 fps (9.2 m/sec)
service ceiling 23,000 ft (7,010 m)
**Power plant**
One 1,100 hp Lycoming T53–L–11A turboshaft
**Payload**
1 man crew and 11 troops or 2 fire-fighters and 1,000 lb
(454 kg) fire-fighting equipment
**First flights**
*HH–43F*: August 1964
**Production**
*HH–43F*: 40 built
**In service**
*HH–43F*: Iran, United States

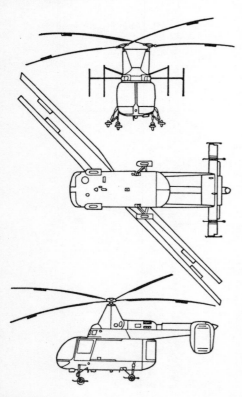

## KAMAN SH–2F 'SEASPRITE'

**Type**
ASW helicopter
3 man crew
**Weights**
normal 12,200 lb (5,805 kg)
maximum 13,300 lb (6,032 kg)
**Performance**
maximum speed 168 mph (270 km/hr)
maximum cruising speed 150 mph (241 km/hr)
ferry range 445 miles (716 km)
initial rate of climb 40.7 fps (12.4 m/sec)
service ceiling 22,500 ft (6,858 m)
hovering ceiling in ground effect 19,260 ft (5,670 m)
hovering ceiling out of ground effect 15,400 ft (4,695 m)
**Dimensions**
main rotor diameter 44 ft 0 in (13.41 m)
length of fuselage 40 ft 4¼ in (12.30 m)
height 15 ft 6 in (4.72 m)
**Power plant**
Two 1350 hp General Electric T58–GE–8F turboshafts
**Armament**
*HH–2C*: One 7.62 mm Minigun machine gun and two
   7.62 mm M–60 machine guns
   *SH–2D, SH–2F*: 2 homing torpedoes
**Variants**
*UH–2A, UH–2B*: Transport helicopters, 42 converted to
   *UH–2C* from 1966–68; *HH–2C*: Conversion of 6 *UH–
   2B* to armed rescue helicopters 1969; *HH–2D*: Conver-
   sion of 67 *UH–2B* to unarmed rescue helicopters from
   1969–1971; *SH–2D, SH–2F*: Conversion of 105 *UH–2*
   and *HH–2* of various series to ASW helicopters from
   1971
**First flights**
Prototype: 2 July 1959
**Production**
Series production from 1961–1966; *UH–2A*: 88 built;
   *UH–2B*: 102 built; conversions to *UH–2C, HH–2C,
   HH–2D, SH–2D* and *SH–2F* from 1966
**In service**
United States

## LOCKHEED C–5A 'GALAXY'

**Type**
Strategic transport
**Weights**
empty 325,244 lb (147,528 kg)
maximum 764,500 lb (346,770 kg)
**Performance**
maximum speed at 25,000 ft (7,620 m) 571 mph
   (919 km/hr)
maximum cruising speed at 30,000 ft (9,150 m) 541 mph
   (871 km/hr)
range with 80,000 lb (36,287 kg) payload 6,500 miles
   (10,460 km)
range with 220,462 lb (100,000 kg) payload 2,950 miles
   (4,745 km)
initial rate of climb 38.4 fps (11.7 m/sec)
service ceiling 34,000 ft (10,360 m)
**Dimensions**
wing span 222 ft 8 in (67.88 m)
length overall 247 ft 10 in (75.54 m)
height overall 65 ft 1½ in (19.85 m)
wing area 6,200 sq ft (576.00 sq m)
**Power plant**
Four General Electric TF–39–GE–1 turbofans each rated
   at 41,000 lb (18,598 kg) st
**Payload**
5 man crew and 10 seats for relief crew and couriers, 75
   troops on the upper and 270 troops on the lower deck,
   or max 264,550 lb (120,000 kg) freight, e.g. two M–60
   tanks or five M–113 personnel carriers or 10 Pershing
   missiles with tow and launch vehicles
**First flights**
Prototype: 30 June 1968
**Production**
8(?) prototypes and pre–production models
81 built from 1969–1973
**In service**
United States

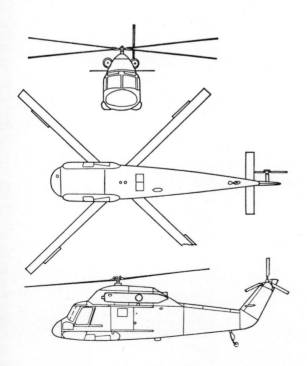

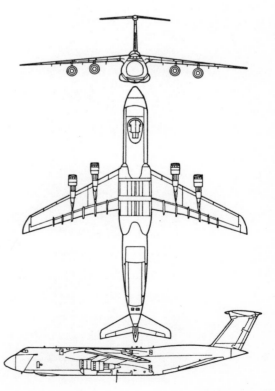

## LOCKHEED C–121C 'CONSTELLATION'

**Type**
Long-range transport
**Weights**
empty 73,134 lb (33,173 kg)
normal 133,000 lb (60,329 kg)
**Performance**
maximum speed at 20,000 ft (6,100 m) 375 mph
  (605 km/hr)
Maximum cruising speed at 23,000 ft (7,000 m) 330 mph
  (533 km/hr)
range 2,100 miles (3,380 km)
initial rate of climb 19.4 fps (5.9 m/sec)
**Dimensions**
wing span 123 ft 5 in (37.62 m)
length overall 116 ft 2 in (35.41 m)
height overall 24 ft 8¾ in (7.54 m)
wing area 1,654.4 sq ft (153.7 sq m)
**Power plant**
Four 3,250 hp Wright R–3350–34 piston engines
**Payload**
4 man crew and 106 troops or 47 stretcher cases or max
  40,000 lb (18,144 kg) freight
**Variants**
*L.749 Constellation, L.1049 Super Constellation*: Civil
  airliner; *EC–121C, D, H, K, L, M, P, R, T*: Electronic
  reconnaissance aircraft; *C–121A, C, G, J*: Transports;
  *WC–121N*: Weather reconnaissance aircraft
**First flights**
Prototype *L.1049*: 13 October 1950;
Prototype *C–121*: 1951
**Production**
169 of various series built as military variants from 1951–
  1955, numerous conversions up to 1969 (?)
**In service**
*C–121A, G, J, WC–121N*: United States;
*L.749A*: France; *L.1049*: India

## LOCKHEED EC–121 'WARNING STAR'

**Type**
Electronic reconnaissance aircraft
Details as for C–121C with the following exceptions
**Weights**
empty 80,612 lb (36,565 kg)
normal 143,600 lb (65,137 kg)
**Performance**
patrol speed 240 mph (385 km/hr)
range/radius of action 2,150 miles (3,460 km)
ferry range 4,400 miles (7,080 km)
**Dimensions**
height overall 27 ft 0 in (8.23 m)
**Power plant**
Four 3,650 hp Wright R–3350–93 piston engines
**Payload**
27–31 man crew
**In service**
United States

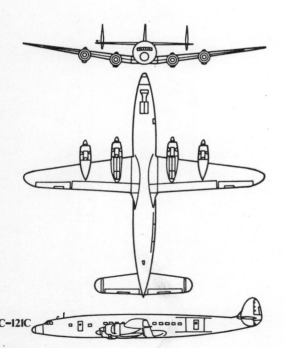

C–121C

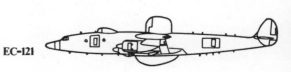

EC–121

## LOCKHEED C–130E 'HERCULES'

**Type**
Medium transport
**Weights**
empty 72,894 lb (33,064 kg)
normal 155,003 lb (70,308 kg)
maximum 175,000 lb (79,380 kg)
**Performance**
maximum speed 380 mph (611 km/hr)
maximum cruising speed at 20,000 ft (6,096 m) 365 mph
    (587 km/hr)
range/w.m.p. 3,650 miles (5,874 km)
range with 19,537 lb (8,862 kg) payload 4,700 miles
    (7,562 km)
initial rate of climb 26.6 fps (8.1 m/sec)
service ceiling 22,640 ft (6,900 m)
**Dimensions**
wing span 132 ft 7¼ in (40.42 m)
length overall 97 ft 8¾ in (29.79 m)
height overall 38 ft 3 in (11.66 m)
wing area 1,745 sq ft (162.12 sq m)
**Power plant**
Four 4,050 hp Allison T56–A–7A turboprops
**Payload**
4 man crew and 92 troops or 64 paratroops or 70 stretcher
    cases or max 45,000 lb (20,412 kg) freight
**Variants**
*C–130A, B, D*: Earlier versions; *C–130F, H*: later series;
*C–130K*: Transport version for Great Britain;
*HC–130B, H, N, P*: Rescue aircraft; *KC–130F, H*:
    Tankers;
*EC–130E, Q, RC–130A*: Reconnaissance aircraft;
*WC–130E*: Weather-reconnaissance aircraft; *LC–130F, R*:
    Ski planes; *AC–130 Gunship*: Night ground-support
    aircraft;
*Lockheed L–100*: Civil version of C–130
**First flights**
Prototype: 23 August 1954; C–130E: 25 August 1961
**Production**
Series production from 1954, approx 1,200 (2,000?) of all
    variants delivered or on order
**In service**
*C–130A*: Australia, United States, Vietnam (South);
*C–130B*: Indonesia, Iran, Pakistan, South Africa, United
    States;
*C–130E*: Argentine, Australia, Brazil, Chile, Canada,
    Colombia, Iran, Israel, Libya, Peru, Saudi Arabia,
    Spain (?), Sweden, Turkey, United States;
*C–130H*: Belgium, Congo, Denmark, Iran, Italy, New
    Zealand, Norway, Venezuela;
*C–130K*: Great Britain (Hercules C.1);
*C–130D, F; HC–130B, H, N, P; KC–130F; EC–130E, Q;
RC–130A, WC–130E, LC–130F, R; AC–130*:
    United States;
*KC–130H*: Saudi Arabia;
*L–100–20*: Kuwait, Philippines

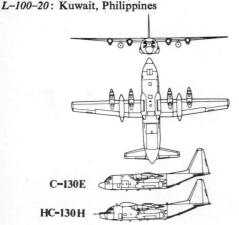

C–130E

HC–130H

## LOCKHEED C–140B 'JETSTAR'

**Type**
Light transport
**Weights**
empty 22,074 lb (10,012 kg)
normal 37,997 lb (17,235 kg)
maximum 42,000 lb (19,051 kg)
**Performance**
maximum speed at 21,200 ft (6,460 m) 566 mph
    (911 km/hr)
maximum cruising speed at 23,000 ft (7,010 m) 570 mph
    (917 km/hr)
ferry range 2,237 miles (3,600 km)
initial rate of climb 86.6 fps (26.4 m/sec)
service ceiling 37,400 ft (11,400 m)
**Dimensions**
wing span 54 ft 5 in (16.60 m)
length overall 60 ft 5 in (18.42 m)
height overall 20 ft 5 in (6.23 m)
wing area 542.5 sq ft (50.40 sq m)
**Power plant**
Four Pratt & Whitney JT12A–8 turbojets each rated at
    3,300 lb (1,497 kg) st
**Payload**
8 man crew and 8–12 troops
**First flights**
Prototype: 4 September 1957
**Production**
Series production from 1961, 46 delivered or on order
    to date
**In service**
Germany (West), Indonesia, Libya, Mexico, Saudi Arabia,
    United States (C–140A, VC–140B)

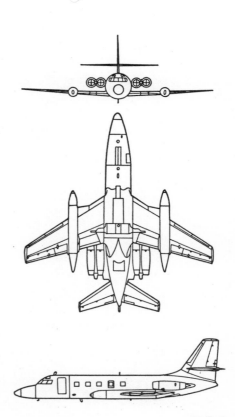

## LOCKHEED C–141A 'STARLIFTER'

**Type**
Strategic transport
**Weights**
empty 133,774 lb (60,679 kg)
maximum 316,105 lb (143,383 kg)
**Performance**
maximum speed 570 mph (917 km/hr)
maximum cruising speed 561 mph (904 km/hr)
range with 70,548 lb (32,000·kg) payload 3,970 miles (6,390 km)
ferry range 6,820 miles (10,977 km)
initial rate of climb 53.5 fps (16.3 m/sec)
service ceiling 40,000 ft (12,200 m)
**Dimensions**
wing span 160 ft 1¾ in (48.81 m)
length overall 145 ft 0¼ in (44.20 m)
height overall 39 ft 3¾ in (11.98 m)
wing area 3,229.2 sq ft (300.00 sq m)
**Power plant**
Four Pratt & Whitney TF33–P–7 turbofans each rated at 21,000 lb (9,526 kg) st
**Payload**
4 man crew and 154 troops or 127 paratroops or 80 stretcher cases and 8 medics or max 94,000 lb (42,638 kg) freight
**Similar**
Ilyushin Il–76 (Candid): Soviet strategic transport, first appeared at the 1971 Paris Air Show
**First flights**
Prototype: 17 December 1963
**Production**
289 built from 1964–1968
**In service**
United States

## LOCKHEED F–104G 'STAR FIGHTER'

**Type**
Single-seat fighter and strike fighter
**Weights**
empty 14,088 lb (6,390 kg)
normal 19,842 lb (9,000 kg)
maximum 28,770 lb (13,050 kg)
**Performance**
maximum speed at sea level (Mach 1.2) 913 mph (1,470 km/hr)
maximum speed at 36,000 ft (11,000 m) (Mach 2.2) 1,450 mph (2,330 km/hr)
maximum cruising speed at 36,000 ft (11,000 m) (Mach 0.95) 609 mph (980 km/hr)
radius of action 684–808 miles (1,100–1,300 km)
ferry range 2,180 miles (3,510 km)
initial rate of climb 833 fps (254 m/sec)
service ceiling 58,000 ft (17,680 m)
**Dimensions**
wing span 21 ft 11 in (6.68 m)
length overall 54 ft 9 in (16.69 m)
height overall 13 ft 6 in (4.11 m)
wing area 196.1 sq ft (18.22 sq m)
**Power plant**
One General Electric J79–11A turbojet rated at 10,000 lb (4,536 kg)/15,800 lb (7,167 kg) st
**Armament**
One 20 mm M61 Vulcan cannon and (as fighter) two-four A1M–9 Sidewinder AAMs or (as strike fighter) max 3,970 lb (1,800 kg) weapon load; e.g. two Bullpup ASMs and three 1,000 lb (454 kg) bombs or one nuclear bomb
**Variants**
*F–104A, C*: Earlier versions; *F–104B, D, DJ, F, CF–104D* Two-seat strike trainers; *CF–104*: Canadian licence-built F–104G; *RF–104G*: Single-seat reconnaissance aircraft; *TF–104G*: Two-seat strike trainer; *F–104J*: Version of F–104G for Japan; *F–104S*: Further development of F–104G for Italy, with more powerful engine (General Electric) J79–GE–19 turbojet rated at 11,872 lb (5,385 kg)/17,902 lb (8,120 kg) st
**First flights**
Prototype: 7 February 1954; *F–104G*: 5 October 1960; *TF–104G*: October 1962; *F104S*: December 1966
**Production**
*F–104A, F–104F*: 310 built from 1955–1960;
*F–104G, RF–104G*: 1,156 built from 1960–1965 plus 50 German repeat orders from 1970–1973;
*TF–104G*:158 built from 1962–1965; *CF–104*: 340 built from 1961–1964; *CF–104D*: 38 built from 1962–1964; *F–104J*: 210 built from 1963–1968; *F–104DJ*: 20 built from 1963–1964; *F–104S*: 205 built from 1968
**In service**
*F–104A, F–104B*: China (Taiwan), Jordan, Pakistan;
*F–104G, TF–104G*: Belgium, China (Taiwan), Denmark, Germany (West), Greece, Italy, Netherlands, Norway, Turkey;
*RF–104G*: China (Taiwan), Netherlands;
*CF–104, CF–104D*: Canada, Denmark;
*F–104J, F–104DJ*: Japan
*F–104S*: Italy

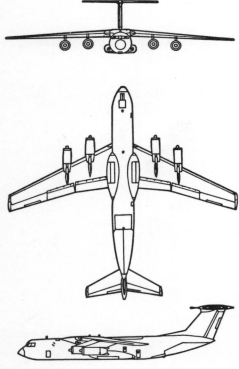

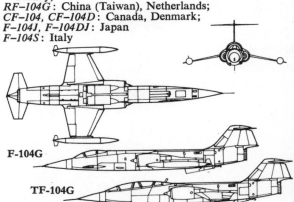

**F-104G**

**TF-104G**

## LOCKHEED P-2H 'NEPTUNE'

**Type**
Maritime reconnaissance and ASW aircraft
6–7 man crew
**Weights**
empty 49,935 lb (22,650 kg)
normal 76,456 lb (34,680 kg)
maximum 80,071 lb (36,320 kg)
**Performance**
maximum speed at 10,000 ft (3,050 m) 356 mph
  (573 km/hr)
maximum cruising speed at 8,500 ft (2,590 m) 207 mph
  (333 km/hr)
patrol speed at 980 ft (300 m) 173 mph (278 km/hr)
range 2,200 miles (3,540 km)
ferry range 3,685 miles (5,930 km)
initial rate of climb 34.4 fps (10.5 m/sec)
time to 9,840 ft (3,000 m) 4 min 0 sec
service ceiling 22,000 ft (6,710 m)
**Dimensions**
wing span 103 ft 10¾ in (31.67 m)
length overall 91 ft 8 in (27.94 m)
height overall 29 ft 4 in (8.94 m)
wing area 999.9 sq ft (92.90 sq m)
**Power plant**
Two 3,500 hp Wright R-3350-32W piston engines plus
  two auxiliary Westinghouse J34-WE-36 turbojets each
  rated at 3,400 lb (1,542 kg) st
**Armament**
Max 8,000 lb (3,630 kg) weapon load in fuselage bay and
  underwing, e.g. two homing torpedoes or two 2,000 lb
  (907 kg) mines or eight 1,000 lb (454 kg) bombs or
  mines or twelve 325 lb (147 kg) depth charges or one
  nuclear weapon in fuselage bay and sixteen 127 mm
  rockets underwing
**Variants**
*P-2E, J-2F*: Earlier versions *SP-2H*: 154 P-2Hs with
  more modern search equipment;
*Kawasaki P-2J*: Japanese further development;
*AP-2H*: Conversion of 4 P-2Hs to night ground-support
  aircraft
**First flights**
Prototype: 17 May 1945;
*P-2E*: 29 December 1950;
*P-2F*: 16 October 1952;
*P-2H*: 26 April 1954;
*P-2J*: 21 July 1966
**Production**
Series production from 1945–1962: Total of 1,195 built
  in 8 different versions, inc *P-2E*: 424 built from 1950–
  1954; *P-2F*: 83 built from 1952–1954; *P-2H*: 359 built
  from 1954–1962, plus 48 Japanese licence-built from
  1960–1962; *P-2J*: 46 built from 1969–1973, plus a
  further 43 planned for delivery by 1976
**In service**
*P-2E*: Brazil, Portugal;
*P-2H*: France, Japan;
*SP-2H*: Argentine, Australia, Netherlands;
*P-2J*: Japan

## LOCKHEED P-3C 'ORION'

**Type**
Maritime reconnaissance and ASW aircraft
10 man crew
**Weights**
empty 62,000 lb (28,123 kg)
normal 133,507 lb (60,558 kg)
maximum 141,998 lb (64,410 kg)
**Performance**
maximum speed at 15,000 ft (4,750 m) 437 mph
  (703 km/hr)
maximum cruising speed at 25,000 ft (7,620 m) 397 mph
  (639 km/hr)
patrol speed at 1,500 ft (475 m) 230 mph (370 km/hr)
radius of action 2,530 miles (4,075 km)
initial rate of climb 48.0 fps (14.6 m/sec)
service ceiling 28,300 ft (8,625 m)
**Dimensions**
wing span 99 ft 8 in (30.37 m)
length overall 116 ft 10 in (35.61 m)
height overall 33 ft 8½ in (10.29 m)
wing area 1,300 sq ft (120.77 sq m)
**Power plant**
Four 4,910 hp Allison T-56-A-14W turboprops
**Armament**
In fuselage bay: 2 nuclear depth charges and 4 torpedoes
  or 8 bombs. On 9 hard points: Max 13,713 lb (6,220
  kg) weapon load
**Payload**
As auxiliary transport: 50 troops and max 4,000 lb
  (1,814 kg) freight
**Variants**
*P-3A, P-313*: Earlier versions; *EP-3E*: Electronic re-
  connaissance aircraft; *WP-3A*: Weather reconnaissance
  aircraft; *P-3F*: Simplified export version of P-3C
**First flights**
Prototype: 25 November 1959;
*P-3C*: 18 September 1968
**Production**
*P-3A*: 157 built from 1960–1966, 12 converted to EP-3E;
*P-3B*: 210 built from 1966–1969;
*P-3C*: 83 delivered or on order from 1968; P-3F: 4(6?)
  built 1973/74
**In service**
*P-3A, EP-3E, WP-3A*: United States;
*P-3B*: Australia, New Zealand, Norway, Spain, United
  States;
*P-3C*: Australia, United States; *P-3F*: Iran

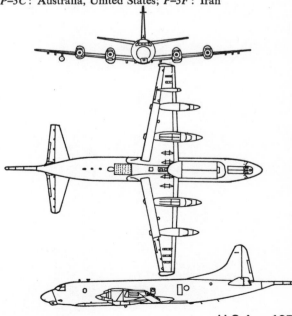

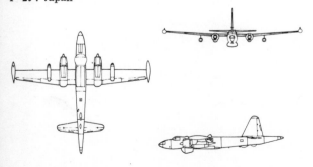

## LOCKHEED S-3A 'VIKING'

**Type**
Shipboard ASW aircraft 4 man crew
**Weights**
empty 26,598 lb (12,065 kg)
normal 41,998 lb (19,050 kg)
maximum 46,002 lb (21,320 kg)
**Performance**
maximum speed 507 mph (816 km/hr)
patrol speed 184 mph (257 km/hr)
maximum cruising speed 403 mph (649 km/hr)
radius of action 2,300 miles (3,700 km)
ferry range 3,455 miles (5,560 km)
initial rate of climb 70.0 fps (21.3 m/sec)
service ceiling 35,000 ft (10,670 m)
**Dimensions**
wing span 68 ft 8 in (20.93 m)
length overall 53 ft 4 in (16.26 m)
height overall 22 ft 9 in (6.93 m)
wing area 598 sq ft (55.56 sq m)
**Power plant**
Two General Electric TF34–GE–2 turbofans each rated
   at 9,275 lb (4,207 kg) st
**Armament**
Max 7,716 lb (3,500 kg) weapon load, e.g. four homing
   torpedoes or four bombs or two depth charges and 4
   mines in two fuselage bays plus bombs, rockets and
   ASMs underwing
**First flights**
Prototype: 21 January 1972
**Production**
8 prototypes and pre-production models, series production
   from 1973, 191 delivered or on order to date
**In service**
United States

## LOCKHEED SR-71

**Type**
Two-seat strategic reconnaissance aircraft
**Weights**
normal 139,993–145,505 lb (63,500–66,000 kg)
maximum 169,757 lb (77,000 kg)
**Performance**
maximum speed at 80,380 ft (24,500 m) (Mach 3.5)
   2,300 mph (3,700 km/hr)
maximum cruising speed (Mach 3.0) 1,980 mph
   (3,186 km/hr)
ferry range 2,983 miles (4,800 km)
service ceiling 80,050 ft (27,450 m)
**Dimensions**
wing span 55 ft 7 in (16.95 m)
length overall 107 ft 4½ in (32.73 m)
height overall 18 ft 6 in (5.64 m)
**Power plant**
Two Pratt & Whitney J58 turbojets each rated at
   34,000 lb (15,422 kg) st
**Armament**
*YF–12A*: Eight AIM–47A AAMs
**Variants**
*A–11*: Earlier version, three converted to YF–12;
*YF–12*: Experimental fighter with eight AIM–47A AAMs,
   one converted to SR–71C;
*SR–71C*: Strike trainer
**First flights**
*A–11*: 1961, *YF–12*: 1964;
*SR–71*: 22 December 1964
**Production**
Approx 26 built from 1964–1970
**In service**
United States

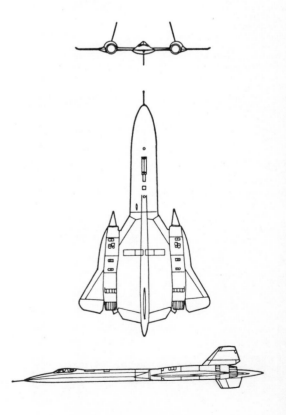

## LOCKHEED T–33 'T–BIRD'

**Type**
Two-seat trainer
**Weights**
empty 8,400 lb (3,810 kg)
normal 11,967 lb (5,428 kg)
maximum 13,007 lb (5,900 kg)
**Performance**
maximum speed at sea level (Mach 0.78) 600 mph
  (996 km/hr)
maximum speed at 25,000 ft (7,620 m) 543 mph
  (874 km/hr)
ferry range 1,345 miles (2,165 km)
initial rate of climb 91.2 fps (27.8 m/sec)
time to 25,000 ft (7,620 m) 6 min 30 sec
service ceiling 47,500 ft (14,480 m)
**Dimensions**
wing span 38 ft 10½ in (11.85 m)
length overall 37 ft 9¼ in (11.51 m)
height overall 11 ft 8 in (3.55 m)
wing area 237 sq ft (22.02 sq m)
**Power plant**
One Allison J33–A–35 turbojet rated at 4,600 lb (2,087 kg)
  st/5,400 lb (2,449 kg) st (with water injection) (CL–30:
  Rolls–Royce Nene rated at 5,100 lb (2,313 kg) st)
**Armament**
Two 12.7 mm M–3 machine guns
**Variants**
T–33A–N: Canadian licence-built (CL–30 Silver Star);
  T–33B and naval version TV–2: Later series; RT–33A:
  Single-seat reconnaissance aircraft; WT–33A: Weather
  reconnaissance aircraft; DT–33A: Target aircraft;
  T–1A SeaStar: Further development, naval trainer
**First flights**
Prototype: 22 March 1948;
T–1A: 15 December 1953
**Production**
T–33A, B: 5,691 built from 1948–1959, additional 210
  Japanese licence-built from 1956–1958; CL–30: 656
  built; T–1A: 271 built from 1954–1958
**In service**
T–33: Belgium, Brazil, Burma, Chile, China (Taiwan),
  Colombia, Denmark, Ecuador, Ethiopia, France,
  Germany (West), Guatemala, Honduras, Iran, Italy,
  Japan, Korea (South), Libya, Mexico, Nicaragua,
  Norway, Pakistan, Peru, Philippines, Portugal, Saudi
  Arabia, Spain, Thailand, United States, Uruguay,
  Yugoslavia;
T–33A–N: Bolivia, Canada, Greece, Turkey;
T–1A: United States;
RT–33A: Iran, Thailand, Yugoslavia

## MARTIN B–57B

**Type**
Two-seat bomber and reconnaissance aircraft
**Weights**
empty 30,000 lb (13,608 kg)
normal 49,500 lb (22,453 kg)
maximum 54,500 lb (24,721 kg)
**Performance**
maximum speed at sea level 520 mph (837 km/hr)
maximum speed at 39,375 ft (12,000 m) (Mach 0.88)
  581 mph (936 km/hr)
maximum cruising speed 478 mph (770 km/hr)
radius of action 1,100 miles (1,770 km)
ferry range 2,650 miles (4,264 km)
initial rate of climb 58.4 fps (17.8 m/sec)
service ceiling 48,000 ft (14,630 m)
**Dimensions**
wing span 63 ft 11¼ in (19.49 m)
length overall 65 ft 5¾ in (19.96 m)
height overall 15 ft 7 in (4.75 m)
wing area 959.3 sq ft (89.19 sq m)
**Power plant**
Two Wright J65–W–5 turbojets each rated at 7,200 lb
  (3,275 kg) st
**Armament**
Eight 12.7 mm Colt Browning machine guns, max 8,000 lb
  (3,629 kg) weapon load in fuselage bay and underwing
**Variants**
B–57A, C, E: Other series, RB–57A, D: Reconnaissance
  aircraft and bombers; RB–57F: Conversion of 17
  B–57Bs to strategic high-altitude reconnaissance aircraft;
  B–57G: Conversions of 16 B–57Bs to night ground-
  support aircraft; EB–57A, D, E: Conversion to ECM
  aircraft; WB–57F: Weather reconnaissance aircraft
  (original designation RB–57F)
**First flights**
B–57A: 20 July 1953;
B–57B: 28 June 1954
**Production**
Series production from 1952–1956, conversions from 1964–
  1970; B–57A: 8 built; RB–57A: 67 built; B–57B: 202
  built; B–57C: 38 built; RB–57D: 20 built; B–57E: 68
  built
**In service**
B–57B: China (Taiwan), Pakistan, United States;
B–57G, EB–57, WB–57F: United States;
RB–57: China (Taiwan), Pakistan

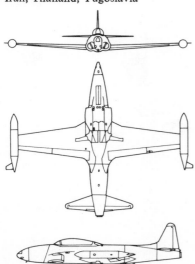

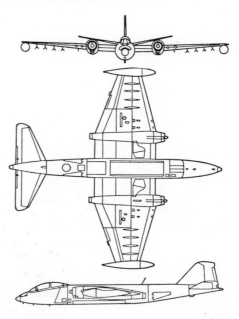

## MARTIN RB-57F

**Type**
Strategic high-altitude reconnaissance aircraft
Details as for B-57B with the following exceptions
**Performance**
service ceiling 101,710 ft (31,000 m)
**Dimensions**
wing span 122 ft 0½ in (37.19 m)
length overall 68 ft 10 in (20.98 m)
height overall 19 ft 0 in (5.79 m)
**Power plant**
Two Pratt & Whitney TF-33-P-11 turbofans each rated at 18,000 lb (8,165 kg) st and two Pratt & Whitney J60-P-9 turbojets each rated at 3,300 lb (1,497 kg) st

## McDONNELL DOUGLAS A-4F 'SKYHAWK'

**Type**
Single-seat shipboard strike fighter
**Weights**
empty 9,998 lb (4,535 kg)
normal 16,301 lb (7,394 kg)
maximum 24,500 lb (11,113 kg)
**Performance**
maximum speed at sea level (Mach 0.88) 674 mph (1,086 km/hr)
maximum speed at 35,000 ft (10,700 m) (Mach 0.92) 612 mph (985 km/hr)
radius of action 341 miles (550 km)
ferry range 2,436 miles (3,920 km)
service ceiling 57,570 ft (14,500 m)
**Dimensions**
wing span 27 ft 6 in (8.38 m)
length overall 40 ft 3¼ in (12.27 m)
height overall 15 ft 0 in (4.57 m)
wing area 260 sq ft (24.16 sq m)
**Power plant**
One Pratt & Whitney J52-P-8A turbojet rated at 9,300 lb (4,218 kg) st
**Armament**
Two 20 mm Mk.12 cannon with 100 rpg and max 8,200 lb (3,720 kg) weapon load; e.g. two Bullpup ASMs or bombs and rockets
**Variants**
*A-4A, B, C, E*: Earlier versions; *A-4G, H, K, M, N*: Later series; *A-4L*: Conversion of A-4C; now as A-4F; *A-4P, A-4Q*: Conversions of A-4B; TA-4F, G, H, J, K: Two-seat strike trainers
**First flights**
Prototype: 22 June 1954;
*A-4F*: 31 August 1966
**Production**
Series production from 1954, over 2,600 delivered or on order to date, inc. 166 A-4A, 542 A-4B, 638 *A-4C*, 500 *A-4E*, 154 *A-4F*, 8 *A-4G*, 108 *A-4H*, 10 *A-4K*, 50 *A-4M*, 50(?) *A-4N*, 200 *TA-4F*, 2 *TA-4G*, 13 *TA-4H*, 185 *TA-4J*, 4 *TA-4K*
**In service**
*A-4B*: Singapore; *A-4E*: Israel, United States; *A-4F*: Argentine, Brazil, United States; *TA-4F, TA-4J*: United States; *A-4G, TA-4G*: Australia; *A-4H, TA-4H*: Israel *A-4K, TA-4K*: New Zealand; *A-4L, A-4M*: United States; *A-4N*: Israel(?); *A-4Q*: Argentine

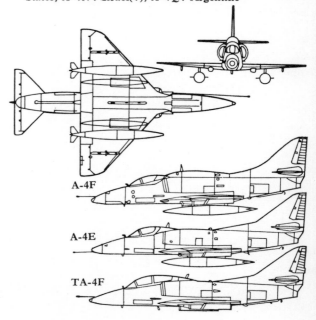

A-4F

A-4E

TA-4F

RB-57F

## McDONNELL DOUGLAS A–4M

**Type**
Single-seat shipboard strike fighter
Details as for A–4F with the following exceptions
**Weights**
empty 10,600 lb (4,808 kg)
**Performance**
maximum speed at sea level (Mach 0.9) 685 mph
  (1,102 km/hr)
maximum speed at 25,000 ft (7,620 m) (Mach 0.94)
  640 mph (1,030 km/hr)
ferry range 2,055 miles (3,307 km)
initial rate of climb 264.1 fps (80.5 m/sec)
**Power plant**
One Pratt & Whitney J52–P–408A turbojet rated at
  11,200 lb (5,080 kg) st
**Armament**
Two 20 mm Mk.12 cannon with 200 rpg and max 9,193 lb
  (4,170 kg) weapon load, e.g. two Bullpup ASMs or
  bombs and rockets
**First flights**
10 April 1970

## McDONNELL DOUGLAS C–9A 'NIGHTINGALE'

**Type**
Aeromedical transport
**Weights**
empty 59,214 lb (26,859 kg)
normal 98,000 lb (44,450 kg)
maximum 108,000 lb (48,988 kg)
**Performance**
maximum cruising speed at 25,000 ft (7,620 m) 565 mph
  (909 km/hr)
ferry range 2,800 miles (4,505 km)
**Dimensions**
wing span 93 ft 5 in (28.47 m)
length overall 119 ft 3¼ in (36.36 m)
height overall 27 ft 6 in (8.38 m)
wing area 1,000.7 sq ft (92.97 sq m)
**Power plant**
Two Pratt & Whitney JT8D–9 turbofans each rated at
  14,495 lb (6,575 kg) st
**Payload**
3 man crew and over 40 troops or 30–40 stretcher cases
  and 4–6 medics
**Variants**
*McDonnell Douglas C–9B 'Skytrain II'*: Transport
*McDonnell Douglas DC–9*: Civil airliner
**First flights**
Prototype *DC–9*: February 1965; *C–9A*: June 1968
**Production**
*DC–9*: Series production from 1965, over 540 delivered to
  date; *C–9A*: 30 built from 1968–1972; *C–9B*: 8 built
  from 1972/73
**In service**
*C–9A, C–9B*: United States

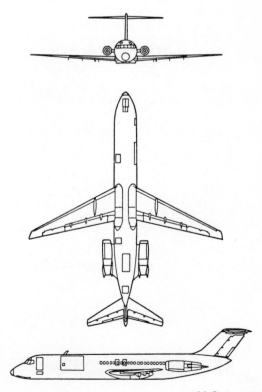

## McDONNELL DOUGLAS F–4B, C, D and RF–4B, C 'PHANTOM II'

**Type**
Two-seat fighter and strike fighter (F–4B, C, D) or reconnaissance aircraft (RF–4B, C)

**Weights**
empty 27,998 lb (12,700 kg)
normal 46,000 lb (20,865 kg)
maximum 54,598 lb (24,765 kg)

**Performance**
maximum speed at sea level (Mach 1.2) 915 mph (1,472 km/hr)
maximum speed at 48,200 ft (14,700 m) (Mach 2.4) 1,583 mph (2,548 km/hr)
maximum cruising speed at 40,000 ft (12,000 m) 575 mph (925 km/hr)
radius of action 404–900 miles (650–1,450 km)
ferry range 2,300 miles (3,700 km)
initial rate of climb 469 fps (143.0 m/sec)
time to 49,200 ft (15,000 m) 2 min 0 sec
service ceiling 71,000 ft (21,640 m)

**Dimensions**
wing span 38 ft 5 in (11.70 m)
length overall 58 ft 3 in (17.76 m)
length overall *RF–4B, C*: 62 ft 9 ¾ in (19.15 m)
height overall 16 ft 3 in (4.96 m)
wing area 530.1 sq ft (49.24 sq m)

**Power plant**
Two General Electric J79–GE–8 or –15 turbojets each rated at 10,913 lb (4,950 kg)/16,000 lb (7,711 kg) st

**Armament**
F–4B, C, D: (as fighter) four AIM–7E Sparrow III and four AIM–9–Sidewinder AAMs or (as strike fighter) max 15,984 lb (7,250 kg) weapon load; e.g. fifteen 1,000 lb (454 kg) bombs; *RF–4B, C*: Cameras and SLAR (Side-looking Airborne Radar)

**Variants**
*F–4A*: Pre-production model; *F–4G*, *F–4J*, *F–4E*: Further developments; *F–4K*, *F–4M*: Fighter and strike fighter for Great Britain with British engines; *F–4N*: Conversion of 178 F–4B from 1972–1976

**First flights**
Prototype: 27 May 1958; *F–48*: 1961; *F–4C*: 27 May 1963; *F–4D*: 8 December 1965, *RF–4B*: 12 March 1965; *RF–4C*: 9 August 1963; *F–4J*: 27 May 1966

**Production**
Series production from 1960: *F–4A*: 47 built; *F–4B*: 635 built; *F–4C*: 583 built; *F–4D*: 825 built; *RF–4B*: 46 built; *RF–4C*: 495 built; *F–4G*: 12 built; *F–4K*: 52 built; *F–4M*: 118 built; *F–4J*: 522 built from 1966–1972

**In service**
*F–4B, G, J, N; RF–4B, C*: United States;
*F–4C*: Korea (South), Spain, United States;
*F–4D*: Iran, Korea (South), United States;
*F–4K, F–4M*: Great Britain

## McDONNELL DOUGLAS F–4E 'PHANTOM'

**Type**
Two-seat fighter and strike fighter

**Weights**
empty 32,629 lb (14,800 kg)
normal 51,810 lb (23,500 kg)
maximum 60,630 lb (27,502 kg)

**Performance**
maximum speed at 40,000 ft (12,200 m) (Mach 2.27) 1,500 mph (2,414 km/hr)
maximum speed at 985 ft (300 m) (Mach 1.2) 900 mph (1,464 km/hr)
maximum cruising speed at 40,000 ft (12,200 m) 575 mph (925 km/hr)
radius of action 155–660 miles (250–1,060 km)
ferry range 2,300 miles (3,700 km)
initial rate of climb 502 fps (153.0 m/sec)
service ceiling 62,340 ft (19,000 m)

**Dimensions**
wing span 38 ft 5 in (11.70 m)
length overall 62 ft 11¾ in (19.20 m)
height overall 16 ft 3 in (4.96 m)
wing area 530 sq ft (49.20 sq m)

**Power plant**
Two General Electric J79–GE–17 turbojets each rated at 11,872 lb (5,385 kg)/17,902 lb (8,120 kg) st

**Armament**
One 20 mm M–61A1 cannon and (as fighter) four–six AIM–7E Sparrow IIIB AAMs and four AIM–9D Sidewinder 1C AAMs and (as strike fighter) max 16,050 lb (7,280 kg) weapon load

**Variants**
*F–4EJ*: Japanese licence-built F–4E;
*F–4F*: Strike fighter with simplified avionics

**First flights**
*F–4E*: 30 June 1967, *F–4EJ*: 14 January 1971

**Production**
*F–4E*: Series production since 1967, 846 delivered or on order to date; *F–4EJ*: 128 ordered; *F–4F*: 175 ordered for delivery from 1973/74

**In service**
*F–4E*: Greece, Iran, Israel, Korea (South), Turkey(?), United States;
*F–4EJ*: Japan; *F–4F*: Germany (West)

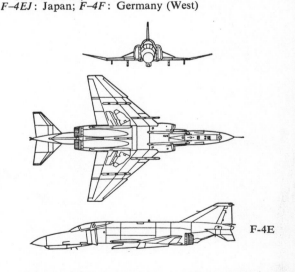

F-4E

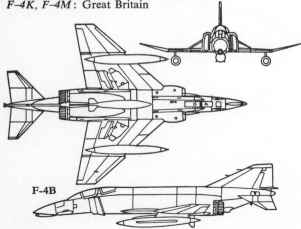

F-4B

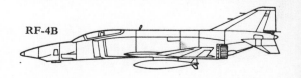

RF-4B

## McDONNELL DOUGLAS RF–4E 'PHANTOM'

**Type**
Two-seat reconnaissance aircraft
Details as for F-4E with the following exceptions
**Weights**
normal 46,077 lb (20,900 kg)
maximum 57,320 lb (26,000 kg)
**Performance**
radius of action 684 miles (1,100 km)
**Armament**
Infra-red, radar and photographic reconnaissance
    equipment
**Production**
Series production from 1967, over 112 delivered or on
    order to date
**In service**
Germany (West), Iran, Israel, Japan

## McDONNELL DOUGLAS F–15A 'EAGLE'

**Type**
Single-seat fighter
**Weights**
normal 40,000 lb (18,144 kg)
maximum 55,930 lb (25,370 kg)
**Performance**
maximum speed at 40,000 ft (12,000 m) (Mach 2.5)
    1,650 mph (2,655 km/hr)
maximum speed at 980 ft (300 m) (Mach 1.2) 913 mph
    (1,470 km/hr)
ferry range 2,980 miles (4,800 km)
service ceiling 62,000 ft (18,900 m)(?)
**Dimensions**
wing span 42 ft 9½ in (13.04 m)
length overall 63 ft 9½ in (19.44 m)
height overall 18 ft 7¼ in (5.67 m)
**Power plant**
Two Pratt & Whitney F100–PW–101 turbofans each rated
    at 19,000 lb (8,618 kg)/27,000 lb (12,247 kg) st
**Armament**
One 20 mm M–61A–1 Vulcan cannon with 900 rpg (or
    one 25 mm GAU–7/A cannon with 750 rpg) and max
    13,230(?) lb (6,000(?) kg) weapon load, e.g. four AIM–
    7F Sparrow and four AIM–9L Sidewinder AAMs
**Variants**
*TF–15*: Planned two-seat strike trainer
**First flights**
Prototype: 27 July 1972
**Production**
20 prototypes and pre-production models, series production
    from 1973, 107 delivered or on order to date; 729 to be
    built by 1978
**In service**
United States

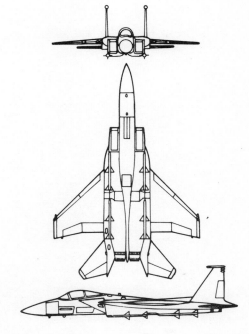

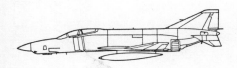

RF-4E

## McDONNELL F–101B 'VOODOO'

**Type**
Two-seat all-weather fighter
**Weights**
empty 27,954 lb (12,680 kg)
normal 39,802 lb (18,054 kg)
maximum 46,672 lb (21,170 kg)
**Performance**
maximum speed at sea level (Mach 0.94) 716 mph
(1,152 km/hr)
maximum speed at 40,000 ft (12,200 m) (Mach 1.85)
1,220 mph (1,963 km/hr)
maximum cruising speed at 36,000 ft (11,000 m) 590 mph
(950 km/hr)
range 1,553 miles (2,500 km)
ferry range 2,200 miles (3,540 km)
initial rate of climb 283.5 fps (86.4 m/sec)
service ceiling 52,000 ft (15,850 m)
**Dimensions**
wing span 39 ft 8 in (12.09 m)
length overall 67 ft $4\frac{1}{2}$ in (20.54 m)
height overall 18 ft 0 in (5.49 m)
wing area 358 sq ft (34.19 sq m)
**Power plant**
Two Pratt & Whitney J57–P–55 turbojets each rated at
11,989 lb (5,438 kg)/14,782 lb (6,705 kg) st
**Armament**
Three AIM–4E or –4F Super Falcon AAMs in fuselage
bay and two underwing AIR–2A Genie ASMs
**Variants**
*F–101A, F–101C*: Fighter and strike fighter;
*RF–101A*: Reconnaissance aircraft;
*TF–101B*: Two-seat fighter and strike fighter
**First flights**
Prototype: 29 September 1954;
*F–101B*: 27 March 1957
**Production**
Series production from 1957–1961; *F–101A*: 79 built;
*RF–101A*: 35 built; *F–101C*: 47 built; *F–101B* and
*TF–101B*: 478 built
**In service**
Canada, United States

## McDONNELL RF–101C 'VOODOO'

**Type**
Single-seat reconnaissance aircraft
Details as for the F–101B with the following exceptions
**Weights**
normal 40,345 lb (18,300 kg)
maximum 48,722 lb (22,100 kg)
**Performance**
maximum speed at 37,700 ft (11,500 m) (Mach 1.58)
1,040 mph (1,673 km/hr)
range/radius of action 1,678 miles (2,700 km)
initial rate of climb 232.9 fps (17.0 m/sec)
**Dimensions**
length overall 69 ft 3 in (21.11 m)
**Power plant**
Two Pratt & Whitney J57–P–13 turbojets each rated at
10,099 lb (4,581 kg)/14,880 lb (6,750 kg) st
**Armament**
5 cameras
**First flights**
12 July 1957
**Production**
166 built
**In service**
China (Taiwan), United States

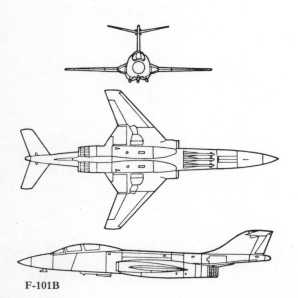

F-101B

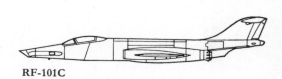

RF-101C

## NORTH AMERICAN (CAVALIER) F–51D 'MUSTANG'

**Type**
Two-seat ground-attack aircraft
**Weights**
empty 7,671 lb (3,480 kg)
normal 10,097 lb (4,580 kg)
maximum 12,500 lb (5,670 kg)
**Performance**
maximum speed at 28,000 ft (8,530 m) 457 mph
  (735 km/hr)
maximum cruising speed 290 mph (467 km/hr)
ferry range 1,980 miles (3,186 km)
initial rate of climb 55.8 fps (17.0 m/sec)
time to 20.000 ft (6.100 m) 7 min 18 sec
service ceiling 40,000 ft (12,200 m)
**Dimensions**
wing span 37 ft 0½ in (11.29 m)
length overall 32 ft 2½ in (9.82 m)
height overall 14 ft 10 in (4.52 m)
wing area 233.1 sq ft (21.66 sq m)
**Power plant**
One 1,695 hp Packard V–1650–7 piston engine
**Armament**
Six 12.7 mm M–2 machine guns with 400 rpg and weapon
  load on 8 hard points, e.g. two 1,000 lb (454 kg) bombs
  and six 127 mm unguided rockets
**Variants**
*TF–51D*: Two-seat strike trainer
*Cavalier Mustang II, Mustang III*: Further developments
**First flights**
Prototype *P–51*: 26 October 1940;
*P–51D*: 1944
**Production**
15,576 of all series built from 1940–1946, inc 7,956 *P–51D*
  (later designation F–51D), over 60 (100?) conversions
  by Cavalier from 1967/68
**In service**
Bolivia, Dominican Republic, El Salvador, Guatemala,
  Haiti, Honduras, Indonesia, Nicaragua

## NORTH AMERICAN F–86D(L) 'SABRE'

**Type**
Single-seat all-weather fighter
**Weights**
empty 13,500 lb (6,123 kg)
normal 18,160 lb (8,237 kg)
maximum 19,952 lb (9,050 kg)
**Performance**
maximum speed at sea level (Mach 0.9) 693 mph
  (1,115 km/hr)
maximum speed at 40,000 ft (12,200 m) (Mach 0.93)
  616 mph (991 km/hr)
maximum cruising speed 547 mph (880 km/hr)
radius of action 270 miles (435 km)
ferry range 767 miles (1,235 km)
initial rate of climb 200 fps (61.0 m/sec)
service ceiling 49,375 ft (15,050 m)
**Dimensions**
wing span 37 ft 2 in (11.32 m)
length overall 40 ft 3 in (12.27 m)
height overall 14 ft 11¾ in (4.57 m)
wing area 289.6 sq ft (26.90 sq m)
**Power plant**
One General Electric J47–GE–33 turbojet rated at
  5,500 lb (2,495 kg)/7,650 lb (3,470 kg) st
**Armament**
*F–86D*: Twenty-four 70 mm unguided rockets in weapon
  tray and two AIM–9B Sidewinder AAMs
*F–86L*: Four 20 mm M–24A–1 cannon and two AIM–9B
  Sidewinder AAMs
**Variants**
*F–86K*: Further development of F–86D
*F–86L*: 981 converted F–86Ds with more modern
  electronics
**First flights**
*YF–86D*: 22 December 1949
**Production**
*F–86D*: 2,504 built from 1950–1955
**In service**
*F–86D*: Korea (South), Philippines, Yugoslavia
*F–86L*: Thailand

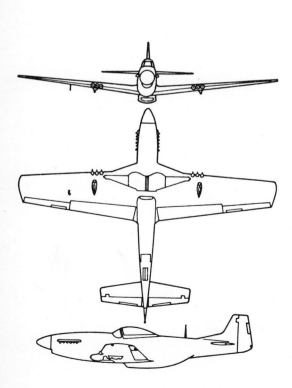

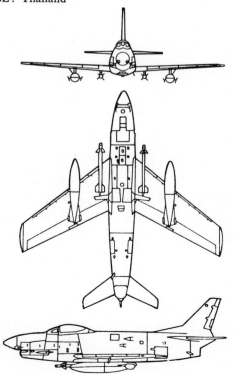

## NORTH AMERICAN F–86K 'SABRE'

**Type**
Single-seat all-weather fighter
(Details as for F–86D with the following exceptions)
**Weights**
empty 13,367 lb (6,063 kg)
normal 18,377 lb (8,335 kg)
maximum 20,772 lb (9,150 kg)
**Performance**
maximum speed at 40,000 ft (12,200 m) 512 mph
    (985 km/hr)
ferry range 746 miles (1,200 km)
initial rate of climb 169.9 fps (51.8 m/sec)
**Dimensions**
wing span 39 ft 1½ in (11.92 m)
length overall 40 ft 11 in (12.47 m)
wing area 314.3 sq ft (29.20 sq m)
**Power plant**
One General Electric J47–GE–17B turbojet rated at
    5,423 lb (2,460 kg)/7,500 lb (3,402 kg) st
**Armament**
Four 20 mm M–24A–1 cannon and two AIM–9B
    Sidewinder AAMs
**Variants**
**First flights**
*YF–86K*: 15 July 1954
**Production**
*F–86K*: 341 built from 1954–1956
**In service**
*F–86K*: Venezuela

## NORTH AMERICAN F–86F 'SABRE'

**Type**
Single-seat fighter and strike fighter
**Weights**
empty 11,133 lb (5,050 kg)
normal 15,190 lb (6,890 kg)
maximum 20,613 lb (9,350 kg)
**Performance**
maximum speed at sea level (Mach 0.98) 677 mph
    (1,090 km/hr)
maximum speed at 36,000 ft (11,000 m) (Mach 0.9)
    599 mph (964 km/hr)
maximum cruising speed 528 mph (850 km/hr)
radius of action 466 miles (750 km)
ferry range 1,525 miles (2,455 km)
initial rate of climb 164 fps (50.0 m/sec)
time to 30,200 ft (9,200 m) 5 min 12 sec
service ceiling 49,210 ft (15,000 m)
**Dimensions**
wing span 39 ft 1 in (11.90 m)
length overall 37 ft 6 in (11.45 m)
height overall 14 ft 9¼ in (4.50 m)
wing area 314.3 sq ft (29.20 sq m)
**Power plant**
One General Electric J47–GE–27 turbojet rated at
    5,908 lb (2,680 kg) st
**Armament**
Six 12.7 mm M–3 machine guns and (as fighter) two
    AIM–9B Sidewinder AAMs or (as strike fighter) max
    2,000 lb (908 kg) weapon load, e.g. two 1,000 lb (454
    kg) bombs or eight rockets
**Variants**
*F 86E*: Earlier version (Canadian licence-built CL–13
    Sabre Mk.2 and 4);
*CA–27 Sabre Mk.30, 31, 32*: Australian licence-built with
    Avon engine;
*CL–13B Sabre Mk.6*: Canadian licence-built with
    Orenda engine;
*RF–86*: Single-seat reconnaissance aircraft
**First flights**
Prototype: 1 October 1947
*F–86F*: 9 March 1952
**Production**
Series production from 1950–1956; *F–86E*: 336 built;
*F–86F*: 1,839 built; *CA–27*: 112 built; *CL–13 and 13B*:
    1,815 built from 1950–1958
**In service**
*F–86E*: Yugoslavia
*F.86F*: Argentine, Burma, China (Taiwan), Colombia,
    Ethiopia, Iran, Japan, Korea (South), Pakistan, Peru,
    Philippines, Portugal, Saudi-Arabia, Spain (C–5), Thai-
    land, Tunisia, Venezuela; *RF–86F*: Japan, Korea
    (South), Yugoslavia
*CA–27*: Indonesia, Malaysia
*CL–13B*: Colombia, Iran, Pakistan, South Africa

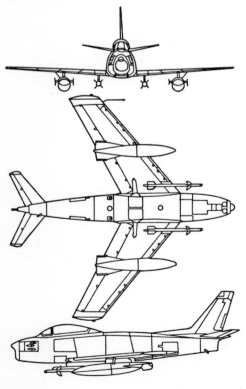

## NORTH AMERICAN F-100D 'SUPER SABRE'

**Type**
Single-seat strike fighter
**Weights**
empty 21,000 lb (9,526 kg)
normal 29,762 lb (13,500 kg)
maximum 34,831 lb (15,799 kg)
**Performance**
maximum speed at 35,000 ft (10,680 m) (Mach 1.3)
862 mph (1,388 km/hr)
maximum speed at 8,000 ft (2,440 m) (Mach 1.1)
810 mph (1,304 km/hr)
maximum cruising speed at 36,000 ft (11,000 m)–46,000 ft
(14,000 m) 565 mph (910 km/hr)
radius of action 550 miles (885 km)
ferry range 1,500 miles (2,145 km)
initial rate of climb 267.4 fps (81.5 m/sec)
time to 32,800 ft (10,000 m) 2 min 30 sec
**Dimensions**
wing span 36 ft 9¾ in (11.82 m)
length overall 49 ft 6 in (15.09 m)
height overall 16 ft 2½ in (4.94 m)
wing area 385.1 sq ft (35.78 sq m)
**Power plant**
One Pratt & Whitney J57–P–21A turbojet rated at
11,700 lb (5,307 kg)/16,950 lb (7,688 kg) st
**Armament**
Four 20 mm M–39E cannon and max 7,500 lb (3,402 kg)
weapon load on six hard points, e.g. 4 Sidewinder
AAMs and 2 Bullpup ASMs, bombs and rockets
**Variants**
*F–100A*, *F–100C*: Earlier versions
**First flights**
Prototype *YF–100A*: 25 May 1953
*F–100D*: 24 January 1956
**Production**
Series production from 1953–1959;
*F–100A*: 203 built; *F–100C*: 476 built; *F–100D*: 1,274
built
**In service**
F–100C: United States;
F–100D, F: China (Taiwan), Denmark, France, Turkey,
United States

## NORTH AMERICAN F-100F 'SUPER SABRE'

**Type**
Two-seat strike fighter and trainer
(Details as for F–100D with the following exceptions):
**Weights**
empty 22,300 lb (10,115 kg)
maximum 40,000 lb (18,143 kg)
**Dimensions**
length overall 52 ft 5¼ in (16.00 m)
**Armament**
Two 20 mm M–39E cannon and max 6,000 lb (2,722 kg)
weapon load, e.g. rockets, napalm tanks and bombs
**First flights**
*F–100F*: 7 March 1957
**Production**
*F–100F*: 333 built

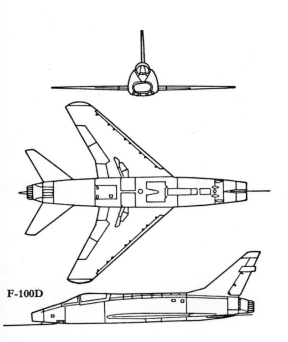

F-100D

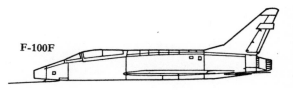

F-100F

## NORTH AMERICAN T-6G 'TEXAN'

**Type**
Two-seat trainer
**Weights**
empty 4,270 lb (1,937 kg)
maximum 5,618 lb (2,548 kg)
**Performance**
maximum speed at 5,000 ft (1,524 m) 211 mph
  (341 km/hr)
maximum cruising speed 170 mph (274 km/hr)
ferry range 870 miles (1,400 km)
initial rate of climb 27.2 fps (8.3 m/sec)
service ceiling 24,750 ft (7,544 m)
**Dimensions**
wing span 42 ft 0½ in (12.81 m)
length overall 29 ft 6 in (8.99 m)
height overall 11 ft 8¼ in (3.56 m)
wing area 253.5 sq ft (23.56 sq m)
**Power plant**
One 550 hp Pratt & Whitney R-1340-AN-1 piston engine
**Variants**
*BC-1, AT-6, T-6*: Earlier versions;
*Harvard*: Canadian licence-built T-6
**First flights**
Prototype NA-26: 1937
*BC-1*: 1938
**Production**
*T-6*: 15,094 built from 1940-1945;
*Harvard*: 555 built from 1940-1954;
*T-6G*: Conversion of 2,068 T-6 and Harvards from
  1949-1950
**In service**
Argentine, Bolivia, Brazil, Cambodia, Chile, China
(Taiwan), Colombia, Congo, Dominican Republic,
Ecuador, El Salvador, Guatemala, Haiti, Honduras,
India, Indonesia, Iran, Laos, Mexico, Morocco, New
Zealand, Nicaragua, Pakistan, Paraguay, Peru, Portugal,
South Africa, Spain (C-6), Switzerland, Thailand,
Tunisia, Turkey, Uruguay, Venezuela (?)

## NORTH AMERICAN T-28A 'TROJAN'

**Type**
Two-seat trainer
**Weights**
empty 5,107 lb (2,318 kg)
normal 6,365 lb (2,887 kg)
maximum 7,462 lb (3,385 kg)
**Performance**
maximum speed at 5,900 ft (1,800 m) 285 mph (455 km/hr)
maximum cruising speed 191 mph (306 km/hr)
ferry range 1,056 miles (1,700 km)
initial rate of climb 31.2 fps (9.5 m/sec)
service ceiling 24,020 ft (7,320 m)
**Dimensions**
wing span 40 ft 1 in (12.22 m)
length overall 32 ft 0¼ in (9.76 m)
height overall 12 ft 8 in (3.86 m)
wing area 268 sq ft (24.89 sq m)
**Power plant**
One 800 hp Wright R-1300-1A piston engine
**Variants**
*T-28B, C*: Naval versions of T-28;
*T-28D, AT-28D* and *Fennec*: Conversions of T-28 to
  light ground-attack aircraft
**First flights**
Prototype XT-28: 26 September 1949;
*T-28B*: 6 April 1953;
*T-28C*: 19 September 1955
**Production**
*T-28A*: 1,193 built from 1949-1953;
*T-28B*: 492 built from 1953-1955;
*T-28C*: 301 built from 1955-1957
**In service**
*T-28A*: Argentine, Bolivia, China (Taiwan), Congo,
  Ecuador, Ethiopia, Haiti, Korea (South), Laos, Mexico,
  Nicaragua, Philippines, Saudi Arabia, Thailand, Vietnam
  (South);
*T-28B*: United States;
*T-28C*: Brazil, United States

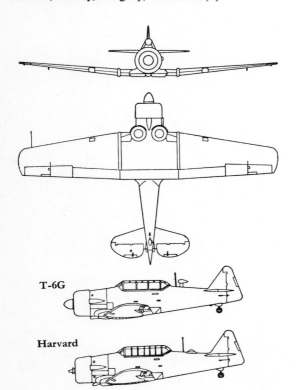

T-6G

Harvard

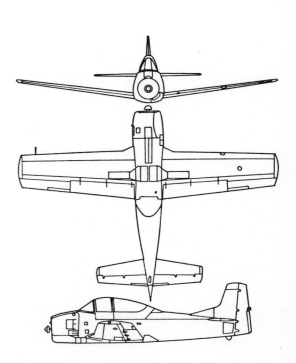

## NORTH AMERICAN T-28D

**Type**
Two-seat light ground-attack aircraft
**Weights**
empty 6,548 lb (2,970 kg)
maximum 11,486 lb (5,210 kg)
**Performance**
maximum speed at sea level 298 mph (480 km/hr)
maximum speed at 18,000 ft (5,500 m) 352 mph
 (566 km/hr)
maximum cruising speed 202 mph (326 km/hr)
ferry range 1,183 miles (1,905 km)
initial rate of climb 63.0 fps (19.2 m/sec)
service ceiling 36,000 ft (11,000 m)
**Dimensions**
wing span 40 ft 1 in (12.22 m)
length overall 32 ft 0¼ in (9.76 m)
height overall 12 ft 8 in (3.86 m)
wing area 269 sq ft (25.00 sq m)
**Power plant**
One 1,300 hp Wright R-1820-56S piston engine
**Armament**
*T-28D*: Max 4,000 lb (1,814 kg) weapon load on 6 hard
 points, e.g. two weapon packs each containing 12.7 mm
 M-3 machine guns, two 500 lb (227 kg) bombs, two
 rocket launchers with eight 70 mm rockets and thirty-
 six 19 lb (8.62 kg) fragmentation bombs
*Fennec*: Four 12.7 mm machine guns and four 330 lb
 (150 kg) bombs
**Variants**
*T-28A, B* and *C*: Trainers
*AT-28D*: Light ground attack aircraft
**First flights**
Prototype *T-28D*: 1961
**Production**
321 *T-28* converted to *T-28D* from 1961–1967;
130 *T-28A* converted to *Fennec* in France from 1960-1961
— *T-28* converted to AT-28D in 1973
**In service**
*T-28D*: Bolivia, Cambodia, Congo, Ethiopia, Laos,
 Morocco, Thailand, United States;
*Fennec*: Argentine

## NORTH AMERICAN ROCKWELL OV-10A 'BRONCO'

**Type**
Two-seat AOP and light ground-attack aircraft
**Weights**
empty 6,892 lb (3,126 kg)
normal 9,916 lb (4,498 kg)
maximum 14,445 lb (6,552 kg)
**Performance**
maximum speed at sea level 279 mph (449 km/hr)
maximum speed at 20,000 ft (6,100 m) 259 mph
 (417 km/hr) (OV-10B: 375 mph (604 km/hr))
maximum cruising speed 194 mph (312 km/hr)
radius of action 228 miles (367 km)
ferry range 1,480 miles (2,220 km)
initial rate of climb 38.7 fps (11.8 m/sec)
service ceiling 27,000 ft (8,230 m)
**Dimensions**
wing span 40 ft 0 in (12.19 m)
length overall 39 ft 9 in (12.12 m)
height overall 15 ft 1 in (4.62 m)
wing area 291 sq ft (27.03 sq m)
**Power plant**
Two 715 hp Garret AiResearch T-76-G-10/12 turboprops
 and (OV-10B) one General Electric J85-GE-4 turbojet
 rated at 2,952 lb (1,339 kg) st
**Armament**
Four 7.62 mm M-60C machine guns with 500 rpg and
 max 3,600 lb (1,633 kg) weapon load on 5 hard points
**Variants**
*OV-10B*: Target-towing aircraft;
*OV-10C, OV-10E*: Export versions of OV-10A
**First flights**
Prototype: 16 July 1965
*OV-10B*: 21 September 1970
**Production**
*OV-10A*: 7 prototypes and 271 production models from
 1966–1969;
*OV-10B*: 18 built from 1969–1971;
*OV-10C*: 32 built from 1970–1973;
*OV-10E*: 16 built from 1972–1973
**In service**
*OV-10A*: United States; *OV-10B*: Germany (West);
*OV-10C*: Thailand; *OV-10E*: Venezuela

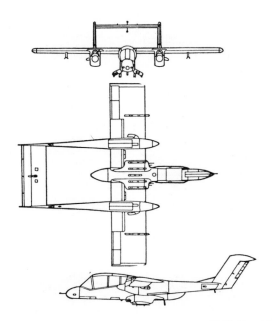

## NORTH AMERICAN ROCKWELL RA–5C 'VIGILANTE'

**Type**
Two-seat shipboard reconnaissance aircraft and bomber
**Weights**
normal 61,729 lb (28,000 kg)
maximum 79,998 lb (36,285 kg)
**Performance**
maximum speed at sea level (Mach 0.95) 684 mph
  (1,103 km/hr)
maximum speed at 40,000 ft (12,200 m) (Mach 2.1)
  1,386 mph (2,230 km/hr)
maximum cruising speed at 40,000 ft (12,200 m)
  (Mach 0.85) 559 mph (900 km/hr)
range with four 333 gal (1,514 l) auxiliary fuel tanks
  3,000 miles (4,820 km)
service ceiling 64,050 ft (19,510 m)
**Dimensions**
wing span 53 ft 0 in (16.15 m)
length overall 75 ft 10 in (23.11 m)
height overall 19 ft 4¼ in (5.90 m)
wing area 769 sq ft (71.44 sq m)
**Power plant**
Two General Electric J79–GE–10 turbojets each rated at
  11,894 lb (5,395 kg)/17,902 lb (8,120 kg) st
**Armament**
Max 8,000 lb (3,630 kg) weapon load on 4 underwing
  hard points, e.g. two 1,000 lb (454 kg) or 2,000 lb
  (908 kg) bombs, two napalm tanks or two Bullpup
  ASMs
**Variants**
*A–5A, A–5B*: Shipboard bombers
**First flights**
Prototype *YA–5A*: 31 August 1958;
*RA–5C*: 30 June 1962
**Production**
*YA–5A*: 2 built; *A–5A*: 57 built from 1959–1963
*A–6B*: 6 built; *RA–5C*: 460 built from 1967–1971; in
  addition twenty-seven A–5A and all six A–6B since
  modified to RA–5C standard
**In service**
United States

## NORTH AMERICAN ROCKWELL T–2B 'BUCKEYE'

**Type**
Two-seat shipboard trainer
**Weights**
empty 8,220 lb (3,728 kg)
normal 12,315 lb (5,586 kg)
maximum 13,284 lb (6,025 kg)
**Performance**
maximum speed at 25,000 ft (7,600 m) 539 mph
  (867 km/hr)
range 951 miles (1,530 km)
initial rate of climb 112.9 fps (34.4 m/sec)
service ceiling 43,965 ft (13,400 m)
**Dimensions**
wing span 38 ft 1½ in (11.62 m)
length overall 38 ft 3½ in (11.67 m)
height overall 14 ft 9½ in (4.51 m)
wing area 255 sq ft (23.69 sq m)
**Power plant**
One Pratt & Whitney J60–P–6 turbojet rated at 3,000 lb
  (1,361 kg) st
**Armament**
Two 100 lb (45 kg) practice bombs or two weapon packs
  each containing one 12.7 mm machine gun or two
  rocket launchers containing 70 mm rockets
**Variants**
*T–2A*: Earlier version with only one Westinghouse
  J34–WE–36 turbojet rated at 3,395 lb (1,540 kg) st;
*T–2C*: As T–2B, but with different engines (two General
  Electric J85–G1–4 turbojets each rated at 2,950 lb
  (1,339 kg) st);
*T–2D*: Export version
**First flights**
*T–2A*: 31 January 1958; *T–2B*: 30 August 1962;
*T–2C*: 10 December 1968;
**Production**
*T–2A*: 217 built from 1958–1961;
*T–2B*: 100 built from 1964–1968;
*T–2C*: 144 built from 1968–1974;
*T–2D*: 12 built 1973
**In service**
*T–2B, C*: United States;
*T–2D*: Venezuela

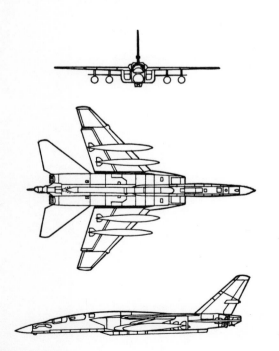

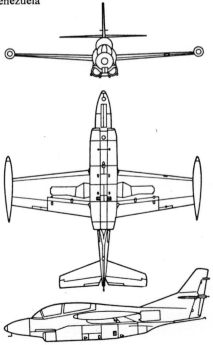

# NORTH AMERICAN ROCKWELL T–39A 'SABRELINER'

**Type**
Trainer and light transport
**Weights**
empty 10,250 lb (4,649 kg)
normal 16,700 lb (7,575 kg)
maximum 17,758 lb (8,055 kg)
**Performance**
maximum speed at 36,000 ft (11,000 m) (Mach 0.82) 540 mph (869 km/hr)
maximum cruising speed at 43,300 ft (13,200 m) (Mach 0.7) 502 mph (808 km/hr)
ferry range 1,725 miles (2,775 km)
service ceiling 44,300 ft (13,500 m)
**Dimensions**
wing span 44 ft 3¾ in (13.53 m)
length overall 43 ft 8¾ in (13.33 m)
height overall 16 ft 0 in (4.88 m)
wing area 342.4 sq ft (31.82 sq m)
**Power plant**
Two Pratt & Whitney J60–P–3A turbojets each rated at 3,000 lb (1,361 kg) st
**Payload**
Trainer: 2 man crew;
Transport: 2 man crew and 4–8 troops
**Variants**
*T–39B, T–39F*: Radar trainers; *T–39D, CT–39E*: Naval trainers;
*Sabreliner Series 40 and Series 60; Sabre 75 and 75A*: Civil variants
**First flights**
Prototype: 16 September 1958
**Production**
*T–39A*: 143 built from 1960–1963; *T–39B*: 6 built; *T–39D*: 42 built; *CT–39E*: 9 built; *T–39F*: — built
**In service**
United States

# NORTH AMERICAN ROCKWELL (AERO) 'COMMANDER' 500B

**Type**
Light transport
**Weights**
empty 4,300 lb (1,950 kg)
maximum 6,750 lb (3,062 kg)
**Performance**
maximum speed at sea level 228 mph (367 km/hr)
maximum cruising speed at 10,000 ft (3,050 m) 218 mph (351 km/hr)
ferry range 1,305 miles (2,100 km)
initial rate of climb 22.3 fps (6.8 m/sec)
service ceiling 21,000 ft (6,400 m)
**Dimensions**
wing span 49 ft 6 in (15.09 m)
length overall 35 ft 2 in (10.72 m)
height overall 14 ft 6 in (4.42 m)
wing area 255 sq ft (23.70 sq m)
**Power plant**
Two 290 hp Lycoming IO–540–B1A5 piston engines
**Payload**
1 man crew and 5–7 troops
**Variants**
*Shrike Commander (formerly Commander 500U), Commander 560, Commander 680FL*: Later series;
*Aero Commander 685, Grand Commander, Turbo Commander*: Further developments
**First flights**
Prototype: 23 April 1948
**Production**
Over 1,000 of all variants built from 1951
**In service**
*Commander 500B*: Colombia, Dahomey, Ivory Coast, Korea (South), Niger, Pakistan, Upper Volta;
*Commander 560*: United States (U–9C, U–9D);
*Commander 680FL*: Greece, Kenya, United States (U–4B)
*Shrike Commander*: Argentine;
*Turbo Commander*: Iran

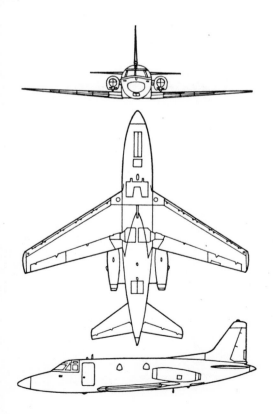

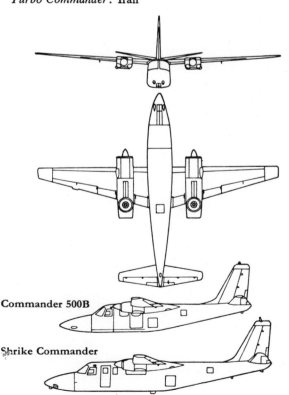

Commander 500B

Shrike Commander

## NORTHROP F–5A

**Type**
Single-seat fighter and strike fighter
**Weights**
empty 8,085 lb (3,667 kg)
normal 14,212 lb (6,446 kg)
maximum 20,576 lb (9,333 kg)
**Performance**
maximum speed at sea level (Mach 0.96) 745 mph
  (1,199 km/hr)
maximum speed at 36,000 ft (11,000 m) (Mach 1.4)
  924 mph (1,487 km/hr)
maximum cruising speed at 36,000 ft (11,000 m) 553 mph
  (890 km/hr)
radius of action 215–550 miles (346–885 km)
ferry range 1,565 miles (2,518 km)
initial rate of climb 478.4 fps (145.8 m/sec)
service ceiling 50,000 ft (15,250 m)
**Dimensions**
wing span 25 ft 3 in (7.70 m)
length overall 47 ft 2 in (14.38 m)
height overall 13 ft 2 in (4.01 m)
wing area 170 sq ft (15.79 sq m)
**Power plant**
Two General Electric J85–GE–13 turbojets each rated at
  2,720 lb (1,234 kg)/4,081 lb (1,851 kg) st
**Armament**
Two 20 mm M–39 cannon with 280 rpg and max 6,200 lb
  (2,812 kg) weapon load on 7 hard points, e.g. four
  Bullpup ASMs or bombs, Napalm tanks, rockets and
  two AIM–9 Sidewinder AAMs
**Variants**
*CF–5A, CF–5D, NF–5A, NF–5B*: Canadian licence-built
  by Canadair;
*SF–5A, B*: Spanish licence-built by CASA;
*RF–5A*: Single-seat reconnaissance aircraft with 4
  cameras;
*F–5E Tiger II*: Further development with uprated 3,500 lb
  (1,588 kg)/5,000 lb (2,268 kg) st engines
**First flights**
Prototype: 3 July 1959;
*F–5A*: October 1963
**Production**
Series production from 1964, over 1,150 delivered or on
  order to date; licence-built in Canada (89 CF–5A, 46
  CF–5D, 75 NF–5A, 30 NF–5B) and Spain (34 SF–5A,
  36 SF–5B from 1968–71)
**In service**
*F–5A, B*: China (Taiwan), Ethiopia, Greece, Iran, Korea
  (South), Libya, Morocco, Norway, Philippines, Thai-
  land, Turkey, United States, Vietnam (South);
*RF–5A*: Greece, Iran, Norway, Turkey, Vietnam (South);
*CF–5A, D*: Canada, Venezuela; *NF–5A, B*: Netherlands;
*SF–5A, B*: Spain (C–9, CE–9)

## NORTHROP F–5B

**Type**
Two-seat strike trainer
Details as for F–5A with the following exceptions
**Weights**
empty 8,361 lb (3,792 kg)
normal 13,752 lb (6,237 kg)
maximum 20,116 lb (9,124 kg)
**Performance**
maximum speed at 36,000 ft (11,000 m) (Mach 1.34)
  884 mph (1,422 km/hr)
**Dimensions**
length overall 46 ft 4 in (14.12 m)
height overall 13 ft 1 in (3.99 m)
**First flights**
February 1964

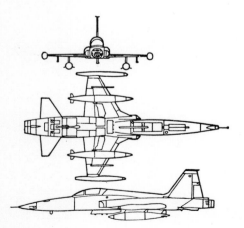

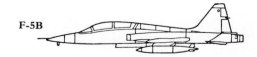

F-5B

# NORTHROP F–5E 'TIGER' II

**Type**
Single-seat fighter and strike fighter
**Weights**
normal 15,400 lb (6,985 kg)
maximum 21,834 lb (9,903 kg)
**Performance**
maximum speed at sea level (Mach 1.0) 760 mph
  (1,223 km/hr)
maximum speed at 36,090 ft (11,000 m) (Mach 1.6)
  1,056 mph (1,700 km/hr)
maximum cruising speed (Mach 1.45) 957 mph
  (1,540 km/hr)
radius of action 173–426 miles (278–686 km)
ferry range 1,595 miles (2,567 km)
initial rate of climb 525.5 fps (160.5 m/sec)
service ceiling 53,500 ft (16,305 m)
**Dimensions**
wing span 26 ft 8½ in (8.14 m)
length overall 48 ft 2½ in (14.69 m)
height overall 13 ft 2½ in (4.02 m)
wing area 186.2 sq ft (17.29 sq m)
**Power plant**
Two General Electric J85–GE–21 turbojets each rated at
  3,500 lb (1,588 kg)/5,000 lb (2,268 kg) st
**Armament**
Two 20 mm M–39 cannon with 280 rpg and (as fighter)
  two AIM–9 Sidewinder AAMs or (as strike fighter)
  max 7,000 lb (3,175 kg) weapon load on 5 hard points
**Variants**
*F–5A, F–5B*: Single-seat strike fighter and two-seat
  trainer
**First flights**
Prototype: 11 August 1972
**Production**
6 prototypes and pre-production models;
Series production from 1973, over 500 delivered or on
  order to date
**In service**
Brazil, China (Taiwan), Iran, Jordan, Korea (South),
  Malaysia, Saudi Arabia, Thailand, Turkey, Vietnam
  (South)

# NORTHROP T–38A 'TALON'

**Type**
Two-seat trainer
**Weights**
empty 7,628 lb (3,460 kg)
maximum 12,050 lb (5,465 kg)
**Performance**
maximum speed at 36,000 ft (11,000 m) (Mach 1.23)
  820 mph (1,320 km/hr)
maximum cruising speed at 39,375 ft (12,000 m) 593 mph
  (955 km/hr)
range 1,100 miles (1,770 km)
ferry range 1,320 miles (2,125 km)
initial rate of climb 499.3 fps (152.2 m/sec)
service ceiling 53,600 ft (16,335 m)
**Dimensions**
wing span 25 ft 3 in (7.70 m)
length overall 46 ft 4½ in (14.13 m)
height overall 12 ft 10½ in (3.92 m)
wing area 170 sq ft (15.79 sq m)
**Power plant**
Two General Electric J85–GE–5 turbojets each rated at
  2,680 lb (1,216 kg)/3,850 lb (1,748 kg) st
**First flights**
Prototype: 10 April 1959;
*T–38A*: May 1960
**Production**
1,189 built from 1960–1972
**In service**
Germany (West), United States

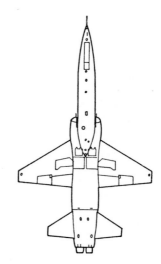

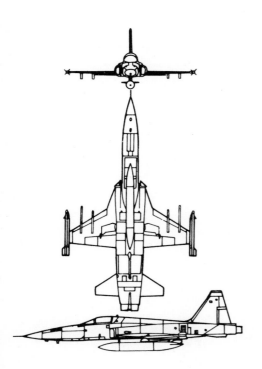

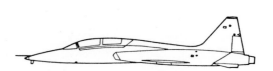

## PIPER U-7A 'SUPERCUB'

**Type**
Liaison and AOP aircraft
**Weights**
empty 930 lb (422 kg)
maximum 1,750 lb (794 kg)
**Performance**
maximum speed at sea level 130 mph (209 km/hr)
maximum cruising speed 115 mph (185 km/hr)
ferry range 460 miles (740 km)
initial rate of climb 16.1 fps (4.9 m/sec)
service ceiling 18,996 ft (5,790 m)
**Dimensions**
wing span 35 ft 4 in (10.77 m)
length overall 22 ft 6¼ in (6.86 m)
height overall 6 ft 7¾ in (2.03 m)
wing area 178.5 sq ft (16.58 sq m)
**Power plant**
One 135 hp Lycoming O-290-D2 piston engine
**Payload**
1 man crew and 1 observer
**Variants**
*PA-18-150 SuperCub*: Civil variant
*U-7B*: Later series;
*L-4 (J-3 Cub)*, *L-18 (PA-18-95 SuperCub)*: Earlier
  versions
**First flights**
Prototype: 1949; *PA-18-150*: 1955
**Production**
Over 9,000 of all series built from 1951 in both civil and
  military variants, inc 105 L-18B, 838 L-18C, 150 U-7A,
  582 U-7B
**In service**
*L-4*: Paraguay; *L-18B*: Turkey;
*L-18C*: Denmark, France, Germany (West), Iran, Israel,
  Italy, Netherlands, Norway, Thailand, Uganda,
  Uruguay;
*U-7A*, *U-7B* (earlier designations L-21A, L-21B):
  Argentine, Greece, Italy, Japan, Portugal, Sweden,
  United States, Uruguay

## PIPER U-11A 'AZTEC'

**Type**
Liaison aircraft
**Weights**
empty 2,933 lb (1,330 kg)
maximum 4,806 lb (2,180 kg)
**Performance**
maximum speed 218 mph (351 km/hr)
maximum cruising speed at 7,510 ft (2,290 m) 208 mph
  (335 km/hr)
range/radius of action 830 miles (1,335 km)
ferry range 1,320 miles (2,124 km)
initial rate of climb 27.6 fps (8.4 m/sec)
service ceiling 21,000 ft (6,400 m)
**Dimensions**
wing span 37 ft 0¼ in (11.28 m)
length overall 30 ft 1 in (9.17 m)
height overall 10 ft 3½ in (3.14 m)
wing area 207.56 sq ft (19.28 sq m)
**Power plant**
Two 250 hp Lycoming IO-540-C45B piston engines
**Payload**
2 man crew and 3 troops
**Variants**
*PA-23-250 Aztec*: Civil light aircraft
**First flights**
Prototype: 1959
*U-11A*: 1960
**Production**
Over 3,000 built from 1959, inc 22 *U-11A*
**In service**
Argentine, France, Uganda, United States (U-11A)

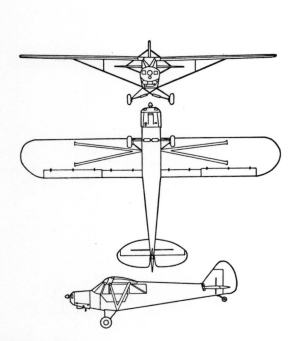

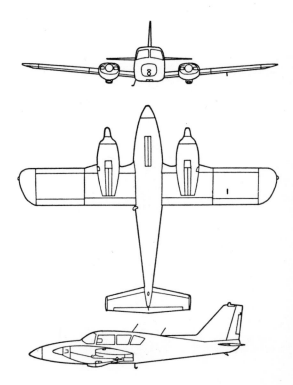

## REPUBLIC F–84F 'THUNDERSTREAK'

**Type**
Single-seat strike fighter
**Weights**
empty 10,106 lb (4,584 kg)
normal 26,032 lb (11,808 kg)
maximum 28,000 lb (12,701 kg)
**Performance**
maximum speed at sea level (Mach 0.91) 695 mph
   (1,118 km/hr)
maximum speed at 20,000 ft (6,100 m) 658 mph
   (1,059 km/hr)
radius of action 450–851 miles (725–1,370 km)
ferry range 2,140 miles (3,443 km)
initial rate of climb 136.8 fps (41.7 m/sec)
service ceiling 45,930 ft (14,000 m)
**Dimensions**
wing span 33 ft 5¼ in (10.24 m)
length overall 43 ft 4¾ in (13.23 m)
height overall 14 ft 4¾ in (4.39 m)
wing area 325 sq ft (30.20 sq m)
**Power plant**
One Wright J65–W–3 turbojet rated at 7,200 lb
   (3,275 kg) st
**Armament**
Six 12.7 mm M–3 machine guns with 300 rpg and max
   6,000 lb (2,720 kg) weapon load, e.g. two 1,000 lb
   (454 kg) bombs, eight 127 mm rockets and two 192 gal
   (870 l) auxiliary tanks
**First flights**
Prototype *YF–84F*: 3 June 1950;
**Production**
3 prototypes; *F–84F*: 2,711 built from 1951–1957
**In service**
Greece, Turkey

## REPUBLIC RF–84F 'THUNDERFLASH'

**Type**
Single-seat reconnaissance aircraft
Details as for F–84F with the following exceptions
**Weights**
normal 26,800 lb (12,157 kg)
maximum 28,000 lb (12,701 kg)
**Performance**
maximum speed at sea level 679 mph (1,093 km/hr)
maximum speed at 35,000 ft (10,500 m) 607 mph
   (977 km/hr)
ferry range 2,200 miles (3,540 km)
initial rate of climb 133.2 fps (40.6 m/sec)
**Dimensions**
length overall 47 ft 7½ in (14.52 m)
height overall 14 ft 11¾ in (4.57 m)
**Power plant**
One Wright J65–W–7 turbojet rated at 7,800 lb
   (3,538 kg) st
**Armament**
Four 12.7 mm M–3 machine guns and 6 cameras
**First flights**
Prototype *YRF–84F*: February 1952
**Production**
718 built from 1951–1958
**In service**
Turkey

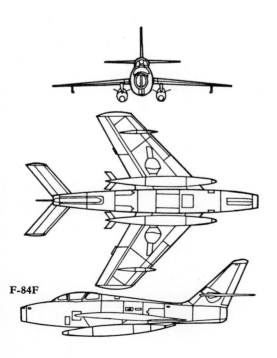

F-84F

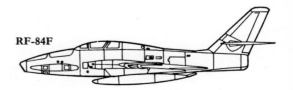

RF-84F

## REPUBLIC F–105D 'THUNDERCHIEF'

**Type**
Single-seat strike fighter
**Weights**
empty 28,000 lb (12,701 kg)
normal 38,140 lb (17,300 kg)
maximum 52,984 lb (24,033 kg)
**Performance**
maximum speed at sea level (Mach 1.11) 855 mph
  (1,376 km/hr)
maximum speed at 36,000 ft (11,600 m) (Mach 2.1)
  1,390 mph (2,237 km/hr)
maximum cruising speed at 39,375 ft (12,000 m)
  (Mach 0.95) 584 mph (940 km/hr)
radius of action 920 miles (1,480 km)
ferry range 2,390 miles (3,845 km)
initial rate of climb 574 fps (175.0 m/sec)
time to 40,000 ft (12,200 m) 2 min 1 sec
**Dimensions**
wing span 34 ft 11¼ in (10.65 m)
length overall 63 ft 3¾ in (19.60 m) (F–105F: 69 ft 1¼ in
  (21.06 m)
height overall 20 ft 11¾ in (6.15 m)
wing area 385 sq ft (35.77 sq m)
**Power plant**
One Pratt & Whitney J75–P–19W turbojet rated at
  17,200 lb (7,802 kg)/26,499 lb (12,020 kg) st
**Armament**
*F–105D*: One 20 mm M–61 Vulcan cannon with 1,029
  rpg, max 12,000 lb (5,443 kg) weapon load, e.g. six
  750 lb (340 kg) bombs or five 1,000 lb (454 kg) bombs,
  two 118 gal (539 l) external auxiliary tanks and one
  102 bal (467 l) auxiliary tank in bomb bay, two ECM
  pods;
*F–105*: Max 11,905 lb (5,400 kg) weapon load, e.g. two
  750 lb (340 kg) bombs, one 171 gal (779 l) external
  auxiliary tank and one 102 gal (467 l) auxiliary tank
  in bomb bay, several ECM pods or AGM–45A Shrike
  anti-radar missiles
**Variants**
*F–105B*: Earlier version
*F–105F*: Two-seat strike fighter, ECM aircraft and
  strike trainer
**First flights**
Prototype *YF–105A*: 22 October 1955;
*F–105D*: 9 June 1959; *F105F*: 11 June 1963
**Production**
5 prototypes; *F–10B*: 75 built from 1957–1959;
*F–105D*: 610 built from 1960–1963;
*F–105F*: 143 built from 1963–1964
**In service**
*F–105B, D, F*: United States

## SIKORSKY S–55 (H–19 'CHICKASAW')

**Type**
Transport helicopter
**Weights**
empty 5,260 lb (2,386 kg)
normal 7,500 lb (3,402 kg)
maximum 7,900 lb (3,583 kg)
**Performance**
maximum speed at sea level 112 mph (180 km/hr)
maximum cruising speed 91 mph (146 km/hr)
range 360 miles (580 km)
initial rate of climb 17.1 fps (5.2 m/sec)
hovering ceiling in ground effect 5,800 ft (1,770 m)
hovering ceiling out of ground effect 2,300 ft (700 m)
**Dimensions**
main rotor diameter 52 ft 11¾ in (16.15 m)
length of fuselage 42 ft 3 in (12.88 m)
height 14 ft 0 in (4.06 m)
**Power plant**
One 800 hp Wright R–1300-3 piston engine
**Payload**
2 man crew and 10 troops or 6 stretcher cases and 1
  medic or freight
**Variants**
*Whirlwind*: British (Westland) licence-built
**First flights**
Prototype: 9 November 1949
**Production**
*S–55*: 1,281 built from 1950–1959, plus 44 Japanese and
  — French licence-built from 1961–1962;
*Whirlwind*: Over 400 built from 1950–1963
**In service**
*S–55*: China (Taiwan), Dominican Republic, Greece,
  Guatemala, Honduras, Korea (South), Philippines,
  Spain (Z–1), Thailand, Turkey, Venezuela, United States
  (UH–19B, UH–19D, UH–19F);
*Whirlwind 2*: Nigeria, Yugoslavia;
*Whirlwind 3*: Brazil, Ghana, Great Britain (HAS.7,
  HAR.9, HAR.10), Nigeria, Qatar

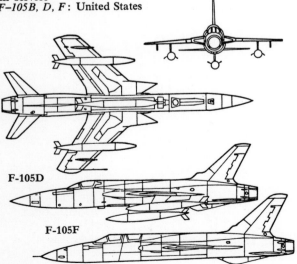

F-105D

F-105F

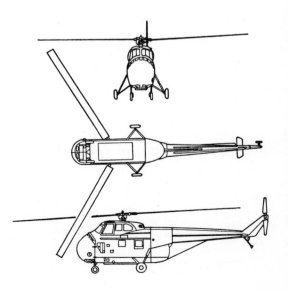

## SIKORSKY S-58 (CH-34A 'CHOCTAW', UH-D 'SEA HORSE')

**Type**
Medium transport helicopter
**Weights** (apply specifically to CH-34A)
empty 7,750 lb (3,515 kg)
normal 12,993 lb (5,897 kg)
maximum 14,000 lb (6,350 kg)
**Performance**
maximum speed at sea level 122 mph (196 km/hr)
maximum cruising speed 97 mph (156 km/hr)
range 245 miles (397 km)
initial rate of climb 18.5 fps (5.6 m/sec)
service ceiling 9,500 ft (2,900 m)
hovering ceiling in ground effect 4,916 ft (1,495 m)
hovering ceiling out of ground effect 2,407 ft (732 m)
**Dimensions**
main rotor diameter 56 ft 0 in (17.07 m)
length of fuselage 46 ft 9 in (14.25 m)
height 15 ft 11 in (4.85 m)
**Power plant**
One 1,525 hp Wright R-1820-84B or D piston engine
**Payload**
2 man crew and 16–18 troops or 8 stretcher cases
**Variants**
*SH-34G Seabat, SH-34J, LH-34D*: ASW helicopters, 4 man crew, homing torpedoes, mines, depth-charges;
*Wessex*: British licence-built S-58 by Westland
*S-58B, S-58D*: Civil versions;
*S-58T*: Installation of 1,525 hp Pratt & Whitney PT6 T-3 Twin Pac turbine powerplant into old S-58 models
**First flights**
Prototype: 8 March 1954
*S-58T*: 19 August 1970
**Production**
1,821 of all variants built from 1954–1969, plus 171 licence-built in France by Sud-Aviation and 40(?) Japanese licence-built by Mitsubishi
**In service**
*CH-34A*: Chad, Belgium, France, Germany (West), Laos, Philippines, Thailand, United States;
*SH-34G*: Germany (West), United States;
*SH-34J*: Brazil, France, Japan, Spain, United States, Uruguay;
*S-58C*: Belgium;
*S-58T*: Chile;
*CH-34C, LH-34D, UH-34D, UH-34E, VH-34D*: United States; *UH-34D*: Laos

## SIKORSKY S-61B (SH-3D 'SEA KING')

**Type**
Amphibious ASW and transport helicopter, 4 man crew
**Weights**
empty 12,083 lb (5,383 kg)
normal 18,626 lb (8,449 kg)
maximum 20,500 lb (9,297 kg)
**Performance**
maximum speed at sea level 166 mph (267 km/hr)
maximum cruising speed 148 mph (238 km/hr)
ferry range 625 miles (1,004 km)
initial rate of climb 40.0 fps (11.2 m/sec)
service ceiling 14,700 ft (4,480 m)
hovering ceiling out of ground effect 6,506 ft (1,983 m)
**Dimensions**
main rotor diameter 61 ft 11¼ in (18.88 m)
length of fuselage 54 ft 9 in (16.69 m)
height 15 ft 3¾ in (4.67)
**Power plant**
Two 1,400 hp General Electric T58-GE-10 turboshafts
**Armament**
Max 840 lb (381 kg) weapon load; e.g. 2 homing torpedoes or depth charges
**Payload**
S-61A: 2–3 man crew and 26 troops or 15 stretcher cases
**Variants**
*SH-3A*: Earlier version, 105 converted to SH-3G and SH-3H, plus 9 converted to RH-3A mine-sweeping helicopters; *S-61A (CH-3B), VH-3A*: Transport helicopters; *HH-3A*: Rescue helicopter; *SeaKing*: British licence-built SH-3D by Westland
**First flights**
Prototype: 11 March 1959
**Production**
*SH-3A*: 255 built from 1961–1965, plus 57 (46?) Japanese licence-built by Mitsubishi from 1964;
*SH-3D*: 74 built from 1965–1972, plus 34 Italian licence-built by Agusta;
*CH-3B*: 6 built; *VH-3A*: 10 built; *HH-3A*: 12 built
**In service**
*SH-3A*: Canada (CHSS-2), Japan, United States;
*SH-3D*: Brazil, Iran, Italy, Spain, United States;
*S-61A*: Denmark, Malaysia (Nuri);
*CH-3B, HH-3A, RH-3A, SH-3G, SH-3H, VH-3A*: United States;
*S-61D-4*: Argentine

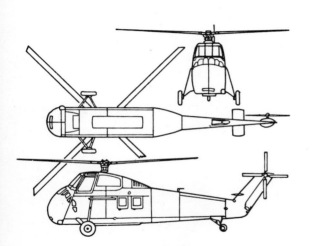

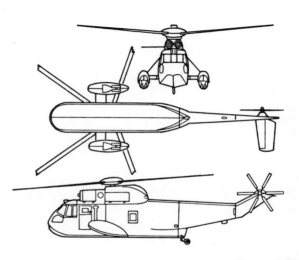

## SIKORSKY S–61R (CH–3E)

**Type**
Amphibious transport and rescue helicopter
**Weights**
empty 13,250 lb (6,010 kg)
normal 21,242 lb (9,635 kg)
maximum 22,050 lb (10,000 kg)
**Performance**
maximum speed at sea level 163 mph (261 km/hr)
maximum cruising speed 144 mph (232 km/hr)
range 465 miles (748 km)
ferry range 780 miles (1,255 km)
initial rate of climb 21.7 fps (6.6 m/sec)
service ceiling 12,205 ft (3,720 m)
hovering ceiling in ground effect 4,101 ft (1,250 m)
**Dimensions**
main rotor diameter 62 ft 0 in (18.90 m)
length of fuselage 57 ft 3 in (17.45 m)
height 18 ft 1 in (5.51 m)
**Power plant**
Two 1,500 hp General Electric T–58–GE–5 turboshafts
**Armament**
Optional: Two weapon pods each containing one 7.62 mm
  Minigun
**Payload**
2–3 man crew and 25–30 troops or 15 stretcher cases or
  max 5,000 lb (2,270 kg) freight
**Variants**
*CH–3C*: Earlier version (with less powerful engines);
  all modified to CH–3E standard;
*HH–3E, HH–3F Pelican*: Rescue helicopters
**First flights**
Prototype: 17 June 1963
**Production**
Series production from 1963; *CH–3C*: 41 built; *CH–3E*:
  42 built from 1966; *HH–3E*: 50 built; *HH–3F*: 58(40?)
  built, licence-built in Italy by Agusta (20 from 1974/75?)
**In service**
United States

## SIKORSKY S–62A

**Type**
Amphibious transport helicopter
**Weights**
empty 4,957 lb (2,248 kg)
maximum 7,900 lb (3,583 kg)
**Performance**
maximum speed at sea level 101 mph (163 km/hr)
maximum cruising speed 92 mph (148 km/hr)
range 462 miles (743 km)
initial rate of climb 19.0 fps (5.8 m/sec)
service ceiling 6,600 ft (2,010 m)
hovering ceiling in ground effect 12,200 ft (3,720 m)
hovering ceiling out of ground effect 1,700 ft (520 m)
**Dimensions**
main rotor diameter 53 ft 0 in (16.16 m)
length of fuselage 44 ft 6½ in (13.58 m)
height 16 ft 0 in (4.88 m)
**Power plant**
One 1,250 hp General Electric CT58–110–1 turboshaft
**Payload**
2 man crew and 12 troops or max 3,017 lb (1,368 kg)
  freight
**Variants**
*C–62C*: Military export and civil version
**First flights**
Prototype: 14 May 1958
**Production**
Series production from 1960; 26 licence-built in Japan
  by Mitsubishi from 1963
**In service**
Iceland, India, Japan, Phillipines, Thailand

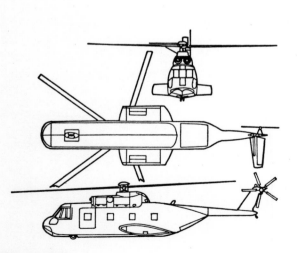

## SIKORSKY HH–52A

**Type**
Amphibious transport helicopter
Details as for S–62A with the following exceptions
**Weights**
empty 5,053 lb (2,306 kg)
normal 8,100 lb (3,674 kg)
**Performance**
maximum speed at sea level 109 mph (175 km/hr)
maximum cruising speed 98 mph (158 km/hr)
range 475 miles (765 km)
initial rate of climb 18.0 fps (5.5 m/sec)
service ceiling 11,200 ft (3,410 m)
hovering ceiling in ground effect 14,100 ft (4,295 m)
hovering ceiling out of ground effect 4,600 ft (1,400 m)
**Power plant**
One 1,250 hp General Electric T58–GE–8 turboshaft
**Production**
99 built
**In service**
United States

## SIKORSKY S–64 'SKYCRANE' (CH–54A 'TARHE')

**Type**
Heavy flying-crane helicopter
**Weights**
empty 19,234 lb (8,724 kg)
normal 38,000 lb (17,237 kg)
maximum 42,000 lb (19,050 kg)
**Performance**
maximum speed at sea level 127 mph (204 km/hr)
maximum cruising speed 109 mph (175 km/hr)
range 253 miles (407 km)
initial rate of climb 28.2 fps (8.6 m/sec)
service ceiling 13,000 ft (3,962 m)
hovering ceiling in ground effect 10,600 ft (3,230 m)
hovering ceiling out of ground effect 6,900 ft (2,100 m)
**Dimensions**
main rotor diameter 72 ft 0 in (21.95 m)
length of fuselage 70 ft 3 in (21.41 m)
height 18 ft 7 in (5.67 m)
**Power plant**
One 4,500 hp Pratt & Whitney T73–P–1 turboshaft
**Payload**
2–3 man crew and interchangeable pod with accommoda-
 tion for 45 troops or 24 stretcher cases or max 15,000 lb
 (6,800 kg) external freight load
**Variants**
*S–64E*: Civil variant of CH–54A;
*CH–54B* (*S–64F*): Further development with uprated
 (4,800 hp) power plant
**First flights**
Prototype: 9 May 1962; *CH–54B*: 30 June 1969
**Production**
CH54A: 3 prototypes, 6 pre-production models; 60 built
 from 1965–1968
**In service**
United States (CH–54A)

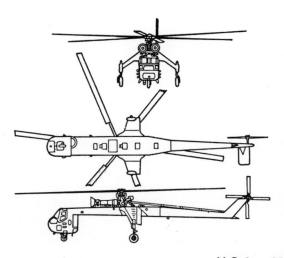

## SIKORSKY S–65A (CH–53A 'SEA STALLION')

**Type**
Heavy transport helicopter
**Weights** (apply specifically to CH–53D)
empty 23,485 lb (10,653 kg)
normal 36,400 lb (16,510 kg)
maximum 42,000 lb (19,050 kg)
**Performance**
maximum speed at sea level 195 mph (315 km/hr)
maximum cruising speed 173 mph (278 km/hr)
range 257 miles (413 km)
ferry range 806 miles (1,297 km)
initial rate of climb 36.5 fps (11.1 m/sec)
service ceiling 21,000 ft (6,400 m)
hovering ceiling in ground effect 13,400 ft (4,080 m)
hovering ceiling out of ground effect 6,500 ft (1,980 m)
**Dimensions**
main rotor diameter 72 ft 3 in (22.02 m)
length of fuselage 67 ft 2 in (20.47 m)
height 24 ft 9 in (7.55 m)
**Power plant**
Two 3,925 hp General Electric T–64–GE–413
  turboshafts
**Payload**
3 man crew and 38–64 troops or 24 stretcher cases and
  4 medics or freight
**Variants**
*CH–53A*: Earlier version;
*CH–53DG*: Export version of CH–53D for Germany
  (West);
*HH–53B, HH–53C*: Armed rescue and recovery
  helicopters, three 7.62 mm Miniguns;
*RH–53D*: Minesweeping helicopter;
*S–65C*: Export version for Austria
**First flights**
Prototype: 14 October 1964
*HH–53B*: 15 March 1967
**Production**
Series production from 1966; *CH–53A*: 106 built;
  *CH–53D*: — built; *CH–53DG*: 110 built, partly under
  licence in Germany by VFW-Fokker from 1972–1975;
  *HH–53B*: 8 built; *HH–53C*: 58 built; *RH–53D*: 30
  built; *S–65C*: 2 built in 1970
**In service**
*CH–53A Sea Stallion, CH–53D, HH–53B, RH–53D*:
  United States;
*CH–53D*: Germany (West);
*HH–53C*: Israel, United States;
*S–65C*: Austria (*S–650E*)

## VOUGHT A–7D 'CORSAIR' II

**Type**
Single-seat strike fighter
**Weights**
empty 19,275 lb (8,743 kg)
normal 30,000 lb (13,608 kg)
maximum 43,722 lb (19,832 kg)
**Performance**
maximum speed at sea level (Mach 0.92) 706 mph
  (1,125 km/hr)
radius of action 528 miles (850 km)
ferry range 3,879 miles (6,243 km)
initial rate of climb 225.7 fps (68.8 m/sec)
service ceiling 52,500 ft (16,000 m)
**Dimensions**
wing span 38 ft 8½ in (11.79 m)
length overall 14 ft 1½ in (14.06 m)
height overall 16 ft 0 in (4.88 m)
wing area 375 sq ft (34.84 sq m)
**Power plant**
One Allison TF41–A–1 turbofan rated at 14,250 lb
  (6,463 kg) st
**Armament**
One 20 mm M–61A–1 cannon with 1,000 rpg and max
  15,000 lb (6,804 kg) st weapon load on 8 hard points
**Variants**
*A–7A, A–7B, A–7C*: Earlier versions
*A–7H*: Two-seat strike trainer
**First flights**
Prototype: 27 September 1965;
*A–7D*: 6 April 1968
**Production**
*A–7A*: 199 built from 1966–1968;
*A–7B*: 196 built from 1968–1969;
*A–7C*: 67 built from 1969–1971;
*A–7D*: 645 delivered or on order from 1968
**In service**
*A–7A, B, C, D, E*: United States

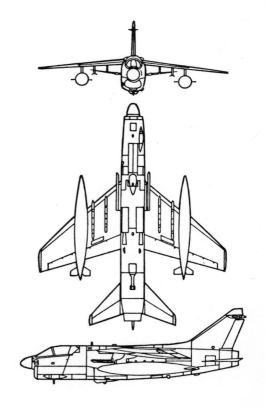

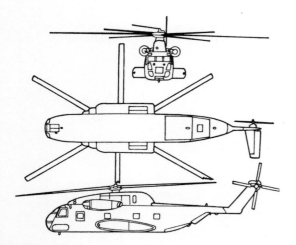

## VOUGHT A-7E 'CORSAIR' II

**Type**
Single-seat shipboard strike fighter
Details as for A-7D with the following exceptions
**Weights**
empty 17,571 lb (7,969 kg)
maximum 42,000 lb (19,050 kg)
**Performance**
ferry range 2,775 miles (4,465 km)
**Power plant**
One TF-41-A-Z (R.R. RB 168-62 Spey) turbofan rated
  at 15,000 lb (6,804 kg) st
**Armament**
Max 20,000 lb (9,072 kg) weapon load
**First flights**
*A-7E*: 25 November 1968
**Production**
551 delivered or on order from 1969

## VOUGHT F-8E & F-8J 'CRUSADER'

**Type**
Single-seat shipboard fighter and strike fighter
**Weights**
normal 28,000 lb (12,701 kg)
maximum 34,000 lb (15,422 kg)
**Performance**
maximum speed at 40,000 ft (12,200 m) (Mach 1.7)
  1,120 mph (1,802 km/hr)
maximum cruising speed at 36,000 ft (11,000 m) 560 mph
  (900 km/hr)
radius of action 600 miles (965 km)
ferry range 1,400 miles (2,253 km)
time to 40,000 ft (12,200 m) 5 min 0 sec
service ceiling 35,327 ft (17,675 m)
**Dimensions**
wing span 35 ft 8 in (10.87 m)
length overall 54 ft 6 in (16.61 m) (RF-8G: 54 ft 3 in
  (16.54 m)
height overall 15 ft 9 in (4.80 m)
wing area 375 sq ft (34.84 sq m)
**Power plant**
One Pratt & Whitney J57-P-20/22 turbojet rated at
  10,7000 lb (4,853 kg)/18,000 lb (8,165 kg) st
**Armament**
Four 20 mm Mk.12 cannon with 84 rpg and (as fighter)
  two-four Sidewinder AAMs or (as strike fighter) max
  5,000 lb (2,270 kg) weapon load, e.g. two AGM-12
  Bullpup ASMs or bombs and rockets; *RF-8*: 5 cameras
**Variants**
*F-8A, B, C, D*: Earlier versions;
*F-8E (FN)*: Shipboard strike fighter for France;
*F-8H, J, K, L*: Updated versions modified from 89 F-8D,
  136 F-8E, 87 F-8C and 63 F-8B;
*RF-8A*: Reconnaissance aircraft, 73 converted to RF-8G
**First flights**
Prototype: 25 March 1955; *F-8E*: 30 June 1961
**Production**
Series production from 1957-1965, conversions from 1966-
  1970; *F-8A*: 318 built; *F-8B*: 130 built; *F-8C*: 187
  built; *F-8D*: 152 built; *F-8E*: 286 built; *F-8E*(FN):
  42 built; *RF-8A*: 144 built
**In service**
*F-8E(FN)*: France;
*F-8H, J, K, L, RF-8G*: United States

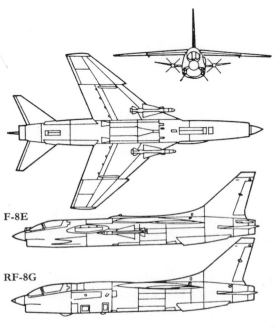

F-8E

RF-8G

## AERO 3

**Type**
Two-seat trainer
**Weights**
maximum 2,647 lb (1,200 kg)
**Performance**
maximum speed at sea level 143 mph (230 km/hr)
maximum cruising speed at 2,953 ft (900 m) 112 mph
  (180 km/hr)
ferry range 423 miles (680 km)
service ceiling 14,100 ft (4,300 m)
**Dimensions**
wing span 34 ft 5 in (10.50 m)
length overall 28 ft 1 in (8.58 m)
height overall 8 ft 10 in (2.69 m)
**Power plant**
One 185 (190?) hp Lycoming 0–435–A piston engine
**Variants**
Aero 2: Earlier version
**Production**
Series production from 1957
**In service**
Yugoslavia

## SOKO G–2A 'GALEB'

**Type**
Two-seat trainer
**Weights**
empty 5,485 lb (2,488 kg)
normal 7,690 lb (3,488 kg)
maximum 9,211 lb (4,178 kg)
**Performance**
maximum speed at sea level 470 mph (756 km/hr)
maximum speed at 20,340 ft (6,200 m) 505 mph
  (812 km/hr)
ferry range 770 miles (1,240 km)
initial rate of climb 74.8 fps (22.8 m/sec)
time to 19,680 ft (6,000 m) 5 min 30 sec
service ceiling 39,375 ft (12,000 m)
**Dimensions**
wing span 5 ft 4 in (10.47 m)
length overall 33 ft 11 in (10.34 m)
height overall 10 ft 8¾ in (3.28 m)
wing area 209.1 sq ft (19.43 sq m)
**Power plant**
One Rolls–Royce Bristol Viper 11 Mk.22–6 turbojet
  rated at 2,500 lb (1,134 kg) st
**Armament**
Two 12.7 mm machine guns with 160 rpg and max 440 lb
  (200 kg) weapon load, e.g. two or four 110 lb (50 kg)
  bombs, or four 57 mm rockets or two 127 mm rockets
**Variants**
*G–3A Galeb*: Further development of G–2A
**First flights**
Prototype: May 1961;
1st production model: February 1963
**Production**
Approx 150 built from 1963–1970
**In service**
Tanzania, Yugoslavia, Zambia

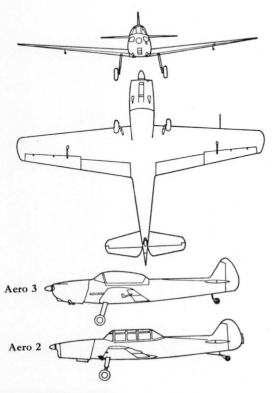

Aero 3

Aero 2

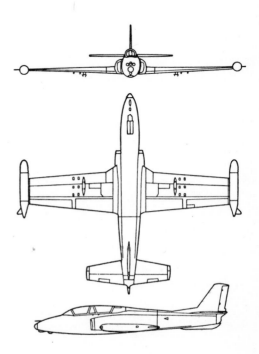

## SOKO J–1 'JASTREB'

**Type**
Single-seat light ground-attack aircraft
Details as for G–2A with the following exceptions
**Weights**
empty 5,759 lb (2,612 kg)
normal 8,757 lb (3,972 kg)
maximum 9,859 lb (4,472 kg)
**Performance**
maximum speed at 19,680 ft (6,000 m) 510 mph
 (820 km/hr)
maximum cruising speed at 16,400 ft (5,000 m) 460 mph
 (740 km/hr)
ferry range 944 miles (1,520 km)
initial rate of climb 68.9 fps (21.0 m/sec)
**Dimensions**
wing span 5 ft 8 in (10.56 m)
length overall 35 ft 1 in (10.71 m)
height overall 11 ft 11 in (3.64 m)
wing area 204.5 sq ft (19.00 sq m)
**Power plant**
One Rolls–Royce Viper 531 turbojet rated at 3,120 lb
 (1,415 kg) st
**Armament**
Two 12.7 mm machine guns with 135 rpg and max
 1,100 lb (500 kg) weapon load on 8 hard points, e.g.
 two 550 lb (250 kg) bombs or six 57 mm or 127 mm
 rockets or two 33 gall (150l) napalm
**Variants**
*J–2 Jastreb*: Light reconnaissance aircraft with 3–5
 cameras
**Production**
*J–1, J–2*: Series production from 1968
**In service**
*J–1, J–2*: Yugoslavia, Zambia

## SOKO P–2 'KRAGUJ'

**Type**
Single-seat light ground-attack aircraft
**Weights**
empty 2,491 lb (1,130 kg)
maximum 3,580 lb (1,624 kg)
**Performance**
maximum speed at sea level 171 mph (275 km/hr)
maximum speed at 5,000 ft (1,500 m) 183 mph (295 km/hr)
maximum cruising speed at 5,000 ft (1,500 m) 174 mph
 (280 km/hr)
ferry range 497 miles (800 km)
initial rate of climb 22.3 fps (6.8 m/sec)
**Dimensions**
wing span 34 ft 11 in (10.64 m)
length overall 26 ft 10 in (7.93 m)
height overall 9 ft 10 in (3.00 m)
wing area 183 sq ft (17.00 sq m)
**Power plant**
One 340 hp Lycoming GS0–480–B1A6 piston engine
**Armament**
Two 7.62 mm machine guns with 325 rpg, two 220 lb
 (100 kg) bombs or two 33 gall (150 l) napalm tanks or
 two rocket launchers each containing twelve 55 mm
 unguided rockets
**First flights**
Prototype: 1966
**Production**
30 (40?) built from 1958–1971/72
**In service**
Yugoslavia

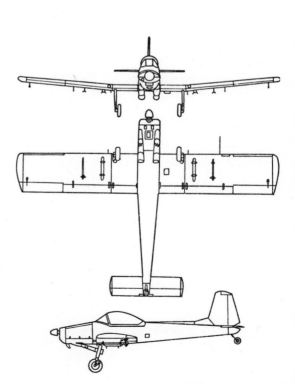

## UTVA–60AT1

**Type**
Liaison and reconnaissance aircraft
**Weights**
empty 2,100 lb (952 kg)
normal 3,192 lb (1,448 kg)
maximum 3,571 lb (1,620 kg)
**Performance**
maximum speed at sea level 157 mph (252 km/hr)
maximum cruising speed 143 mph (230 km/hr)
range 485 miles (780 km)
ferry range 590 miles (950 km)
initial rate of climb 21 fps (6.4 m/sec)
service ceiling 17,000 ft (5,200 m)
**Dimensions**
wing span 37 ft 5 in (11.40 m)
length overall 26 ft 11½ in (8.22 m)
height overall 8 ft 11 in (2.72 m)
wing area 194.5 sq ft (18.08 sq m)
**Power plant**
One 270 hp Lycoming G0–480–B136 piston engines
**Payload**
1 man crew and 3 troops or (U–60AM) 2 stretcher cases
   and 1 medic or max 908 lb (412 kg) freight
**Variants**
*U–60H*: Floatplane
*UTVA–66*: Further development
**First flights**
Prototype: *UTVA–56*: 22 April 1959;
*UTVA–60*: 1960; *UTVA–66*: 1967
**Production**
*UTVA–60*: Series production from 1960
**In service**
*UTVA–60, UTVA–66*: Yugoslavia

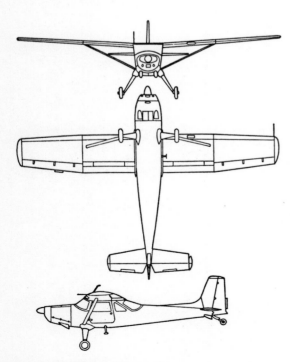

# Weaponry

## AIRCRAFT ARMAMENT
Abbreviations

| | | | |
|---|---|---|---|
| CAL | = Calibre | RW | = Round weight |
| GW | = Gun weight | | (machine-gun) |
| L | = Length | s/min | = Shots/minute |
| LW | = Launch weight | SW | = Shell weight |
| M | = Mach | | (cannon) |
| R | = Range | $v_0$ | = Muzzle velocity |
| RF | = Rate of fire | | |

## Guns
The difference between machine-guns and cannon lies not in the weapons themselves, but in the ammunition they use. While machine-guns fire metal-cased bullets, cannon employ shells fitted with rotating rings.

Aircraft of the Western powers are armed with machine-guns as well as cannon. The advent of the armed helicopter and, in part, the counter-insurgency (COIN) ground-attack aircraft has given a new lease of life to the machine-gun. Special emphasis is placed upon high rates of fire and muzzle velocity. Cannon calibres are generally in the 20 to 30 mm range. The United States keeps to a standard 20 mm calibre.

In contrast the Soviet Union first introduced larger calibres: cannon of 23 and 37 mm calibre, which were not replaced by 30 mm weapons until much later. Machine-guns are only occasionally to be found in older types of aircraft. The Soviet emphasis was laid upon shell weight, with a limited overall weapon weight being achieved at the expense of rate of fire and muzzle velocity.

## FRANCE
*7.5 mm A–52 machine gun*
GW 24.31 lb (11 kg), RW 9.0 g, $v_0$ 2,707 ft/sec (825 m/sec), RF 700 s/min
Army weapon, employed in helicopters.
*20 mm MG151 cannon*
GW 92.6 lb (42 kg), SW 90g, $v_0$ 2,362 ft/sec (720 m/sec), RF 780 s/min
German World War II design, employed in helicopters.
*30 mm DEFA552 cannon*
GW 176.4 lb (80 kg), SW 224 g, $v_0$ 2,674 ft/sec (815 m/sec), RF 1,100–1,500 s/min
Equips French aircraft and G.91R.3
*30 mm DEFA553 cannon*
GW 187.4 lb (85 kg), SW 244 g, $v_0$ 2,674 ft/sec (815 m/sec), RF 1,200–1,300 s/min
Equips latest French aircraft and A–4H.
The 20 mm DEFA621 cannon is currently under test for helicopter employment.

## GREAT BRITAIN
*20 mm Mk.5 cannon*
GW 99.2 lb (45 kg), SW 122 g, $v_0$ 2,789 ft/sec (850 m/sec), RF 800 s/min
Hispano-Suiza design licence-built since beginning of World War II, equips Canberra
*30 mm Aden Mk.4 cannon*
GW 198.4 lb (90 kg), SW 276 g, $v_0$ 1,969 ft/sec (600 m/sec), RF 1,200 s/min
Equips British fighters and strike fighters.

## SWITZERLAND
*20 mm HS–804 cannon*
GW 99.2 lb (45 kg), SW 120 g, $v_0$ 2,723 ft/sec (830 m/sec), RF 750–800 s/min
Equips A 32A Lansen and Venom FB.50

## SOVIET UNION
*12.7 mm UB machine-gun*
GW 48.5 lb (22 kg), RW 48 g, $v_0$ 2,625 ft/sec (800 m/sec), RF 1,000 s/min
Equips MiG–15UTI
*20 mm B–20 cannon*
GW 55.1 lb (25 kg), SW 96 g, $v_0$ 2,625 ft/sec (800 m/sec), RF 800 s/min
Equips maritime reconnaissance aircraft.
*23 mm NR–23 cannon*
GW 86 lb (39 kg), SW 196 g, $v_0$ 2,264 ft/sec (690 m/sec), RF 850 (650)[1] s/min.
Nudelmann–Richter design. Equips fighters, strike fighters, bombers and transports.
*30 mm NR–30 cannon*
GW 145.5 lb (66 kg), SW 410 g, $v_0$ 2,559 ft/sec (780 m/sec), RF 900 s/min
Equips all cannon-armed aircraft entering service after 1955.
*37 mm NS–37 cannon*
GW 227 lb (103 kg), SW 735 g, $v_0$ 2,264 ft/sec (690 m/sec), RF 400 (450)[1] s/min
Nudelmann–Suranov design. Equips older-type fighters and strike fighters
[1] theoretical (figure obtained from practical tests)

## UNITED STATES
*7.62 mm M–60C, D machine-gun*
GW 22 lb (10 kg), RW 9.5 g, $v_0$ 2,799 ft/sec (853 m/sec), RF 550 s/min
Derivative of army weapon, employed in helicopters and ground-attack aircraft.
*7.62 mm M–37C machine-gun*
GW 30.9 lb (14 kg), RW 9.5 g, $v_0$ 2,799 ft/sec (853 m/sec), RF 550 s/min
Derivative of tank machine-gun, employed in helicopters
*7.62 mm Heligun machine-gun*
RW 9.5 g, $v_0$ 2,799 ft/sec (853 m/sec), RF 4,000 s/min
Twin-barrelled rotating machine-gun, employed in helicopters.
*7.62 mm M–134 Minigun or GAU–2B/A machine-gun*
GW 48.5 lb (22 kg), RW 9.5 g, $v_0$ 2,799 ft/sec (853 m/sec), RF 3,000 or 6,000 s/min
Six-barrelled rotating machine-gun, employed in helicopters and (podded) in 'Gun Ships'.
*12.7 mm M–2 machine-gun*
GW 83.8 lb (38 kg), RW 45 g, $v_0$ 2,930 ft/sec (893 m/sec), RF 500–650 s/min
Army weapon, employed in helicopters.
*12.7 mm M–3 machine-gun*
GW 64 lb (29 kg), RW 45 g, $v_0$ 2,841 ft/sec (866 m/sec), RF 1,200 s/min
Equips F–84, F–86, G.91R.1, also in weapon packs.
*20 mm M–11 cannon*
GW 229.3 lb (104 kg), SW 110 g, $v_0$ 3,199 ft/sec (975 m/sec), RF 700 or 4,200 s/min
Naval weapon, twin-barrelled, in weapon packs for strike fighters.
*20 mm M–24A1 cannon*
GW 114.6 lb (52 kg), SW 130 g, $v_0$ 2,749 ft/sec (838 m/sec), RF 750–850 s/min.
Licence-built Hispano-Suiza design. Equips F–86K.
*20 mm M–39 cannon*
GW 111 lb (63 kg), SW 104 g, $v_0$ 3,300 ft/sec (1,006 m/sec), RF 1,200–1,500 s/min
Equips F–100, F–5.
*20 mm M–61, A, Vulcan or GAU–4 cannon*
GW 200–211 lb (114–120 kg), SW 104 g, $v_0$ 3,399 ft/sec (1,036 m/sec), RF 6,000–6,600 s/min
Six-barrelled rotating cannon, equips F–104, F–105, F–4E, in weapon pods.
*20 mm M–12 cannon*

GW 101.4 lb (46 kg), SW 110 g, v₀ 3,199 ft/sec (975 m/sec), RF 1,000 s/min

Equips only carrier-borne aircraft
*40 mm M–5 automatic grenade-launcher*
SW 170 g, RF 250 s/min
Equips helicopters

In addition trials are currently being carried out with a large number of grenade-launcher and cannon prototypes for helicopter employment. The French 30 mm DEFA553 cannon is being produced under licence and used to equip aircraft delivered to Israel. The 30 mm GAU–8/A and 25 mm GAU–7/A are under development for the A–10A and the F–15A respectively.

**Air-to-Air Missiles (AAM)**
AAMs equipped with an *Infra-red homing head* necessitate orthodox fighter tactics: the attacking aircraft must close the enemy from the rear. This position is particularly difficult to achieve if the attacker has only a marginal advantage in speed. In addition this homing head possesses disadvantages in bad weather (rain and fog).

With AAMs equipped with *Radar-guidance* attacks can also be mounted along an intersecting course; beam attacks are also possible. They can be carried by attacking aircraft which are slower than their target. But this method of guidance is affected by ground-echo at low-altitude.

The majority of AAMs are fitted with either proximity-fuses or proximity and contact-fuses.

**FRANCE**
*Matra R.511*
L 10.14 ft (3.09 m), LW 397 lb (180 kg), M 1.8, R 4.4 mls (7 km), Radar
*Matra R.530*
L 10.76 ft (3.28 m), LW 430 lb (195 kg), M 2.7, R 11.2 mls (18 km), Radar or Infra-red

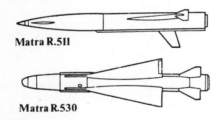

**Matra R.511**

**Matra R.530**

**GREAT BRITAIN**
*Firestreak*
L 10.47 ft (3.19 m), LW 300 lb (136 kg), M2+, R 5.0 mls (8 km), Infra-red
*Red Top*
L 11.48 ft (3.50 m), LW 300 lb (136 kg), M 3, R 6.8 mls (11 km), Infra-red

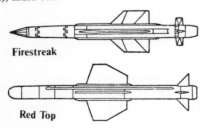

**Firestreak**

**Red Top**

**JAPAN**
*AAM1*
L 8.53 ft (2.60 m), LW 154 lb (70 kg), M 2.5, R 4.4 mls (7 km), Infra-red

**SOVIET UNION**
While nearly all Western fighters and strike fighters are built to carry various types of AAMs, in the Eastern bloc almost every aircraft type is equipped with a different missile. The names quoted below are the official NATO code designations.

*Alkali*
L 6.99 ft (2.13 m), LW 201 lb (91 kg), R 3.7 mls (6 km), Radar for MiG–17, MiG–19, Su–9, Yak–25
*Anab*
L 13–15.09 ft (3.96–4.6 m), LW 500 lb (277 kg), R 6.2 mls (10 km) Infra-red or radar for Su–9, Su–11, Yak–28P
*Ash*
L 15.4–18 ft (4.69–5.49 m) LW 441 lb (200 kg), R 6.8 mls (11 km), Infra-red or radar for Tu–28
*Atoll*
L 9.15 ft (2.79 m), LW 154 lb (70 kg), R 1.8 mls (3 km), Infra-red for MiG–19, MiG–21
*Awl*
L 15.09 ft (4.6 m), R 5.0 mls (8 km), Infra-red for MiG–25

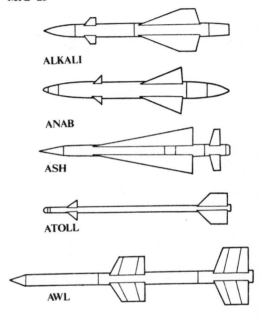

**ALKALI**

**ANAB**

**ASH**

**ATOLL**

**AWL**

**SWEDEN**
*Rb24*
L 9.19 ft (2.8 m), LW 159 lb (72 kg), M 2.5, R 4.4 mls (7 km) Infra-red
Licence-built *Sidewinder*
*Rb27* (HM–55)
L 7.15 ft (2.18 m), LW 150 lb (68 kg), M 2.5, R 5.6 mls (9 km), Radar
Licence-built *AIM–4E Falcon*

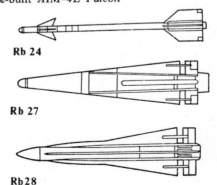

**Rb 24**

**Rb 27**

**Rb 28**

## UNITED STATES

*AIM–9B Sidewinder 1A*
L 9.19 ft (2.8 m), LW 159 lb (72 kg), M 2, R 4.4 mls
  (7 km), Infra-red
*AIM–9C Sidewinder 1B*
L 9.19 ft (2.8 m), LW 159 lb (72 kg), M 2.5, R 6.2 mls
  (10 km), Radar
*AIM–9D Sidewinder 1C*
L 9.51 ft (2.9 m), LW 185 lb (84 kg), M 2.5, R 6.2 mls
  (10 km) Infra-red
*AIM–4A Falcon*
L 6.89 ft (2.10 m), LW 126 lb (57 kg), M 2, R 5.0 mls
  (8 km), Radar
*AIM–4C Falcon*
L 6.5 ft (1.98 m), LW 110 lb (50 kg), M 2, R 5.0 mls
  (8 km), Infra-red
*AIM–4D Falcon*
L 6.63 ft (2.02 m), LW 134 lb (61 kg), M 2.5, R 5.6 mls
  (9 km), Infra-red
*AIM–4E Super Falcon*
L 7.15 ft (2.18 m), LW 141 lb (64 kg), M2.5+, R 5.6 mls
  (9 km), Radar
*AIM 4F Super Falcon*
L 6.73 ft (2.05 m), LW 146 lb (66 kg), M 2.5, R 6.8 mls
  (11 km), Radar
*AIM–4G Super Falcon*
L 6.76 ft (2.06 m), LW 146 lb (66 kg), M 2.5, R 6.8 mls
  (11 km), Infra-red
*AIM–26A Nuclear Falcon*
L 6.99 ft (2.13 m), LW 249 lb (113 kg), M 2, R 5.6 mls
  (9 km), Radar, Nuclear warhead
*AIM–26B Falcon*
As AIM–26A, but with conventional warhead
*AIM–47A Falcon*
L 12.01 ft (3.66 m), LW 800 lb (363 kg), M 6, R 46.6 mls
  (75 km), Infra-red or Radar. Also with Nuclear warhead
*AIR–2A Genie*
L 9.55 ft (2.91 m), LW 820 lb (372 kg), M 3, R 5.6 mls
  (9 km), Unguided, Nuclear warhead
*AIM–7E Sparrow IIIB*
L 12.01 ft (3.66 m), LW 399 lb (181 kg), M 3.5, R 16.2 mls
  (26 km), Radar.
*AIM 7F* Similar
*AIM–54A Phoenix*
L 12.99 ft (3.96 m), LW 838 lb (380 kg), R 68.4–99.4 mls
  (110–160 km), Radar

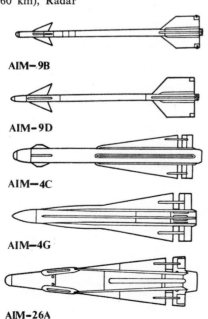

**AIM–9B**

**AIM–9D**

**AIM–4C**

**AIM–4G**

**AIM–26A**

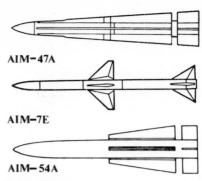

**AIM–47A**

**AIM–7E**

**AIM–54A**

## Air-to-Surface Missiles (ASM)

ASMs constitute the main armament of strike fighters and
bombers to an ever-increasing degree. They can be
launched during the approach to the target while still out
of range of the defences. Some are also used as decoys
(to simulate an aircraft target). Other types are intended
specifically to destroy radar installations. They home automatically on to the transmitter. More and more ASMs
are being employed especially in the anti-shipping role.

## FRANCE

*Nord A.S.12*
L 6.14 ft (1.87 m), LW 165 lb (75 kg), R 3.7 mls (6 km),
  Wire-guidance
*Nord A.S.20*
L 8.53 ft (2.60 m), LW 315 lb (143 kg), R 4.4 mls (7 km),
  Radio-guidance, Licence-built in Germany
*Nord A.S.30*
L 12.80 ft (3.90 m), I W 1,146 lb (520 kg), R 7.5 mls
  (12 km), Radio-guidance
*Nord A.S.30L*
L 11.81 ft (3.60 m), LW 838 lb (380 kg), R 6.8 mls (11 km),
  Radio-guidance
*Matra Martel A.S.37*
L 12.99 ft (3.96 m), Radio and Radar-guidance

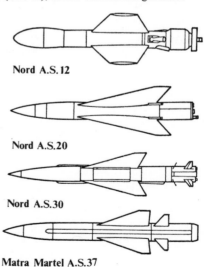

**Nord A.S.12**

**Nord A.S.20**

**Nord A.S.30**

**Matra Martel A.S.37**

## GERMANY

*Kormoran*
L 14.44 ft (4.40 m), LW 1,323 lb (600 kg), R 24.9 mls
  (40 km), Inertia navigation

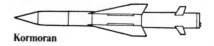

**Kormoran**

## GREAT BRITAIN
*Martel AJ168*
L 12.0 ft (3.66 m), Radio and television-guidance
*Blue Steel*
L 34.84 ft (10.62 m), R 230 mls (370 km), Inertia navigation

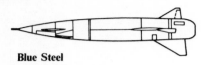

**Blue Steel**

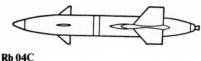

**Rb 04C**

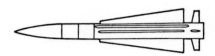

**Rb 05A**

## SOVIET UNION
The names quoted below are the official NATO code-designations. The majority of the missiles are intended for the anti-shipping role.

Performance details are estimated
*Kangaroo*
L 49.9 ft (15.2 m), R 298.3 mls (480 km). For Tu–20
*Kelt*
L 31.0 ft (9.45 m), R 99.4 mls (160 km). For Tu–16
*Kennel*
L 25.92 ft (7.9 m), LW 6,610 lb (3,000 kg), R 93.2 mls (150 km). For Tu–16
*Kipper*
L 31.0 ft (9.45 m), R 124.3 mls (200 km). For Tu–16
*Kitchen*
L 35.99 ft (10.97 m), R 198.8 mls (320 km). For Tu–22
*Soviet Air-to-Surface Missiles*

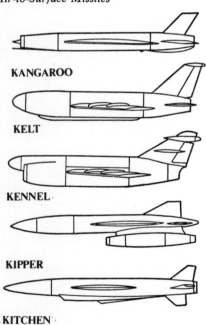

**KANGAROO**

**KELT**

**KENNEL**

**KIPPER**

**KITCHEN**

## SWEDEN
*Robot Rb04C*
L 14.6 ft (4.45 m), LW 1,323 lb (600 kg), Autopilot-control.
*Robot Rb04D* Similar
*Robot Rb04E*
Improved version of *Rb04C*
*Robot Rb05A*
L 11.77 ft (3.75 m), LW 661 lb (300 kg), Radio-guidance

## UNITED STATES
*AGM–12A Bullpup*
L 10.5 ft (3.2 m), LW 571 lb (259 kg), R 5.6 mls (9 km) Radio-guidance
*AGM–12B Bullpup A*
L 10.5 ft (3.2 m), LW 571 lb (259 kg), R 6.8 mls (11 km), Radio-guidance. *AGM–12E* Similar
*AGM–12C Bullpup B*
L 13.58 ft (4.14 m), LW 1,786 lb (810 kg), R 9.9 mls (16 km). Radio-guidance. *AGM–12D* with Nuclear warhead but otherwise similar
*AGM–28B Hound Dog*
L 42.03 ft (12.81 m), LW 10,145 lb (4,602 kg), R 786 mls (1,265 km), Inertia navigation, Nuclear warhead.
*AGM–45A Shrike*
L 10.01 ft (3.05 m), LW 390 lb (177 kg), R 9.9 mls (16 km), Radar-guidance
*AGM–53A Condor*
L 20.01 ft (6.10 m), LW 2,500 lb (1,134 kg), R 46 mls (74 km), Television and Automatic-guidance
*AGM–65A Maverick*
L 8.07 ft (2.46 m), LW 474 lb (215 kg), Television and Automatic-guidance
*AGM–69A SRAM[1]*
L 14.01 ft (4.27 m), LW 2,240 lb (1,016 kg), R 138 mls (222 km), Inertia navigation, Nuclear warhead
*ADM–20C Quail*
L 12.83 ft (3.91 m), LW 1,208 lb (548 kg), R 400 mls (640 km), Inertia guidance, Anti-radar-device
*AGM–78A Standard ARM[2]*
L 14.01 ft (4.27 m), LW 1,301 lb (590 kg), R 15.5 mls (25 km), Radar-guidance
[1] SRAM = Short-Range-Attack-Missile
[2] ARM = Anti-Radar-Missile

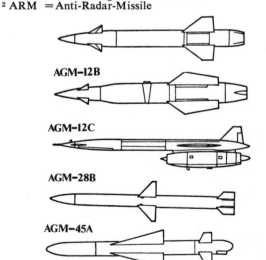

**AGM–12B**

**AGM–12C**

**AGM–28B**

**AGM–45A**

**AGM–53A**

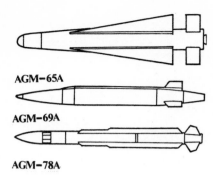

AGM–65A

AGM–69A

AGM–78A

## Unguided Rockets

The advantages of rockets over guns are twofold—their simpler method of firing, and their larger calibre. This means that a bigger warhead can be delivered on target. To compensate for the spreading effect use is made of high speeds, stabilizing fins, and the firing of rockets in salvoes. The line of flight of unguided rockets is governed by the direction of the whole aircraft at the moment of launching.

### FRANCE
*37 mm SNEB Rocket*
LW 2.21 lb (1.0 kg). In packs of 16 and 36 rockets, sometimes also housed in nose of auxiliary fuel tanks.
*68 mm SNEB Rocket*
LW 9.5–13.9 lb (4.3–6.3 kg). In packs of 19 or 36 rockets, sometimes also housed in nose of auxiliary fuel tanks.
*120 mm Rocket*
LW 60 lb (27.2 kg). Obsolescent

### GREAT BRITAIN
*51 mm Rocket (2")*
In packs of 12, 19, 24, 31 and 37 rockets. Also integral launching trays
*76.2 mm Rocket (3")*
LW 81.6 lb (37 kg), in packs of 6 rockets or individually mounted

### ISRAEL
*82 mm Rocket*
In packs of 6 rockets

### ITALY
*50 mm Rocket*

### SOVIET UNION
*35 mm Rocket*
In packs of 8, 16 and 19 rockets
*137 mm M100 Rocket*
LW 34.4 lb (15.6 kg). Individually mounted
*190 mm TRS–190 Rocket*
LW 101.4 lb (46.0 kg). Individually mounted.
*212 mm ARS–121 Rocket*
LW 256 lb (116 kg). Individually mounted

### SPAIN
*37 mm INTA S9 Rocket*
In packs of 18 and launchers of 54 rockets
*57 mm Rocket*
*70 mm Rocket*
In packs of 6 and 18 rockets
*100 mm INTA S–12*
In packs of 6 rockets

### SWEDEN
*75 mm M57 Rocket*
LW 15.4 lb (7.0 kg). In packs of 19 rockets or individually mounted

*135 mm M56 and M60 Rocket*
LW 92.6 lb (42.0 kg). In packs of 6 rockets or individually mounted
*145 mm Rocket*
Obsolescent
*180 mm Rocket*
Obsolescent

### SWITZERLAND
*80 mm R–80 SURA Rocket*
LW 26.2 lb (11.9 kg). Individually mounted

### UNITED STATES
*70 mm FFAR[1] Mighty Mouse (2.75") Rocket*
LW 18.7 lb (8.5 kg). In packs of 7, 16 and 19 rockets
*127 mm ZUNI (5") Rocket*
LW 106.9 lb (48.5 kg). In packs of 4 and 7 rockets, also individually mounted
*127 mm HVAR[2] (5") Rocket*
LW 136.7 lb (62 kg). Obsolescent
[1] FFAR = Folding-Fin Aerial Rocket
[2] HVAR = High-Velocity-Aircraft-Rocket

## Bombs
Only the more important of the numerous types of bombs currently in service are listed below. Little is known of the types employed by the Eastern bloc, but it is safe to assume that they correspond in the main to those of the West.
*General Purpose Bomb (GP):*
Because of the ratio of explosive to overall weight (approx 50%), also known as 50% bomb. Employed in many roles in the 100 lb (45 kg) to 4,000 lb (1,800 kg) weight range, fitted with nose and tail-fuses, some also with time-fuses.
*Armour Piercing Bomb (AP):*
Also known as 15% bomb. Employed against targets protected by armour or concrete, tail-fuse only.
*Semi-Armour Piercing Bomb (SAP):*
Also known as 30% bomb. Employed against targets protected by medium-thickness armour, mainly tail-fuses.
*Light Case Bomb (LC):*
No fragmentation effect, increased explosive content.
*Fragmentation Bomb (FRAG):*
Increased fragmentation effect, employed on anti-personnel operations. Also as cluster ("ripple") bombs in canisters.
*Incendiary Bomb (INC)*
*Fire Bomb (Napalm):*
Employed against combustible targets, tanks and field-works. As an anti-personnel weapon its effect is achieved by the removal of oxygen from the air. The very thin-walled bomb is normally first attached to the aircraft's bomb-pylon and then filled. The mixture is composed of petrol, to which is added napalm-powder. In emergencies auxiliary fuel tanks can also be employed as fire-bombs.
*Flare, Photoflash or Target Identification Bomb.*
*Practice Bomb*
*Nuclear Weapons:*
Obviously no specific details are available about these bombs. The lightest, capable of delivery by future NATO strike fighters, has an approx weight of 2,000 lb (907 kg)
*Depth Charge:*
Serves in the ASW role. Known types include those of the United States, 325 lb (147.5 kg); France, 353 lb (160 kg); and France/United States, 386 lb (175 kg). The American Mk.101 Lulu nuclear depth charge is a special case.
*Smart Bomb:*
Television or laser-guidance. Television-guidance is performed manually from a monitor in the launch-aircraft via a camera installed in the bomb, or automatically by pre-setting the objective for the camera prior to launch.
Laser-guidance is achieved by illuminating the objective in a Laser-beam from the launch-aircraft or from an accompanying aircraft; the infra-red sensors in the bomb guide it to the target automatically. A further possibility lies in automatic homing from heat sources, e.g. vehicle

engines, by infra-red guidance.

**Aircraft torpedoes**
Despite the introduction of new and improved models after the Second World War, the importance of the torpedo as an anti-surface-vessel weapon has waned drastically. Although the height of release has now risen to above 328 ft (100 m) and speeds too have increased, modern anti-aircraft defences have rendered the conventional torpedo attack, with its requisite straight and level approach flight, all but impossible. For operations against surface vessels most countries have replaced the torpedo by the ASM.

But homing torpedoes are still in general use in the ASW role. They are fitted with search equipment with a range of up to 1,094 yds (1,000 m) and are designed for use in depths of up to 985 ft (300 m).

**FRANCE**
*L4 Homing Torpedo*
Calibre 583 mm, Weight 1,190 lb (540 kg)
**GREAT BRITAIN**
*Mk.30 Homing Torpedo*
**UNITED STATES**
*Mk.34 Homing Torpedo*
Calibre 483 mm, Weight 1,387 lb (629 kg.) Obsolescent
*Mk.43 Homing Torpedo*
Calibre 254 mm, Weight 320 lb (145 kg)
*Mk.44 Homing Torpedo*
Calibre 324 mm, Weight: Model 0 507 lb (230 kg)
Model 1 520 lb (236 kg)
*Mk.46 Homing Torpedo*
Calibre 324 mm, Weight 683 lb (310 kg)
*Anti-surface-vessel Torpedo*
Calibre 583 mm, Weight 2,150 lb (975 kg)

# *Glossary & Abbreviations*

**Air Forces** (section)
(?) information uncertain
– no information available
*Squadrons*: Total given includes fighter, strike fighter, ground-attack, bomber, reconnaissance, maritime reconnaissance and ASW, transport and helicopter squadrons, but NOT liaison and AOP squadrons nor training squadrons.
*Operational aircraft*: These include fighters, strike fighters, ground-attack aircraft, bombers, reconnaissance and ECM aircraft, maritime reconnaissance and ASW aircraft plus transports, but NOT liaison and AOP aircraft nor trainers. Army aviation is the only exception: Here liaison and AOP aircraft are also classed as "operational aircraft"— as their role differs from those of the Air Forces and Naval Air Arms.
*Helicopters*: Include all helicopters, regardless of operational function, i.e. also armed and attack-helicopters.

**Aircraft** (section)
*Weight empty*: The combined weight of airframe, power plant(s) and standard equipment. The different interpretations of standard equipment by individual nations can result in differing figures.
*Normal take-off weight*: Encompasses empty weight plus load, the latter comprising crew, fuel, lubricants and payload.
*Maximum take-off weight*: The highest permissible take-off weight dependent upon runway conditions, local authorities and/or flight characteristics.
*Maximum speed*: The highest speed it is possible to achieve in horizontal flight for a limited period, under ideal conditions and at a fixed height above ground level.
*Maximum cruising speed*: Highest possible speed over longer periods. Not to be confused with economical cruising speed for maximum range.
*Patrol speed*: Quoted mainly for maritime aircraft as optimum search speed.
*Radius of action*: (Often referred to as penetration range) The distance an aircraft can fly in any one direction, dependent upon its returning to base.

*Range*: The distance an aircraft can fly at the optimum cruising speed for any given weight *with* a fixed payload fuel capacity (inc auxiliary tanks) without refuelling.
*Ferry range*: The distance an aircraft can fly at the optimum cruising speed for any given weight *without* payload at the most favourable altitude and with maximum fuel capacity (inc auxiliary tanks) without refuelling.
*Initial rate of climb*: The maximum rate of climb near ground level, generally in relation to normal take-off weight.
*Service ceiling*: Generally taken as the height at which rate of climb drops to 1.64 ft/sec (0.5 m/sec).
*Hovering ceiling*: The maximum height at which a helicopter can remain stationary in both horizontal and vertical planes. Because of ground-effect this ceiling is dependent upon the height of the machine above ground level.
*Static thrust* (st): the static thrust of its turbojet engines is given in lb (kg) without/with afterburning.

**Abbreviations**
| | |
|---|---|
| AAM | Air-to-air missile |
| AOP | Aerial observation post |
| ARM | Anti-radar missile |
| ASM | Air-to-surface missile |
| ASR | Air-sea rescue |
| ASW | Anti-submarine warfare |
| ECM | Electronic counter-measures |
| fps | feet per second |
| hp | horse-power |
| kg | kilograms |
| m | metres |
| mph | miles per hour |
| m/sec | metres per second |
| rpg | rounds per gun |
| s/l | sea-level |
| sq ft | square feet |
| sq m | square metres |
| st | static thrust |
| STOL | Short take-off and lift |
| VTOL | Vertical take-off and lift |
| w.m.p. | with maximum payload |

# Insignia

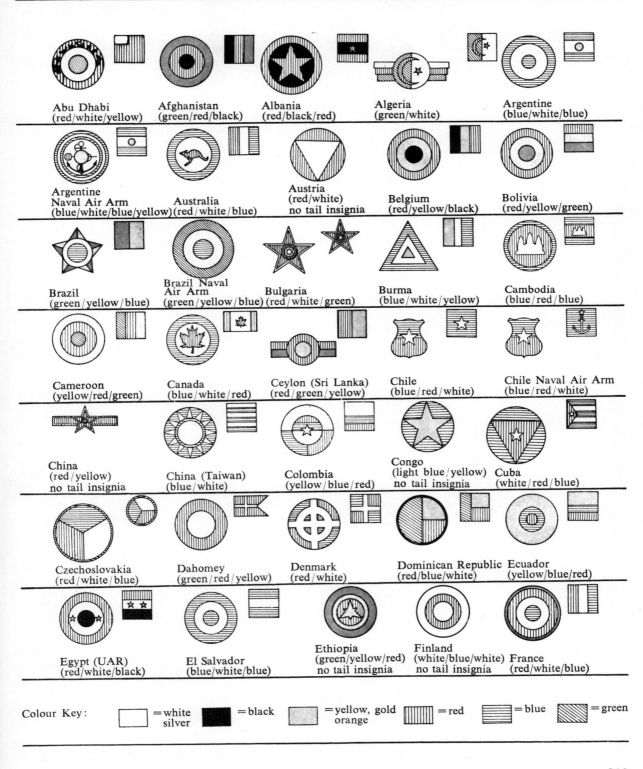

Abu Dhabi
(red/white/yellow)

Afghanistan
(green/red/black)

Albania
(red/black/red)

Algeria
(green/white)

Argentine
(blue/white/blue)

Argentine
Naval Air Arm
(blue/white/blue/yellow)

Australia
(red/white/blue)

Austria
(red/white)
no tail insignia

Belgium
(red/yellow/black)

Bolivia
(red/yellow/green)

Brazil
(green/yellow/blue)

Brazil Naval
Air Arm
(green/yellow/blue)

Bulgaria
(red/white/green)

Burma
(blue/white/yellow)

Cambodia
(blue/red/blue)

Cameroon
(yellow/red/green)

Canada
(blue/white/red)

Ceylon (Sri Lanka)
(red/green/yellow)

Chile
(blue/red/white)

Chile Naval Air Arm
(blue/red/white)

China
(red/yellow)
no tail insignia

China (Taiwan)
(blue/white)

Colombia
(yellow/blue/red)

Congo
(light blue/yellow)
no tail insignia

Cuba
(white/red/blue)

Czechoslovakia
(red/white/blue)

Dahomey
(green/red/yellow)

Denmark
(red/white)

Dominican Republic
(red/blue/white)

Ecuador
(yellow/blue/red)

Egypt (UAR)
(red/white/black)

El Salvador
(blue/white/blue)

Ethiopia
(green/yellow/red)
no tail insignia

Finland
(white/blue/white)
no tail insignia

France
(red/white/blue)

Colour Key:  □ = white
silver  ■ = black  ▨ = yellow, gold
orange  ▥ = red  ▤ = blue  ▧ = green

France Naval
Air Arm
(red/white/blue)
Germany (West)
(black/red/gold)
Germany (East)
(black/red/gold)
Ghana
(red/yellow/green)
Great Britain
(blue/white/red)

Great Britain
(blue/red)
(on camouflaged surfaces)
Greece
(blue/white/blue)
Guatemala
(blue/white/blue)
Guinea
(green/red/yellow)
no tail insignia
Haiti
(white/blue/red)
no tail insignia

Honduras
(blue/white/blue)
Hungary
(red/white/green)
India
(red/white/green)
Indonesia
(red/white)
Indonesia Naval
Air Arm
(red/white)

Iran
(green/white/red)
Iraq
(black/white/green)
Ireland
(green/white/red)
no tail insignia
Israel
(white/blue)
no tail insignia
Italy
(red/white/green)
no tail insignia

Ivory Coast
(green/white/orange)
Japan
(white/red)
no tail insignia
Jordan
(black/white/green)
Kenya
(black/red/green)
Korea (North)
(blue/white/red)
no tail insignia

Korea (South)
(blue/white/red)
no tail insignia
Kuwait
(green/white/red/black)
Laos
(white/red/white)
Lebanon
(red/white/green)
Libya
(red/black/green)

Madagascar (Malagasy)
(red/green/white)
Malaysia
(blue/yellow)
Mauritania
(green/yellow)
Mexico
(red/white/green)
Mongolian
People's Republic
(red/white)

Morocco
(green/red/yellow)
Netherlands
(red/white/blue)
New Zealand
(blue/white/red)
Nicaragua
(red/blue/white and
blue/white/blue)
Niger
(orange/white/green)

Niger (Alternative) (orange/white/green)   Nigeria (green/white/green)   Norway (blue/white/red) no tail insignia   Oman (white/red/white)   Pakistan (green/white)

Paraguay (red/white/blue)   Peru (red/white/red)   Philippines (blue/white/red) no tail insignia   Poland (red, white)   Portugal (white/red and green/red)

Rhodesia (green/white/gold)   Rumania (blue/yellow/red)   Saudi Arabia (green/white/green)   Senegal (green/yellow/red)   Singapore (red/white/red)

Somali (blue/white)   South Africa (white/blue/yellow and red/white/blue)   Spain (red/yellow/red)   Soviet Union (red)   Sudan (yellow/blue/green)

Sweden (yellow/blue /yellow) no tail insignia   Switzerland (red/white)   Syria (green/white/black)   Tanzania (blue/green/yellow)   Thailand (red/white/blue/white/red)

Togo (red/yellow/green)   Tunisia (red/white) no tail insignia   Turkey (red/white/red)   Uganda (black/yellow/red) no tail insignia   Upper Volta (black/white/red)

United States (blue/white/red) no tail insignia   Uruguay (blue/red/white)   Naval Air Arm (yellow star)   Venezuela (yellow/blue/red)   Vietnam (North) (red/yellow)

Vietnam (South) (yellow/red)   Yemen (red/white/black)   Yugoslavia (blue/white/red)   Zambia (orange/green/red/black)

221

# Index

224